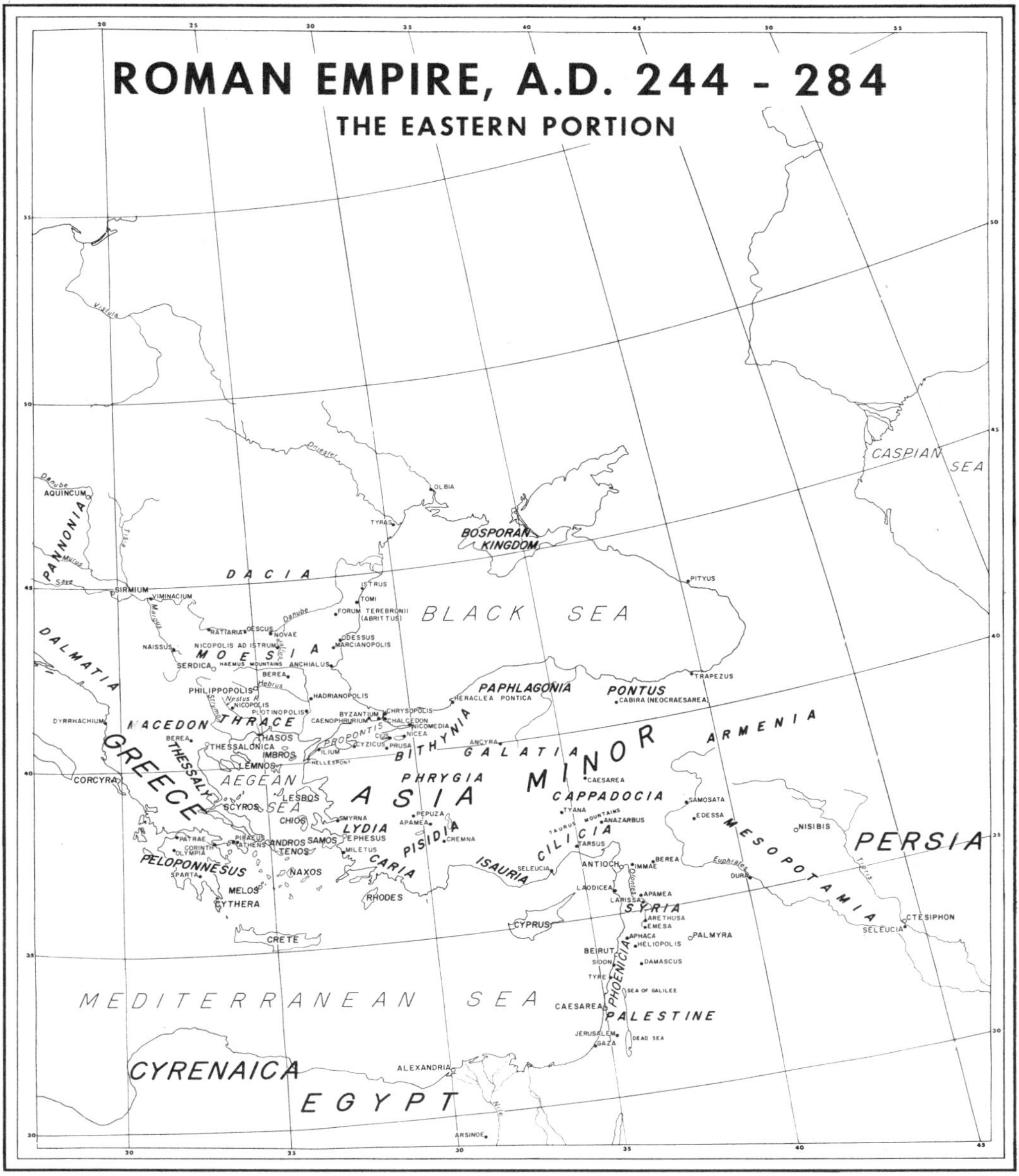

ROMAN EMPIRE, A.D. 244 - 284
THE EASTERN PORTION
Vistula
Danube
AQUINCUM
PANNONIA
Murus
Save
SIRMIUM
VIMINACIUM
DACIA
Dniester
OLBIA
TYRAS
BOSPORAN KINGDOM
ISTRUS
TOMI
FORUM TEREBRONII (ABRITTUS)
BLACK SEA
PITYUS
CASPIAN SEA
DALMATIA
RATIARIA
OESCUS
NOVAE
NAISSUS
NICOPOLIS AD ISTRUM
ODESSUS
MARCIANOPOLIS
MOESIA
SERDICA
HAEMUS MOUNTAINS
ANCHIALUS
BEREA
Hebrus
PHILIPPOPOLIS
HADRIANOPOLIS
Nestus R.
NICOPOLIS
PLOTINOPOLIS
DYRRHACHIUM
MACEDON
THRACE
BYZANTIUM
CHRYSOPOLIS
CAENOPHRURIUM
CHALCEDON
NICOMEDIA
HERACLEA PONTICA
PAPHLAGONIA
PONTUS
CABIRA (NEOCRAESAREA)
TRAPEZUS
ARMENIA
BEREA
THESSALONICA
THASOS
PROPONTIS
CIUS
NICEA
CYZICUS
PRUSA
BITHYNIA
ANCYRA
GALATIA
GREECE
THESSALY
IMBROS
ILIUM
HELLESPONT
LEMNOS
AEGEAN SEA
CORCYRA
LESBOS
SCYROS
CHIOS
PHRYGIA
ASIA MINOR
CAESAREA
CAPPADOCIA
SAMOSATA
EDESSA
NISIBIS
PERSIA
PEPUZA
APAMEA
SMYRNA
LYDIA
EPHESUS
CREMNA
PISIDIA
TYANA
TAURUS MOUNTAINS
ANAZARBUS
CILICIA
TARSUS
MESOPOTAMIA
Tigris
Euphrates
PATRAE
PIRAEUS
CORINTH
ATHENS
OLYMPIA
ANDROS
SAMOS
TENOS
MILETUS
CARIA
ISAURIA
SELEUCIA
ANTIOCH
IMMAE
BEREA
DURA
PELOPONNESUS
SPARTA
NAXOS
MELOS
CYTHERA
RHODES
LAODICEA
Orontes
APAMEA
LARISSA
SYRIA
ARETHUSA
EMESA
CYPRUS
CRETE
PALMYRA
CTESIPHON
SELEUCIA
APHACA
HELIOPOLIS
BEIRUT
SIDON
DAMASCUS
TYRE
PHOENICIA
SEA OF GALILEE
MEDITERRANEAN SEA
CAESAREA
PALESTINE
JERUSALEM
GAZA
DEAD SEA
CYRENAICA
ALEXANDRIA
EGYPT
Nile
ARSINOE

Library of
Davidson College

THE AGE OF THE SOLDIER EMPERORS

THE AGE OF THE SOLDIER EMPERORS

IMPERIAL ROME, A.D. 244-284

by

GEORGE C. BRAUER, JR.

NOYES CLASSICAL STUDIES

NOYES PRESS
Park Ridge, New Jersey

Copyright © 1975 by George C. Brauer, Jr.
Library of Congress Catalog Card Number: 75-13569
ISBN: 0-8155-5036-7

Published in the United States by
NOYES PRESS
Noyes Building
Park Ridge, New Jersey 07656

Library of Congress Cataloging in Publication Data

Brauer, George C
   The age of the soldier emperors : Imperial Rome, A.D. 244-284.

   (Noyes classical studies)
   Bibliography: p.
   Includes index.
   1. Rome—History—Empire, 30 B.C.-284 A.D.
2. Roman emperors. I. Title.
DG305.B7   937'.6'06   75-13569
ISBN 0-8155-5036-7

PREFACE

As a professor of English, I became interested in the ancient past through two factors. One was the kind of literature I teach—that of the eighteenth century, when the influence of classical literature, Roman even more than Greek, was of course enormous. The other was my hobby, the collecting of Greek and Roman coins. The hobby developed into an enthusiasm, if not an obsession, and led me into reading in the fields of ancient history and culture.

It may have been partly because coins of the mid-third century after Christ are plentiful that I became especially interested in that age. The more I read, the more attractive this late period of classical civilization became. What proved most fascinating was the determined resistance that Roman leaders in the mid-third century put up to both inimical external forces and internal agents of decay. The pagan and Christian thought of this crucial era also appealed to me, and the obscurity surrounding some of its very important figures and events acted, perhaps, as a challenge. The result is this book.

Its faults are my own. But special thanks are due to Mr. F. Coates Crewe of C & M Studios, Columbia, South Carolina, for the photographs; Mr. Michael T. Holland, Department of Geography, University of South Carolina, for the drawing of the maps; Miss Janet Coe Sanborn, Department of History, Cleveland Public Library, for helpfulness exceptional even among librarians; and Professor Richard H. Chowen, Department of History, University of South Carolina, for enlightening and stimulating conversations on a wide variety of topics all concerned with ancient Rome.

Columbia, S.C.
April, 1975

George C. Brauer, Jr.
Professor of English
University of South Carolina

CONTENTS

	Introduction	1
1.	The Roman World of Philip the Arab	3
2.	Decius and the Christians	19
3.	Cyprian and the Christians	38
4.	The End of Decius	51
5.	The Reign of Gallus	58
6.	The Empire as a Tired Old Man	68
7.	Heretics and Martyrs	97
8.	The Closing Years	121
9.	Son of the Captive Emperor	127
10.	Gallienus at Rome	145
11.	The Philosopher	152
12.	Chaos Compounded	162
13.	Claudius Gothicus	177
14.	The Advent of Aurelius	188
15.	The Overthrow of Zenobia	198
16.	The Hermit	218
17.	Aurelian Triumphant	225
18.	Reform, Benevolence and Death	233
19.	The Next Hero	239
20.	Probus	243
21.	Carus and His Dynasty	257
22.	Prospect	265
	Bibliography	268
	Index	276

LIST OF ILLUSTRATIONS

Philip the Arab, radiate. Obverse of an *antoninianus* 5
Otacilia Severa, diademed. Obverse of an *antoninianus* 9
Antelope. Reverse of an *antoninianus* of Philip the Arab 9
Lion. Reverse of an *antoninianus* of Philip the Arab 15
Philip Junior. Obverse of a tetradrachm of Alexandria 15
Trajan Decius, laureate. Obverse of a *sestertius* 21
Isis nursing Horus. Reverse of a *denarius* of Julia Domna 37
Trajan Decius, radiate. Obverse of a double *sestertius* 55
Herennius Etruscus, as Caesar. Obverse of a *sestertius* 55
Trebonianus Gallus, laureate. Obverse of a bronze of Antioch 59
Emperor with branch and transverse sceptre. Reverse of an
   antoninianus 59
Aemilian, radiate. Obverse of an *antoninianus* 65
Emperor in military dress. Reverse of an *antoninianus* 65
Gallienus, laureate. Obverse of a tetradrachm of Alexandria 85
Roman eagle. Reverse of a tetradrachm of Alexandria 85
Military trophy. Reverse of an *antoninianus* of Gallienus 93
Valerian, radiate. Obverse of an *antoninianus* 96
Two snakes curled around a bow case. Reverse of a *cistophorus* 107
Postumus, radiate. Obverse of an *antoninianus* 123
Hercules. Reverse of an *antoninianus* of Postumus 126
Macrianus Junior, radiate. Obverse of an *antoninianus* 131
Emperor of Orient or Sol. Reverse of an *antoninianus* of
   Gallienus 135
Gallienus, radiate. Obverse of an *antoninianus* 151
Sol. Reverse of an *antoninianus* of Gallienus 161
Diana of Ephesus. Reverse of a *cistrophorus* 165
Claudius Gothicus, radiate. Obverse of an *antoninianus* 187
Aurelian, laureate. Obverse of a *dupondius* 191
Severina, diademed. Obverse of an *antoninianus* 191
Vabalath, laureate. Obverse (?) of an *antoninianus* 199
Aurelian, radiate. Reverse (?) of an *antoninianus* 199
Sol and enemy. Reverse of an *antoninianus* 211
Valerian, laureate. Obverse of a *sestertius* 224

Victorinus, radiate. Obverse of an *antoninianus* 226
Tetricus, radiate. Obverse of an *antoninianus* 226
Aurelian receiving glove from Jupiter. Reverse of an *antoninianus*..231
Severina and Aurelian. Reverse of a *dupondius*..............................232
Tacitus, laureate. Obverse of a tetradrachm of Alexandria................238
Probus, radiate. Obverse of an *antoninianus*...................................245
Sol in four-horse chariot. Reverse of an *antoninianus* of Probus ...249
Probus, radiate and helmeted. Obverse of an *antoninianus* 256
Carus, radiate. Obverse of an *antoninianus* 259
Carinus, radiate, as Caesar. Obverse of an *antoninianus* 259
Numerian, radiate, as Caesar. Obverse of an *antoninianus*................263
Diocletian, radiate. Obverse of an *antoninianus* 263
Victory with wreath and palm branch. Reverse of a *sestertius*
 of Decius 267
Zeus Ammon. Reverse of a tetradrachm of Philip the Arab................275

Introduction

I have been told about an ancient Chinese curse that goes: "May you live in interesting times." If such a wish is a curse, the middle part of the third century A.D. qualifies as one of the most cursed of all ages. The years between A.D. 244 and 284 pushed interesting times beyond the point of chaos.

Ancient ways of life were collapsing in those years. The calm ideality of classical art had become difficult even to copy. Cities, the hearts of ancient civilization, had begun to forget their heritage, some of them because they had fallen into poverty, others because they were raped and ravaged by barbarians. Much of the countryside also succumbed to the barbarians, who burned and plundered as they swept through.

Like an old mosaic, the empire was fragmented—cracked and torn not only by invading West Germans and Goths but by civil dissention. Revolt, usurpation, and murder were now the expected in national politics. Gaul, joined by Spain and Britain, formed its own Roman Empire; the Oriental state of Palmyra broke from Rome and tried to rob her of her fairest Eastern provinces. Meanwhile Persia harassed the empire. So did social injustice; so did invincible plague. Inflation escalated; coins that carried the emperor's image were shamelessly debased.

The traditional gods and goddesses, such as Mars, Jupiter, and Minerva, were being crowded out. Several times the government tried to stop the spreading menace of Christianity by demanding worship of the emperor and tormenting those who refused to worship. Christians quarreled with one another as zealously as they assailed the pagans. In addition to Christianity, a wide choice of mystic Eastern creeds competed for converts. Diverse philosophical and ethical ideals and confusion as to the aims of art aggravated the incoherence.

But the great men of the time fought this chaos—some of them desperately like the Emperor Gallienus, some of them very competently like the Emperor Aurelian, some of them spiritually like Plotinus or St. Antony. They did what they could although they had no vision of the age that would come out of the agony. Diocletian made himself emperor in 284; no one could know that under him and later under Constantine the Roman world would be reorganized into a viable thing.

The decades before Diocletian have often been viewed as the nadir of the Roman experience. Recently, however, scholars have started to see a certain amount of glory in them—the glory, for instance, of philosophical questing, religious fervor, stubborn self-sacrifice, and almost superhuman military achievement. These were years of birth as well as of disruption. They were the years that made the renewed empire possible.

1 The Roman World of Philip the Arab

In A.D. 248 Rome observed the thousandth year of her life. The celebration, scheduled for 247, had had to be delayed a while, since in 247 the emperor had not yet returned to the city from war against barbarians. But to the people in the capital, the festivities must have seemed well worth the wait.

Games in circus and Colosseum were timeworn entertainments for the oversophisticated Roman mob, but the thousandth anniversary was marked by the so-called Secular Games. These were supposed to take place at intervals of 110 years, although in actuality they were not that regularly spaced. The Secular Games rendered official gratitude to the gods for the coming of a brand new age, together with prayers for the new age's glory. Their rarity and their relevance to national welfare, plus the pure thrill of being alive for the thousandth year of the greatest city on earth, gave the delayed celebration an enormous importance.

The emperor tried to provide spectacles equal to so significant an occasion, and he struck coins in commemoration of it. On some of the coins he depicted the exotic animals, such as lions, antelopes, and elephants, that were used in the games. Coins struck with his wife's portrait showed hippopotamuses on the reverse. Other pieces represented the goddess Roma enthroned in her temple, or the babies Romulus and Remus suckled by the she-wolf before there was a Rome.

The ceremonies went on for several nights and days. Thousands of torches in the hands of the throng glowed on the Campus Martius, where holy pageants were performed, and on the Palatine and Capitoline Hills. Wheat, barley, and beans were passed out to the crowd. People danced and drank much wine.

The sacred college of the Fifteen Men, keepers of the Sibylline Books, presided over the ceremonies. In all the gravity of his office as high priest of the state religion the veiled and togate emperor carried out changeless rituals at the altars. Along the Tiber he burned lambs and black she-goats to the Fates, who caused men to prosper or fail. He sacrificed white bulls to Jupiter the Best and the Greatest, king of gods and patron of Rome; a spotless heifer to Jupiter's wife Juno, patroness of Rome; a pregnant black sow to Mother Earth, who gave the empire food in abundance or held it back and made men starve. He offered cakes and burned incense to Ilithyia, goddess of childbirth, without whose assistance the empire's population dropped. Matrons knelt to Juno in supplication for blessings. Twenty-seven aristocratic youths and twenty-seven highborn young virgins, their lives unpolluted by the death of either parent, chanted ancient hymns to Apollo and his chaste sister Diana.[1]

Through the sacrifices, the offerings, the prayers, and the holy songs the people thanked the gods and solicited their favor for the present and the future—the age that had freshly dawned. With divine help perhaps the Romans could renew the virtues that made their ancestors supreme over men and preserve the empire that their ancestors had won. Some of the residents of the capital may actually have hoped for this. Others were probably too beaten by circumstance to hope at all.

Whatever the new age might bring, the present bore only a faint resemblance to the solid, valorous days of old Rome. For instance, Roman citizenship, which had once been the privilege of the few, was now common to the whole Mediterranean area and beyond. Gauls, Syrians, Dacians and Dalmatians were Romans. The emperor, Philip, happened to be a Roman Arab, born in a small town east of the Sea of Galilee. Theoretically Philip had achieved the throne by obtaining the approval of army and senate in time-honored fashion, but actually the senate's confirmation had come only after Philip persuaded the army to do away with the previous emperor, the noble boy named Gordian. That had been in 244. Gordian and Philip (prefect of the Praetorian Guard) were on campaign against Persia. Philip sent back word to the senate that Gordian had died of disease, and the senate did not bother to question the information. That assembly, like other survivals from an older Rome, had lost much of its vigor.

Rather surprisingly, perhaps, Philip turned out to be a good emperor. He had a strong sense of what was wrong with the empire and a strong urge to do what he could about it. A hard, intelligent, self-made man, he felt that possibly he could give the gods a little assistance at shaping the forthcoming age.

When Philip took the throne in 244 the empire was probably sicker than ever before. Rulers earlier in the century—the cruel Caracalla with

Philip the Arab (244-249), radiate. Obverse of an antoninianus or double denarius. 21 mm.

his military posturing, the extravagant and effeminate Elagabalus, the weak Severus Alexander, the rapacious Maximin, and the mild young Gordian—had done their world little good. Elagabalus' extravagance, for example, had helped to sap the national finances. But much more disastrous than imperial improvidence was the fact that wars had to be fought and that money had to be found to fight them. On the southeast frontier a strong new Persia threatened the empire—a Persia that had succeeded the exhausted Parthian kingdom as overlord of the Iranian plateau a couple of decades earlier and was ambitious to revive the glories of the long-gone Persia of Cyrus and Darius. On the northeastern borders an assortment of hungry barbarian nations waited to grab whatever they could. Having no conception of a national debt, the empire never kept a reserve fund on hand to finance costly campaigns against enemies such as Persians or barbarians. The wars must be paid for by the present population of the empire, and poor and rich came to hate a demanding government.

To make things worse, the army, coddled by Caracalla and his father Septimius Severus, was poorly disciplined and eminently selfish. It fought not for Rome but for its own profit. Loyal to the man that rewarded it the most, it would willingly kill an emperor and give the imperial command to a more promising aspirant, just as it had killed the boy Gordian and proclaimed Philip. Immensely proud of itself as the force that made civilization secure, the army also expected to be served and fed by the lands through which it marched. It took peasants from the fields and put them to work on its own projects. It requisitioned the oxen that were needed for plowing and made them pull its own baggage carts. It confiscated the wine, wheat, barley, and olives necessary for the preservation and enjoyment of life, and it quartered itself noisily on private property. Sporadically the government remunerated the populace in small degree for suffering inconveniences from the soldiers, but often there was no remuneration at all, except the assurance that civilization was still secure.

Like the army the civil servants—the minor and major officials—held the poor down. Quite a few of these officials had been born into slavery but had obtained their freedom and then accumulated power through deviousness and a nonchalant attitude about other people's money. Some independent peasants managed to rise to prosperity in spite of all the ways to drag them under, but many farmers preferred not to be independent at all—to be tenants, serfs in almost a medieval sense, not yet bound to the soil but subject to the whims, fortunes, or misfortunes of their landlords. Other people turned to robbery; bands of thieves roamed the countryside, well organized, desperate, compassionless, feared almost as much as the soldiers. The poor in the cities were as badly off as the country poor, who at least had open fields to work in rather than the festering squalor of the slums.

Fortunately, many children died—and not quite so many were being born, it seems, as had been born a century before, in spite of official prayers to the goddess of childbirth.[2] If a baby did not sicken of his own accord, his mother and father might leave him out in the fields until he starved to death or was eaten by a hungry dog. Or they could sell him into slavery and get a little money for the rest of the family.

But the poor did not suffer alone. Taxation and exorbitant exactions, in kind as well as in coin, fell heavily on people of property for the simple reason that those people could probably pay. The government bore down greedily on the middle and upper classes, and members of the dreaded secret police lurked in the background to scout out the vulnerable and exploit them, level false charges against them, and seize their possessions for the state.

The development of levies for the so-called crown gold illustrates the trend. During the early days of the empire various communities, grateful to the emperor for one reason or another, had presented gold crowns to him as tokens of appreciation. Later on, emperors demanded these crowns, which often weighed many pounds apiece and became a significant source of the imperial revenue. By the early third century the provincial cities were regularly taxed to provide the crowns, and additional taxes were levied to produce other crowns for special occasions, such as military victories. The custom had gotten out of hand.

Some people, of course, prospered—clever craftsmen whose products would always be in demand, a few landowners who found ways around taxation, and especially the newly rich, who were shrewd and unscrupulous enough to take advantage of the economic instability and even to profit from the tight tyranny of the imperial government. In many towns guilds existed for the benefit of particular kinds of merchants, tradesmen, or artisans—bakers' guilds, dyers' guilds, fullers' guilds. Trade and industry went on in the cities just as farming and stockherding occupied those portions of the country where land had not been abandoned in despair. Tarsus wove its fine linens, Sidon cast its bronzes, and Gaza crushed its grapes for wine. At Damascus the swordmakers already practiced a skill that would call forth the admiration of knightly Crusaders hundreds of years later. Near Cyzicus men quarried marble; outside Antioch, in the voluptuous pleasure gardens of Daphne, beautiful bodies carried on the same lucrative business that they had carried on for centuries. Desert caravans poured into Palmyra with their wares. At Alexandria on the coast of Egypt the great lighthouse pointed the way to the crowded harbor where ships took on cargoes of green glass perfume bottles, jeweled gold earrings, ivory carvings, and load after load of grain for the people of Rome. The cities were not idle, though ragged men tramped their streets starving and the rich saw insolvency around the corner.

Each city had its council or governing body, consisting of several hundred members in the case of the large Eastern communities. The necessary civic business, such as the passing of town legislation and the appointment of magistrates, was taken care of by these assemblies. The councillors, called decurions, were usually the city's wealthiest men, since a considerable amount of property was a qualification for membership, and they held their seats for life. These decurions were the provincial aristocracy, the upper class outside Rome.

In former years there had been something great about belonging to a city council, especially one in a famous Eastern metropolis such as Ephesus or Antioch. The councils were modeled after the governing bodies of Greek cities in the age before Rome, and it was generally agreed that whatever the Greeks had devised was excellent. During the first and second centuries A.D., when cities were flourishing, the decurions took it upon themselves to donate lavishly to the local welfare. This gave them a chance to satisfy their burning civic pride, to exhibit their wealth and importance, and perhaps to perpetuate some of their fame. They raised magnificent temples, baths, fountains, gates, and theatres in the cities, established colonnaded marketplaces to protect shoppers against sun and rain, and had their names engraved in marble. They also contributed money for the games their cities liked to hold. If the council appointed them to municipal offices they very likely put on their own games, paying for the runners, the wrestlers, the dancers and musicians that the people loved. If plague came, or an earthquake or a famine, the decurions financed the relief of the suffering. Even when there was no famine they sometimes handed out money or free bread to the citizens, or free wine so that everybody could have a good time. Theirs was the glory, and they enjoyed it.

But in the third century, as taxation increased and prosperity wavered, all that changed. Membership in a city council became a dreaded thing, an obligation to be avoided if possible because it could lead to financial ruin. Decurions were still expected to give abundantly for the benefit of their communities, even if they no longer had the means. Besides, the imperial government, relying on the ancient principle that an individual existed for the good of the state and must sacrifice his private interests to the state if necessary, rendered compulsory many of the contributions from decurions for the welfare and pleasure of their fellow citizens. Members of city councils were now forced to provide food or funds in time of distress, patronize local organizations, and pay for games or for repairs on buildings that had been erected in a more affluent age. If the decurions managed to hand over what the state demanded of them, they received no recompense. If they could not fulfill the demands or if for some reason they refused, the government would confiscate their property.

These compulsory contributions were called liturgies. Council members who had been appointed to municipal offices were most liable to them because any office entailed expensive duties. The offices themselves were liturgies in a sense, being compulsory appointments that drew no salaries. The most hated liturgy of office was the job of collecting taxes, paid in agricultural produce as well as in coin. This duty was usually

Otacilia Severa (wife of Philip the Arab), diademed. Obverse of an antoninianus. 22 mm.

Antelope. Reverse of an antoninianus of Philip the Arab struck for the Secular Games of 248. Inscription: SAECVLARES AVGG. 21 mm.

assigned to members of the council with the most money—the First Ten as they were called in some cities, or the First Twenty as they were called in others. Like the rest of the offices, the collection of revenue was supposed to be an honor and consequently did not merit a salary. If one of the First Ten or the First Twenty could not squeeze the full tax out of the depressed city residents and the poor farmers on the surrounding lands, his own estate was seized by the government, as might be expected. But to prevent that disgrace he could of his own free will cede his property to the state.

The rule was the same all over: an office-holder was personally responsible for the perfect execution of his job, and financial punishment followed failure. Public spirit was low. Nobody wanted to become known as a rich man in his city, or to keep his city beautiful. The greatest achievement was obscurity.

In addition to taxation and liturgies, the government found another answer to the expensive proposition of running an empire. It debased the coinage. The process was very gradual, but by the time Philip became emperor it had passed the danger point. For centuries the standard silver coin had been the **denarius** (a piece about the size of a dime), and for a long time the **denarius** had remained relatively pure. But toward the end of the second century A.D. its silver content sank to about 70 percent and then 60 percent, and in the early third century the **denarius** was only half silver, if that. Coins remained in circulation much longer then than they do today; fifty years were probably an average life for a coin. Handling the silver of former emperors, people knew that the money of Rome was steadily deteriorating. Inflation resulted.

In A.D. 214 the emperor Caracalla had introduced a new silver denomination, which several decades later supplanted the **denarius.** We do not know what he called it but we term it the **antoninianus** because one of Caracalla's names was Antoninus. It presumably counted as two **denarii** although it weighed only as much as one and a half. Of course this "double **denarius**" or whatever it was called was no purer than the single **denarius**. It was discontinued about 219, but in 238 it reappeared in quantity. During the reign of the boy Gordian (238-244) the coin was occasionally copper inside and adulterated silver outside; and the coating soon wore off in splotches that corrupted a man's faith in the administration.

Philip could not improve the currency, and in so far as we know he did not make the attempt. Even the showiest base-metal coin of his day, the shiny brass **sestertius**, looked shrunken beside the broad, thick **sestertii** issued in the previous century by great emperors such as Hadrian and Marcus Aurelius. The majority of the coins that Philip struck to celebrate the thousandth anniversary in 247/8 were these reduced **sestertii** and the **antoniniani** or "double **denarii**." On the obverse his subjects could see his strong, beak-nosed portrait, with the short whiskers then in fashion and, on **antoniniani**, the radiate headdress that made emperors look like sun gods; but the glitter was meretricious.

Although he could do nothing about the coinage, he exerted himself earnestly to strengthen the empire in other ways. His first important act as emperor, for instance, was to make peace with the Persians against whom he and Gordian had been campaigning. It was not an embarrassing treaty from the Roman point of view. Rome kept Mesopotamia and the region known as lesser Armenia, so that her borders remained intact. She had to pay the Persians a considerable sum of money, but there was nothing very disgraceful about that. The senate felt that Philip deserved to be granted the title **Persicus Maximus**, or "Supreme Conqueror of the Persians."

Most important, there was peace. For a while at any rate, the empire's diminished resources would not have to be drained off for campaigns in the heart of the Orient.

From the East Philip traveled to Rome, stopping at Berea in Macedonia to preside at games held in his honor. He reached the capital in July of 244. As part of his effort to reign well, he immediately began a policy of pleasant relations with the senate that was to last for the rest of his life.

During the republic the senate had conducted the affairs of the state with dignity, intelligence, and much firmness. Under its direction Rome had concluded advantageous treaties with foreign powers, had been victorious over Greeks, Asiatics, and Carthaginians, and had acquired much territory. The senate of A.D. 244, on the other hand, was not a policy-making body. Most of its legislative and judicial functions too had already gone over to the emperor or the emperor's servants. It was even relinquishing its right to appoint magistrates for the city of Rome.[3]

But the memory of its golden days made the senate a vital tradition, a thing to revere in spite of its decadence, a living idol from a better time. The wise and good Marcus Aurelius, best of rulers, had treated this idol with great honor, and Philip wished to imitate Marcus. The senators, besides, were rich and therefore powerful, and Philip respected the power of riches. Although senators were not allowed to engage in commerce, which was demeaning, they owned enormous tracts of land throughout the empire, and they were exempt from liturgies. Philip could afford to approach these men without insolence, to offer them small courtesies, and to praise their opinions. The Roman world might benefit, as well as himself.

Perhaps because he came from a remote corner of the empire, the Arab region east of the Sea of Galilee, Philip sympathized with provincials and tried to help them. He built roads in the provinces, partly to enable troops to march back and forth with ease but also to render the necessary journeys of farmers and tradesmen less rough. In his homeland, on the site of the town where he was born, he founded a city named after himself—Philippopolis, the City of Philip—providing it with baths, temples, a theatre, and a main avenue bordered by colonnades. Philippopolis was the only totally new city erected in the middle of the third century; a hundred years before, new cities were being founded all over. There must have been some egotism in Philip's gesture, but there was probably also a desire to promote the economy in that area, and to give his fellow Arabs more of the amenities of Roman civilization.

In Italy, he dispatched some marines from the naval base at Ravenna to a town on the Umbrian coast to take care of swarms of thieves and pirates that were robbing by land and sea. At Rome too he performed good works. For instance, he built a reservoir on the far side of the Tiber and held three distributions of money for the citizens of the capital. These largesses may just have been a matter of keeping popular support. The people who lived in Rome were used to receiving money from the emperors every now and then, just as they were used to having free food doled out to them. Their rulers had bestowed such favors on them since early in the empire; it was part of the system. But three distributions in a five-year reign amounted to more than the average. Philip was being as generous as his means allowed.

Whatever Philip's good intentions were, however, the age was too strong for them. It overbalanced his benefactions and made them seem puny. He could not lighten the taxes. He could not lift the liturgies. He could not keep his officials or his soldiers from oppressing the poor. He could not change the temper of the troops, who remained arrogant and mercenary, just as they were when they gave him the throne. The situation looked as hopeless as the coinage. It grew worse when, about 245, a semi-barbaric tribe of Thracian stock known as the Carpi crossed the Danube, which at that point formed the border of the empire. They spread over Lower Moesia (now Bulgaria), raiding and slaughtering. The Roman governor could not stop them with the troops at his command. Other barbarians—apparently a Germanic nation called the Quadi—crossed the Danube too, seeing how weak Rome was, and plundered. Philip, following his duty, left Rome for the Danube area.

We know very little about these barbarian invasions. We are not sure when they started, when they ended, or just where the battles took place. The campaigns are almost totally unrecorded. The Carpi were in many respects civilized people. Like their ancestors in the time of Trajan, they worked in silver, made hoes and sickles of iron, painted geometric designs on pottery, and built houses and forts of stone and brick.[4] But to Philip's softer contemporaries far from the frontier, one barbarian must have seemed a great deal like another. They came, killed, looted, drank, raped, stuffed themselves, and then passed on, leaving desolate land and dead Romans behind. In the country they burned the fields and took the animals; when they captured a city they smashed and looted. It was always the same.

Many cities in Lower Moesia and the Balkan provinces of Macedonia and Thrace had been issuing sorry-looking copper coins. Because coinage now stopped in some of the cities, we assume that the barbarians got there. When Philip returned to Rome in 247 the senate gave him the titles "Conqueror of the Carpi" and "Conqueror of the Germans." We suppose that the Germans were the Quadi and that he defeated them somewhere as well as the Carpi. The only precise detail we have is that at some time during the campaign the Carpi took over a fort in the Danube region and charged out of it against the Romans but were crumpled by an elite corps of the Roman army, the Moorish javelin men. These superb fighters from Africa rode bareback, protecting themselves with small shields. They could send their javelins accurately into a man's lungs or his brain.

After coming back to Rome Philip had the grateful senate confirm his son Philip Junior as his partner in the imperial office. Philip Junior was already "Caesar" and "Prince of Youth," which implied that he would succeed to the throne. He now received the title "Augustus," which we very loosely translate as "Emperor." The boy was about ten years old. His father evidently hoped to establish his own family as the imperial dynasty.

He obtained for his wife the title borne by eminent empresses in other reigns, "Mother of the Augustus and of the Camp and of the Senate and of the Fatherland," an appellation that gave her a certain supramortal character. Earlier he had had the senate declare his father divine. Possessing a deified father had been an advantage for an ambitious emperor ever since the reign of Augustus himself, whose adoptive father, Julius Caesar, became a god not long after assassination. The Secular Games that followed Philip's return to Rome, hollow as they may have been in many respects, were a good chance to suggest that the new era should be equated with the new dynasty, the great dynasty. Philip must have been an indomitable optimist or an irrepressible propagandist. The age of iron had not broken him yet.

Eusebius, a church historian who lived in the early fourth century, claims that Philip was also a Christian. According to Eusebius, the emperor went at Eastertime to pray with other Christians at the building they used as a meeting place. But the man in charge of the congregation would not let him in. The man stipulated that first Philip would have to confess his great sinfulness and agree to sit in the area reserved for penitents. He implied that Philip had more crimes against his name than most people did. But the emperor was humble and eager. Having bared the bloody recesses of his heart, he went piously inside and joined the others in prayer.

The story is almost certainly a legend, but Philip did show tolerance and respect for Christianity and was probably interested in it. Although

Christianity was still above all the faith of the depressed, it was beginning to draw adherents from the upper classes. Philip would not have been the first imperial personage to harbor curiosity about it. The emperor Severus Alexander, who reigned between 222 and 235, may even have kept a statue of Jesus Christ in his private chapel along with statues of Abraham, Alexander the Great, and others. When that ruler's mother happened to be at Antioch she had sent for Origen, probably the greatest churchman of the age, to talk to her about Christianity. Origen later wrote letters to Philip. But in so far as we can make out, Philip's enthusiasm for Christianity did not extend beyond an open-minded appreciation for a creed that he had probably heard a lot about while he was growing up east of Galilee.

It was probably the late spring or early summer of 248, not long after the Secular Games, when news reached Rome calculated to try Philip's self-confidence and obscure his dynastic visions. The troops on the Danube, the same troops whom he had led against the Carpi and the Germans, had revolted against him and chosen one of their officers as emperor.

Not much later the dreaded Goths raided the Danube lands. They hoped that in the confusion as to who was really emperor they would be able to pillage without having to fight Roman legions. Besides, they were justifiably angry because the Roman government had not paid them the money that had been promised them by Philip's immediate predecessor, the boy Gordian. Probably Rome could not afford to pay it. But the Goths had waited long enough; now they would take.

Other tribes, including the Carpi, joined them. Led by two war-chieftains, Argaith and Guntheric, they surged down into Lower Moesia and ravaged. They even besieged its capital, Marcianopolis. Trajan had founded this city near the Black Sea coast when the empire was on the offensive and had named it after his sister Marciana. The residents—Greeks, Italians, and Thracians accustomed to a certain amount of urban sophistication—resisted the barbarians under the command of their governor, a Thracian himself. The walls had recently been rebuilt, and from behind these strong new barricades they defeated two assaults. According to the sixth century Gothic historian Jordanes, they also paid the Goths to stop bothering them. The barbarians turned back to the Moesian countryside, where the peasants tilled their fields or the fields of their masters, herded cattle, and fished the rivers. A few of the landowners probably started converting their villas into forts, as more were to do later on; but the Goths overran everything.

Philip seems to have been more disturbed by the revolt of the army than by the Gothic invasion. The troops had made him emperor several years before, killing the boy Gordian. Now perhaps it was his own turn to go. He stood in the senate, which had always liked him so much, and pleaded

Lion. Reverse of an antoninianus of Philip the Arab struck for the Secular Games of 248. Inscription: SAECVLARES AVGG. 22 mm.

Philip Junior (son of Philip the Arab) as co-Augustus. Obverse of a potin tetradrachm struck at Alexandria. 23 mm.

rhetorically for help. If the senators were disappointed in him, he said—if they thought that somebody else could do a better job—perhaps they would accept his abdication. But the senators, the grave rich men he had cultivated, said nothing.

If Philip's offer to abdicate was sincere, he probably made it in the hope of saving his life. There would be less reason for the new man or his troops to kill an abdicated emperor, an ex-ruler retired to private status. But Philip may not really have contemplated giving up the imperial purple. He may just have been looking for sympathy and support.

Finally a distinguished senator named Decius spoke. The revolt, he asserted, was nothing to worry about. The usurper, named Pacatian, did not have enough backing. The senate should not exaggerate the situation. Decius proved to be right. Pacatian was soon murdered by his own soldiers.

But troubles multiplied. One or two men tried to make themselves emperors in the Eastern provinces, where Philip's brother Priscus governed. Priscus' administration was rigid if nothing worse; heavy taxes and liturgies caused the population to welcome any ambitious upstart who promised good times. A usurper named Jotapian was proclaimed emperor in Cappadocia, the mid-eastern part of Asia Minor. He struck coins with his own radiate portrait on them, but fortunately for Philip he was killed by his troops like Pacatian. It may have been as early as Philip's reign that another usurper, called Uranius, announced in Syria that he was the real emperor. He too issued a few coins—in gold, to pay his soldiers. We know scarcely anything about his regime—which can hardly be called a regime, since he did not even have much of Syria to rule over. But we do know that he kept holding out until 253 or 254, long after Philip was dead.[5]

While these men nipped at the Eastern provinces the Goths ravaged the Danube lands. Philip had been much impressed by Decius and decided to put him in command in Moesia and Pannonia (now Hungary). Decius' duties, in addition to defeating the Goths and their barbaric allies, would be to punish people who had followed Pacatian and calm down the Roman soldiers, who were still uneasy and undisciplined after Pacatian's murder, ripe for another usurper if one would offer himself.

At first, we are told, Decius declined the assignment. He seems to have been sincerely unwilling to push himself forward; the life of a senator and great landowner was evidently enough for him. He may have realized, besides, that if he succeeded in the difficult job the whimsical troops were likely to proclaim him emperor. He apparently did not want that. On the other hand, he may have been pretending a reluctance that he did not feel.

At any event he did undertake the arduous job. Jordanes says that when he got to the Danube he cashiered some of the soldiers for not stopping the Goths, and that instead of going humbly home they joined the barbarians. On the whole, however, Decius put things efficiently in order. He defeated the Goths, punished the rebels, and soothed his remaining soldiers by giving them their back pay. In June of 249 they declared him emperor.

Unlike other usurpers proclaimed by their legionaries, he did not immediately start issuing coins in his own name and with his own portrait. This would suggest that even now he did not actually want the imperial office. According to the twelfth century chronicler Zonaras, he also wrote Philip a letter assuring him that as soon as he returned to Rome he would turn in the imperial insignia with which the troops had invested him. But his sincerity is still open to suspicion. In an age when it was not rare for a military man to hope for supreme command, and at a time when Philip's reputation had surely passed its peak, Decius may have thought he stood an excellent chance to succeed to world power.[6]

There was, at any rate, no immediate way out of the honor with which the troops had overwhelmed him. If he refused to rule now, they would of course kill him. For his own safety if for no other reason he had to be an emperor, at least for the time being.

With his enthusiastic legions he set out toward Italy. Philip did not believe the letter about eventually turning in the imperial insignia any more than he would have believed the smile of an assassin. If Philip indulged in self-reproaches, there was abundant material to reproach himself with. He should never have trusted Decius, or handed him so much authority, or put him in a situation where he could perform like a hero. Decius was a much more serious threat than Pacatian and the others. Desperate, Philip gathered his own army and marched off to meet this usurper who had said a year before that usurpers were nothing to worry about.

Decius' soldiers were hardy, confident, and fresh from their Danube victories. Philip's were not, but they evidently outnumbered Decius'. In September 249 the armies fought near Verona.

Philip died in the battle; we do not know how. If we are to believe the historians Zosimus and Zonaras, his son Philip Junior, twelve or thirteen years old, died at the same time. The historian Aurelius Victor, however, says that when the news of Decius' victory reached Rome the Praetorian Guards murdered the boy in their camp.[7] It makes little difference how the young prince was killed. The dynasty of Philip the Arab ended with him.

Philip had, at any rate, tried his best, both administratively and militarily, even though in the light of the problems that he faced, his accomplishments from 244 to 249 had not been great. His final defeat is often adduced as proof of the well known fact that emperors were made and unmade by the army, not the senate. But in a way his reign really does begin a new age. Like him, his successors—or most of them anyway—were going to try their best, fighting inconceivable odds, struggling with soldierly stubbornness to rescue the ailing empire.

Notes to Chapter 1

1. Zosimus gives a circumstantial account of the Secular Games in general, without mentioning those of Philip, in **Historia Nova,** II. 1-7. Presumably the ceremonies observed for the thousandth anniversary resembled those observed for other Secular Games.

2. On the question of depopulation see F. Oertel in **Cambridge Ancient History,** XII (1956), 237-38 (concerning Italy only) and 267-68, and A. H. M. Jones, **The Later Roman Empire 284-602: A Social Economic and Administrative Survey** (Norman, Oklahoma, 1964), I, 25-26. But see also Fergus Millar, **The Roman Empire and its Neighbours** (New York, 1968), p. 243.

3. See W. Ensslin in **Cambridge Ancient History,** XII, 372-74.

4. See D. Berciu, "The Dacians in the First Century AD: The Roman Conquest," in Millar, **Roman Empire and its Neighbours,** esp. pp. 270, 275, 278-80.

5. See Ensslin in **Cambridge Ancient History,** XII, 92-93.

6. Among those who question Decius' apparent reluctance to be emperor are A. Alföldi in **Cambridge Ancient History,** XII, 222-23, and Sir Ronald Syme, **Emperors and Biography: Studies in the Historia Augusta** (Oxford, 1971), p. 198. But see also Ensslin in **Cambridge Ancient History,** XII, 93-94, and H. M. D. Parker, **A History of the Roman World from A. D. 138 to 337,** revised with additional notes by B. H. Warmington (London, 1958), pp. 154-55.

7. See Parker, **History of the Roman World,** p. 155.

2 Decius and the Christians

The new emperor had, like Philip, been born far from the capital. Philip's birthplace was an Arabian town; Decius' was the town of Budalia in the province of Lower Pannonia, now roughly Hungary. This was a part of the empire where Romanization had come slowly, brought mainly by the legions. But in the third century there were villas on the Pannonian plains and the fierce tribesmen who entered the Roman army were some of the most loyal defenders of Roman power.

Decius' father may have been stationed in Pannonia as a military officer at the time of the boy's birth. Both father and mother were aristocrats; the mother belonged to a proud Italian family. Decius himself had followed a typically aristocratic career of public service to the state, eventually occupying high stations which probably included that of City Prefect of Rome.[1] Close to sixty when he won the throne, he had a firm, lean, determined, dead-serious face with sucked-in cheeks, a harshly lined forehead, thin lips, and a long, narrow nose.

When he reached Rome in the fall of 249 and appeared before the senate he received the ringing acclamations customary at the beginning of a reign. Six hundred senators, shouting as one man, hailed him as emperor, blessed by the gods, victorious. Before the battle near Verona in which Philip died, the senators had declared Decius a public enemy. But now that lapse in foresight was forgotten. Perhaps at the senators' suggestion, perhaps at his own, he was even given the additional name Trajan, connoting the hero-emperor of a century and a half before who had led hard troops to triumph after triumph. Trajan had won many of his battles in the same general region, the Danube frontier, where Decius had recently been fighting, so in a way the adoption of the name was appropriate. As a result of his victories Trajan had added the trans-Danubian province of Dacia to the empire, making the Roman world vaster than ever, and had had a famous column set up in his honor. His name held the virtues and greatness of Rome.

At the capital Trajan Decius devoted himself to projects such as the completion of the baths started by Marcus Aurelius' son Commodus in the preceding century, and, as was to be expected, he also distributed cash to the people. These acts would contribute to his own glory, just as the name Trajan would if he did not disgrace it. Knowing that the barbarians might attack the Balkan provinces again at any time, he ordered the road on the south bank of the Danube to be repaired—the military highway that the legions would use in time of war. He also had subsidiary roads repaired and bridges rebuilt in the area. At his command, road repair went on also in Asia Minor, through which troops would have to march if there was a war in the East. When trouble came, he would be ready. Not that he neglected less vulnerable parts of the empire, such as northern Africa and Spain, where no danger was anticipated. If reconstruction was necessary anywhere he ordered it done. He would prove himself a good emperor.

It may have been the time he spent in the Danubian and Balkan provinces—either as a child, if that was where he grew up, or later in command of his army—that nurtured his strong sense of the dignity and supremacy of Rome. While half-Greek Asiatics in soft old cities such as Ephesus and Antioch rolled in luxury and lechery and did not care very much about the empire, the new, tough Romans in these harder provinces cared about it a great deal. For the farmers in Pannonia and Moesia and the men from the Illyrian mountains, especially those who fought in the legions, to be a Roman meant to be part of a solemn and noble tradition. These men still felt the exaltation of belonging to a nation that had beaten its enemies and had made most of the known world into its own empire.

The Romans of old had achieved all this through valor and devotion and with the help of the gods of the state. Jupiter, Juno and Minerva, Mars Propugnator and Venus Victrix, Neptune who watched over battles at sea, Vesta the goddess of the sacred hearth—these and other divine beings had given Rome glory in return for proper ritual and sacrifice. But the worship of many of these deities was in serious decline, not only in the East but over most of the empire. Philip's Secular Games had not left that impression, and of course it is true that a great many Romans still regarded the national gods with undiminished veneration. But other people, as they looked around and saw the misery of men and remembered stories of the prosperous past, wondered whether the traditional protectors of the state were worth praying to any more.

They may have expressed their feelings in cynical jokes or they may not have expressed them at all, but, consciously or unconsciously, they

Trajan Decius (249-251), laureate. Obverse of a sestertius. 28 mm.

turned from the national gods. Some were drawn toward Oriental deities whose rites were much more emotional than the formal Roman rituals, and who, like Isis the Egyptian goddess, dangled the promise of immortality in front of their devotees. Some tried to find a single, all-inclusive divinity, since monotheism was growing and the plethora of classical gods with their tangled legends and jurisdictions proved only a hopeless confusion. Some, in the countrysides of Gaul or Syria, adored the local deities of their ancestors and paid little attention to the gods of Rome.

Here and there, temples to the primary divinities of the state were run down because contributions had fallen off, or were even abandoned. Sometimes scabby flesh, fat, and hoofs were offered to the gods in sacred ceremonies. The government did not for this reason attack the various non-Roman cults that were flourishing, since it was felt that even local gods, pleased if people worshipped them, would do whatever they could to help the empire; in that sense all gods were Roman. But the situation still did not promise good fortune for the nation.

At least the cult of the emperor retained strength. Perhaps it was stronger than in previous ages. It was especially popular in the East, where, ever since Augustus, the emperor had been adored. In any self-respecting Eastern city and many in the West stood a temple dedicated to the imperial cult, with priests to perform the ritual. The emperor was not only the most powerful and the richest man in the world, he was the state personified, a human being who surpassed humanity because he was also Rome. Men swore solemn oaths by invoking his name. On his coins—the silver-coated double **denarii** that flooded the markets—he wore the radiate crown that associated him in people's minds with the sun god. He was the comrade of the gods who cared for the state, and he had been delegated by them to lead the state. Through him a man worshipped Rome itself. While his cult prospered, Rome could not be entirely lost.

According to many people, the Christians had less Roman spirit than any other group in the empire. They never worshipped the gods of the state, saying either that those gods did not exist or that they were actually devils in masquerade. From the Roman standpoint, therefore, the Christians were atheists. They did not worship the emperor either, although they prayed their one God to keep him healthy. When they were faced with the alternatives of obeying their God or helping the empire, they of course were committed not to help the empire. They called themselves soldiers of Christ and considered their kind of service more important than military service in defense of Rome. Christ was their emperor, and the actual emperor was irrelevant to them. Once in a while they announced that the imperial government itself was a fabric of evil, a Satanic machine, although they were gradually becoming more reconciled to its presence.

Large segments of the Roman populace—especially those who still had faith in the national divinities—said that the gods were angry. The troubles of the times—the barbarian menace, the abject poverty, the injustice—were punishments which the tutelary deities had unleashed because they were no longer honored as much as they deserved. As the worst offenders, the Christians should be made to sacrifice to the deities who protected Rome and let her prosper. All non-Christians, even those not especially interested in the Roman gods, would gladly render such sacrifice. Men saw no reason why Christians should not do it too. They should also be forced to admit the divine nature of the emperor, and the fact that he derived his authority from the gods. Then perhaps the troubles would abate, and people might be happier, and Rome might regain some of her majesty.

Decius himself took this approach. As an aristocrat brought up in the service of the empire, and as successor to an emperor who had tried hard to make the Roman world better, he felt that it was part of his sacred mission to get rid of disruptive, jarring elements in the state. As a soldier he favored compulsion: if people refused to be persuaded, they should be coerced. He probably also realized the psychological advantage, both to himself and to his empire, of concentrating his subjects' attention on one loathed object during this period of misfortune. He therefore decided to loose what later ages have termed the first great persecution of the Christians. It was the best way to pull the old empire together.

Up to this time, 250 A.D., the Roman government had not done much to check the spread of Christianity. The religion was illicit, which meant that technically anybody convicted of being a practicing Christian could be put to death. But that stipulation was seldom enforced. The imperial policy was to tolerate all religions, no matter how absurd or fantastic some of the local ones seemed, unless they involved obnoxious habits such as human sacrifice or unless, like Judaism in the past, they led their adherents to make war on Rome. Christianity, being subversive, suffered persecution occasionally, but only at rare intervals and not for long at a time.

The persecution that Nero instituted after the burning of Rome in 64—the one that probably gave both Peter and Paul the deaths of martyrs—was apparently no more than local. Burgeoning Christian centers in the East were not damaged by it. It had a dramatic side when Christians were fastened to crosses at night in the gardens on the Vatican, covered with pitch, and lighted as torches, but the faith soon recovered from the shock. With few exceptions, Christians were then left alone for a generation or more. Because the letters of Pliny the Younger survive we happen to know the policy of the emperor Trajan toward Christians early in the second century. Trajan ordered that those who were turned in by informers should, if convicted, be punished. But he added that no official effort should be made to hunt out Christians, and that if a man recanted and started worshipping the gods of Rome, he must be pardoned. Perhaps

Trajan felt that this offer of pardon for recantation was the best way to diminish the Christian ranks. At any rate his anti-Christian measures were not extreme.

During the succeeding decades Christianity—a creed with no temples, no wealth, and a short history—built up its strength and organized itself into a well-administered, widespread religion. In 176, toward the end of his reign, the emperor Marcus Aurelius, who could understand Stoic virtue and ancient Roman piety but could not understand Christianity at all, began a persecution. There was much anti-Christian agitation in Gaul and Asia Minor at the time and a few recalcitrant Christians lost their lives, but Marcus Aurelius died in 180 and the persecution faded soon after. The next one, early in the third century during the reign of Septimius Severus, was directed at recent converts to Christianity, and some converts were turned into martyrs before it all ended in a couple of years. The warrior-emperor Maximin, who reigned from 235 to 238, aimed a persecution at the Christian clergy, particularly the bishops, but many provinces do not seem to have been affected by it at all and ordinary members of the congregations did not have to be afraid of losing their lives.

The persecutions may even have bolstered Christianity by emphasizing the unity of this faith which stood alone against the whole Roman world and by making brave martyrs out of the few who were punished by death. Some new converts may even have come into the faith because they assumed that what a man or woman is eager to die for must be worthwhile. But the main attraction of Christianity was undoubtedly its assurance of salvation from sin and an eternal life of happiness for the good. In spite of the resentment of most of the Roman public and the scorn of many government officials, that assurance of redemption and immortality, preached by nameless missionaries in the late first century and throughout the second and into the third, brought people in.

To poor and miserable laborers trying to stay alive in polluted times, to slaves mistreated by harsh masters, and to rich sophisticates jaded with the luscious evils of Antioch or Alexandria, the Christian message must have been almost inexpressibly beautiful. In the early days of Christianity men often said that the Second Coming was imminent, and they looked forward to the Day of Judgment and the end of the sorry old world within their own unhappy lifetimes. As the decades wore on the Second Coming looked farther and farther off, but by that time Christianity was established. It was especially attractive to people who had been brought up to believe that whatever happened to an individual was fated—inexorably fixed by the stars—and that no one could do anything about his destiny.

Hardly anybody questioned astrology during this period; its practitioners, sometimes called Chaldeans, were everywhere, gravely informing their tremulous patrons what the stars foretold. To learn that a man was not caught in fate—that he was master of his own actions—that he could do good or evil as he wished, fashion his own destiny, and earn everlasting reward—was to be set suddenly and overwhelmingly free.

Some of the Oriental mystery religions, such as the cult of Isis the Egyptian goddess, and the cult of Mithra, Persian sun god and champion of good, also held out the hope of immortality and a release from fate. These mystery religions with their exotic rituals and intense adherents were the greatest rivals of Christianity during the days of its spread. They too offered the chance of exaltation, of spiritual union with the divine. Mithraism stressed heroic virtues and nobility of soul and had a ceremony very much like the Christian communion. For a long time there was no way of telling which Oriental faith would come out ahead. In the second century Isis worship outpaced Christianity by a long distance.[2] Quite a few people belonged to two or three of these Eastern religions so as not to miss out on whichever one happened to be truest.

But Christianity possessed certain advantages over other creeds from the East. According to it, Christ had already come down at a definite time in the not-very-distant past and made salvation an accomplished fact. There were no cycles to be gone through first, no vaguenesses and eventualities, not even any secret ceremonies or hypnotic trances. Redemption had occurred. The story of Christ, besides, was clearer and more immediate than the stories about Mithra killing a supernatural bull or the dismemberment and resurrection of Isis' husband Osiris. People knew what mangers were, and shepherds, and the crucifixion of criminals, and a teacher followed by his disciples. Christianity was close to everyday experience.

Mithraism, anyway, was mainly for men; it had attracted the soldiers first and had been carried by them to far parts of the empire, and it does not seem to have welcomed women. This, of course, put it at a decided disadvantage. As for the cult of Isis, some people found its white-robed, tonsured, cymbal-banging, effeminate Egyptian priests objectionable. In the cult of the Great Mother, an immemorially aged creed founded on fertility, the priests wore women's clothes and castrated themselves in ecstatic devotion to their goddess, and that was offensive to some people too. Adherents of both the Great Mother and Mithra used the **taurobolium**, the bath in the blood of a bull. On a latticework over a pit a bull would be slaughtered; the blood would gush from his neck, and the person standing underneath would let it flow over himself and let it drip into his mouth and eyes. This dramatic ceremony, which (unlike most ceremonies in the Eastern cults) was public, attracted many people, but for others the simple Christian baptism had more appeal.

So did the Eucharist, not only because of its sacred meaning but because it was something that everybody could share. The group participation which characterized Christianity, and which was felt in the weekly gatherings of the congregation as well as in the celebration of the Eucharist, did not necessarily differentiate this religion from other faiths that had come out of the Orient. But it set Christianity far apart from the official religion of the Roman state. The rituals for the Roman gods were usually administered by a few priests who had learned the archaic formulas, no longer comprehended by other Romans, and the formal acts; and the rest of the people, though perhaps onlookers, were non-participants. Some Romans converted to Christianity because they were hungry for a religion in which they could do more than just watch.

What annoyed ordinary Romans most about Christianity was probably its exclusiveness—the fact that Christians did not like to associate with non-Christians but stuck to one another in a clannish self-sufficiency. Rich Christians shied away from political careers, which would bring them into intimate contact with powerful pagans, oblige them to keep quiet about the gods they hated, and perhaps even require them to torture accused criminals or finance games in which men killed men or beasts killed men. Even poor Christians shied away from playing or feasting with neighbors who might contaminate them with a touch of idolatry. Christian men shunned service in the army, which would train them to fight rather than to be peacemakers and force them to march behind the legionary standards that the troops adored almost as gods. By the middle of the third century this aloofness was decreasing; Christians were mixing with pagans more and more and a few were even joining the imperial bureaucracy or the army. But during the years when Christianity was trying to grow the exclusiveness was very apparent, and it repelled many potential converts.

If a man was able to get past it, however, he discovered that Christian clannishness was also brotherly love. The members of this religious community actually addressed one another as "brother" and "sister." In place of the convivial, rollicking pagan feast they held an **agape** or "love feast" which emphasized the group's family feeling. It did not seem to make much difference whether they were humble, influential, or somewhere in between; they were "brothers" and "sisters" anyway, and in a world of class gradations this appeared remarkable. They practiced charity in the broad sense of love for their fellow human beings, as long as their fellows were Christians. They helped one another as if it was the natural thing to do. Now and then one of them even said that all their possessions should be held in common. This was an extreme position and in the third century it was seldom heard any more, but the Christians still gave generously from whatever they had to give, taking care of their own people while other Romans starved. At the capital and in other large cities the Christian church had minor officials whose duty was to distribute to the poor whatever the church could afford. Hundreds of the penniless depended on these handouts.

Meanwhile those who knew no better attacked the "love feast" as an incestuous orgy in which brothers had sex with their sisters, and some persons claimed the Eucharist was a cannibalistic ceremony at which

Christians ate the flesh of a child and drank his blood. These notions were fading out in the third century, just as the "love feast" itself was giving place to the Eucharist, but other calumnies kept coming.

Angry pagans said, for instance, that Christ had been a common magician — and a charlatan at that, unlike the many expert magicians who wandered through the empire performing real miracles. They declared that Christians themselves were sorcerers — that Christians used their wizardry to cause storms, famines, and plagues. Intellectuals reared in the tradition of Greek culture called the Christians barbaric, illiterate, ignorant; and since the church often opposed Hellenic art and literature and drew much of its membership from the uneducated poor, this charge was hard to refute. Other people laughed at the Christians for deprecating wealth and its enjoyments or for protecting their virginity rather than getting married and having a family. Others criticized them as uncharitable because they refused to donate money for baths, temples, and gymnasiums, the marks of civilization.

But the Christians increased in spite of all that, in the third century more than in the preceding two. They were to be found primarily in large cities and good-sized towns, where many persons used Greek or Latin rather than some local tongue with only pagan affiliations. In cities the devout could be tightly organized into a community with a bishop in charge and priests and deacons under him.

Most of the Christians in Gaul during the second century were probably immigrants from the East who had come to cities such as Lyons to find markets for what they made with their hands and sold in their shops, but by the middle of the third century some of the native Celts had been converted. There were Christians in Spain and on the island of Crete. In Greece the university city of Athens, where philosophies and religions proliferated, had a Christian community. The apostle Paul himself, of course, had founded one at Corinth. Christians held their assemblies at Sparta, once the military examplar of the Greek world, now a peaceful provincial town. Asia Minor (present-day Asiatic Turkey) was the biggest stronghold of Christianity. Its main cities, such as Nicomedia, Nicaea, and Smyrna, contained flourishing congregations, and even the more Hellenized of the rural areas had some. Christians at Ephesus, as at Corinth, could point to Paul as the founder of their church.

The Syria-Phoenicia area was not far behind Asia Minor. Its ancient ports such as Tyre and Berytus had Christian organizations that could compete for followers with priests of Isis or the Great Mother. At Antioch, capital of Syria and third largest city in the empire, the Christian nucleus antedated Paul. Not many Jews in Palestine had converted to Christianity since the early days of the new religion, and the land was tightly controlled by Rome. But although Jerusalem had been wrecked and rebuilt since the time of Jesus, whatever Christians lived in that city now forbidden to Jews could still walk in places sacred to him. The once-independent Arab kingdom of Osrhöene, east of the Euphrates, had been an officially Christian nation since about the beginning of the third century. Outside the empire there were even Christians in Persia.

Aside from Antioch, the great Christian centers of the empire were probably Alexandria in Egypt, Carthage in North Africa, and of course Rome. Christianity came early to Alexandria. Although for a while the religion was hardly important enough to mention along with the cult of Isis and multifarious other creeds of this Graeco-Roman-Egyptian metropolis, the Alexandrian Christians had asserted themselves intellectually in recent years and their writings were widely known. Fron Carthage, great and opulent Roman heir to the Punic capital, Christians had gone out to form congregations in other North African cities. By 256, only a few years after Decius' persecution, eighty-seven of those cities had bishops.[3] As for Rome, out of a population of about a million, at least 30,000 were Christian by the mid-century—perhaps as many as 50,000.[4]

Christianity was still very much a minority religion, but it had become a significant one. It was certainly worth persecuting.

Decius' edict or edicts against the Christians are lost, but from their effects it would seem that the persecution had two stages. At first the government went after the leaders, arresting them, incarcerating them, and perhaps executing them if they did not demonstrate belief in the national gods. The bishop of Rome, Pope Fabian, was put to death on January 20, 250, and the Christian community at the capital was in such chaos and terror that nobody could be elected to succeed him for fifteen months. The bishops of Antioch and Jerusalem were shut up in prison, and both of them apparently died there although Chrysostom says that Babylas of Antioch was beheaded. Quite a few ecclesiastics decided that they could benefit their flocks more if they were alive than if they were martyrs and consequently went into hiding. In Asia Minor, for instance, a zealous churchman named Gregory, who had been ordained a bishop about ten years before, climbed to safety in the hills, inviting his congregation to do the same.

The second stage of the persecution may have started as early as February 250. The whole population of the empire was commanded to sacrifice to the gods of Rome under the eyes of an official commission. The act of sacrifice might be only a gesture, such as sprinkling incense on an altar that stood before the temple of a god or before the emperor's statue, or eating a little meat from a sacrificed animal. But it was a gesture implying loyalty to the national ideals, and it would force soft Christians to deny their Christianity and hardened ones to declare themselves. Throughout the provinces commissions were set up to administer the edict. People who sacrificed were handed certificates saying that they had done so. Presumably, if they were secret Christians they could then go back to worshipping the Christian God. Those who refused to sacrifice could look forward to exile, perhaps the confiscation of their property, very likely torture, and maybe a bloody death.

Some Christians no doubt avoided sacrifice simply by waiting the thing out in obscurity. Others bought certificates of sacrifice from bribable officials. But even with these drawbacks, Decius' persecution was much more thorough than any of the previous ones. It involved the whole empire rather than just certain areas; it involved laymen as well as clergymen, followers as well as leaders; and it was designed to catch all social classes.

In June of 250 it intensified. Members of the secret police, efficient and deadly, skulked through the cities and villages ferreting out the hidden, the suspect, the hopeful. Men and women reported on Christian neighbors; it was a good way for them to get revenge on these people of brotherly love for paying them no attention in the past. Many Christians, of course, broke and sacrificed, and then went home to answer their screaming consciences. The stronger were whipped till their skin hung down like rags, clubbed into senselessness, or stretched slowly on the rack till their joints came apart. In prison they lay in chains, given only enough food and water to keep them from dying before they recanted.

At Smyrna in Asia Minor a priest named Pionius was questioned in the marketplace in front of a crowd of angry Greeks and Jews yelling for his death. The officials jailed him, and the police beat him up in an effort to persuade him to sacrifice. Even a rhetorician came and delivered a speech, but Pionius was not won over. The governor of the province examined him, found him stubborn, and ordered him to be burned alive in the stadium. Burning was a favorite form of execution because people thought that if a Christian's body was demolished it could not be resurrected. With Pionius died a priest who belonged to a group of heretics termed the Marcionites. This man too had declined to sacrifice, and although orthodox Christians would not have called him their brother, it was not for the Roman establishment to try to distinguish between one subversive sect and another.

A more pleasant story, but not a true one, comes from Ephesus. Seven young men hid in a cave near the city, as many of their co-religionists were probably doing. They fell asleep. When they woke up they felt hungry and decided to sneak back into Ephesus for some bread. Their hunger was understandable since, as they soon discovered, they had been sleeping for almost two hundred years. In the meantime the Roman Empire had become Christian.

At Caesarea on the coast of Palestine the authorities jailed Origen, the most famous Christian in the Roman world, a man in his middle sixties. Origen had been born into a Christian family at Alexandria. Living in one of the primary centers of Hellenic culture, he studied Greek disciplines such as geometry and Greek philosophies such as Platonism as a boy, but he also studied the Bible ardently, searchingly, greedily. About 202, during the persecution of Septimius Severus, his father was beheaded. Not intimidated, Origen used to give Christians the kiss of peace as they were being led off to death.

Soon after his father's execution the bishop of Alexandria appointed Origen to the headship of the Catechetical School, a lay society for advanced examination of Christian ethics and theology. He was eighteen at the time—intense, full of things to say, burning with love of God. At the Catechetical School he taught matters such as logic, mathematics and astronomy as preliminaries to ethical and theological investigation, and supported Christian training with Greek philosophical thought. It was partly because of him and his predecessor at the school, Clement, that Christianity began to free itself from the charge of anti-intellectualism and near-illiteracy that had embarrassed it earlier. Even pagans came to hear Origen teach.

He kept himself poor, ate little and sometimes did not eat at all, abstained from wine, slept on the floor, and wore nothing on his feet for years. By these measures he avoided some of the temptations of the beautiful world—the meretricious world of Alexandria, second in size only to Rome, crowded with things to attract the senses. While still a young man, according to a story, he removed his testicles for the same reason.

About the year 230, having run afoul of the bishop of Alexandria and other churchmen, he went to Palestine, where he had friends and where he had been ordained a priest. For the rest of his life he taught at Caesarea on the coast, occasionally making a journey somewhere to argue against a heresy or talk with some famous person but mainly gathering around himself at Caesarea the same kind of eager pupils that he had attracted at Alexandria. Origen turned Caesarea into a thriving Christian center. Interested pagans and ardent young Christians flocked to this city founded by Herod the Great. He spent some of his time teaching, some of it corresponding with other leaders of the church, including prominent Eastern bishops, and much of it in writing. He even sent a letter to the emperor Philip and to Philip's wife, since they were curious about Christianity. According to Epiphanius, a fourth century bishop, he produced 6,000 volumes. These were scrolls, not individual books, but even so—and even if Epiphanius exaggerated—Origen's literary output must have been remarkable. Experts in shorthand came to Caesarea to take down his dictation, and many scribes went there to make copies for distribution through the Christian world.

Most of his writings are lost, but we still have some, in fragments if not in entirety, and we know about others. His commentaries on the books of the Old and New Testaments, started while he was still at Alexandria but continued at Caesarea, approached the Bible from a symbolic and allegorical standpoint instead of a literal one and looked forward to the fascination with figurative interpretation that was to overwhelm the High Middle Ages. One of his most influential works, a piece of painstaking scholarship rather than an original literary effort, was the **Hexapla**, a comparative edition of the Old Testament. In parallel columns he set down six versions of the Old Testament: the Hebrew in Hebrew characters; the Hebrew transliterated into Greek characters; and four Greek translations, one of which, the so-called Septuagint, had been done at Alexandria in Ptolemaic times for Jews who had lost the knowledge of Hebrew. He emended the Septuagint and added passages from the other Greek translations in a desire to establish it as the authoritative text.

About 247 he allowed his sermons to be taken down in shorthand and copied out for the edification of Christians all over. Probably the next year —in any case soon before Decius became emperor—he wrote the treatise **Contra Celsum** or **Against Celsus**, an attack on an opponent of Christianity who had lived during the reign of Marcus Aurelius in the preceding century. Although Celsus' book has not come down to us, from Origen's refutation we can gain some idea of what it said, since Origen quoted passages in order to challenge them. Celsus called Christ a magician and urged Christians to participate like everybody else in the affairs of the empire rather than sitting back when civilization was endangered. He made considerable use of Platonism. But Origen, with his own extensive knowledge of Greek philosophy, relied heavily on Platonic ideas in his rebuttal; it was a case of a cultivated Christian employing Greek weapons against a Hellenist. Origen also argued that the church was infinitely more important that the empire and must always be served first. This was an impolitic opinion to publicize in a time of violent anti-Christian feeling, just before the outbreak of the persecution.

At Caesarea, Roman officialdom fastened Origen down with iron chains in prison, put him in the stocks and had his feet pulled out farther and farther; but the officials let him live. As the most notorious Christian in the state, life was perhaps more than he might have expected. He was not good for much afterwards, however. He held on as a mutilated man for three or four more years and then died of his own accord.

The bishop of Alexandria from about 247 on was a very capable and likeable man named Dionysius. Trouble had started at Alexandria before Decius announced the persecution—toward the end of Philip's reign in fact, just after Dionysius became bishop. Perhaps the trouble was inherent in the nature of this great, excitable port. People of many origins—native Copts, Nubians, Greeks, Syrians, Spaniards, Italians, Phoenicians—had come to Alexandria over the centuries to work at the docks, weave linen, blow fine blue-green glass, carve idols, practice astrology, make the papyrus plant into paper, worship Isis or God or Serapis, set themselves up as prostitutes or pimps, grow rich on trade, drive demons out of the possessed, swell the complex bureaucracy of the prefect or governor, concoct love potions, and make fun of the administration.

The Alexandrians were a reckless, fickle people, touchy and easy to rouse. Being intensely civilized they often let their indignation off as satire, but a savage fury lay under their laughter: they liked to form factions and riot. Most of their riots were relatively small but bloody affairs, soon forgotten. But under Trajan they had turned against the Jews, who occupied a whole section of the city at the time, and massacred the whole Jewish population. Now, at the beginning of Dionysius' episcopate, they rose against the Christians.

Dionysius himself described the pogrom in correspondence which the fourth century churchman Eusebius has preserved in his **Ecclesiastical History.** The correspondence does not give the cause for the outbreak, but presumably Dionysius' assumption of office had nothing to do with it. Perhaps some of the Alexandrians resented Christians for being successful in business; the economic motive is at least a possibility in this merchant city. No doubt the unpatriotic attitude of many Christians annoyed some of the population, and so did their religious aloofness, a strange thing in a metropolis where cults and ideologies brushed together in the streets.

The pogrom began with a minor incident. A mob captured an old Christian named Metras and tried to make him blaspheme his God. He would not give in. They bloodied him with clubs and poked the pointed ends of reeds into his eyes. Then they took him outside the city and finished him off by throwing rocks at him.

With their appetites whetted by the taste of Metras' death, they went after a Christian woman named Quinta. Dionysius does not say whether they took her to the temple of some Greek or Roman god or of some Eastern deity. At any rate they ordered her to worship the idol there. When she turned out to be as recalcitrant as Metras they tied her feet together and dragged her through Alexandria, into the dust and over the pebbles, beating her as they dragged. In the same place where Metras had been stoned they stoned her too, hitting her legs and her back and her head until she died.

Then they ran wild—swarmed into the homes of their Christian neighbors, grabbed whatever was valuable, pulled the furniture out into the streets and made fires with it, screaming insults at the Christians and probably mauling or raping those that they could catch. One of their victims was named Serapion after the Graeco-Roman god Serapis. They cracked his arms and legs and threw him down from the top of his house, head first.

There lived at Alexandria a very old woman who had managed to preserve her virginity throughout her life and was famous for it. They knocked her teeth out. Near the city they amassed a great pile of combustible material and set it on fire. Having tied up the ancient virgin, they told her that they would put her on top of it to roast to death unless she repeated the blasphemies they suggested. She requested a breathing space to make up her mind, and they granted her that and let her out of her bonds. The fire flared, and it looked as if she would give in. But a woman who had resisted sex all her life, in order to stand pure some day before her God, was not about to bow to idolators. Before anybody could stop her she jumped into the fire and was incinerated.

The rioters burned many other Christians—those who would not give in—and the whole Christian community cowered and hid. But finally the mob somehow turned on itself; Dionysius talks vaguely about a civil war within it. If Eusebius had not published the bishop's correspondence the whole pogrom and the civil war that followed would probably be just a couple of the many anonymous events in this unquiet city, pushed out of memory by events that crowded after.

When the Christians thought that the trouble was over Decius became emperor and the edict was announced. The pogrom was now official at Alexandria. Many Christians, unable to stand any more, rushed off to sacrifice, exclaiming that they had never been Christians anyway and stretching out their eager hands for the certificate that would give them official approval. Others resisted and were dragged screaming to the altars and stopped resisting there. One by one their names were pronounced and, cringing with shame as well as fear, they rendered their devotion to the demon idols, probably even to Decius himself. Some had to lie locked in prison for a while, and suffer their flesh to be beaten by scourges and torn away by iron scrapers, before they would consent to disobey their God. But eventually they too went through the motions of sacrifice and received their certificates.

Christians not bound to Alexandria by little children, old parents, or a lucrative business scattered into the desert or the mountains. The hardiest stayed alive there, but many succumbed to thirst or hunger, failed to protect themselves against a wild animal, or were dispatched by robbers. They could not go to a town because even the towns had their examining boards. Quite a few of them were apprehended and were carried back in misery.

As soon as the edict reached Alexandria the prefect or governor of Egypt sent military men after Bishop Dionysius. Thinking that he must be hiding somewhere, they searched all over for him, inside the city and out—along the roads, in the fields, on the water. He was at home, but they did not find him there because they did not look in so obvious a place. He stayed at home for four days, evidently believing that God wished him to preserve his life for the sake of the Christian community; but on the fifth day he escaped from the city along with his household and some of his congregation. They went west, in the direction of Libya.

But Dionysius and four of his followers did not get far. It was sunset, probably on the day after the flight from Alexandria, when a centurion and a detail of soldiers found them. Under guard, the five captives turned around and started back toward the capital. Dionysius does not say where the main part of his flock was. Perhaps these people succeeded in hiding whereas Dionysius and his friends did not try to avoid the soldiers.

Their prison that night was a building in the town of Taposiris, about thirty miles from Alexandria. Dionysius lay like his four companions on a hard bed, with only his linen gown between himself and the straw.

The Christian clergy had not yet been forbidden to marry, although people in the congregations occasionally suggested that a bishop or priest was more admirable when he proved to be superior to the interests of the flesh. Dionysius may have had a son named Timothy who had come along on the flight. Otherwise Timothy was simply a young follower or disciple of Dionysius who looked up to him as a spiritual father.[5] But Timothy had not been with Dionysius and the four others when the soldiers arrested them. The young man came back later, learned what had happened in his absence, and discovered where the bishop and the rest had been taken. As he was pacing in a state of high agitation, not knowing what to do, an Egyptian peasant noticed him and asked what was bothering him. The peasant, it turned out, was on his way to a wedding feast. It must already have been fairly late at night, but he had plenty of time because the country people generally celebrated weddings until dawn; that was one of their few pleasures in a life of labor.

After listening to Timothy's story the peasant went on to the feast, where his friends were already eating and drinking. He told them that several Christians were being held prisoner in Taposiris. These people apparently resented government authority, as represented by the soldiers, more than they resented Christians. Jumping off the couches on which they had been reclining at the tables, they rushed to the building where Dionysius and his companions were lying on their beds of straw. The soldiers took one look at the noisy crew and ran.

When they broke into the building Dionysius assumed that they were a gang of bandits. (Egypt, like other parts of the empire, was full of robbers, mostly poor men who had turned to thievery because it was the best way to earn a living.) The bishop's clothes were lying beside his bed. He grabbed them and held them out to these raucous men, telling them to take the garments and let him alone. They kept shouting at him to get up, to get out of the building, to escape while he had the chance, and suddenly he realized that they were trying to save him from martyrdom.

He was not at all pleased. He had been looking forward to dying for the faith, and he did not wish to postpone a death which he felt sure would come soon. He urged them to cut off his head.

The suggestion possibly sobered them a little. In any case they rejected it. He yelled at them to let him be, or to slice his head off before it was too late. The peasants decided they would have to save this Christian from himself as well as from the soldiers. They lifted him out of his bed. Furious, he managed to drop to the floor, where he lay on his back screaming. The peasants had had enough. They grabbed his hands and feet and dragged him outside. Then they handed him over to the four other Christians, who held him as securely as they could. His companions took him out of the town and, to make the contemplated journey to safety easier, they found an ass and put him on it.

With two of these friends Dionysius ended up in a remote part of Libya, dry and dismal. There he stayed for the rest of the persecution.

While he waited, people in Alexandria who did not submit to Decius' decree achieved the martyr's crown. Even though so many did submit, he heard glorious stories about Christians who had persevered until the end. Some of these recalcitrants were women—virgins as brave as the one who had jumped on her own funeral pyre during the pogrom and, perhaps more surprisingly, mothers of large families who would rather die than go back to their children after denying their religion. A poor old man called Julian, who had the gout or arthritis so badly that he could not even stand, much less walk, was carried to the judge by two fellow Christians. One of these men took the easy way out, but Julian and the other one refused to admit the Roman gods. They were hoisted onto camels and paraded through the city, the people screaming at them and pounding them with sticks as they went by. Then they were covered with quicklime. It ate their bodies just as efficiently as fire would have done. In the people's estimation, it was as good a way of preventing the bodies from being resurrected.

From other parts of Egypt too, there came accounts of savagery to Christians—for instance, the story of the Christian steward who declined to sacrifice to the gods when his powerful employer ordered him to. As the steward kept on saying no, his employer grew steadily angrier and let out a string of dirty names. Since these only made the steward more obstinate the man grabbed a strong stick and rammed it up the Christian's bowels.

Because Christians of the mid-third century did not avoid military service as scrupulously as their predecessors had done, the army was not the 100 percent loyal group that the government would have wished. Not many Christians had infiltrated it; in the main it carried out the persecution to the best of its considerable ability. But there were occasional soldiers who, being secretly Christian, could not properly enforce the edict. One of these men raised such objections to the treatment of poor old crippled Julian that the crowd had to shout him down, after which he was beheaded.

Several soldiers, on duty in court while a prisoner was being questioned as to Christianity, suddenly started moaning and groaning. It looked as if the prisoner was about to repudiate his faith, and the soldiers, who had no doubt heard many other people do the same thing, could not stand it this time. They rolled their eyes, gnashed their teeth, looked up toward heaven, stretched out their arms, wiggled in distress, and wailed. This naturally attracted the entire attention of the judge, the various officials, and all the listeners, including other Christians soon to be examined. Before anybody could stop the soldiers they rushed up to the prisoners' dock and announced that they were Christians. Their conduct, according to Dionysius, inspired the other Christians and terrorized the authorities. The men marched out in triumph, leaving the astonished court to pick up the pieces behind them. Dionysius does not say what ever happened to them.

Reports of official cruelty were of course exaggerated: many committees were reluctant to subject Christians to torture or dissolve them in quicklime. Even at Alexandria the governor could show leniency. A boy of about fifteen was brought before him one day along with three native Egyptians or Copts. The three men would not speak or act against the faith, and the boy was just as determined. The governor talked to him as a father, tried to persuade him to relent, argued with him and did not win the arguments: the boy gave intelligent answers and stood for no sophistry. Torture was tried; it did not affect him any more than conversation. In consideration of his courage in the torture chamber, his sensible replies, and his youth, the governor let him go free for the time being, telling him to repent. The three men were burned to death right away.

Notes to Chapter 2

1. For this probability, and Decius' age in 249, see Syme, **Emperors and Biography**, pp. 196-97.

2. On this point see T. M. Lindsay in **Cambridge Medieval History**, I (1964), 90.

3. Michael Grant, **The Climax of Rome: The Final Achievement of the Ancient World AD 161-337** (Boston and Toronto, 1968), p. 232. For most of the other material on the spread of Christianity I am indebted to Monsignor Louis Duchesne, **Early History of the Christian Church from Its Foundation to the End of the Third Century** (New York and London, 1909), pp. 143, 184-85, 188-91, 240, 285, 288, 326-27, 330-31, 351, and Kenneth Scott Latourette, **A History of the Expansion of Christianity** (New York and London, 1937-45), I (**The First Five Centuries**), 85-106. See also Grant, **Climax**, pp. 232-33, and Joseph Vogt, **The Decline of Rome**, translated by Janet Sondheimer (New York, 1967), pp. 45, 70-71.

4. See G. A. Williamson (ed.), Eusebius, **The History of the Church from**

Christ to Constantine (Baltimore, 1965), p. 282, n. 2, and Latourette, **Expansion**, I, 95.

5. See Roy J. Deferrari (ed.), Eusebius Pamphili, **Ecclesiastical History** (New York, 1953-55), II, 68, n. 7.

Isis nursing Horus. Reverse of a denarius of Julia Domna, wife of Septimius Severus (193-211). 17 mm.

3 Cyprian and the Christians

In 248 or the beginning of 249, while the pogrom was going on in Alexandria, a middle-aged man named Cyprian was elected bishop of Carthage. He had been a Christian for only two years and a priest for one, but in the opinion of most people he eminently deserved this important bishopric.

His disciple and biographer, the deacon Pontius, has this to say about him:

> So much sanctity and grace beamed from his face that it confounded the minds of the beholders. His countenance was grave and joyous. Neither was his severity gloomy, nor his affability excessive, but a mingled tempering of both; so that it might be doubted whether he most deserved to be revered or to be loved....And his dress was not out of harmony with his countenance, being itself also subdued to a fitting mean. The pride of the world did not inflame him, nor yet did an excessively affected penury make him sordid....[1]

In addition, he was active, forceful, clear-headed, strong-willed, used to issuing orders, inexhaustible, and extremely intelligent.

Until recently he had been carrying on a law practice. Very successful, he was well known among influential people at Carthage. Then he became acquainted with a Christian priest and everything changed. When he was baptized into the illegal religion in 246 he gave up law and just about everything else that had been part of his life. He stopped reading the books on which he had been brought up, the great literary heritage of Graeco-Roman civilization, and turned only to the Bible and religious writings such as those of Tertullian, leader of Carthaginian Christians in the preceding generation, thereby laying himself open to the charge of anti-intellectualism that many well educated pagans still leveled at Christians. He distributed much of his ready wealth among the poor, sold his estates and devoted the proceeds to the relief of the underprivileged, opened his house to the needy and dirty, put money in the blind man's hands and the widow's lap, and started living with the modesty that he considered appropriate to a Christian, apparently to the displeasure of his wife. To free his mind from carnal impediments he also resolved to have no sexual experiences for the rest of his life.

During more than a generation before Cyprian became a Christian, the church at Carthage had been unmolested by the government. The persecution of Maximin (235-238) does not seem to have affected the city, and the last martyrdoms had occurred there under Septimius Severus about 203. The safe and easy living since then had allowed the church to grow of course, but also to become slack and a little flabby. A number of Christians were educators, which meant that they read and expounded the illustrious works of Greek and Roman literature that Cyprian had abandoned. They admired pagan masterpieces such as the **Iliad** and the **Aeneid**, they enjoyed the stories about gods and goddesses, and they taught their pupils to admire and enjoy such abominations. A few—recent converts, perhaps—were even sculptors, fashioning statues of naked gods and obscene goddesses to be placed in heathen temples. People whose occupations compromised their Christianity could plead Paul's words in 1 Corinthians: "Let every man abide in the same calling wherein he was called." But with the purists that convenient text did not go far as an excuse.

There were Christians who made their money from selling incense for use in the temples, and Christians who entered professions the church explicitly forbade, becoming gladiators or prostitutes. Hundreds of Christians went to the games to cheer at the skill men showed in murdering one another. Hundreds went to the theatres to watch the incestuous story of Oedipus unfold or to see a mime, by far the most popular form of drama, in which lewd plots about the erotic entanglements of the gods, the suggestive gestures, and the bare flesh tickled the audience's taste for the prurient. "The matron," said Cyprian, "who perchance had gone to the spectacle a modest woman, returns from it immodest." As for the males in the audience, they "are emasculated, and all the pride and vigour of their sex is effeminated in the disgrace of their enervated body; and he is most pleasing there who has most completely broken down the man into the woman." The actors in mimes

> ...picture Venus as immodest, Mars adulterous; and that Jupiter of theirs not more supreme in dominion than in vice, inflamed with earthly love in the midst of his own thunders, now growing white in the feathers of a swan, now pouring down in a golden shower, now breaking forth by the help of birds to violate the purity of boys....Men

imitate the gods whom they adore, and to such miserable beings their crimes become their religion.[2]

At home ladies had their hair dyed and artificially curled in pride, spread cosmetics on their cheeks, emphasized their eyes by edging them with black powder, and gazed lovingly at themselves in silver mirrors. Their husbands pulled the whiskers out of their chins, disfiguring the appearance that God had given them. In law and commerce men cheated one another for the feel of a few extra coins. Cyprian, like Tertullian before him, was appalled as he looked at the Christians of Carthage.

What he objected to was of course not true of a great many Christians — simple, honest, quiet, pious people, trying to avoid pride if they ever discovered anything to be proud of, eschewing luxury if it ever came their way, not cultivating sex to the point of lechery, too poor to be guilty of avarice. But particularly among the middle and upper classes — and Christianity was no longer attracting only the downtrodden — worldliness was penetrating. Even some of the poor, as far as they were able, relished things that had made their heathen ancestors happy. The same was true at Alexandria, Antioch, Ephesus, and Rome — throughout the Christian world, in fact. Bishops themselves, God's representatives, sometimes did surprisingly well in business, seizing estates, charging interest on loans, and selling commodities for a fat profit. All this was one reason why, when Decius started his persecution, so many Christians either hurried off to sacrifice or agreed to sacrifice after very little persuasion. They did not have the hard, lean, almost fanatical religiosity of earlier Christians. They did not have the strength to resist.

Cyprian had been bishop of Carthage for about a year when Decius announced the persecution. From what we can tell, his office so far had not been easy. The Carthaginian bishopric was the primary one in all of northern Africa outside Egypt and Cyrenaica; bishops in other African cities looked to it for advice and leadership, so the responsibility was great and taxing. In addition, there was the problem of how to reform the lax and worldly Christians.

There was a more personal problem too. Although Cyprian commanded the high respect of almost all his associates and the intense devotion of many, a few disapproved of his election. This minority — composed, it would seem, of several of his priests and an influential layman or so — felt that Cyprian's rise had been too rapid, that the episcopal chair should be occupied by a more seasoned Christian. It was perhaps because of their opposition that he had at first declined the bishopric and even tried to avoid his enthusiastic supporters. He had finally accepted the promotion because he believed that his God meant him to have it; God had designated him, and there was nothing that anybody could do about it. But his opponents kept working against him. They probably resented his austerity and the authority with which he gave orders. They may also have envied his benevolence and suspected that it was a show; and they certainly interpreted him as conceited and ambitious. He may have been both, but if so, he did not know it.

In the middle of all this the persecution struck, and in its earliest stage it was aimed primarily at the leaders of the church. Cyprian would have been among the first to go up for trial. But like Dionysius of Alexandria, he did not wait to be brought before the authorities. He escaped to a hiding place outside Carthage, where he remained for the next eighteen months, while in the city the Christians were performing the pagan sacrifices or, here and there, risking their lives by refusing.

According to his biographer Pontius, whom there is no cause to doubt, it was not fear for his own safety that made Cyprian go into hiding. Since he believed so strongly that God had ordained him bishop of Carthage, he had to preserve his life and freedom. Otherwise he could not attend to his duties and lead his flock. He would have liked nothing better than the crown of a martyr, but he must not seek it.

The best way to look after the Carthaginian Christians from his retreat was through correspondence. He sent out many letters—a few of them to Rome or other distant places, but most of them to Carthage. He wrote to his priests and deacons, still carrying on there in unremitting peril, and to those who had made the shameful sacrifice in front of the commission, and to those who had admitted being Christians and were waiting for death. He advised the persecuted to pray, and to be a united group of brothers rather than falling apart under stress. He told them that if they had been united and virtuous in the first place the persecution might never have descended on them. He described a vision of a young man (Christ) sitting with his chin in his hand, sorrowful that his commandments were not obeyed any more, while an evil man (the persecution) caught Christians in a net with God's permission, since the Christians had been bad. He consoled them by adding that he himself had received divine assurance that peace would return to the church in time.

Meanwhile, those not in hiding attacked him. Along with a letter from Rome announcing the death of Pope Fabian as a glorious martyr came a letter, evidently from the distracted, frightened, confused, hysterical clergy at Rome, intended for the clergy at Carthage rather than for Cyprian. The purport was that Cyprian should be ashamed of himself for deserting his people when they needed him most, like a hired shepherd who runs away from the sheep when a wolf creeps up. There was even the implication that Cyprian no longer had the right to call himself bishop of Carthage, and that he should be replaced by a better man.

Cyprian did not take this humbly or even calmly. He sent the letter back to Rome, intimating that he could not believe the Roman clergy could really have written it. He also sent to Rome copies of thirteen wise and bracing letters that he had written to various Christians at Carthage. When the Roman churchmen read these letters they would surely realize that Cyprian was doing his part, and was staying alive for that purpose only. They did realize this, and they wrote to him to tell him so. They also appointed one of their most distinguished members, a man named Novatian who would be a good candidate for pope when they finally came to filling the vacant see, as the secretary who would handle future correspondence with Cyprian.

In spite of the reversed opinion of the Roman clergy quite a few of the Christians at Carthage, not convinced by Cyprian's real motive for hiding, thought that if their bishop could run away to keep from being killed, they could swear they were heathens to keep from being killed. People in the congregation perhaps had friends, sons, wives, or fathers who had been scourged, clubbed, clawed, and pulled apart on the rack, and had died glorifying God. Those were the heroes and heroines. It was easy for Cyprian to urge courage and virtue from concealment. If he was in prison waiting to be brought out for the lions, his counsel would carry more weight.

For this reason, and also from terror or from love of their families, and even from unwillingness to lose their property, many Christians at Carthage continued to cave in, just as many at Alexandria were doing. Some declared that they had never been Christians; some said they had tried Christianity once but had returned to the gods of Rome a long time ago; some said that they certainly did not want to be Christians from now on. These people who repudiated their religion were called the lapsed, or the fallen. They draped over the back of their heads the long white veil that Romans wore when pouring incense to the gods or tasting the meat of sacrificial animals; they advised their friends to join them; they brought little children along by the hand to deny Christ in front of the idols; and they revered those few who were steadfast enough to do none of these things.

The faction that had never wanted Cyprian to be bishop naturally capitalized on his absence, dropping snide comments about his irresponsibility, cowardice, and unchristianity, scattering calumnies among the harassed priests and the demoralized congregation at Carthage. This faction was headed by a rich layman named **Felicissimus, which meant** "the happiest, the most blessed." Most of the other members of the group seem to have been discontented priests. Felicissimus was determined to defeat Cyprian one way or another, to ruin this pretentious autocrat who had not been a Christian long enough to act like one when trouble came. He must have known Cyprian's real reason for going into hiding, but even this reason could be construed as an instance of outrageous pride. Surely Cyprian should not think that only he himself was qualified to direct the Carthaginian congregation.

Cyprian knew what was going on at Carthage and followed the machinations of Felicissimus' faction. But what worried him most was that not enough of the lapsed were really distressed about what they had done. They carried on as usual.

Occasionally, it was true, a story would spring up about divine punishment being meted out to one of the fallen. There was the man who, the moment he had rejected Christ, became a mute. There was the woman who went to the public baths right after eating the sacrificial meat, compounding her recent sin with the sin of immodesty. A demon entered into her:

> ...there, unclean as she was, [she] was seized by an unclean spirit, and tore with her teeth the tongue with which she had either impiously eaten or spoken. After the wicked food had been taken, the madness of the mouth was armed to its own destruction. She herself was her own executioner, nor did she long continue to live afterwards: tortured with pangs of the belly and bowels, she expired.[3]

Not only at Carthage but in many parts of the empire, however, it was relatively easy for the lapsed to obtain re-entry into the church. Technically, an apostate from Christianity was supposed to wait until the end of his life, and undergo specific forms of public penance, before being taken back into the bosom of the faithful. But with so many thousands of apostates this hardly seemed feasible. In actual practice, all that one of the lapsed had to do was to go to somebody who had admitted being a Christian and was consequently in jail waiting to be tortured or killed. These steadfast men and women, the unyielding few, were termed confessors because they had confessed their Christianity in front of the examiners. The fallen Christian, tearful and prayerful, could tell the confessor how sorry he was to have lapsed, how abysmally ashamed he felt, how terrible it was to be outside the church, and how greatly he would like to get back in. Then the confessor would absolve him from his drastic error and assure him he could re-enter the church. The confessor might even give him a signed statement saying that he should be permitted to participate in communion again.

This slackness enraged Cyprian. In his view only God could judge the lapsed. He came also to feel that bishops, as men appointed by God, possessed the authority to absolve the fallen and readmit them to the church; or in emergency situations, such as the mortal illness of one of the lapsed, a duly constituted board of priests and deacons could readmit a man without the bishop's permission. But confessors were another matter.

They could be very admirable in their own way: "With what praises can I commend you, most courageous brethren?...The tortured stood more brave than the torturers; and the limbs, beaten and torn as they were, overcame the hooks that bent and tore them...Oh, what a spectacle was that to the Lord...."[4] But even so, they were not entitled to interfere in affairs that were the clergy's business. They could plead for the fallen if they liked, but they must not readmit. They were usurping one of the most important episcopal prerogatives. Cyprian could not sit back and see that happen.

Since the confessors had stayed firm through excruciating torment, were hungering and thirsting now in their bug-infested cells, and would perhaps be earning the crown of martyrdom in a few days, they thought they had as much right as anybody to say who could come back into the church. The Holy Ghost, they believed, had bestowed this right on them in appreciation of their strength of character. The veneration with which the rest of the Christians regarded them, extolling them as warriors of Christ, possibly gave some of them an exalted conception of their place in the universe. One of them, a certain Lucian, even claimed to have been deputed to absolve the fallen in the name of a member of the congregation who had already died a martyr.

The confessors were, of course, most holy men and women. Some of the holiest, overcome by the ideals of their community, were very happy at the chance to be martyrs—hungered for martyrdom much more eagerly than Bishop Dionysius had done at Taposiris, longed for it with a sweet and powerful yearning, coveted the trappings of applause and honor as the beast bit or the body burned, and imagined the rich reward. To a few of these confessors, it felt good to be greatly honored even before they tasted glory. It felt good to receive the fallen and say, "Do not worry, sinner. I have the power to let you back into the church." They grew indiscriminate about whom to readmit. After a while they were readmitting almost everybody—the careless as well as the penitent, the brash as well as the chastened. They even started issuing broad letters of readmission covering a whole group of people, such as a family. Not all the confessors did this kind of thing, but the practice was spreading. Lucian was the most flagrant offender.[5]

Felicissimus and his faction encouraged this unselective granting of pardons—perhaps to bother Cyprian, perhaps to undermine his authority and ingratiate themselves with the greater part of his congregation, or possibly because they really felt that leniency toward the lapsed was the justest policy. The priests in Felicissimus' faction readily accepted the letters of reinstatement and welcomed back the hardened along with the humble.

According to Cyprian, this helter-skelter pardon of the lapsed to favor was as great an outrage as the idea of interference by confessors in a bishop's proper function. A man or woman, he maintained, must be truly repentant—prostrate in public, heavy with regret—before being considered for reinstatement in the church. Nobody should be allowed to take communion whose shame and sorrow had not been demonstrated in word and deed, tested and proved beyond doubt. He told these fallen souls: "You must pray more eagerly and entreat; you must spend the day in grief; wear out nights in watchings and weepings; occupy all your time in wailful lamentations; lying stretched on the ground, you must cling close to the ashes, be surrounded with sackcloth and filth; after losing the rainment of Christ, you must be willing now to have no clothing ...."[6] The disgusting spectacle must be stopped—the spectacle of unrepentant sinners tumbling over one another to get statements of readmission—people who had dropped incense to idols scrambling and crawling to take communion. "Do we believe that a man is lamenting with his whole heart, that he is entreating the Lord with fasting, and with weeping, and with mourning, who from the first day of his sin daily frequents the bathing-places with women; who, feeding at rich banquets, and puffed out with fuller dainties, belches forth on the next day his indigestions, and does not dispense of his meat and drink so as to aid the necessity of the poor?"[7] Cyprian held that God did not want this Christian chaff. Neither did Cyprian want it.

He was still in charge of the Carthaginian church, and the church would have to do as he prescribed. He wrote letters to his clergy, to the fallen, and to the confessors, praising the ones who did not absolve the lapsed. Except for emergency cases—in other words, people at the point of death—the question of who could or could not be restored to the church's good graces must be postponed until he himself was able to return to Carthage. He would take care of it then. He would not be especially autocratic; he contemplated consulting his clergy and congregation on matters of readmission or rejection. But nobody was allowed to do anything until he was again in the city.

Meanwhile the persecution slacked off. Barbarians had unintentionally helped the Christians by invading the Balkans. Decius' attention was diverted from the persecution, and the government's attention consequently faltered too. By the end of the year 250 the violence had dwindled to occasional roughness, and in the spring of 251 it petered out.

On the whole, the persecution had not been a remarkable success from Decius' point of view. The government had forced enormous numbers of Christians to recognize the Roman gods and deny their own God, but there were still a great many who had kept their religion a secret or (like Cyprian) avoided being caught. These people were neither confessors nor lapsed souls but just Christians as usual. As for those who had fallen, they probably felt even less loyal to Roman ideals than before, and of course they were rushing back to the church they had repudiated, blocked only by men with rigid principles such as Cyprian. Making martyrs of the most unflinching had only given the Christians models to look up to and had emphasized the underlying toughness of the church; even a few pagans were impressed by the martyr-heroes.

If the purpose of the persecution was to pull the empire together by cutting out the most blatantly disloyal element or by forcing the most disaffected inhabitants to worship the national gods, the persecution had failed. Its greatest accomplishment was to demoralize Christianity a little by making so many people lapse. Its other main accomplishment was one that nobody had intended: to crack Christian unity by creating the question of whether to take back the fallen.

Dionysius now proceeded from the parched recesses of Libya to Alexandria, and at Rome it was time to choose a pope to replace the long-dead Fabian. Easter fell on March 23rd in 251. Not long after that Cyprian came out of hiding. He had already tried to prepare for his return to Carthage by sending bishops of two other African cities there as his representatives, ordering them to inform Felicissimus of excommunication from the church. Felicissimus and several malcontent priests spearheaded a schism. The most turbulent of these splinter-priests, named Novatus, had made Felicissimus his deacon. Several weeks before going back to Carthage Cyprian wrote sharply to the Christians there, warning them that to follow the factionalists was to follow the devil and that nobody who joined these heretics could ever re-enter the true church.

So, although he had chafed to get back, he returned to a split community. The venomous Felicissimus had been busy as usual—whispering, implying, inciting, catering to discontent—and many of the Christian eyes that looked at Cyprian now were resentful. A large number of his priests, deacons, and subdeacons must have rallied around him, and the more conscientious Christians probably agreed that he had a point. His mere presence—his obvious sincerity, his piety, his concern for the flock that had strayed and been ravaged, and his devotion to the best interests of the church as he saw them—must have drawn people to him.

But others could not forget that he had been living in security all these months. Here, they thought, was the coward bishop, back when everything was safe, and instead of apologizing he was dictating to them. He refused to receive the people who had yielded through terror while he himself was ensconced in his secret retreat, away from the claws of the government. At least he could extend a little Christian mercy toward the fallen. Felicissimus and the maverick priest Novatus had stayed in Carthage working with the people throughout the persecution. These men showed mercy; they understood the lapsed and did not want to keep them out of God's church. But now Cyprian and his friends would not even let Felicissimus take communion. So ran the talk.

Cyprian seems to have proceeded calmly, ignoring Felicissimus' party whenever he could. Novatus, fortunately, did not have to be dealt with right now. He had gone to Rome to stir up trouble for Cyprian there, but so far his machinations among the Roman clergy had not borne bitter fruit. Meanwhile it was time to rebuild the church in Africa; and as a prerequisite, it was time to define. The matter of the lapsed had to be settled once and for all. A policy had to be agreed on and set down plainly for Christian communities all over North Africa to follow.

Cyprian called a council of the North African bishops—not the first Christian council by any means, but a larger one than many. Prelates came from cities in Tingitana, in Mauretania proper, in Numidia, in Byzacium. It was to be expected that they should assemble at the seat of their spiritual leader, the greatest city on the continent except for Alexandria. They came in the spring and stayed into summer, deciding questions of grave importance for the recuperating church.

On the lapsed they supported Cyprian. That was perhaps not surprising since his views, although they had sounded too authoritarian to some Carthaginians, were pretty much those of the clergy at Rome. There were two kinds of fallen Christians. The less heinous offenders had bribed venal officials into giving them certificates of sacrifice. They had never really recognized the heathen gods at all, but since they pretended to have sacrificed—since they displayed a certificate that satisfied the heathen government—they were in a sense denying Christianity. The council ruled that these lesser offenders would have to undergo a term of penance before being allowed back into the church, and the length of time would vary with the seriousness of the individual cases.

As for the majority of the lapsed—those who had actually performed the odious sacrifice—if they were truly penitent they could be readmitted to the church just before death. In other words a man's hope of salvation was not to be entirely cut off because he had sacrificed. To deny him this hope unequivocally would be to send him in his despair "to Gentile ways and to worldly works," or perhaps make him "pass over to heretics and schismatics," as Cyprian explained.[8] But until death approached he would remain unforgiven.[9]

While the council was in session, or possibly even before all the bishops had assembled at Carthage, news came that a pope had been elected in Rome and his name was Cornelius. The council dispatched a letter of congratulation. But there was trouble. A little while later news came that a pope had been elected and his name was Novatian. The split at Carthage was minor compared to the split at Rome.

In the capital the maverick priest Novatus had been intriguing very much in the spirit of worldly churchmen of the Renaissance. His object was to prevent the election of Cornelius as pope, since Cornelius, like most other prelates, approved of Cyprian's position on the lapsed. If an anti-Cyprian pope could be elected, then perhaps Cyprian could be declared ineligible to be bishop of Carthage for having vacated his see during the persecution. Novatus went to the Roman confessors, who, like the Carthaginian confessors, were insulted by Cyprian's rigorous stand. He went all over breeding discord, rupturing relationships among the

Roman Christians, strengthening his party through underhanded devices. He even went to the prominent theologian named Novatian, the man whom the Roman clergy had appointed to handle its correspondence with Cyprian and others a short while before.

Novatian received him graciously but, in so far as we know, did not at that time change his own position on the lapsed, which was the same as Cyprian's. As a matter of fact, Novatian in his capacity as secretary to the Roman clergy had written letters for distribution all over Roman Christendom, advising the same treatment of the fallen that Cyprian was upholding. Novatian also believed that Cyprian was the legitimate bishop of Carthage. It would seem, then, that he and the priest Novatus had little to draw them together. Certainly he was not Novatus' candidate for pope. But Christian politics were shifting and vicious, and in the very near future Novatian and Novatus were to be thrown together as opponents of the controversial Cyprian.

Novatian was ambitious to be pope. Even during the persecution, when people wondered who would be chosen as bishop of Rome if conditions were ever settled again, his name was frequently mentioned. Actually he was a more distinguished man than Cornelius. An elegant master of Latin prose, he wrote nine works that we know of. Only two survive: **On Jewish Meals**, interpreting the Old Testament taboos against unclean foods allegorically rather than literally, and **On the Trinity**, treating the complex question of the nature and components of the Trinity in a learned and orthodox manner and in the process attacking four or five of the period's popular heresies.

We are in the dark about most aspects of the papal election in the spring of 251—for instance, whether the priest Novatus caused much trouble at this time, or any at all, in his campaign to get somebody elected who would eject Cyprian from his bishopric. We can be certain only that whatever Novatus' attempts may have been he failed, and that Cornelius was elected.

But the eminent Novatian would not admit that Cornelius was pope. He himself was much more erudite; he had defended the faith in eloquent works; he had conducted the correspondence of the Roman clergy; his friends had expected him to be bishop of Rome. And if the minority faction that went ahead to elect Novatian represented the Roman church, Cornelius was pope illegally, though sixteen bishops had consecrated him.

Novatian sent to some obscure part of Italy for three bishops who were friends of his, telling them to come to Rome in a hurry so that they could act as arbitrators in the disputed election. They were simple men, not accustomed to the devices of ambitious priests. When they arrived Novatian got them drunk and, while they were sick and reeling, had them consecrate him as bishop of Rome by the ceremony of the laying on of hands, which represented the sanction of the Holy Ghost.

At least, that is the story as Cornelius tells it in one of his letters. Naturally prejudiced, Cornelius is perhaps not to be relied on for unembellished truth. Until this point at any rate, Novatian's reputation had been that of an upright, admirable man as well as a learned one. But his ambition had been wounded painfully—perhaps enough to make him resort to a trick.

One of the three simple, drunken bishops tearfully repented afterwards.

The other two evidently did not, and Cornelius' party dismissed them from their sees.

There was no final authority to appeal to on the question of who was really bishop of Rome. Whichever one was accepted by the majority of Christians, or at least of Christian leaders, would end up the winner. It looked very much as if Cornelius was ahead so far, partly because he had been consecrated by sixteen bishops in contrast to Novatian's three. He also knew how to vilify his rival, whom he described as a perjurer and hypocrite, a wild animal whose friendships were those of a wolf.

Cornelius claimed, for instance, that Novatian, lying very ill in bed at the time he was baptized, had not been baptized by immersion, which was the approved way, but only by a sprinkling. In fact, the whole ceremony had been the work of Satan. He also said that many clergymen and even laymen had opposed Novatian's ordination as priest. He announced that during the persecution the pusillanimous Novatian, terrified of torture and martyrdom, had denied being a priest, had refused to help his Christian brothers in their distress because they would identify him as a Christian himself, and had told the deacons he did not want to be a priest any more since he was interested in some other religion. Cornelius even claimed that at the present time, while Novatian was handing out the holy bread of the Eucharist, he would make the recipients swear an oath by the body and blood of Christ that they would not join Cornelius. But much of this, if not all of it, was just scandalmongering.

In the struggle for support the three most critical sees aside from Rome itself were Antioch, Alexandria, and Carthage. Both men sent out representatives to these cities and to others. The bishop of Antioch decided in favor of Novatian, and his decision was potentially a very influential one, especially in the churches of Syria. He planned to hold a council at Antioch to support Novatian, but it may never have met. The poor in Asia Minor liked Novatian, but their feelings did not count for a great deal.

At Alexandria, Bishop Dionysius came out for Cornelius but was less vehement on the issue than some of the other ecclesiastics, whose partisanship lacked good manners and reason. Dionysius suggested mildly that perhaps Novatian could withdraw his claim, since he surely did not want to embroil the church in a savage internecine fight so soon after the persecution and since he probably would rather not be pope anyway.

Of course Novatian did not take this suggestion seriously.

The council at Carthage was genuinely perplexed for a while as to who was the real pope, and it looks as if Cyprian was perplexed too. Everybody waited to hear from two delegates, both of them North African bishops, who had been dispatched to Rome to find out what was going on there. The two delegates sent back a report that Cornelius had been legally elected pope, and the churchmen who carried this report to the council had been present at Cornelius' election and could vouch for its legitimacy. That settled the matter. Novatian was a false pope, a false Christian.

Like the council Cyprian felt satisfied that Cornelius had been designated by God. He and Dionysius of Alexandria exerted all the influence they could to get Cornelius approved by Christians everywhere. The bishop of Carthage had made another enemy.

Some time after this—perhaps as late as the autumn of 251—a council of sixty bishops met at Rome under Cornelius' leadership. They agreed with what the council at Carthage had done about the lapsed. They also expelled Novatian from the church.

Notes to Chapter 3

1. Pontius the Deacon, **The Life and Passion of Cyprian, Bishop and Martyr**, in **The Writings of Cyprian, Bishop of Carthage**, translated by the Rev. Robert Ernest Wallis (Edinburg, 1880-82), I, xviii-xix.

2. Cyprian, **Writings**, I, 7. From Epistle I, "To Donatus." (Oxford edition places this among the treatises.)

3. **Ibid.**, I, 368. From Treatise II, **On the Lapsed.**

4. **Ibid.**, I, 33-34. From Epistle VIII (Oxford edition: Ep. X), "To the Martyrs and Confessors."

5. See Hans Lietzmann in **Cambridge Ancient History**, XII, 538; Duchesne, **Early History of the Christian Church**, pp. 293-94; Cuthbert Hamilton Turner, **Studies in Early Church History** (Oxford, 1912), p. 113; and for a particularly harsh treatment of the confessors, T. A. Lacey (ed.), **Select Epistles of St. Cyprian Treating of the Episcopate** (London and New York, n. d.), p. xv.

6. Cyprian, **Writings**, I, 375. From Treatise II, **On the Lapsed.**

7. **Ibid.**, I, 372. From Treatise II.

8. **Ibid.**, I, 142. From Epistle LI (Oxford edition: Ep. LV), "To Antonianus."

9. See Alban Butler, **Lives of the Saints**, edited, revised, and supplemented by Herbert Thurston, S. J. and Donald Attwater (New York, 1956), III, 563-64; Lacey (ed.), **Select Epistles of St. Cyprian**, pp. xviii-xix; Lietzmann in **Cambridge Ancient History**, XII, 539; and Edward White Benson, **Cyprian: His Life, His Times, His Work** (London and New York, 1897), pp. 156-59. See also Epistle LI in Cyprian, **Writings**, I, 133-52.

4 The End of Decius

The barbarians who distracted Decius' attention from the Christians were the Goths.

These people were East Germans—much less civilized than the West Germans whom Romans had been fighting for two or three centuries and who by this time were advanced enough to practice agriculture and appreciate Roman money. The Goths at some time in their past had crossed the cold Baltic Sea from Scandinavia in unsafe vessels and under the leadership of warrior chiefs. By the first century A.D. they were established on the south shore of the Baltic and had gone south from there along the Vistula River in what is now Poland. The Romans did not worry about them—these shaggy hunters, fishers, and fighters in an obscure, chilly, uninviting world a long distance from the borders of the empire.

But early in the third century A.D. the Goths were on the move again, trekking southeast toward the mouths of the Danube and the Don. When other barbarians opposed them they waged wild warfare, blood-splashed, drunk with the smell of battle, performing the great and savage deeds that were their only claim to glory. Perhaps their exceptional killings would get preserved in heroic tales and recited at night when there was nothing better to do than to remember how wonderful it was to make war. They swept down toward the north shore of the Black Sea, and in this area some of them settled—along the rivers leading into the Black Sea from the north, in the region we call the Ukraine. It was a rich and pleasant land, with broad steppes in the east toward the Don, thick oak forests west of the Dniester, and plenty of game everywhere.

Across from them, on the south shore of the Black Sea, lay the Roman provinces of Asia Minor. To the west was Roman Dacia; to the southwest,

Roman Moesia and Thrace. All these provinces, with their cultivated fields and prosperous cities, looked very attractive to barbarian eyes. For a while the Goths let them alone, but the temptation was too great. First they attacked the Black Sea towns of Olbia and Tyras, which had flourished many centuries ago as isolated commercial outposts of the Greek world but had been weakened by the onslaughts of Scythians and other barbarians and proved an easy prey.[1]

Then, in the year 238, a Gothic army crossed to the west bank of the Danube in the province of Dacia and attacked Istrus, another ancient Greek port, near the mouth of the river. The boy emperor Gordian III bought them off with the promise of a yearly payment of money. Toward the end of Philip's reign in 248, as we have seen, they surged into the province of Lower Moesia and besieged its capital, Marcianopolis, angry because the Roman government was not keeping up the payments. As Philip's general, Decius defeated them. Now, in 250, they were back, breaking the peace of Decius' own reign.

Decius had two teenage sons. It was probably in the spring of 250 that he sent the older one, Herennius Etruscus, to the Danube region at the head of seasoned troops. The soldiers were the same ones, apparently, that had marched from the frontier into Italy in 249 to drive Philip from the throne. We know scarcely anything about Herennius Etruscus except that his portraits on coins depict him as a serious youth with close-cut hair. Decius no doubt believed that sending him to war against barbarians would be excellent training for the imperial command which might eventually be his. It would harden him for the hard life he would have to live if he lived at all. His performance on the campaign could also be an important factor in his favor when the army and senate came to choosing Decius' successor as emperor. He had probably grown up in the Danube region anyway, so that he knew it well. But his younger brother was left in the luxury and safety of Rome.

Decius himself marched to the frontier soon after his son—most likely during the summer of 250, while the persecution that he had inaugurated half a year before was at its height. We lose track of the son for a long time; we do not know whether he was distinguishing himself on the frontier. As for the father, he may not have tried to deal with the Goths immediately but went instead to Dacia, north of the Danube, to clear out the Carpi, who had allied themselves with the Goths and were ravaging the already ravaged province. He evidently succeeded against the Carpi. Like Philip's campaigns in the Balkan region, Decius' come to us in garbled, cursory reports.

The Goths were led by Kniva, the astute battle-king whom they would follow anywhere against any odds. Kniva sent one army through Moesia and across the Haemus range that separated Moesia from Thrace. The mountain passes were easy to get through since no Roman troops defended them. In Thrace the Goths roared on toward the large city of Philippopolis, spoiling the land as they went, gorging themselves on the convenient crops.

Philippopolis, City of Philip, had been founded around the middle of the fourth century B.C., probably on the site of an older town, by Philip II of Macedon, father of Alexander the Great. He had named it after himself and had apparently started it off as a penal colony. Twenty-five miles to the north rose the Haemus mountains. Around the city stretched a fertile plain, with peasant villages scattered over it, and the Hebrus River flowed past. Silver and gold could be mined near by. Grain grew abundantly. So did grapes for the wines for which Thrace was famous; the province adored the great god Dionysus, who was worshipped drunkenly and orgiastically in the mountains. The climate around Philippopolis was also fine for roses, and the city became a center for rose perfume.[2] With all these advantages it could not help flourishing. Greeks, native Thracians, and Italian immigrants mingled in its streets. At the time the Goths sat down outside it, the population is supposed to have been about 100,000. To the Goths it must have looked magnificent.

Decius evidently wrote the citizens a letter which was read to them by Priscus, the governor of Thrace, while they were assembled in the stadium. That, at least, is what is told us by Dexippus, an Athenian who lived in these times. Although the emperor naturally hoped they would be courageous under siege, he warned them to be cautious. They were not used to walking the streets armed, since Roman civilians were not normally permitted to carry arms. He seems to have had some suspicion that with weapons in their hands these Thracian Romans might revolt. He probably also suspected the troops stationed at Philippopolis under Priscus. It would not be the first time that soldiers took advantage of a war to rebel against their emperor.

While one of the Gothic armies was busy besieging Philippopolis, King Kniva took his other army to Novae, in Moesia on the south side of the Danube. Jordanes, the Gothic historian who lived several centuries later, says that Kniva's army contained 70,000 men. This was a great many Goths to invest the town of Novae without taking it, and Jordanes may have been exaggerating. In any case the Goths withdrew when Gallus, governor of Moesia, advanced.

But the withdrawal was not a retreat. Kniva with his army sauntered down the valley of the Jatrus River, a Danube tributary. They no doubt fattened themselves as they went, at the expense of the Moesian peasants and landowners. They were headed for Nicopolis, City of Victory, which the emperor Trajan had named in commemoration of his defeat of Slavic barbarians called the Sarmatians when he was piling up glories for Rome. Nicopolis lay about as far north of the Haemus range as Philippopolis lay south of it. When King Kniva reached this city it was crowded with peasants from the farmlands outside. They had rushed to get into the comparative safety of its walls as peasants in the Middle Ages rushed to get behind the walls of castles—frantic, taking their few possessions along with them, outrunning the savage men who had probably swarmed over their fields already and confiscated their cattle.

Decius, apparently having finished with the Carpi in Dacia, marched with his troops to Nicopolis and defeated the Goths there, costing them perhaps as many as 30,000 casualties. Kniva was now really in retreat —south over the Haemus mountains into Thrace, with Decius and his confident Romans chasing. But the Romans chased too hard. Forced marches through the rugged hills were not invigorating even for a victorious army. At the city of Berea on the south side of the mountains Decius had to rest his troops. While they were taking their breathing spell, the Goths attacked. The screaming, skin-clad men were suddenly on top of them, hewing with their vicious short swords and protecting themselves with round shields. By the time the Romans had recovered from the shock they were cut to pieces. When the Goths had killed enough men to satisfy their lust for glory they looted the camp.

Kniva had proved himself a great war leader again. He turned southwest now and joined his other army, which was still besieging Philippopolis. But either shortly before he got there or shortly after, the situation at the terrified city changed. Priscus, military governor of Thrace and prime protector of the city, used the emergency for his own advantage: he revolted against Decius. His men proclaimed him emperor, and he proceeded to join the Goths. Very likely the barbarians promised safety for Priscus and his troops when Philippopolis was taken.

With the Goths and the Roman army both against them, the citizens were of course doomed. The Goths stormed in, impatient to swill the wines and seize the riches of this city of rose perfume. They seem to have massacred everybody.

We do not know what happened to Priscus, but he was never heard from again.

While the Goths disported among the corpses of Philippopolis and ran wild over Thrace, Decius tried to recuperate. Meanwhile the fickle mob at Rome, disheartened by the news from the front, thought that another emperor might do better and proclaimed a certain Valens. He was quickly overthrown, but even so, Decius must have realized about this time that his own great ambition to restore the ancient virtues of the empire was plummeting toward failure.

The money, among other things, continued to be discouraging. The silver-coated **antoniniani** or double **denarii** were looking baser and baser. In an attempt at propaganda Decius had started issuing some **antoniniani** that carried the portraits of deified emperors from the past, such as Augustus, Trajan, and Marcus Aurelius, men who represented true Roman

Trajan Decius (249-251), radiate. Obverse of a double sestertius. 33 mm.

Herennius Etruscus (son of Decius) as Caesar. Obverse of a sestertius. 28 mm.

gravity and grandeur. But their solemn faces on the pseudo-silver coins only pointed up the contrast with the present. Decius had also instituted a new coin, a double **sestertius**. Thick and heavy, made of shiny brass, this piece was calculated to impress. His stern radiate portrait on the obverse connoted Roman dignity, but the allegorical female on the reverse, sometimes a winged Victory and sometimes the Happiness of the Age standing with caduceus and horn of plenty, must have seemed an irony.

Then of course there was the slackening in the anti-Christian campaign; Decius did not have time to check subversive groups right now. Only one thing could give him back the respect of his subjects and the power to carry on the reunification of the empire. He needed a great victory over the Goths.

They were going home now, dragging their loads of booty, still despoiling the countryside, jubilant and insolent. They had had a wonderful war and it was time to relax with their women. North through Thrace they went and north through Moesia, probably traveling close to the Black Sea. Decius caught up with them somewhere around the mouth of the Danube. He had stationed his general Gallus, governor of Moesia, in the area, so that Gallus' troops as well as his own could be hurled against the barbarians.

The battle took place near an obscure spot called Abrittus or Forum Terebronii, in a marshy, ugly tract of country that was probably not Decius' choice. Whether Gallus helped at all, we do not know. He may have done as much harm as he could. The relatively reliable historian Zosimus, who wrote in the late fifth century, says that Gallus, ambitious to be emperor, betrayed Decius by making a clandestine compact with the Goths.

Kniva's men, according to Zosimus, were drawn up in three divisions. The first was protected in front by a stretch of swamp, but Decius attacked and drove the Goths before him and was conqueror so far. He made the second barbarian division retreat too. The great victory that he had to have moved closer.

But it may have been in one of these two engagements that his teenage son crumpled with a Gothic arrow in him. According to Jordanes, the boy's father saw him drop. The emperor loved the son he had sent to war, but there would be time to praise him and cry for him later, after the battle was won. Right now he must not let the prince's death discourage the men. So he shouted that the loss of one soldier was not that important for the Roman state. No man should mourn the emperor's son.

The third Gothic division looked small, but it was placed on the other side of a bog. According to Zosimus, this was where Gallus really played foul. He signaled the emperor to attack. Decius led his men into the bog and they got stuck. While they were floundering in the mire, the Goths sent their javelins raining down on them. The Romans fell bleeding into the ooze. Decius was one of those who fell.

His body and his son's body were never found; they lay with thousands of others decomposing in the swamp. The senate declared them both to be gods, but their defeat ranked among the worst that the empire ever suffered from barbarians. Not since Teutoburg Forest in the reign of Augustus, when Germans annihilated three legions, had Roman lordliness been so insulted. The barbarians could laugh at Rome as they climbed out of the mud and continued on toward their camps near the Dniester or the Don. Decius' vision of a sturdy new empire held no more truth than his coins. It was up to the next man to remake Rome. The next man, of course, was Gallus.

Notes to Chapter 4

1. But see Norman H. Baynes, **Byzantine Studies and Other Essays** (London, 1955), p. 220, where he maintains that Olbia was occupied by the Goths after 248 rather than in the reign of Severus Alexander (222-235) as is generally assumed, and that Tyras was not occupied by the Goths until the reign of Gallienus (253-268).

2. See A. H. M. Jones, **The Cities of the Eastern Roman Provinces**, 2nd edition (Oxford, 1971), pp. 4-5, 21, and Theodor Mommsen, **The Provinces of the Roman Empire: The European Provinces**, edited by T. Robert S. Broughton (Chicago and London, 1968), p. 324.

5 The Reign of Gallus

After the surviving Roman troops had proclaimed Gallus their emperor, he made a treaty with the Goths. It was not an advantageous one from the Roman point of view, but perhaps it was all that could be accomplished under the circumstances. According to this agreement the Goths could continue on to their homes with the staggering amount of loot that they had taken from Philippopolis, from other cities and towns in Moesia and Thrace, and from the estates of prominent landowners. They could also keep the Romans whom they were dragging with them as captives. Many of these prisoners were citizens of Philippopolis—prosperous men and matrons a short while ago, now being forced along to some barbarian camp near the Black Sea. Finally, the treaty assured the Goths a yearly payment of gold by the Roman government.

Having made this humiliating peace, Gallus set out for Rome, where the senate confirmed the army's choice of him as emperor. At the capital, citizens who had seen the boastful splendor of Philip's Secular Games less than four years before may have blamed Gallus for the national disgrace. But more of them probably blamed Decius, who had, after all, let the Goths do as they wished in Roman territory and then had let them kill him, the first Roman emperor ever to die in battle against the nation's enemies. Gallus' treachery in the swamp does not seem to have been generally known, although it may have been rumored. It may not even be a fact; we have only the word of the historian Zosimus. Little is known about Gallus except that he came of an ancient Etruscan family and that he did not have the vigor of either Philip or Decius. Whether he was capable of betraying his emperor and gathering the reward cannot be determined.

He adopted as his own son Decius' remaining son, Hostilian—the boy who had been left in Rome while his brother and father went off to fight

Trebonianus Gallus (251-253), laureate. Obverse of a bronze struck at Antioch. 29 mm.

Emperor standing with branch and transverse sceptre. Reverse of an antoninianus of Volusian. 21 mm.

the Goths. He also had the senate make Hostilian co-emperor with himself. These may have been elaborate gestures of hypocrisy. If so, they probably fooled the Roman populace and may have fooled the senators too. The senate gave the title **Augustus** to Gallus' real son Volusian, a young man somewhat older than Hostilian; so there were now three co-emperors, one of whom had all the power.

No record exists of Gallus' relationships with his expanded family, or of whether the real and the adopted son cooperated with each other or detested each other. Decius' widow, Hostilian's mother, went into retirement. Gallus' own wife did not take the title **Augusta**, or empress; this title remained the exclusive honor of Decius' widow, and again the impression is that Gallus was showing an extraordinary amount of thoughtfulness toward the family of his departed chief.

It was apparently toward the end of the year that Decius' son Hostilian died. The report that he succumbed to the plague then raging in Rome may have been true. The historian Zosimus, however, says that Gallus arranged the boy's death. This makes Zosimus' picture of the new emperor a consistent one, but again we have no way of gauging its veracity.

Even if Gallus was not the villain that Zosimus claims he was, he evidently had no bright-burning vision of reshaping the empire. At least he did not exert himself as Philip and Decius had done. The temper of the times may have been partly responsible for this. People who had been discouraged when Philip came to the throne seven years before were more discouraged now. Some of them clung to the memory of old Roman valor and the persuasion that Rome was eternal, but nobody could deny the actual fact: the empire could be raided and roundly defeated by barbarians in skins, and obliged to accept an ignominious peace treaty. It looks as if Gallus was content to maintain the miserable status quo without trying to make the world better.

He did not even do much against the Christians. Early in 252 there were rumors of a renewal of the persecution—rumors that terrorized Christians in Carthage and everywhere else—but if Gallus actually did renew the persecution he does not seem to have pushed it very energetically. Pope Cornelius was arrested at Rome and kept in prison until he died in the summer of 253, but we do not know of a great deal else that can be attributed to Gallus' anti-Christian program. The new pope, Lucius, was exiled but not killed, and about the end of Gallus' reign or the beginning of the next reign he was allowed to come back to Rome.

Even if Gallus had been more dynamic he might have been prevented from action by the plague. The primitive medical accounts of the period do not make it perfectly clear just what kind of a plague this was, but bubonic seems to be the most likely guess. It had started in the slums of Egypt in 251 or possibly as early as 250, when Decius was still reigning; and it spread, invisible and horrible, through the cities of the empire, knocking people over, knocking out whole families, piling up the bodies.

The symptoms were a high fever, vomiting, and diarrhoea. Sometimes it infected the eyes or attacked the extremities. Occasionally somebody recovered from it, but with the loss of his putrefied feet or a whole leg. Other victims ended up deaf or blind. Most people, however, simply died. Gibbon estimates that half the population of Alexandria was killed by the pestilence, and although his careful eighteenth century mind may be indulging in an overcalculation here, he probably is not far wrong. If the boy Hostilian had really been murdered, attributing his death to the advent of the plague at Rome was the most plausible course that Gallus could have taken. Cyprian's biographer Pontius says that at Carthage the sickness

> ...invaded every house in succession of the trembling populace, carrying off day by day with abrupt attack numberless people, every one from his own house. All were shuddering, fleeing, shunning the contagion, impiously exposing their own friends, as if with the exclusion of the person who was sure to die of the plague, one could exclude death itself also. There lay about the meanwhile, over the whole city, no longer bodies, but the carcases of many....[1]

The emperor decided that in this emergency more sacrifices than usual should be offered to the gods. He struck coins dedicated to Apollo as a giver of health, but Apollo was as deaf as some of the victims. Gallus also did what he could to ensure the proper burial of the dead at Rome, so that they would not litter the streets any longer than absolutely necessary. Except for that, he was not able to help his subjects.

At Carthage Cyprian organized the Christians and instructed them to be merciful even to the heathen in this communal distress. He urged the rich to contribute money for whatever relief money could bring, and asked the poor to contribute their services by caring for the stricken. The plague, he said, "examines the minds of the human race, to see whether they who are in health tend the sick; whether relations affectionately love their kindred; whether masters pity their languishing servants; whether physicians do not forsake the beseeching patients; whether the fierce suppress their violence; whether the rapacious can quench the ever insatiable ardour of their raging avarice even by the fear of death...."

Some of the Christians could not understand why the plague did not let them alone and attack only pagans. God did not seem to be watching out for his own people. Cyprian explained that Christians were subject to the same ills of the flesh as other human beings—to more ills, in fact, since Christians were Satan's prime targets. In his view, the plague gave them a chance to show how firm, how Job-like they could be in a time of agony. "What a grandeur of spirit it is to struggle with all the powers of an unshaken mind against so many onsets of devastation and death!"

Besides, their thoughts ought to be directed toward heaven; they should not regret having to leave "the captivity of earth." For good Christians, the plague was "a departure to salvation."[2] They should think of it in that light; and perhaps a number of them did.

In May of 252 another council met at Carthage under Cyprian's leadership. The Christians at this time were telling each other that Gallus was going to revive the Decian persecution in all its fury. The purpose of the council was to decide what to do in the face of the threatened terror, and that question concerned the lapsed. Cyprian, who had been maintaining so strongly that no sacrificers to pagan gods could be readmitted to the church except at the point of death, now changed his mind. The important point, he announced, was that the church present a united front against the anti-Christian government. Christianity needed as many soldiers as it could get to fight the fight of the Cross against the false and cruel gods of Rome. The council therefore decided that any lapsed Christian who demonstrated an eagerness to join this battle, and who had been performing penance piously since he made sacrifice to the gods, should be readmitted to the church. Such a person did not have to wait until he was dying to be taken back. Sincerity was the criterion.

Meanwhile Novatian, excommunicated but not unbeaten, was trying to establish himself as pope in opposition to Cornelius, who had not yet been imprisoned by the emperor. No one knows exactly when Novatian started revising his views on the lapsed. It may even have been as early as Cornelius' election to the papacy.[3] At any rate he gradually adopted a platform that was more purist, or puritanical, than Cyprian's former one. He ended up with the conviction that none of the lapsed could ever be readmitted into the church, even if they had only bought certificates of sacrifice without actually sacrificing, and even if they were on their deathbeds.

The church, Novatian came to believe, had no power to forgive the fallen under any circumstances; and Cyprian and other bishops, in exercising that power, were insulting Christ. The church was too high and holy a body to contaminate itself with people who had dropped into apostasy. Once a man had denied Christianity he was out forever, no matter what. He should still tear his hair, wail and moan, and hate himself for being such a sinner, but the most abysmal penance would never get him back into the church. He belonged in hell.

The fact that Novatian's position on the lapsed grew increasingly austere while Cyprian's grew increasingly lenient furnished the two Christian leaders with an excellent cause of contention. But their antagonism really had a basis in Cyprian's support of Cornelius as pope. Cyprian had been backing Cornelius with as much energy as he was capable of, and he was capable of a great deal. He had sent out urgent letters to other bishops, championing Cornelius over Novatian.

It was now clear that Novatian would not win his campaign for the papal chair, but Novatian still maintained that he was the true pope and that his own brand of Christianity was the true church. Cyprian's church, he said, was sullied by the readmission of the lapsed. Every fallen Christian who was taken back in—no matter how he castigated himself in penance— brought a little filth into the edifice of God. The great Cyprian himself was a channel for filth. Of course Cyprian affirmed that Novatian was not even a legitimate Christian since he no longer took communion in the church of Rome.

Full of the spirit of their pagan ancestors, then, they wrote and spoke vituperation. The technique was an old one, a traditional part of Roman rhetorical training for centuries, a disputatious, almost litigious, very vicious manner.[4] Neither man really triumphed and both of them may have shed a little Christian humility in the process. They certainly shed some brotherly love.

Novatian was eager to install a healthy branch of his church at Carthage. He sent a delegation to Carthage to get a Novatianist church organized there, with its own bishop. What seems to have happened is that the Novatianists set up a certain Maximus as bishop but at about the same time Felicissimus' party, still hating Cyprian but not ready to accept Novatian, set up its own bishop—a man named Fortunatus, one of Cyprian's old enemies.[5]

So Carthage now had three men claiming to be bishop just as Christianity had two men claiming to be pope. While the empire cracked apart from various causes, one of its most divisive elements was divided against itself. Most of the Carthaginian Christians must have sided with Cyprian, especially since he had relaxed his rigid stand toward the lapsed. But there were a number of people who, having disliked Cyprian from the beginning, rushed to join one of the rival churches. The bishops of most of the other cities in North Africa seem to have stayed loyal to Cyprian and Cornelius, although a few—apostates or heretics already—became prelates in Felicissimus' faction because the orthodox church offered them no future. Several North African clergymen, as inflexible toward the fallen as Novatian himself now was, joined Novatian's church out of strong conviction.

Felicissimus made the four-or-five-day voyage to Rome to persuade Pope Cornelius to recognize his own man, Fortunatus, as the legitimate bishop of Carthage. But Cornelius, after wavering, rejected the appeal,[6] and soon after that the emperor had the pope arrested and shut up in prison.

Nobody knows what happened to Felicissimus. He may have died at Rome lamenting the failure of his latest effort against Cyprian. He may have died en route to Carthage, or lived on in obscurity somewhere, no longer able to incommode the great. As for his faction at Carthage, it collapsed. Its more innocent members fell over one another in their hurry to get back into Cyprian's church.

But Novatian lived for several more years, and the church he had fathered lived for a long time. There were Novatianist communities not only in North Africa but in Gaul, Spain, the Orient, and Rome itself. Most of the men and women attracted to Novatianism were religious conservatives. They certainly did not expect anybody to consider them heretical. Their doctrine was sound and orthodox. They did not cherish the popular heresies that Christ had never been incarnated, that the God of the Old Testament was a tyrant, or that the world was entirely evil. They accepted the same dogma that Cyprian and Cornelius accepted and performed the same rituals in the same way. They differed from other Christians only on the question of the lapsed and the conception of the Christian fabric. They saw in Novatianism the old church, the church as it should be, the clean and holy virgin uncorrupted by the world. The church of Cornelius and Cyprian had compromised with mundane life, they said—had temporized with sin. It was foul with the smell of the fallen. Only the church of Novatian preserved the wishes of Christ inviolate.

Many Novatianist communities were established in Asia Minor, especially the area called Phrygia, and in other parts of the East, and they flourished. They were still strong in the fourth century, when Constantine made Christianity a permitted religion and when the government and in time the empire were largely Christianized. The legacy of Novatian continued after the Western Roman Empire was gone and the Eastern had become what we know as the Byzantine Empire. The question of the lapsed was now an antique issue; newer disputes had arisen to engross contentious ecclesiastics. The Novatianists seemed so mild in contrast to many of the disputants that most people evidently accepted them as ordinary Christians. But although there was less and less reason for the existence of the Novatianist church, and although its adherents probably kept dwindling, it lingered on as a separate entity until the seventh century. Only then were the last Novatianists absorbed into the common Christian body.

While Gallus sat helpless in 252 and the plague struck city after city, Persia struck also. Shapur of Persia, King of Kings, a strong and ambitious monarch who had already held the throne for ten or eleven years, invaded Armenia and forced its boy ruler to run to Roman territory for refuge. The collapse of Armenia meant that Rome had lost its buffer against the powerful Persian realm, Rome's greatest enemy by far. Shapur proceeded into Roman territory, looting and ravaging the rich province of Syria with its green farms and great cities. Gallus did not lead an army against him.

In the harassed Balkans, meanwhile, the peace that Gallus had bought

Aemilian (253), radiate. Obverse of an antoninianus. 21 mm.

Emperor in military dress, sacrificing from patera at altar; military standard at left. Reverse of an antoninianus of Aemilian. 21 mm.

with his ignominious treaty was short-lived. Gallus' promise to pay an annual tribute in gold to King Kniva's Goths was irrevelant to other Goths, not subject to Kniva. These people, plus other barbarians such as the Carpi and the Burgundians, saw that Moesia and Thrace were still prostrate after King Kniva's expedition, too weak to defend themselves against a swarming enemy. A few of the landlords may have had a chance to fortify the central building complexes on their estates by putting walls around them, thickening the walls already in existence, or erecting towers designed for defense as well as surveillance. But most of the big farms were open, and their peasant protectors could do little against warriors.

There were still Roman troops in the Balkans for the barbarians to cope with, but Roman soldiers had been beaten by Kniva and could be beaten again. The Romans were infected with the plague anyway and could not do anything properly, and their emperor did not amount to much. And the provinces were tempting, still containing much to pillage. Philippopolis might be a bleak ruin, but other parts of the Balkans promised a great deal. It was a good time to take.

But the barbarians had not reckoned with Aemilian, governor in Moesia, who now marches briefly and obscurely into history. Aemilian must have had considerable ability as a general. We do not know the details, but in some way he defeated the barbarian invaders and even chased them back into their own territory. Neither the empire nor the barbarians had expected this, but anybody could have predicted what came next. Aemilian's soldiers, intensely proud of a general who could turn the tables on the invaders and resurrect some of Rome's buried glory, proclaimed him emperor.

Leaving the provincials to take care of themselves in case there were still predatory Germans lurking around, Aemilian and his enthusiastic legionaries set off for Italy to drive Gallus from the throne. In consternation, Gallus realized that action was essential. He sent for his highly respected general Valerian, in command of troops on the Rhine frontier. Valerian was to hurry to Italy to help defeat this usurper, and Gallus hoped he would arrive in time, although the distance was against it.

In May of 253 Aemilian's army marched down into Italy—fierce Illyrians and Dacians from the Balkans, on fire with a patriotism that would have looked childish in the capital, still in high spirits over their recent victory and confident of another one, sure that they were doing the right thing by pushing the supine Gallus from power and putting a great general in his place.

Gallus, with his son and whatever soldiers he could muster, ventured out of Rome to defend his throne and life. Valerian had not yet arrived with his troops from the Rhine.

The armies of Gallus and Aemilian met at Interamna, about fifty miles north of Rome. It appears that they did not even fight. Gallus' soldiers looked at themselves and the enemy and realized that the enemy outnumbered them too heavily. They probably also sensed the spirit of Aemilian's men. They knew, besides, that a new emperor always distributed gold coins to his loyal army. Then they thought about Gallus, who did not deserve thinking about for long.

They killed Gallus, they killed his son, and they joined Aemilian.

The general Valerian, still on his way to Italy from the Rhine, heard about Gallus' death, and so did his troops. He did not demur when they hailed him as emperor. He marched on down, prepared to fight.

Aemilian had a short reign. Perhaps he was inept. Perhaps the soldiers saw that he was a better general than ruler. Perhaps the soldiers were just reckless, fickle, spoiled, and in need of another distribution of gold; or else they did not believe that risking a war with Valerian's troops was worth while. Toward the end of summer they murdered the man they had idolized three months before.

Notes to Chapter 5

1. Pontius, **Life and Passion of Cyprian**, in Cyprian, **Writings**, I, xxi.

2. Cyprian, **Writings**, I, 462, 460, 463, 461. From Treatise VII, **On the Mortality**.

3. See Lacey (ed.), **Select Epistles of St. Cyprian**, pp. xxii-xxiii; **New Catholic Encyclopedia** (New York, 1967), X, 535; **Encyclopaedia of Religion and Ethics**, edited by James Hastings and others (Edinburgh and New York, 1908-27), IX, 400; and Turner, **Studies**, p. 119.

4. On this point see **Encyclopaedia of Religion and Ethics**, IX, 400.

5. See Duchesne, **Early History of the Christian Church**, pp. 301-02; Lacey (ed.), **Select Epistles of St. Cyprian**, p. xxv; Encyclopaedia of Religion and Ethics, IX, 400; and especially Benson, **Cyprian**, pp. 225-28.

6. See Benson, **Cyprian**, pp. 228-29.

6 The Empire as a Tired Old Man

Valerian was about sixty when he became emperor. After the death of Aemilian he proceeded to Rome, where the senate gave him a warm welcome, confirmed his imperial titles, and even named his son Gallienus co-emperor. Valerian may have asked the senate to grant his son this honor, but quite possibly it was the senate's own idea, a way of showing confidence in the dynasty that had just been born.

There were reasons why the Roman people, at least the senate, should have hoped for great things from the new reign. Most aristocrats of ancient Roman family probably liked to think that Valerian was an aristocrat of ancient Roman family himself. It was somewhat unusual to have that kind of emperor. Even as far back as the late first century the rulers of the Flavian dynasty had been, in origin, country people rather than members of the city aristocracy, and their connections had approached middle class vulgarity.

In the golden second century the emperors, though very aristocratic, had been of largely provincial stock. More recently, emperors could come from anywhere. Septimius Severus, from Africa, had prided himself on his Punic blood. His wife had been a Syrian lady, so that their son Caracalla was a Syro-African hybrid. Elagabalus and Severus Alexander were Syrians. Maximin was a low-class Thracian; Philip, an Arab; Decius, apparently an Illyrian. It must have felt good to have someone at the head of the state who could be called a Roman in the old sense—urbane, magnanimous, closely connected with the city from which the empire had grown, and devoted to the way of life that must not fail.

Up to this point Valerian had enjoyed a distinguished career.[1] Fifteen years previously, for instance, he had been active in the opposition that the senate, with a burst of old-fashioned vigor, put up against Maximin, a brutal emperor with no aristocratic sympathies. He was also a very competent general—the one man whom Gallus had called for in desperation when his own imperial fabric was crumbling, the man whom Aemilian's victorious soldiers preferred to the general they themselves had named emperor. He had never been an irresponsible firebrand, and if after a few years he should grow too slow with age, and show overcaution or forget to make up his mind about pressing problems, there was his son Gallienus to act swiftly and strongly. Gallienus, about thirty-five years old in 253, could gradually take over as his distinguished father faltered.

It was an attractive picture; it charmed many of the senators and some of the other citizens throughout the empire. But too many Romans could not afford such rhapsodies. They loved to read idyllic Greek romances but they knew that life was bitter. The plague, for instance, was still doing its work of death. If it abated in one place it sprang up in another place; the gods in their anger kept punishing the empire with this relentless thing that nobody could fight. Some cities suffered from famine. Barbarian invasions and unsettled conditions in general meant that trade between many parts of the empire had fallen way off, and trade to distant places such as India had just about stopped.

Gold coins were smaller and scarcer. The "silver" **antoniniani** or double **denarii** contained forty percent silver at the most and looked false and dirty even to begin with. Cities in the Greek East turned out local token coinages in bronze that were so crude as to be almost barbaric; Greek engravers had forgotten the numismatic art in which they had once excelled. Inflation, of course, kept spiraling upward. In the East the Persians were overrunning parts of Asia Minor and the rich, highly civilized province of Syria. Pirates on the Black Sea swooped down on merchant shipping and no big Roman fleet was there to protect the trading vessels. On land, all over the empire, the destitute and the tax-ridden resorted more and more to brigandage, and many people feared the robber bands more than they feared the plague.

Barbarians ransacked east and west. When Valerian marched toward Italy with the legions of the Rhine to defend Gallus against the usurper Aemilian, barbaric tribes in Germany had taken advantage of the soldiers' absence by swarming across to the west bank of the Rhine and southwestward into Gaul, so that a portion of the empire that had seen peace for many generations was suddenly swamped in savage war.

Meanwhile the Goths seem to have attacked some of the coastal cities of Asia Minor. Most of the province of Dacia or present-day Rumania, the large area east of the Danube that Trajan had added to the empire a century and a half earlier, was now Roman in name only. West Goths, Gepids, and other barbarians were streaming into it and taking possession. Posses of citizens probably tried to fight them off and got mutilated in the process. Within two or three years after Valerian gained the throne in 253, inscriptions were no longer being carved on imperial monuments in Dacia because there were no more imperial monuments, and coins were no longer being struck at the Dacian cities for the local population. Some of the Roman inhabitants stayed stubbornly on, especially in a narrow area between what is now the Temes River and the Danube, but in Dacia as a whole the light of Rome had just about gone out.

Goths raided the prostrate provinces of Moesia and Thrace again in 254, since the Danube frontier was now inadequately defended and since the Goths had learned not to respect Rome. Frightened peasants converged on the rude but serviceable towers that had begun to bristle over the Thracian countryside, and holed up there with their wagons of meager belongings and their animals until the Goths came and dragged them out. Greece was terrified that the barbarians would come down as far as its helpless cities. The Greeks hastily barricaded the historic pass of Thermopylae, where heroes of a vanished age had died to a man rather then surrender their land to Persians. The Athenians hurried to rebuild the walls around their own city. Those walls had been left in ruins since Sulla besieged Athens in 86 B.C.; they had not been needed in the long years of the Roman peace.

As it happened, the Goths did not go all the way to Athens on this incursion, but the Athenians were not at all sure that there would be no other incursions. Not only in Greece but throughout the empire, in fact, cities were starting to build walls against the barbarians. In some cases the old walls had crumbled long ago like Athens'. Other cities had expanded outside their original fortifications during the centuries of tranquility, so that new ones had to be erected to enclose the suburbs. A number of cities even tore down their own temples and proud public edifices for stones. It was a sad thing, this admission that the time of peace and safety was over. By no means all the cities were endangered, of course. Many of those in the Orient still flourished and felt secure, and so did Carthage, Alexandria, Rome herself, and London. But the threat hovered over enough of them to cause grave alarm. To a Greek or Roman, cities were the acme of civilization. If barbarians menaced the cities, civilization itself was in peril.

Many Romans, surrounded by danger and destruction, came to think of the world and especially the empire as an old man, assailed by the ills incident to age and too decrepit to combat those ills. They had a sense of living in a twilight, a dim and strengthless senescence. Energy had belonged to the young Rome of the republic, when the armies took up all challenges and defeated their enemies, or to the middle-aged, mature Rome of the earlier empire, which had guarded the peace and guaranteed prosperity. But all that civilization could do now was to lie down and take the blows. There was no point in energy any more—no point in fighting battles that had to be lost.

Cyprian, writing to a pagan, had this to say about his own time:

> ...the world has now grown old, and does not abide in that strength in which it formerly stood; nor has it that vigour and force which it formerly possessed.... In the winter there is not such an abundance of showers for nourishing the seeds; in the summer the sun has not so much heat for cherishing the harvest; nor in the spring season are the corn-fields so joyous; nor are the autumnal seasons so fruitful in their leafy products. The layers of marble are dug out in less quantity from the disembowelled and wearied mountains; the diminished quantities of gold and silver suggest the early exhaustion of the metals ...the husbandman is failing in the fields, the sailor at sea, the soldier in the camp, innocence in the market, justice in the tribunal, concord in friendships, skilfulness in the arts, discipline in morals.

Cyprian was evidently not worried about being charged with rhetorical exaggeration, because he added:

> We see grey hairs in boys—the hair fails before it begins to grow; and life does not cease in old age, but it begins with old age. Thus, even at its very commencement, birth hastens to its close; thus, whatever is now born degenerates with the old age of the world itself; so that no one ought to wonder that everything begins to fail in the world, when the whole world itself is already in process of failing, and in its end.[2]

The bishop went on to put a Christian construction on the whole situation: the world was deteriorating because God was angry at it for being so evil and pagan. But many harried non-Christians would have accepted his view of the enervated empire.

The broad group of people known as the West Germans, who had lived on the south coast of the Baltic Sea between the Oder and the Elbe, began pushing south and west some time after 1000 B.C. This was before the East Germans, principally the Goths, started their own migrations from southern Sweden. The West Germanic peoples penetrated farther and farther into the continent, fighting one another and fighting the Celtic tribes that were there already—tribes somewhat more sophisticated than the West Germanic ones. The invaders gradually drove the Celts into other regions and established themselves throughout what is now Germany. It was a land of marshes, occasional meadows, and vast reaches of thick, dark forest where deer ranged and wolves prowled.

For a long time they pastured sheep on the meadows and hunted much of their food and clothing in the woods, as they had done in their former home on the Baltic and as the Goths continued to do. But gradually, during the first century A.D., more and more of them turned to agriculture. They planted the places where the great trees did not stand too thick. By the early third century they had even chopped down some of the trees. Agricultural villages dotted the German wilderness now—units of farming people clustered together for mutual protection. Recently, leading families in some districts had started erecting great wooden halls surrounded by outbuildings such as stables and workshops and by the huts of the peasants that tended the land for their superiors. There was less independence in these primitive manorial arrangements than in the hamlets or the open spaces where each free man was his own master, but at least there was a strong communal spirit.

War as well as work bound communities and tribes together. A free man was a warrior first and a farm-owner second. Like their eastern cousins the Goths, these West Germanic men valued war as the main aim of life and war-glory as life's prime reward, and their women encouraged them. Their gods were mainly war gods—the implacable Woden, for instance, and thunder-throwing Thor. They worshipped fertility goddesses too, although not so much now as they had done in their dim past, when they used to sacrifice fats, hazel nuts, dogs, horses, cereals, pigs, and sometimes people to the reproductive principle. They had few temples but they had sacred groves, where the trees grew tall and majestic, and here the warriors would leave their weapons as sacrifices to some bloody god of battle. As everybody knows, they believed that if they died nobly in combat they would be translated to Valhalla, the afterlife reserved for the fiercest fighters.

Some of the tribes had kings and some had chiefs, but in both cases the political organization was remarkably democratic. Most of the power was wielded by the tribal assembly, consisting of all the free men—in other words, the warriors. Slaves, captives, and women, as might be expected, had no voice; but the warriors were peers and held the authority. A king was a chief who could trace his pedigree back to a god. If the warriors wanted to be led by another king when he died, they elected one. The new king had to be from the same family since it was the only family in the tribe with a godly origin. But the free men could make up their minds not to have a king at all.

If a tribe was headed by a chief rather than a king, this man too owed his office to election; and when he died the assembled warriors would choose another chief, probably from a different family, to lead them. But neither a king nor a chief could decide important questions for a tribe, such as whether to go to war, whether to ally with another tribe against a common enemy, or whether to move to a greener part of the forest. That kind of decision was up to the whole assembly of free men.

The most important aspect of these people's social structure has acquired the Latin name **comitatus**. It was, of course, war oriented. A **comitatus** was a band of young men attached to a war leader—perhaps the king or chief of a tribe or perhaps one of the sturdiest fighters in the tribe, with many deaths to his credit. The young men were committed to defending their war leader in battle, fighting for him with all their vigor and skill, and, if necessary, dying for him without demur. Bravery and loyalty were the great virtues. There were stories of cowards—craven men who had deserted their leader when he was relying on them—but the youths of the **comitatus** did not need these bitter tales to steer them away from fear.

The **comitatus** conferred status reciprocally. The war leader enhanced his fame by the number of valiant youths he could attract into his own band, and the young men acquired reflected glory from belonging to the band of a notable warrior. In return for their strong arms and spearplay the war leader would give then weapons and feast them at his table, which meant letting them stuff themselves with mutton and drink themselves drunk. They drank beer most of the time, or honey-sweet mead, but after the Roman traders came they learned to like wine too, and some of them preferred it to beer. While they were drinking they would tell of what they had done in battle, or of what their leader or some other distinguished warrior had done, or of what they themselves would do when the next battle came. The drunker they got the more extravagant they got, whetting one another's battle taste and appetite for fame, until finally they would hurl great Beowulfian boasts. They would try to prove these boasts when next they went into battle.

The West Germans did not fight scientifically as the Romans did. Their raids on one another were mere whimsical, spur-of-the-moment affairs, maybe even the outcome of a drunken dare. Nobody knew when a tribe was going to attack, or where, or probably even why. This sometimes discomposed the Romans, who, on the whole, preferred a more rational enemy.

In modern times many explanations have been offered for the Germanic attacks on the empire in the second and third centuries. The Great Wall of China had repulsed Asiatic barbarians striking toward the east, so these hordes started striking westward and set off among barbaric nations a chain reaction that eventually traveled all the way to Germany. A tribe within Germany itself would sometimes decide to migrate because its neighbors had become too powerful or its food too scarce, and in migrating it would displace other tribes, so that again a chain reaction was set off that drove barbaric armies against the barricades of civilization.

But the Germans themselves, if asked what caused them to attack the empire, might have replied that a man grew restless for glory. A quick, clean raid on the Romans was as good a way to gain glory as any. Besides, the empire was rich. Romans had a reputation for golden wealth. Their fields were fertile, their cities were full of things to loot. Two good reasons for warfare were fame and booty. They were sufficient explanations in themselves.

Most of the West Germans did not wear helmets when they fought against Rome or each other; they rushed into battle with their long hair blowing in the breeze. Their shields were wooden or wicker, and their favorite weapon was an iron-pointed spear which they sometimes heaved at the enemy ranks and sometimes held onto until they could stick it into an enemy at close quarters. A few of them also carried short swords for hand-to-hand fighting, but the majority felt that the spear could do enough damage by itself. The West Germans fought mainly on foot, although certain tribes were famous for their mounted warriors. Whether they ran or rode into combat, they shouted their battle cries and screamed for blood. To the Roman legionaries war was a business, practical and well regulated. Not to these men from the forests.

Barbarian contact with the Roman world, however, was certainly not confined to contact at spearpoint. The enterprising Roman merchants who sold wine among the Germans, plus luxury items such as silver plate and drinking cups, made themselves known to tribes all over Germany, as far as the Baltic itself. As they bargained for the amber, furs, and yellow-haired slaves that they would take back to the empire, they unintentionally acquainted the Germans with more civilized ideas and customs. Sometimes, besides, a barbarian would enlist as an auxiliary in the Roman army. Sometimes a tribe located close to the border would agree to act as a buffer between the empire and other tribes and consequently acquire some appreciation for Roman ways of doing things. Barbarians living near the Rhine had dealings with relatives on the western or Roman side of the river—thoroughly Romanized Germans from around imperial centers such as Cologne or Trier—or with Romanized Celts who inhabited the same area.

In addition to gaining a strong relish for wine, some of the Germans developed competence in raising the grapes and making the wine themselves. Barbarians also came to imitate Roman techniques for growing grain. They learned how to weave cloth, blow glass, and manufacture pottery according to Roman methods. They learned about Roman gods such as the Dionysus who appeared so often on the silver cups, or Jupiter, whose weapon, like Thor's, was the thunderbolt. They even gained some conception of a more complex system of social classes than their own, a conception reflected in the newly built mansion-halls whose owners lorded it over the surrounding farmers.

Of course not all the West Germans were exposed to so much influence and there were some aspects of Roman civilization that they knew about but proudly rejected. They scorned the soft life of the cities, for instance, and most of the time they did not try to imitate Roman military practices. They felt no interest in the orderly operation of Roman provincial bureaucracy. But they were changing through Roman contact even so.

They were also changing politically. When the historian Tacitus wrote about the Germans at the end of the first century A.D. they were divided into a chaos of jealously independent tribes, some weak, some powerful, some dominating one area and some controlling another. But from about 200 A.D. on, various West Germanic tribes started uniting into confederations. One such amalgamation, consisting of tribes east of the Rhine between the Main River and the Alps, was called the Alemanni. Its name apparently meant that "all the men" in that area belonged to it. The Alemanni had first made themselves known to the Romans early in the third century, when the emperor Caracalla carried on a war against them. The other great confederation was called the Franks. It consisted of tribes living east of the Rhine where the river flowed through what is now northern Germany and the Netherlands to empty into the North Sea. The name Frank, which meant "free," distinguished the men of this group from their tamed cousins in the westernmost or Roman part of Germany, the men who had to obey Roman laws and keep Roman manners.

It was the Franks that took advantage of the general Valerian's departure for Italy in 253 with many of the troops stationed on the Rhine. By the time the usurper Aemilian was killed and Valerian was proclaimed emperor, the Franks were streaming across the river and through Roman territory. The records of what happened next are scarce—almost nonexistent—but we know that the Roman citizens were psychologically unprepared for barbarian invaders. We know what the land was like before the Franks came.

There had been no serious threats to this frontier and the pleasant country behind it for generations. The Romans who had come here from warmer climates, the Romanized Germans, and the Romanized Celts lived together in peace, trusting the soldiers at the great camps, small fortresses, and barricades along the frontier to keep the peace intact. In their cramped, unheated barracks behind battlemented stone walls the legionaries, men who had signed up for a quarter of a century of service, maintained their regulated lives. Most of them had been born and brought up in the area they were protecting, so that their surroundings were not exotic.

The camps had store rooms; workshops for making bricks, weapons, clay pots, and tools; a shrine for the military standards that were carried in front of the legion into battle and regarded as quasi-divine; luxurious accommodations for the legionary commander; hospital quarters; and perhaps even baths for the men's relaxation. Some of the troops planted the fields owned by the legion outside the fort. Since soldiers were now allowed to marry, a few lived with their wives in special barracks or in town. The majority remained bachelors, but the towns provided them with women. War seldom came, but when it did these men were on hand to fight for the province and the emperor. The population that they guarded did not need to worry.

At Cologne (Colonia Agrippinensis) on the Rhine—originally a settlement for a Germanic tribe, later a military outpost for a while, and by the third century a great city—civilians processed leather, fashioned buff earthenware bowls and cups and jugs, made clear glass vessels and wound threads of colored glass around them in fanciful designs. The rich entertained one another in homes modeled after the town houses of Italy—stately, spacious dwellings centered around courtyards shut off from the noise of the streets, deep inside city blocks whose fringes were rented to shopkeepers. The rooms in these houses were floored with mosaics—triangles, octagons, trapezoids and medallions, pictures of panthers, goats, flowers and happy satyrs, pictures of good things to eat such as quail and oysters, composed of hundreds of thousands of pieces of white or yellow slate, black and gray limestone, blue and green glass.

Outside Cologne stretched vast grainfields possessed by the rich and worked by tenant peasants. In the snow-clogged winters of this climate the great villas on the estates, like the homes of the rich in town, were heated with air that came from a furnace room and flowed under the floors. Otherwise the villas resembled those of the more benevolent Italian peninsula, with porticoed galleries, terraces and gardens open to the sun. Like the town houses, they had elaborate mosaic floors on which men hunted bears or gladiators killed each other in colored glass. Up and down the Rhine in good weather sailed boats loaded with grain, timber, fish, pork, and barrels of wine. Celts and Germans lived in permanent settlements outside the forts so that they could sell to the soldiers, and these settlements —crude, raucous villages to begin with—sometimes grew into important cities, like Mogontiacum (Mainz) or Bonna (Bonn).

Farther west from the Rhine, on the banks of the Moselle, stood Trier (Augusta Treverorum), surrounded by great estates like Cologne and doing a very brisk business in white wine, grain, and cattle. One of its monumental gates, the double-arched, double-towered Porta Nigra, may have been standing by this time, impressing visitors then as it impresses tourists today. Trier rivaled Cologne in the amenities of civilization. At the taverns one could buy the region's wine—not the best wine, which went to the tables of the rich, but vintage of the current year or the year before, good enough to get drunk on. At the Amphitheatre, which accommodated 20,000 and was incorporated into the city wall, the citizens could enjoy tasty food and drink while they watched wild animals tear each other apart; and at the baths, built in the early second century, they could swim, dip into frigid water, boil in hot water, loll in lovely warm water, stroll through the marble halls discussing town gossip or commercial deals, and, if they wished, build up their bodies by violent exercise in the gymnasium. They could do what people did at Rome itself, or in the luscious cities of the East.[3]

The records are so meager that we do not know where the Franks struck when they started crossing the Rhine in 253. Spontaneous and loosely organized, they probably came in a series of raids extending over several years, led by chiefs whose names have not come down to us. They did not occupy; they swept through. We cannot be sure that they attacked the great cities at this time, though the riches of those flourishing commercial centers must have been a strong temptation to the war leaders and their bands of fierce young men. Certainly they swamped the smaller places, looting and killing and passing on. The gracious villas of wealthy landowners, defended by cowering peasants if at all, were easy prey. Tramping over the mosaic floors, the Franks must have wondered at the intricate designs and shaded pictures that were beyond their power to copy, and at the warmth that came through the floors and made it seem like summer inside. But more important, there were silver platters to grab and good wine to drink; there were bronze statues, marble busts, and tables of polished wood and silver to cart off, and cattle and strong peasants to take back to the Rhineland, and slave girls to rape in their mistresses' beds. Sometimes a villa would be deserted when the Franks roared up to it — the silver cups and dishes gone, the jewels and money gone, the people vanished, everything still; but at least the beautiful house and the fields could be burned.

Valerian sent his son Gallienus to stop the Franks. It was probably late in 254 when Gallienus got to the Rhine, although again we cannot be sure, and he probably stayed there until sometime in 258.[4] He was in his middle or later thirties: a man with a lean, sharp, aristocratic face, long, narrow eyes, a brief mustache, and hair that curled down over his forehead and down the back of his neck, curled in sideburns in front of his ears and continued down his chin in a short, thick beard. He was tall and carried himself like a Roman nobleman. Intellectual and artistic matters interested him; they had apparently not interested Decius or Gallus. But there was no time for such things now. As co-emperor with his father and living symbol of the majesty of Rome, he must crack the Franks.

He made Cologne his headquarters and evidently walled the city. He entered into an alliance with a Germanic chief, according to which this barbarian would fight off other Germans for Rome's sake. He worked his soldiers hard but probably paid them largely in gold, which they were glad to accept because Roman gold, unlike silver, was not adulterated. With his troops at his back he fought on the German side of the Rhine as well as on the Roman side, preventing some bands of Franks from crossing, and defeating others as they were in the act of coming over. He seems to have repaired several forts along the river, strengthened strategic settlements such as Novaesium (Neuss) and Antumnacum (Andernach), and built up the defenses of Trier in case the other places should fall.

That is nearly all we know about several years of warfare on the Rhine.

The battles Gallienus lost and the battles he won are forgotten. Late Roman historians who wrote about Gallienus portrayed him as irresponsible, supine, and effeminate, lying at ease in the Rhineland, dining and drinking like some Nero or Vitellius. According to his principal biographer, a man calling himself Pollio who wrote his life for the **Augustan History**, Gallienus had the habit of reclining on beds of roses in the spring. For a long time nobody questioned this picture. Gibbon accepted it in the late eighteenth century because it did not occur to him to doubt it. In our own century we have reassessed the late Roman historians on the basis of archaeological, numismatic, epigraphic, and other evidence and have found them unreliable at best, and we have reassessed Gallienus and found him remarkably energetic. The impression now is that he rushed around the Rhineland fighting Franks and blocking up holes in the wall of fortifications, making the best of a chaotic situation. But we are sure of next to nothing about his struggle to fend off this dark time for the empire.

Whatever he did, Gallienus did not really succeed. But perhaps success was impossible because the forces against it were too strong. The Roman army strung along the Rhine frontier was not sufficient to keep the barbarians back. While Gallienus fought in one spot, they would probably break through somewhere else.

About 257 the Franks came pouring into what is now northern France. Some of them may have looted Paris, a less important place than Trier or Cologne but well worth raiding. Later they pushed on down into warm southern Gaul, a fruitful, peaceful land of wheat farms and olive orchards, as Roman as Italy herself. About 259 they penetrated all the way to Spain, killing and pillaging; ravaged the wine country around the Mediterranean port of Tarraco (Tarragona); fell on Tarraco itself and flattened the city. There were no soldiers to prevent the Franks from roaming wherever they wanted, seizing whatever they liked. A branch of the barbarians may have gotten all the way to the coast of Mauretania or Morocco—again, not to stay but just to raid.

Meanwhile, about 256 or possibly even a couple of years earlier, the other great confederation of West Germanic tribes, the Alemanni, moved against the empire. The points they struck lay south of the Rhine crossings used by the Franks and east toward Switzerland. First they attacked the **limes**, the barricade marking the empire's border—massive earthen ramparts or wooden palisades, reinforced in some parts with stonework, with a ditch behind and rectangular, balconied watchtowers at intervals. For a long time the **limes** had determined entry into the empire. Nobody was allowed in at night, or even in the daytime if he carried a weapon. Everybody had to pay a transit tax before being let through, and of course people could enter only at specific points. The **limes**, in other words, illustrated the Roman talent for keeping things organized and under control. But when the Alemanni assailed this barricade it was abandoned for good.

Soldiers stationed along the **limes** in the watchtowers or forts must have been overwhelmed by the barbarian droves and killed. Perhaps some ran away. The border was open and Roman regulation disappeared.

Again, our information as to what went on comes from very meager records or the significant lack of records. A number of Romans had been living for a long time on the right or east side of the southern Rhine in an area which, for want of a better term, we call the **Agri Decumates** or "Tenth Land" although Roman administrators themselves may not have called it that. This area, protected by the **limes**, extended south from Mainz almost to Lake Geneva and eastward along the north bank of the Danube. The more affluent Romans of the region were not rich owners of great estates like the landlords around Cologne and Trier but prosperous members of the middle class who lived respectably in comfortable dwellings, with peasants to work the land. From this period on, there are no inscriptions or monuments from the area. With the collapse of the **limes** Roman civilization east of the Rhine and north of the Danube ended.

Places on the west side of the river around present-day Rheinzabern had been producing shiny red-orange pottery decorated with leaves and tendrils in relief, but the pottery now ceased to be made. Some of the Alemanni, probably not until 258 or 259, pushed through the province of Raetia (now part of Switzerland and western Austria) into northern Italy.[5] Others turned to Gaul, like the Franks, and burned, looted, and slaughtered in the fair land.

Hoards of coins from this period that keep turning up in France testify that all over Gaul the terrified citizens were burying their wealth. They hoped to dig it up when conditions were more secure, but they never came for it. The Alemanni no doubt carried some of the strong citizens off as slaves, or the rich for ransom. As for the old, the sick, and the otherwise troublesome, the Alemanni killed them rather than be bothered with them. The lucky ones escaped with a few possessions or none at all, and perhaps ended up in caves in the Rhone valley, where they lived miserably until they died. Some of these people had been used to obsequious service, delicate wine, and soft couches.

According to Gregory of Tours, who wrote in the seventh century, one of the Alemannic leaders was a king named Chrocus. He is a doubtful, half-legendary figure who may never have existed, but even if there was no Chrocus or if he did not live until a long time after the reign of Valerian and Gallienus, this barbarian as he comes down to us through Gregory of Tours could not have been very different from actual Alemannic chieftains of the time. His evil mother, Gregory says, suggested that he gather an army together and invade Gaul, and implicit here is the casual nature of these invasions. He was proud and pitiless. Temples were not sacred to him. The strong Germanic gods would protect the Germans and these civilized gods of the Gauls were impotent to save their own shrines. At what is now Clermont in Auvergne, for instance, Chrocus sacked the famous ancient temple of Vasso Galatae, which had a double wall thirty feet thick. The interior shone with marbles and mosaics. He destroyed it all. He also, according to Gregory, made the Christians suffer, and no doubt he did if any got in his way. To him, they were like other Romans. But at Arles, on the Rhone near the Mediterranean coast, he was captured — Gregory does not say by whom — and tortured and put to death by the sword. Gregory comments that he certainly deserved that.

His people went on, doing as much harm as they were capable of. Gallienus, helped by able officers, kept trying hard, but he could not push back the whole West Germanic world. At least the Germans had no interest in occupying any of the invaded territory on a permanent basis except the **Agri Decumates**, land which was, after all, on the barbarian side of the Rhine. All they wanted from the rest of the empire was war and plunder. The devastated provinces picked up what was left, started rebuilding and replanting, and dreaded the next onslaught.

While all this was happening in the West the empire was fighting Persia in the East. The Persia that the Romans had to contend with was a young and patriotic country, unfortunately for the empire. After the wars of Alexander the Great (336-323 B.C.) there was no Persia for several centuries. During most of that long interval the land was controlled by the Parthians, who fought Rome from time to time, traded widely, and dominated much of mid-Asia. In A.D. 224 Ardashir the Persian overthrew the last Parthian ruler and in 226 he had himself crowned king. After five and a half centuries Persia was a nation again. Ardashir looked back to the super-kingdom of Cyrus and Darius and wanted to reconstitute it, supported by powerful nobles whose nationalism he nourished. He established Zoroastrianism as the national religion, defeated Scythian tribes, defeated Indians beyond his eastern borders, and made war against the Romans, who owned lands that had been part of ancient Persia, particularly Asia Minor, Mesopotamia, and Syria.

When Ardashir died in 241 his son Shapur succeeded to the Persian throne. King of Kings, King of the Kings of Iran and non-Iran, earthly counterpart and companion of the prime god Ahura-Mazda, lord over far-flung provinces from Mesopotamia to India and from the Caspian to the Arabian Sea, master whose greatest nobles fell on the ground when they approached his presence, Shapur was ambitious. He had been trained on his father's vision of an even greater Persia, the ancestral Persia that must be equaled by the present. He was a resolute, high-spirited, compelling man, quick to act, intelligent, imperious. Almost at once he attacked the Romans. It was on campaign against Shapur that the boy emperor Gordian was killed by his own soldiers in 244, and it was with Shapur that Philip the Arab concluded a peace treaty after Gordian's death.

The Persian watched the Roman Empire weaken in the next few years. He struck again in 253 while Gallus was still emperor, chasing the child monarch out of Armenia and so depriving Rome of a valuable buffer kingdom, then harassing the Roman provinces of Mesopotamia and Syria. Valerian inherited this war when he became emperor, and like the West Germanic incursions it went on for years. What Shapur evidently did was to launch a new invasion annually, wearing down the Roman East.

Even in the mid-third century Syria was an excellent land to invade, still rich and long experienced in the ways of civilization. Its fields were fruitful; its caravans and merchant fleets handled much of the empire's trade. Its great cities, mingling Greek culture with customs and attitudes of the Orient, were centers of intellect and beautiful sinks of luxury. The law school at Beirut, established about a generation before Valerian, was already making Beirut the greatest center for the study of law in the East. At Emesa the sun was worshiped in a cult of splendor. Oriental philosophies and religions, both rational and mystic, could be picked up on the streets of Damascus, most ancient of living cities; so could almost anything else. Antioch was the third largest city in the empire, a cosmopolis where the world came to buy, sell, and live intensely.

Into this desirable land rode King Shapur backed by his nobles. Persia anticipated the Europe of the Middle Ages in its haughty landed aristocracy. There was not much of a middle class. The nobles were reared in a military tradition, learning to ride their great horses well, to cast the lance, to draw the bow on horseback, and to use the sword. Their principal pastime was hunting, and there were still lions to shoot from horses as their ancestors had shot them in the days of Cyrus and Darius. The most potent nobles governed provinces, but even the lesser nobles presided over vast territories. The society was aristocratic in an almost elementary sense. The nobles expected to be honored, to live a life of authority over inferiors, and to perform strenuous duties for superiors. The peasants, much like serfs of the European Middle Ages, were tied to the soil. Taxes kept them poor and powerless. In the event of a war they had to march on foot behind their master, who levied them in the name of the king from whom he held his lands.

The most sensational part of the Persian army was the **clibanarii** or cataphracts, drawn, apparently, from the lesser nobles and the knights. The cataphracts were a heavy cavalry. They were protected by metal helmets covering all of the face except the eyes, coats of overlapping iron or bronze plates extending down to the knees, and mailed greaves on their lower legs.[6] They carried swords and enormous lances like the ones we associate with tournaments. The huge horses, like the riders, were encased in armor, with greaves on their legs, spiked forepieces on their heads, and mail coats hanging down from the back on both sides. The Persians had borrowed the idea of cataphracts from the Parthians but had improved on it until now these armored aristocrats on armored horses were almost impenetrable. An enemy who saw this flashing host come thundering down on him would be at a severe psychological disadvantage.

The cataphracts, the great nobles, the levies of peasants, and perhaps various subject peoples in an assortment of Oriental costumes roamed through Mesopotamia and Syria for several years adding to the misery of the empire. In spite of his ambitions Shapur did not attempt a permanent occupation of Syria, but he must have greatly enriched his own country and strengthened Persian patriotism at the same time.

We do not know much more about this Persian-Roman war than we do about the Frankish and Alemannic invasions, and the chronology is confused and disputed.[7] It would seem that in 254 the Persians took Nisibis in Mesopotamia, one of the most important Roman fortress-cities in the East. With this guardian of the frontier disposed of, it was much easier for them to cross Mesopotamia whenever they wished and pour into Syria. At the city of Emesa the priest-king Uranius had been ruling for several years as an independent monarch, striking his own coins on the Roman model. He probably used his own army to combat the Persian threat, but there is no proof that he beat the Persians back from his city-kingdom. There is not even any indication of what the Roman legions in the East were doing against the Persians, if anything. Presumably the legionaries tried to fight them off in these years when the legions on the Rhine were trying to fight off the Germans. But the battles are buried in the earth.

Meanwhile a Persian army led by the king's son, Prince Hormizd, invaded Asia Minor and took the city of Tyana in Cappadocia north of the Taurus mountains. The new invasion meant that the Cappadocian farmers, like the Syrian farmers, had to sit by in agony and see their fields despoiled, their sheep herded off to become lamb and mutton for Persian stomachs, and perhaps their buildings burned. If a Roman army had swept through the land in pursuit of the Persians it would have confiscated whatever was left. But the Cappadocians were evidently spared this second depredation; no Roman army chased the Persians. Even so, these farmers had been turned into beggars.

About 256 Prince Hormizd also took Dura, the southernmost Roman outpost on the west side of the Euphrates, garrison city for troops drawn from the Orient whose duty was to defend the middle Euphrates region against Parthians first, later Persians, and always marauding nomads. It was probably also in 256 that Shapur captured Antioch. The empire could hardly have been dealt an uglier blow than the seizure of this city, commercial capital of the Orient, showplace for Roman splendor, and headquarters of the Roman army of the East. The most opulent merchants had princely residences at Antioch, and there were shining temples, arcaded avenues, slums that stayed awake all night, and ingenious sophistications of pleasure. Soldiers who were billeted here on their way to a campaign must have found the theaters, taverns, baths, and bagnios detrimental to their moral strength, but their officers apparently did not try to keep them out of these sources of civilized enjoyment. Even the emperor Caracalla had discovered that the army he brought here in 213 to fight the Parthians was being emasculated by the city's gorgeous sinfulness.

A few of Antioch's inhabitants claimed to be pure Greeks. They spoke Greek and looked proudly back to the time before the Romans, when Macedonian kings of the house of Seleucus ruled in Antioch. Some of the more temporary inhabitants, such as the governor and his staff and the army men, knew Latin. The mass of the Antiochenes were native Syrians, Oriental in their outlook, Syriac-speaking although they could probably get along fairly well in Greek. There were also Jews, Arabs from the desert, Egyptians, Cilicians, Palmyrenes, in fact people from all over the East, even Persians.

One of the richest citizens of Antioch about this time was a certain Mariades. The Greeks called him Kyriades, but his name in its original form was not Greek but Syrian and meant "my lord perceives." Mariades had the expensive honor of serving on Antioch's town council. He was in other words a decurion, one of those influential citizens who a century before had purchased glory for themselves by donating money to their city and erecting buildings there but who now were compelled by the Roman government to make heavy involuntary contributions called liturgies. A story, probably pure fiction, says that Mariades had to flee from Antioch after stealing silver and gold from his father. Another story, which sounds more plausible, says that one of the liturgies assigned to Mariades was that of providing horses for a public entertainment but that instead of fulfilling his civic duty in the expected manner he embezzled public funds. Perhaps he was just greedy or perhaps, like other decurions of the period, he was being ruined by the liturgies and had to get money from somewhere.

At any rate he was found out and expelled from the council in shame. Since Antioch did not promise him much of a future after that, he went to Persia and offered his services to King Shapur. Whatever the real reason for his treason to the empire may have been, Shapur no doubt welcomed this aristocratic Roman citizen and rewarded him liberally from the inexhaustible supply of Persian gold. Mariades seems to have accompanied Prince Hormizd on the Persian invasion of Asia Minor and may also have helped Shapur raid Syria prior to 256. His most important activity was to hand Antioch over to the Persians.

There is disagreement as to whether Mariades' betrayal of Antioch took place in 256 or several years later, when Shapur captured the city a second time, but 256 is perhaps the more likely date.[8] A sizeable pro-Persian party was operating in Antioch at the time. Some of the citizens, especially those in the lower classes, felt little sympathy toward Roman imperialism with its bureaucratic hierarchy, its plentiful regulations, its shabby money, and its iron hand over the poor. They would have preferred to be citizens of Persia. This strong new nation with its energetic king and its broad, flat, real silver money exercised an almost romantic appeal. Besides, Persia was an Eastern country, and these Antiochenes felt spiritually closer to it than to an empire with its base in Europe.

If Mariades had a conscience, he could tell his conscience that he was not betraying Antioch by opening the city to the Persians. He was betraying only that part of it that stayed loyal to Rome—the administration, his former friends who had expelled him from the council, wealthy merchants, and members of the middle and lower classes who either still felt some affection for Rome or considered Rome the lesser of two evils. This party, however, was probably the predominant one at Antioch out of mere habit: the city had been accustomed to Roman rule for three centuries and prided itself on being an integral and illustrious part of the empire. But in the middle of the third century the pro-Persian faction may have been a more demanding, more dynamic force.

What apparently happened is that Shapur's army encamped outside the city, hesitant to launch an attack until it had ascertained just what was going on inside. The administration and the wealthy citizens panicked and fled, taking along official records and as many material possessions as they or their slaves could carry; and humbler persons who feared Persia more than Rome probably fled too. But many of the poor, learning that Mariades was with the Persian army, stayed. Some of them probably thought that since Roman rule had been so undistinguished for the past ten years or so, any change would have to be a change for the better. Others must have been violently pro-Persian.

It sounds as if Mariades had been instrumental among the pro-Persian extremists for quite a while. Perhaps his subversive activities, rather than any embezzlement of public funds, had been the cause of his dismissal from the council and his defection to King Shapur. Whether he actually re-entered Antioch now and spoke to the citizens in favor of Shapur we do not know. But whatever he did, he seems to have had so much charisma that the citizens decided to allow the Persians to come in. This is by no means certain; there may have been a siege before the Persians poured through the gates. But it is more probable that they marched in unopposed.

Free in this rich and famous city, Shapur's army went wild. If the pro-Persian faction had willingly let the army in, it soon regretted that friendly gesture. The citizens who had fled had had to leave much behind, and the Persians sacked the great houses, sacked the temples, took whatever they could get—jewels and gold vessels for the armored nobles on their horses, food for the serfs. The Persians also set fire to the buildings, until much of the beautiful city was blazing into ashes.

We do not know how Mariades reacted to this turn of events. It is

Gallienus (253-268), laureate. Obverse of a potin tetradrachm struck at Alexandria, 256-7. 22 mm.

The Roman eagle, wreath in beak. Reverse of a potin tetradrachm of Valerian struck at Alexandria, 256-7. 21 mm.

possible that he had expected something of the sort, since the Persian army was a raiding expedition anyway and since one of the best means to retain the loyalty of troops was to give them a chance to loot. There is a tradition that members of Mariades' own pro-Persian faction killed him in rage. There is another tradition that King Shapur, having used Mariades to the fullest degree and figuring that a man who could betray his own city could betray a monarch, had him executed. Both traditions illustrate poetic justice very nicely, but neither may be valid.

When the Persians left Antioch they took with them Bishop Demetrianus, who had presided over the city's Christians since 252. They also took other intellectuals and men with technical knowledge. These captives constituted an unusual kind of booty but perhaps a very valuable one. It was of course an ancient custom to make prisoners of strong men who would be good slaves, rich men whose families would pay heavy ransom, and pretty girls, and no doubt the army brought some of these people back to Persia too. But Shapur was a calculating monarch. He expected the educated captives to be of use to his country. He settled them in Persia and gave them problems to solve.

All this time the emperor Valerian, it seems, had been disappointing expectations. We have no account of what he was doing during the first several years of his reign, but that in itself is significant. It looks as if he could not have done much except send his son to the Rhine to drive off the Germans. He was, after all, getting older. There is a possibility that he went to Syria as early as 254 to deal with the Persians, but most scholars today feel that he did not reach the East until 256.[9]

Perhaps shortly before setting out for the Orient—certainly before the end of 256—he divided the empire administratively with his son. Valerian took the East and Gallienus the West. The division did not mean that the two halves of the empire were separate entities. Valerian and Gallienus were still co-emperors, and coins with Valerian's portrait were often struck in the West and coins with Gallienus' portrait in the East. But father and son had their own territorial responsibilities from now on, and soon each had his own body of advisors and his own Praetorian Prefect. Soon also, an estrangement would be evident between the two men. The details of the administrative division of the Roman world are entirely lost. Possibly Gallienus forced his father into it. Possibly the younger man was already itching for more power and impatient of his father's slow pace and vacillation.

When Valerian reached the East he may have finished off Uranius, the priest-king at the city of Emesa, unless the Persians had finished him first. At any rate this minor usurper, who had succeeded in maintaining his own independent city-kingdom in the middle of Roman Syria for several years, is not heard from any more. Valerian probably did not have to retake Antioch. Very likely Shapur left no garrison there except perhaps a token garrison that could not put up much resistance. Having denuded the city and scarred it by fire, the king had gone back to Persia with his treasure and his captives. Rome was humiliated, Persia enriched.

The emperor apparently started rebuilding the parts of Antioch that had been destroyed. He probably used troops for this purpose; Roman soldiers were of course trained builders as well as farmers and fighters. He even seems to have begun the construction of a fortress-palace. But his headquarters was evidently not Antioch but Samosata in Commagene, the Graeco-Oriental city from which the satirist Lucian had come in the preceding century. On the northern Euphrates, northeast of Syria and just east of Asia Minor, Samosata was strategically situated. From it Valerian could watch the roads into both Syria and Asia Minor and spring to action against any Persian army that chose to march along them. Although Samosata was close to Persia itself, the strong Roman garrison at Edessa, not many miles to the southeast, could guard it against enemy attack.

Perhaps while the emperor was still at Antioch or perhaps while he was ensconced at Samosata planning destruction for the Persians, a new trouble broke over the empire. In some ways this proved worse than the Persian trouble.

The Borani lived in south Russia not far from the Goths. About the year 256 the urge to invade Roman provinces set them in motion as it was moving the Franks and Alemanni against the Rhineland and Gaul far to the west. The Borani aimed at a part of the empire not yet bothered by barbarians—the eastern and southern coasts of the Black Sea. They were original in another way too: they invaded by ship.

Since they did not have a fleet of their own they borrowed one. The Russian peninsula now called the Crimea, which dips down into the Black Sea from the north, formed at that time a little nation called the kingdom of the Bosporus. Greek trading centers, busy outposts of civilization on the edge of the barbarian wilderness, had existed there since long before Roman times for the purpose of shipping wheat to Athens and other Hellenic cities. In the third century A.D. Greek-descended aristocrats owned the rich grainfields, treated the natives like serfs, used the natives to plant and harvest the grain and to fight off wandering bands of predatory barbarians, and sold the grain to Greek merchants from Asia Minor or Europe. Many of the common people in the trading cities were skilled navigators or oarsmen with an intimate knowledge of the Black Sea coastline. It was from the Bosporan kingdom that the Borani obtained their ships, plus the men to sail them.

During the preceding two centuries this kingdom, a Roman protectorate, would never have agreed to supply transportation for enemies of the Roman peace. A Roman garrison was quartered there. The Bosporan rulers, who considered themselves Greeks although they intermarried with Slavs from the hinterland, struck coins in gold and later in electrum with the portrait of the reigning Roman emperor on the reverse. But recently the royal house had been overthrown, and the country was embroiled and confused. In this situation it was not hard for the Borani to persuade the Bosporan leaders to furnish ships against Rome and sailors to man them.

With the Bosporan seamen performing the labor, the Borani sailed eastward across the Black Sea. Along the shore the terrified people ran to the widely scattered Roman fortresses, where they could count on some protection for their lives even if their fields were despoiled. These people were probably used to piratical raids on shore as well as on the open water, since piracy was an ancient tradition here. Although the Borani had the same objective as the pirates—booty—they were a whole nation on a raiding expedition, and on the coasts of the Black Sea that was a new and frightening thing.

But the Borani did not land until they got close to Pityus, a Caucasian port. Walled against barbarian attacks, Pityus was the remotest point of Roman control along the Black Sea shore, where Roman control was spotty at best. Behind the city stood the pine forests of the Caucasus. To the southeast, at the eastern extremity of the sea, lay Colchis, the strange land where Jason had come to seize the Golden Fleece in the days of hero-entrepreneurs and had involved himself with Medea the sorceress.

An officer named Successianus commanded the Roman garrison at Pityus when the Borani attacked. He seems to have been a military man of extraordinary ability, especially at defensive warfare. Evidently his presence and leadership inspired his men to much greater effort than they would have put forth otherwise. The Borani could do nothing against him. He not only warded them off, he killed them in large numbers. According to the historian Zosimus, the Borani were also becoming afraid that the Roman troops at the fortresses up and down the coast would come to the relief of Pityus. So they withdrew, leaving behind them a great many dead as testimonies to the excellent generalship of Successianus.

The Borani had not thought out their campaign very well. They had made no arrangements for retaining the Bosporan ships, which had already sailed back to the Bosporan kingdom. Either they had felt overconfident when making their deal or else, with barbaric carelessness about the future, they simply had not bothered to cope with the problem of the return trip. Now that the problem was on them, they seized as many vessels as they could find on the coast and crowded into these. Although Zosimus does not say so, they must have seized men to sail these ships also, since their own nautical skill could not have improved greatly. In hit-and-miss fashion, then, they got back to their homeland, and it looked as if the people along the Black Sea could breathe easily.

But the next year the Borani launched another venture against civilization. This time they were careful to secure Bosporan ships and sailors for the duration of the expedition. Again they sailed east. Their immediate objective, as in their previous campaign, was Pityus.

The emperor Valerian, meanwhile, had summoned Successianus to Syria. Apparently Valerian felt that the general who had defended Pityus so ably against the Borani could be of great help against the Persians. Valerian even appointed Successianus to the office of prefect of the Praetorian Guard and, according to Zosimus, discussed the restoration of Antioch with him. Like most of the decisions of Valerian that we know about, the decision to make use of Successianus proved very unfortunate. Of course the emperor could not foresee that the Borani would repeat their assault on Pityus, and employing such a distinguished officer against the Persian hordes certainly seemed more sensible than keeping him in an isolated post in the Caucasus, where he could be of no enormous service to the empire. But the Borani must have considered Successianus' absence an invitation to themselves. The troops at Pityus, without him to command them and encourage them, quickly folded. The Borani took the city.

Very conscious of the importance of guaranteeing transportation, they pressed some of their captives into service on the Bosporan ships—Roman soldiers, perhaps, and natives of Pityus who knew how to handle oars. Full of their victory and eager for more plunder, they did not think of going home. They sailed on down past Colchis, rounding the eastern tip of the Black Sea, attacked a temple to Artemis near the mouth of the Phasis River, and skirted the sea's southern shore toward the city of Trebizond or Trapezus. Everything was working in their favor this time. Even the summer weather was tranquil, without the storms that sometimes tore up the Black Sea.

Trebizond had been a Greek outpost long before it became an outpost of imperial Rome. When Xenophon the Athenian, struggling tortuously back from Persia with the ragged remains of his army in 400 B.C., sighted Trebizond he and his troops realized that they were again in a Greek place, that the perilous Orient was behind them. The city prospered as a Black Sea port in the next few centuries and still prospered under the empire. Goods being carried between Europe and Armenia, Persia, or even mid-Asia passed through it. Hadrian built an artificial harbor for it in the second century A.D. Richer than Pityus, Trebizond was the answer to a barbarian's dream of plunder.

It looked harder to take than Pityus. A double wall enclosed it. The normal garrison, besides, had been strengthened by an additional 10,000 troops. But the soldiers at Trebizond were like too many other soldiers throughout the empire. They were practical professionals. They had joined the army as men might enter any other career that offered a fair chance of being lucrative. The glory of the empire did not stir them. Committed to defending not only the population of Trebizond but people from the surrounding country who had swarmed into the city in terror, they did not really care whether these helpless citizens lived or died. What interested them was their pay in money and kind, plus donations from emperors who wanted to retain their loyalty, plus whatever else came free and whatever they could legally grab, such as booty if there was a big war (in this respect they did not differ much from the Borani). The amenities of a large port like Trebizond interested them too. They enjoyed the wine, the Pontic girls, the baths and other luxuries of the town.

According to Zosimus these soldiers didn't even bother to climb to the lookout posts on the walls and watch the barbarians beginning the siege. There would be time for watchfulness and for fighting later, perhaps. But the Borani were not as stupid as the soldiers apparently thought. They felled trees in the neighborhood and dragged them to the unmanned walls. They scaled the walls quietly at night by means of the trees while the legionaries were getting drunk or sleeping off their stupor, and entered the city. The soldiers were surprised. Many of the troops escaped from Trebizond by a gate that the barbarians did not control, leaving the inhabitants to the mercy of tribesmen who had no mercy. Troops that did not escape via the gate were exterminated. The Borani ran through the town, pillaging temples, taverns, and the residences of the rich and destroying the proudest buildings as the Persians had done at Antioch. They gathered up the money that was so plentiful in the prosperous port, not forgetting to seize the wealth that people from the countryside had brought with them when they ran to the city for refuge, and they took many captives.

Then they spread out into the countryside itself, and in the days that followed they ravaged the whole area, the part of Asia Minor known as Pontus. There is no record of what happened, but some of the action can be deduced from a letter written by Gregory, bishop of Cabira or Neocaesarea, an inland town about one hundred fifty miles to the west of Trebizond. Gregory, a highly educated man who came from a prominent Pontic family, had been converted to Christianity at Beirut in Syria by Origen, the great Christian teacher from Alexandria who had made Beirut a center for the expanding religion. The convert had been bishop of Neocaesarea since about 240, had been very energetic in evangelistic work in this remote part of Asia Minor, had fled to the mountains with his flock to escape the Decian persecution, and must already have established himself as the leading Christian in the whole region by the year 257, when the Borani came. As an ecclesiastic of authority, he wrote in these troubled times a letter usually called the Canonical Epistle, probably meant for some nearby bishop and dealing with the problem of Christians who had used the Borani invasion for their own private ends.

After the Borani had been through an area, robbing the houses and farms, killing the owners or taking them prisoner, some Christians would, according to Gregory, pounce on whatever the Borani had left (buried silver perhaps, or the fields and herds). They rationalized that they were just reimbursing themselves for their own losses, but Gregory warned that "if it is not lawful to aggrandize oneself at the expense of another, whether he be brother or enemy, even in the time of peace, when he is living at his ease and delicately, and without concern as to his property, how much more must it be the case when one is met by adversity, and is fleeing from his enemies, and has had to abandon his possessions by force of circumstance!"[10]

Other co-religionists were still more reprehensible. When desperate people who had escaped from barbarian captivity came to them for succor, these Christians forcibly detained the refugees, profiting from their destitution and probably putting them to work like slaves. Some Christians even joined the barbarians—showed them the way to Roman houses and villages, and helped the Borani hang or strangle other Romans. The most opportunistic of all apparently went ahead of the barbarians, entering houses from which the owners had just fled and confiscating whatever possessions the owners had abandoned in their frantic haste.

Women whom the Borani had raped were in a different category: they of course were innocent. But for these greedy Christians, these people who fattened themselves on destruction and death, Gregory prescribed public penances. He says nothing about how they felt when they returned home with a dead man's silver and tried to face their neighbors after guiding the Borani against a nearby hamlet that now lay burned and silent. There were problems of conscience in the wake of the barbarian invasions.

The next year the Goths, much impressed by the glittering loot that the Borani brought back from Pontus, decided to stage their own expedition against Asia Minor. It was very well planned. Instead of borrowing ships from somebody else they built their own, using captives for the construction work and wisely employing merchants who traded with them to supervise the whole project. They waited for winter to sail, and since there was not much point in sacking territory that the Borani had already sacked they chose to sail south along the west coast of the Black Sea, the shores of Moesia and Thrace.

Meanwhile their land army proceeded along the coast parallel to the fleet. Past the ancient cities of Istrus and Anchialus went the Goths on foot and on shipboard, and past Tomi where the sophisticated love-poet Ovid had been exiled from Rome by Augustus to live among the trousered natives and scorn them in an age when the Goths were not heard of. The littoral populations of course cringed as the Goths advanced. At a lake near Byzantium the fishermen hid from them among the marsh-weeds, but the Goths found them and commandeered their fishing boats for the land army. With everybody now afloat they headed for Chalcedon across the straits from Byzantium, founded by the Greeks of Megaris in the seventh century B.C. and one of the most prosperous ports on the Propontis.

The Roman garrison at Chalcedon was as slack as the garrison at Trebizond. When the soldiers saw the barbarians coming some of them made excuses to leave. Zosimus is again our principal source. According to him they said that they had an appointment with a general somewhere else. Others did not offer an excuse at all: they just left. The Goths now had an entry into Asia Minor. Screaming through Chalcedon, they seized money, armor, and weapons abandoned by the soldiers, and anything else that struck their fancy.

The rich and helpless land lay open to them, and they overran it at their pleasure, burning and looting, capturing and killing. City after city fell to them — Prusa, Cius, Phrygian Apamea, the beautiful Hellenistic metropolis of Nicea and its rival Nicomedia, gracious capital of Bithynia. After pillaging Nicea and Nicomedia and passing on they turned around, went back to those two cities and burned them. As in other invaded lands, some of the homeless became brigands because organized thievery would at least keep them above the subsistence level. Others starved.

Meanwhile the emperor Valerian, to whose treasury they had been paying their taxes, declined to send them a good general at the head of a strong army to drive the barbarians off. All he did was to dispatch a military officer to Byzantium on the European side of the water to supervise its defenses in case the Goths decided to attack Europe. Valerian may have felt that all the good generals and strong armies were needed for the Persian war. But apparently he was also afraid of giving anyone too much power. A man invested with the command of a potent military force against the Goths could, after defeating the barbarians, use the army to make himself emperor. Cynical and venal, the soldiers would follow any popular leader as long as he paid them. Valerian therefore chose to ignore the seriousness of the Gothic invasion of western Asia Minor. Its population paid the sacrifice for his security.

In that same year, 258, the Alemanni broke through the portion of the **limes** stretching across central Europe between the Main and the Danube. They invaded the province of Raetia, which is now part of Switzerland and western Austria, and swept on south into northern Italy. One band wandered down the Italian peninsula as far as Rome herself, unwalled, unarmed, and psychologically unprepared for war. The senate, panicked into decisive action, mustered an army of citizens laced with members of the Praetorian Guard.

But the day had not yet come when Germanic warriors would enter the sacred city. Outnumbered by the senate's makeshift army, the band of Alemanni withdrew to fields where the taking was easier. With other bands, they despoiled northern Italy, insulting the empire by their very presence on Italian soil, treating Italy like any other invaded province. They penetrated to Ravenna on the Adriatic, where Roman fleets had

Military trophy consisting of captured cuirass and arms. Seated on each side, a German prisoner with hands tied behind back. Inscription: GERMANICVS MAX. V. Reverse of an antoninianus of Gallienus struck 258-9 at Lugdunum (Lyons) in Gaul. 21 mm.

anchored since the reign of Augustus. It looked as if nothing could stop them.

Gallienus was still occupied with trying to stem the Germanic incursions into Gaul. But now he hurried from the Rhine and across the Alps with whatever troops he could spare, one legion. Soldiers from the province of Noricum, east of Raetia, and from Pannonia joined him, and he also picked up another legion in Italy, plus the Praetorian Guardsmen stationed at Rome. The twelfth century historian Zonaras says that Gallienus' fighting force finally amounted to 10,000 men but that there were 300,000 Alemanni. Zonaras probably exaggerated the size of the Germanic host; barbaric forces that assaulted the empire were in general not nearly that large. But even so, Gallienus must have been seriously outnumbered. Nevertheless, he defeated the Alemanni decisively near Milan. They went back where they had come from, having done much damage and enjoyed a good invasion. The Romans of northern Italy tried to resume their industries and their diversions as if no catastrophe had happened. But the shock of seeing untamed Germans ranging across Italian fields could not easily be forgotten.

It was five years—perhaps a little more—since Valerian made himself emperor. The situation, bad enough at the beginning of his reign, had mounted to a crisis of alarming seriousness. Even though the tireless Gallienus won victories such as the one near Milan, neither he nor his inept father seemed able to cope with all the forces opposed to the empire. Barbarians had been allowed to ravage Roman dominions in the Rhineland, in Gaul, in the Balkans, on the coasts of the Black Sea, in Asia Minor, in Switzerland and Austria, in northern Italy itself, and even in North Africa, where a confederation of Moorish tribes under a desert chief named Faraxen was nipping at the southern frontier of the African provinces. At the same time Rome's most civilized enemy, the renewed and vigorous Persia, had been permitted to raid Asia Minor and Syria and to capture Antioch, third city of the empire.

One of the basic troubles was the army's general slackness, poor discipline, and mercenary orientation. Another trouble was that the imperial frontiers were too long and the imperial armies too small and not sufficiently mobile. The legions lived in permanent camps, strategically placed but widely separated. Not enough men could be assembled rapidly at any one spot on a frontier. And while one point was being defended an enemy could break through at some other point, whose garrison had perhaps been withdrawn to help defend the first point.

About 258 Gallienus tried to ameliorate this situation by creating a mobile cavalry corps and perhaps also mobile units of horsemen and foot soldiers combined. The new cavalry corps was made up of Dalmatians—brave Illyrian fighters whose Roman patriotism was stronger than that of most soldiers—plus, perhaps, legionary cavalry, mounted Arab bowmen, and the Moorish troops who threw javelins adroitly from horseback. He later stationed this corps at Milan, from which it could be rushed to whatever danger spot needed it most. This would do some good. But while the enervated old empire was lying down and taking blow after blow, one mobile cavalry corps could not accomplish a great deal.

Notes to Chapter 6

1. Syme, however, doubts the claim of the **Augustan History** that the senate elected him censor under Decius. See **Emperors and Biography**, p. 215.
2. **Writings**, I, 425-27. From the **Address to Demetrianus**.
3. For the above information on Cologne, Trier, and surrounding areas I am indebted to Olwen Brogan, **Roman Gaul** (Cambridge, Massachusetts, 1953), pp. 73-74, 111, 113, 118, 148, 151; Otto Doppelfeld, **The Dionysian-Mosaic at Cologne Cathedral**, translated by Barry Jones (Chicago, 1969), **passim**; Peter La Baume, **Colonia Agrippinensis: A Brief Survey of Cologne in Roman Times**, translated by Barry Jones (Chicago, 1969), pp. 15-16, 18, 58; Peter La Baume, **The Romans on the Rhine** (Chicago, 1969), pp. 12-17, 59-60, 68, 75-76; Paul MacKendrick, **Romans on the Rhine** (New York, 1970), pp. 46-58, 134, 141-53, 211-14, 217-21, 229-34; Mommsen, **Provinces of the Roman Empire: The European Provinces**, pp. 123-24, 176; M. Rostovtzeff, **The Social and Economic History of the Roman Empire**, 2nd edition, revised by P. M. Fraser (Oxford, 1957), I, 223-25; and Edith Mary Wightman, **Roman Trier and the Treveri** (New York and Washington, 1971), **passim**.
4. On the matter of the dates see Alföldi in **Cambridge Ancient History**, XII, 154-58, 181-82; Martin Bang in **Cambridge Medieval History**, I, 201; Brogan, **Roman Gaul**, p. 63; Léon Homo, "L'Empereur Gallien et la Crise de l'Empire Romain au IIIe Siècle," **Revue Historique**, CXIII (May-August 1913), 12; Mommsen, **Provinces: European**, p. 171; and Parker, **History of the Roman World**, p. 167.
5. On the date see Alföldi in **Cambridge Ancient History**, XII, 154-55, 158, 182.
6. The term **cataphracts** had in Hellenistic times been applied to ships whose rowers were protected by a deck over their heads. See F. E. Adcock, **The Greek and Macedonian Art of War** (Berkeley and Los Angeles, 1967), pp. 39-40. An excellent description of cataphracts occurs in the **Ethiopica** by the third century novelist Heliodorus. See Heliodorus, **An Ethiopian Romance**, translated with an Introduction by Moses Hadas (Ann Arbor, 1957), pp. 230-31.
7. See Alföldi in **Cambridge Ancient History**, XII, 170-71; Arthur Christensen in **Cambridge Ancient History**, XII, 132-36; Glanville Downey, **A History of Antioch in Syria from Seleucus to the Arab Conquest** (Prince-

ton, 1961), pp. 253-61, 587-95; Richard N. Frye, **The Heritage of Persia** (London, 1962), pp. 212-13; Grant, **Climax**, pp. 24-25; David Magie, **Roman Rule in Asia Minor to the End of the Third Century after Christ** (Princeton, 1950), I, 707-08, and II, 1568-69 (n. 29); Ramsay MacMullen, **Enemies of the Roman Order** (Cambridge, Massachusetts, 1966), p. 363; Parker, **History of the Roman World**, pp. 165, 168-69, and notes by Warmington, pp. 389-92; and Freya Stark, **Rome on the Euphrates** (New York, 1967), p. 264. In the following account I have relied most heavily on Downey.

8. Downey, **History of Antioch**, pp. 253, 256-57.

9. See, for example, Downey, **History of Antioch**, p. 259; Magie, **Roman Rule in Asia Minor**, II, 1568; and Parker, **History of the Roman World**, pp. 168-69, with Warmington's note, p. 390.

10. **The Works of Gregory Thaumaturgus, Dionysius of Alexandria, and Archelaus**, translated by Rev. S.D.F. Salmond (Edinburgh, 1871), p. 33.

Valerian (253-260), radiate. Obverse of an antoninianus. The dark spot to the right of the portrait is an area where the silver coating has worn off. 23 mm.

7 Heretics and Martyrs

During the early years of the reign of Valerian and Gallienus the Christians, no longer persecuted, tended to their own affairs while catastrophes broke and multiplied over the empire.

Cyprian exerted himself unremittingly on behalf of the church. Under his leadership the great councils of African bishops now met at Carthage every spring and perhaps in the fall as well to discuss matters of ecclesiastical policy. Their fame spread over the Christian world, and Cyprian became the best-known of living Christians.

The city of Arles in southern Gaul had a bishop who supported the Novatianist schism. Cyprian, finding this man's presence on the Christian scene intolerable, wrote to the new pope at Rome, named Stephen, demanding that the Novatianist bishop be replaced. But from a rigorous point of view Stephen was a lax pontiff. He felt inclined to show indulgence toward the Novatianists. Besides, he did not appreciate being told what to do by the bishop of Carthage. Cyprian had antagonized another fellow Christian, this time the pope.

But relations between the two men would probably have calmed down to mutual forbearance if another controversy had not arisen to tear the church apart. This one concerned the rebaptism of heretics. The question was whether people who had been baptized into a heretical sect, and now wanted to become members of the orthodox Christian body, needed to go through another baptism under some priest of the orthodox church. Cyprian said that they did: there could be only one true church, and consequently baptism administered by any man outside that church was not a sacrament and did not carry the hope of salvation. The point had already been established in the preceding generation by a council held at Carthage about the year 220. Most of the bishops in the cities of the Roman East agreed with Cyprian, but Pope Stephen did not.

Although the baptism of babies was becoming common by the middle of the third century, there were many people who avoided being baptized until late in life. They conceived of baptism as a washing away of all their previous sins—a complete rinsing of the wrongs they had committed against God and man, so that they could stand pure before God and be admitted to heaven. But they reasoned that if they were baptized too young this cleansing would not have a great deal of point. They would just dirty their souls all over again afterwards and perhaps lose their chance for a happy immortality. It would be convenient if they could be baptized every few years, or even oftener if they were especially wicked, but the church maintained that this was impossible. Therefore the wisest course was to wait until they were old and had accumulated a great many sins, then have all the sins removed at once by the water of salvation. Delaying baptism until just before death was the best timing of all.

Many of the people who had been baptized into Novatianism, therefore, had never been baptized previously even though they were mature if not elderly individuals and considered themselves Christians of long standing. The whole matter of rebaptism had come up because certain Novatianists had grown disenchanted with the new sect and wanted to come back into the orthodox church. According to Pope Stephen their Novatianist christening was as good as a christening administered by one of his own bishops. After all, in doctrine and dogma the Novatianists did not differ from other Christians. They were not heretics in the usual sense—adherents of false doctrine—but were just schismatics or members of a separate church. Besides, in the view of Stephen and other Christians at Rome baptism was no more important than the ceremony of the laying on of hands at confirmation, through which the Holy Spirit was conveyed to the confirmed person.[1]

Firmilian of Cappadocian Caesarea, one of the most highly respected bishops in Asia Minor, violently objected to Stephen's position. At Alexandria Bishop Dionysius objected more mildly, hoping for peace within the church. But at Carthage Cyprian, supported by the African bishops in council assembled, wrote Stephen a letter implying that the papal position was so lax as to be unacceptable from a Christian point of view. The pope denied audience to the African churchmen who brought this letter and instructed Christians at Rome not to be hospitable to them. He declared that he would not change his views, and indicated that the churches in Africa and the East would have to conform to them. He even threatened to excommunicate defenders of false doctrine such as Cyprian, whom he called Antichrist.

At Carthage in September of 256, eighty-seven bishops voted that no baptism outside the true church could possibly be valid. Nobody mentioned Pope Stephen by name, but one of the African bishops observed that any man who did not agree with the Carthaginian council was a Judas, a betrayer of the bride of Christ. The Christian brotherhood was ruptured. The Roman church and the churches in Africa and the East had reached a stalemate; neither side would budge. It was perhaps fortunate for the future of Christianity that in the summer of 257 Pope Stephen died. Dionysius of Alexandria now succeeded in his efforts to bring about peace.

Behind the whole controversy lay the unwillingness of the African and Eastern bishops to accept the supremacy of Rome. Cyprian, for instance, felt that all Christian bushops were the heirs of the apostles, that they were all appointed by God, and that consequently there was, or should be, a parity among them. But in actual fact the Roman see had moved into a rather dominant position and its authority continued to grow. Located in the capital of the world, toward which the thoughts of all men turned, it could hardly have avoided importance if it had wished. It was, besides, the ultimate church of Peter and Paul, both of whom had died at Rome. Like other Western churches Carthage had gone along with Roman dominance in the past. But Cyprian insisted that no bishop, even the successor to St. Peter,[2] had the right to dictate to other bishops. The pope could claim a symbolic pre-eminence because Christ had looked on Peter as the foundation stone of the Christian structure, but the pope was not intended to have any more actual power than any other bishop.

At Rome and in the West generally, where generations had been accustomed to centralized control and the sanctity of tradition, it was easy to accept the pope as a superior lawmaker and model of what everybody else should do. But Eastern churches, several of which could say proudly that they antedated the Roman church, were never very happy about the prestige of the Roman see. It was not surprising that they sided with Cyprian. The Eastern Christians cherished the individualism, freedom of speculation, and even eccentric self-expression that belonged to the Greek way of life.

That is perhaps one reason why most of the heresies that disrupted the early church sprang up and developed in the East, from Alexandria on through Syria and Asia Minor. Christian thinkers in these areas, using at times the logical techniques of Greek philosophers, indulged in far-flung speculations on such questions as the nature of Christ, the nature of the Trinity, and the nature and origin of evil—matters that would continue to disturb Christianity for centuries. Wildly inventive and eager to argue, Easterners came up with theory after theory, creed after creed. Their sects intertwined with one another, borrowed from one another, contradicted one another, fought off attacks by orthodox Christianity, polemicized and proselytized. The majority of these sects had originated in the second century, but they had not withered by the middle of the third. Although most Christians in the East did not of course become heretics, the proliferation of questionable beliefs made it an exercise of some difficulty for them to keep their orthodoxy intact.

The good Bishop Dionysius of Alexandria devoted himself to refuting two heresies in Africa. One of his efforts was directed toward a part of Egypt called Arsinoë in the area now known as the Fayoum, southwest of modern Cairo. The Christians here were following the teachings left them by a bishop named Nepos who had died not long before. Nepos had written a book interpreting the Bible literally whereas the current trend in the church was to interpret it allegorically. He took the references to a millennium in the Apocalypse to mean that there would actually be a golden age of a thousand years on earth and that during this happy time man would be able to indulge his sexual appetites in uninterrupted bliss. The notion of a thousand-year golden age, though without the emphasis on sex, had already occurred in Jewish thought about the coming of the Messiah.

Dionysius went to Arsinoë to see what he could do about the heresy, which had split whole communities from the orthodox church. He called the leaders of the communities together—the priests and other teachers—intending to speak to them against the concept of a millennium and too literal an approach to Scripture. The result is a good illustration of Greek rationalism in action in a Christian setting. The priests and teachers had brought along Nepos' book as an irrefutable piece of logic, and for three full days they and Dionysius discussed it calmly, philosophically, and fairly. Dionysius wrote later in a tract against the heresy:

> On that occasion I conceived the greatest admiration for the brethren, their firmness, love of truth, facility in following an argument, and intelligence, as we propounded in order and with forbearance the questions, the difficulties raised and the points of agreement; on the one hand refusing to cling obstinately and at all costs . . . to opinions once held; and on the other hand not shirking the counter-arguments, but as far as possible attempting to grapple with the questions in hand and master them.[3]

What especially delighted Dionysius was that at the end of the three days the most influential heretic admitted that he had been wrong, and with him all the others apparently returned to orthodox belief.

But that was an extraordinary event. Most of the heresies were much more stubbornly rooted, and some were widespread. The fact that Dionysius later felt obliged to write a tract called **On Promises** against Nepos' position suggests that even in the case of this heresy a three-day discussion had not in the long run accomplished quite as much as he had hoped.

The other heretical doctrine that Dionysius combated was called Monarchianism. It had spring up, probably in the late second century, in Asia Minor, although the Monarchians that troubled Dionysius lived west of Egypt in Cyrenaica, now Libya.

The time had not yet come when people would riot over the precise nature of the Trinity, but the Trinity was already a crucial problem for Christians in the Greek East and a great deal of philosophical energy was expended on it. A definition of the Holy Ghost was not nearly so pressing as a definition of the Son and his relationship to God the Father. Many Christians were confused because Jesus Christ in the Bible was described in very human, even pathetic terms and yet at the same time was supposed to be non-human, the divine Son of God. It was all very well for pagans to worship man-gods, people thought. But Christianity was presumably opposed to that sort of thing. People also wondered how Christ, if he was not exclusively divine, could really save the human race as he had promised to do. A divine savior-principle satisfied many Christians much more than a savior-God who was in some sense man.

A way out of the dilemma of Christ's identity had been offered since the early days of Christianity by philosophically inclined Christians, especially those with a knowledge of Plato. They spoke of Christ as the **Logos** or "Word." God was basically unknowable, they explained, but He had communicated with mankind by expressing Himself in a visible, human form that man could understand. The **Logos** or Christ was God's translation of Himself into comprehensible terms.

But the Monarchians took this idea much further. They declared that the Word was co-eternal with God the Father and had always been within Him. At the birth of Christ it assumed another form, but it was still God and nothing else. What the Monarchians were doing was negating the human aspect of Jesus—his humility, his struggles, his sorrows. Their aim was to reduce the Trinity to a single divine essence. The term **Monarchian** implied unity, rule by a oneness. There were no real distinctions among the three persons of the so-called Trinity, the Monarchians maintained. Father, Son, and Holy Ghost were just three modes or appearances of the same substance. Therefore the Father became His own Son when He adopted the mode of Christ.

It is perhaps difficult for a less religiously oriented age to appreciate the violent feeling with which people reacted to such subtleties of religious reasoning. Many Christians rushed into the new doctrine as the only way to truth. Orthodox leaders even before Dionysius, on the other hand, were outraged by the Monarchian position. They remarked with pious sarcasm that according to the Monarchians, God the Father sat at His own right hand. They also pointed out that if pushed to its logical extreme, Monarchianism meant that God the Father had suffered on the cross. In fact they started referring to the Monarchians as Patripassians, "those who make the Father suffer." Sabellius, the Monarchian whose disciples were active in Cyrenaica, was annoyed, but the name stuck.

Despite the jeers and orthodox pamphlets the Monarchian heresy had a sturdy growth. In Cyrenaica the Monarchians had taken over many of the Christian congregations by the mid-third century, and it is doubtful that Bishop Dionysius' efforts toward eradicating the heresy were very effective. In the excitement of controversy, Dionysius himself went too far in the opposite direction. He made the rash pronouncement that God the Father differed from the Son as a boat builder differs from his boat—a dip into heresy of which Dionysius repented when the pope issued a rebuke.

The Monarchian sect was still operating in the mid-fourth century. Even after organized communities of Monarchians died out their main point—the single substance of the Godhead—remained to trouble Christianity. Various individuals, whether they said so or not, continued to dislike the idea of a partly human Christ. Here was the germ of Monophysitism, which split the church into hostile camps in the fifth and sixth centuries and caused councils and debates, definitions and redefinitions, loss of temper and loss of life.

Much less subtle than the Monarchians, and probably closer to the lunatic fringe, were the Encratites. They were never organized as a group at all but existed within other heresies and perhaps within orthodox Christianity itself in certain localities, especially in Asia Minor. There had always been an ascetic strain in Christianity. Even in these days before monks and nuns the church admired her voluntary virgins, male and female, such as the chaste ancient lady who threw herself into the fire during the anti-Christian pogrom at Alexandria. Origen, we recall, was said to have castrated himself as a young man, and Cyprian, a husband, relinquished all sexual experience after his conversion. The Encratites carried asceticism about as far as it would go. They did not eat meat or drink wine, using pure water even at communion. They did not own worldly goods. Shuddering at the ways of the flesh, they did not practise sex and did not even marry.

In their ardent abstinence they were, they believed, following Christ's example and showing that the world and all it contained were to be despised. The orthodox church could not disapprove of their moral rigor, but it objected when the Encratites announced that nobody except an Encratite could be a Christian. The church also criticized the Encratites for accepting as Gospel the so-called Apostolic romances, such as the "Acts" of Peter, Andrew, and Thomas, which mixed chaste propaganda with fantastic adventure.

A heresy that condemned the reproduction of the human species was probably not designed for a very long life, but the Encratites propagated through conversion. Although from the standpoint of the church they were never a very serious threat, they continued to attract followers even in the mid-fourth century at Antioch, the cities of Asia Minor and Rome itself.

They renounced meat and property, wine and sex, partly because they looked on all matter as fundamentally evil and did not believe that the being who created this foul world was the God that should be worshipped. They were in this sense very close to Gnosticism—not an organized religion or even an organized philosophy but an attitude that attracted both Christians and non-Christians from Persia on through the whole of the Roman Empire, especially Mesopotamia, Syria, and Egypt, in the second and third centuries. Because Gnosticism stressed sublime knowledge, or **gnosis**, and perhaps because its mythological trappings were complicated, it appealed particularly to educated Greeks and other intellectuals. It certainly constituted as big a problem for early Christianity as the nature of the Trinity or of Christ.

Gnosticism was basically an attempt to account for the presence of evil and suffering in a world supposedly governed by a divine principle that was good, and an attempt to offer a way out of the evil and suffering. There were many varieties of Gnosticism, but all Gnostics agreed about one thing: the world was poorly planned and eminently mismanaged. Animals had to eat one another to live, earthquakes and floods destroyed the innocent in droves, good people sickened and wept, sexually excited human beings acted as bestially as rats. The whole thing was a purposeless, humiliating, filthy mess. Gnostic leaders explained that this was true because the world and all the matter in it had been created by the Demiurge, who was an evil principle, or at best, a relatively ignorant one.

Christian Gnostics believed this evil or ill-informed principle to be the creator-God of the Old Testament and said that he was to be despised rather than adored. They thought that a much higher deity than this creator existed—the principle of good, the God from whom Jesus Christ emanated. But they and other Gnostics also postulated hierarchies of abstractions called Aeons, such as Mind, Truth, Wisdom, and Design, which had relationships and adventures almost in the manner of Greek gods and goddesses, so that complex mythologies developed. Some Gnostics conceived of the Fall as the fall of Wisdom rather than of man and announced that the world must have been made after the Fall, not before, since the world was the product of evil. Some conceived of 365 heavens, only the last and lowest of which was the home of the power that made the world, the God of the Jews.

Gnostics usually treated Christ as an abstraction, perhaps one of the Aeons, sent down by the supreme, good God in human guise to enlighten man and save him from the Demiurge. They therefore gave Christ no more humanity than the Monarchians did, and they regarded the Passion as a fiction. Man, they said, was redeemable because alongside his evil qualities that came from the Demiurge—for instance, his goatish lusts, his cruelty, and his filth—he had a divine element that came from the ineffable God. Contemplation of the ineffable God and of the good in man, and knowledge of how to cultivate this divine good element, perhaps by hating the world's fleshly vices, were the sublime **gnosis**. Through them man could free himself from the evil of matter.

Occasionally the Gnostic attitude would be incorporated in some established group that paid much more attention to Christian writings and Christian beliefs than Gnosticism in general did but still managed to be heretical. One of these groups was the Marcionites, who were very strong in the third century and even in the fourth and fifth. Their founder and organizer, Marcion, was brought up in the second century in Pontus, the same part of Asia Minor where, over a hundred years later, the Borani invaders were to provide violent proof that the world is evil. According to a story which may have no truth in it, Marcion's father, a bishop, excommunicated him for having sex with a virgin. About A.D. 140 he went to Rome, where he presented a large sum of money (200,000 sesterces) to the church. But in the next several years he earned notoriety among the Christians of Rome by proclaiming that Christ was not the son of the God of the Old Testament, the Messiah heralded by the prophets, but that his father was a greater, higher, and far better God, not mentioned in the Old Testament. The Old Testament God, the Yahweh of the Jews, was not evil in Himself but was the originator of evil since He had fashioned the world.

This doctrine made the church uncomfortable. Feeling that if it could not accept Marcion's pronouncements it could not accept his money either, it gave him back the whole amount. Not much bothered by this expression of no confidence, Marcion proceeded to attract converts and worry the church even more. It was probably a number of years after first challenging orthodox Christianity that he come across Polycarp, distinguished bishop of Smyrna on the Aegean coast of Asia Minor, and asked, "Do you know who I am?" The bishop assured him that he recognized the oldest son of the devil.

Marcion's scorn for the material world, like that of many other Gnostics, took a very ascetic turn. The world was a shameful thing, a false and scarlet rose that had to be avoided. Marcionites were Encratites in their shuddering recoil from the pleasures that the God of the Old Testament had created. Not only did Marcion forbid the use of wine at communion, but he did not allow anybody who was married to celebrate communion or even to be baptized. His hatred of the body went so far that he denied it the chance of resurrection. Only the soul would be resurrected, according to him.

Marcionites and Gnostics in general sound anti-Semitic in their violent antipathy toward the Old Testament. Many early orthodox Christians sound the same. Ever since Paul had preached to the Gentiles and opposed Judaic elements in the new faith there had been a very anti-Judaic bias to Christianity. But it was not Jews that the Marcionites and orthodox Christians opposed so much as Judaic doctrine with its emphasis on justice rather than love. The Marcionites paid a great deal more attention to Christ than the Gnostic philosophers did. According to Marcion and his followers the Yahweh of the Old Testament had a fine legal mind but could not transcend His own system of right and wrong, reward and punishment, license and taboo. Sometimes, in fact, He was disturbingly vengeful, and sometimes He was as tyrannical as the most wilful human king. Christ, on the other hand, stood for lovingkindness and mercy. This was because Christ was the visible aspect of the supreme God of good, the divinity that the unconverted Jews did not recognize. This supreme God, Marcion said, is unknowable; in fact Marcion called Him the Stranger God. But He had revealed Himself sufficiently through Christ so that men could see that He was charitable rather than inflexible, merciful rather than inexorably just. Judaism and Christianity were therefore antithetical, and man must choose between them.

Marcionites proclaimed that Christ had shown himself to be the son of the compassionate God of good through his sacrifice on the cross for the redemption of humanity. They went on to say that Christ had suddenly come to earth in the fifteenth year of the reign of Tiberius, or A.D. 29, having the appearance of a mature man. The stories about his being born to the Virgin Mary in a stable, about the shepherds and the wise men coming to see him, and about his boyhood dispute with the doctors in the Temple were nonsense. Christ had had no boyhood at all. These stories implied a being who had been created—a being related to the creator-God of the Old Testament, who had made only evil.

The conception of a Savior with no human past is called Docetism. It brought the Marcionites close to other Gnostics since they also refused to see Christ in human terms. Naturally, it obliged Marcion to throw out quite a bit of the New Testament. The Judaism that he found among the Evangelists obliged him to throw out more. He was left with an expurgated Gospel according to St. Luke, which he thought to have been composed under Paul's influence, and ten of Paul's epistles. Only Paul, he felt, understood the true nature of Christ since only Paul had received revelation direct from God—and even some of Paul's writings had been charged with Judaic ideas after his death. Marcion changed Luke and the ten epistles to fit his own conception of the truth. This kind of editing was easy to perform in an age when the New Testament did not yet exist in a standard version or even in an unquestioned canon. But even so, orthodox Christianity was dismayed again.

Marcion aimed to establish not a sect but a church. We know little about this church except that it was very well organized, probably with a hierarchy of ecclesiastics just as was true of orthodox Christianity. In fact it is possible that orthodox Christianity borrowed some ideas on administration from Marcionism. The firm structure of the Marcionite church was certainly one reason it stayed so strong in the third century and even later.

Its zealous, fanatical approach was probably another. The Marcionites, like ordinary Christians, had their martyrs, men unafraid to die for the faith. The Marcionite priest Metrodorus was burned to death in the stadium at Smyrna during the persecution under Decius.

Certain variants crept into the creed. For instance, Marcion's pupil Apelles rejected the idea that Christ on earth had had no body and said that his body had been fashioned from the four elements. Another variant divided the God of the Old Testament into two—the God of justice that Marcion had talked about and a malevolent God. By the mid-third century many Christians thought of the Marcionites as people who believed in three Gods, one good, one just, and one bad. But whatever variants were introduced, Marcion himself was always venerated as the master and the speaker of truth, who sat in heaven at Christ's left hand just as St. Paul sat on the right.

The strange people called the Ophites, who lived mainly in northern Asia Minor, are a much more shadowy sect. None of their writings have come down to us, and they were probably less interested in recording their doctrines than in practicing their private cult. Like the Marcionites they were basically a Gnostic group, with no use for this terrible world or the God who created it. But comments about them by Christian authors suggest that the Ophites were Christian in only a very peripheral sense.

Asia Minor was such a maelstrom of popular pagan cults that pagan religious elements sometimes affected the beliefs and customs of people who were ostensibly Christian. This is what happened with the Ophites. They attributed supernatural powers to charms, amulets, and secret formulas. Their rituals, from the little we know about them, must have been largely magic. And although the Ophites were divided into a number of sub-sects that emphasized different things, most of these people placed much importance on snakes.

There had been snake cults in Asia Minor for many centuries. In the second and first centuries B.C., cities of Asia Minor issued great quantities of silver coins that showed a snake coiling out of a mystic chest on the obverse and, on the reverse, two snakes winding their bodies together around a bow-case. Serpents were usually associated with health. The health god Aesculapius, a very popular deity since Hellenistic times, was depicted with a snake twining around his staff. The Ophites apparently transferred this ancient veneration of the serpent to God's enemy, the serpent in the Garden of Eden.

They called the God of the Old Testament a "cursed God" and said that His decrees must not be obeyed. Some of their sects revered Cain, the Sodomites, and Judas because those people had transgressed God's commands. They esteemed the serpent of Eden for the same reason. To them the snake was a symbol of freedom, of opposition to immutable law, of rebellion against the oppressive authority wielded by a monstrous God. Some Ophites regarded the serpent as a Christ figure, a type of the Re-

Two snakes coiled around a bow case. Reverse of a cistophorus struck at Tralles in Asia Minor, second century B.C. 27 mm.

deemer himself. Others did not believe in a Redeemer and thought of the serpent as a vital life force. The principal Ophite sect, in a ritual whose exact symbolism has been forgotten, let a serpent crawl out of a sacred chest on the altar and wrap himself around the communion vessels.

In the second century some orthodox Christian priests in northwestern Asia Minor pulled off a raid on the Ophites and killed their snakes. But snakes were not hard to come by and the Ophites recuperated. Although they were never so numerous as to constitute a real threat to Christianity, they were still practicing their mystic rites in the mid-third century, competing with other heresies, and appalling more conventional Christians.

The sect that came to be called the Montanists was a much bigger problem for the church. The Montanists did not borrow as much outright from paganism as the Ophites did, but they were affected by the pagan life of the region where the heresy first gained a foothold and was still centered, Phrygia in west-central Asia Minor. Their founder, named Montanus, may have been a priest of the goddess Cybele before converting to Christianity. Whether he was a priest or not, Phrygian worship of this goddess must have influenced his fervent religiosity. Cybele, the Great Mother, Mother of Gods and Men, accompanied by lions and honored by eunuchs playing tambourines, was the descendant of matriarchal deities and fat fertility queens from the dim and primitive past. She was not worshipped with formal correctness as the state gods of Rome were, but with wild emotion. In the second and third centuries A.D., and probably for many centuries before, her cult was a mystery religion. Her devotees flung themselves around in rapturous seizures, had fits of adoration, mounted to ecstasy, saw visions, and experienced trances in which they did not sense the physical world but something else. All this Phrygian frenzy found its way into Montanism.

Some time in the second half of the second century Montanus, an enthusiastic Christian now, started having prophetic trances. They were apparently a kind of self-induced madness during which he thought that the divine spoke through him. In John 14:16 Christ had promised to send the Holy Spirit as a solace to man: "And I will pray the Father, and he shall give you another Comforter, that he may abide with you for ever." This comforter was called the Paraclete, and it was supposedly the Paraclete that expressed himself through Montanus. The words of solace, often uttered in riddles and strange tongues, were that Christ would soon make a reappearance, a Second Coming. Conveniently enough for the Phrygians, this Second Coming was scheduled for the little town of Pepuza in Phrygia itself.

There was much anxious expectation of an Advent in the second century. Many Christians believed that they might live to see the Second Coming, that it might occur next year or even next week. Orthodox churchmen found nothing wrong in all that. What the churchmen objected to was Montanus' extravagant claims and his manner of prophesying.

He claimed that the Apostles and Christ himself had left an incomplete message and it was up to the Paraclete to finish this message by delivering predictions and other comments through his chosen instrument Montanus. Orthodox churchmen naturally considered this view extreme if not prideful. Montanus' manner of prophesying, besides, was not at all Biblical. The prophets of the Bible had been in a state of ecstasy when they received a message from the divine, but the ecstasy had not, as with Montanus, been actual madness. In addition, they had always returned to sanity before delivering the message, whereas Montanus uttered the words of the Paraclete while he was still in a frenzy. His prophesying was therefore irrational. Ecclesiastics feared that it was really the work of some demon inhabiting his body. They may not have said that it also came close to the frenetic abandon of the cult of Cybele.

In spite of opposition the ecstatic Christianity caught on quickly in Phrygia and spread to other places. Among Montanus' converts were two women, Priscilla and Maximilla, who possessed his own prophetic gift. He approved of their wish to leave their husbands. Free of these encumbrances, they threw themselves into his movement, falling into trances, foreseeing the advent of Christ at Pepuza, predicting turmoil and revolution, and calling on people to forsake their sins and prepare to meet Jesus. The orthodox clergy felt sure that demons lived in these shrieking women. A bishop from Thrace tried to exorcise Priscilla, and two Phrygian bishops tried to drive the demon out of Maximilla. But no devil emerged from either lady.

Like revivalist creeds of the present day, Montanism appealed to the masses. Gnosticism was a philosophy as much as a religion, and its stress on sublime knowledge or **gnosis** as the way to salvation was too subtle for ordinary men to bother with. Although many people got excited about Monarchianism, even that heresy lost some directness in its definition of the Trinity and dehumanization of Christ. But Montanism was as direct as a religion could be. Montanus and the prophetic women spoke in a frenzy that pulled on the emotions of the Phrygians. Their own little town of Pepuza, of all places, was from now on to be called the New Jerusalem. People swarmed to Pepuza—most of them country folk from Phrygian fields and hills, because although Christianity in general was centered in sophisticated cities, this popular religion was rural. At the countrified New Jerusalem they waited for Christ and were fed by Montanist priests. They listened in great crowds to Montanus and the others, who perhaps addressed them in the vulgar Phrygian tongue. They had convulsions, went into hysterics, screamed and foamed, and fainted with the intensity of their fanaticism.

They fasted rigorously on Wednesday and Friday, food being far from the spirit. Many of them separated from their spouses, as Priscilla and

Maximilla themselves had done, because the Montanist leaders kept lauding virginity and expounding on the sinfulness of sex. If husband and wife continued to live in the same house they lived chastely, never lying together. With the Second Coming so imminent they must keep their bodies pure.

In most respects Montanism did not differ from ordinary Christianity. For instance the Montanists accepted the orthodox view of the Trinity and of salvation, and they did not condemn the God of the Old Testament or reject most of the New Testament. But because of the ways in which they did go against the main body of Christianity they were excommunicated by Christian councils in Asia and attacked in pamphlets, which they answered by tracts of their own. Grotesque stories about their customs arose—for instance, that they pricked babies, sometimes fatally, to obtain blood for their rites. That was a libel that in former years had been applied to orthodox Christians. Closer to the truth, perhaps, was the report that the Montanists put their fingers on or in their noses when they prayed; they evidently considered this pose a sign of humility. It may also have been true that at Montanist ceremonies seven virgins, dressed in white and carrying lights, wept over the sins of humanity until they had stirred the congregation to hysterics. Since the Montanists granted so much importance to women, and since they tended to be hysterical anyway, this rumor does not sound entirely incredible.

Like the Marcionites, the Montanists were well organized. Their church had bishops, priests, and deacons like the orthodox church, and the holy city of Pepuza had its patriarch. Christians looked with interest at what they considered an innovation on Montanus' part: his preachers were paid salaries. The regular collection of money helped the Montanist church to prosper. Toward the end of the second century a splintering occurred when some Montanists became attracted to Monarchianism, creating a heresy within a heresy. But strict Montanism survived the split just as it survived the deaths of Montanus, Priscilla, and finally Maximilla, and the rumor that both Montanus and Maximilla had hanged themselves. About the year 205 Tertullian, the austere, fierce, aggressive, uncompromising Carthaginian priest whose writings Cyprian later thought so highly of, left the orthodox church for Montanism. Tertullian, one of the greatest churchmen in the generation before Cyprian, was the Montanists' most illustrious convert. Although he did not endorse all aspects of Montanism, such as its unusual respect for women or its belief that Christ had chosen Pepuza for his reappearance, he certainly helped to make the sect a formidable worry for the orthodox church.

Gradually the Montanists seem to have tempered their asceticism and even their fanaticism, but they clung to their hope in Pepuza. From all over Phrygia, from other parts of Asia Minor, from Egypt, and perhaps even from Rome, they traveled to the holy city on yearly pilgrimages, so that Pepuza continued to boom. In the area around this town there were many Montanist villages, each with its bishop. The sect probably diminished in size when the first fervor had worn itself out, but it persisted. In the fourth century Montanists worshipped in Constantinople. Justinian felt obliged to persecute Montanists in the sixth century, and in 722 the Byzantine emperor Leo III tried forcibly to convert them. They resisted such measures by shutting themselves up in their churches and setting the churches on fire. In time some of them joined other heresies. But there were die-hard Montanists even when the Turks took over in Phrygia.

Despite all the divisive factors in the church—the Novatianist schism, the argument with Pope Stephen about rebaptizing Novatianists, the thriving heresies, and of course the persecution under Decius—Christianity was still a grave problem to the empire during Valerian's reign. In 257 Valerian decided to renew the persecution.

Bishop Dionysius of Alexandria thought that the emperor had been persuaded to take this action by one of his principal ministers, a man named Macrianus. But it is more likely that Valerian had his own motives. Some official act was urgently needed to distract the citizens of the empire from the barbarian depredations, the Persian war, and the plague. In addition, persecution of the Christians might be a means of cementing the empire if that could still be done. Decius' aim of firing the patriotic spirit of the Romans by attacking the most unpatriotic religion was hardly realizable any more and may never have been realizable, but that was no reason for not trying it again. Valerian may even have believed that the catastrophes of his administration were due partly to Christianity, whose stubborn existence still insulted the national gods.

His first edict against the Christians, probably issued from somewhere in the Orient in the summer of 257, was mild in comparison with Decius' decrees. Members of Christian congregations were not required to sacrifice to the gods of the state. Only the bishops, priests, and deacons had to do this. Perhaps Valerian hoped that if the pastors yielded the flocks would follow. Clergymen who refused to sacrifice were to be exiled.

The edict also made it a mortal crime for Christians to meet together or to enter their own cemeteries. The government apparently confiscated the cemeteries and whatever buildings the Christians used as churches in an age before the church building as such existed—in some cases, probably, the villas of prominent persons who belonged to the faith. The theory was that the sect could not survive if it could not meet; Christians customarily held assemblies and performed rituals in their burial places, whether catacombs or not.

Since the edict did not make laymen sacrifice to the gods there was very little of the lapsing that had characterized the Decian persecution. But laymen were sometimes caught in the prohibition against holding meetings and entering cemeteries. It seems that outside Rome some soldiers noticed a young acolyte carrying bread and wine into one of the cemeteries, probably the one that we now call the Catacomb of Callixtus. They grabbed him; he fought to keep the Eucharist out of their profane hands; he was killed. Men, women, and children commemorating the deaths of two recent martyrs at a crypt near another tomb were evidently trapped inside the crypt by soldiers and smothered under a rain of sand and stones, with the priests and deacons still holding the sacred vessels in their hands.

Records as to the sufferings of the clergy tend to be vague. We know that Cyprian's enemy, Pope Stephen, died at the beginning of the persecution, perhaps as a result of it—he may have been in prison or en route to exile for refusing to sacrifice. But it is possible that he died from some other cause.

The governor of the province of Numidia, in North Africa to the west of Carthage, sentenced bishops, priests, and deacons to the mines if they did not perform sacrifice and persisted in holding meetings, together with laymen who went to the meetings. Being sent to the mines was one of the worst fates that a man could suffer in antiquity. Even at the enlightened Athens of the fifth century B.C., men who worked in the silver mines were subjected to horrible conditions and did not last long. In Numidia, those about to start a living death in the mines were clubbed first. The hair was shaved off one side of their heads, so that if they managed somehow to escape they could be spotted easily and brought back. Breathing foul air in the dark tunnels or choking from the smoke of the smelting furnaces, allotted a minimum of bread, dragging iron fetters on their feet, wearing bug-infested rags if anything on their filthy bodies, and beaten when they could not work, they had a hell on earth. Nine of these men were bishops who had recently sat in council at Carthage.

Naturally the government went after Christian leaders, although it was not unduly severe toward them. Dionysius of Alexandria, with a priest and several deacons, had to appear before Aemilian, the deputy governor of Egypt. Aemilian tried hard to persuade him to renounce Christianity, hoping that his example would influence others. The lords Valerian and Gallienus were kind, the governor said. They would not disturb Dionysius as long as he worshipped the gods of the empire and gave up the unnatural Christian gods. But Dionysius, who had been bishop of Alexandria for almost ten years and had expected to become a martyr early in Decius' persecution, was not about to respond to the kindness of Valerian and Gallienus. He explained that Christians adored only one God, that they prayed to Him assiduously for the safety of the empire, and that they would not worship any other gods.

The governor called Dionysius and his companions ungrateful and exiled them to Cephro in Libya. He reminded them not to enter the cemeteries or hold meetings of any kind. But other Christians joined them at this obscure spot, and they proceeded to hold many meetings and even to proselytize the Libyan heathens. Aemilian later moved them nearer Alexandria. Dionysius considered this unfair.

On August 30, 257, Cyprian appeared before the governor in Carthage, a man named Paternus. He gave essentially the same answer that Dionysius gave at Alexandria and that Christians who did not defect customarily gave: that Christians prayed loyally to God for the health of the emperors but that they could not worship the Roman gods. The governor asked for the names of Christian priests who lived in the area. Cyprian refused to divulge any names. He remarked, perhaps with some sarcasm, that the governor himself had been wise enough to forbid men to inform on others; and he assured Paternus that it would not be hard to find the priests anyway.

Paternus exiled him to the small and pleasant town of Curubis on the Gulf of Tunis about fifty miles from Carthage. The sky was sunny, the air and the water were fresh, and the fields around were green. Cyprian's faithful deacon Pontius went along, and so did other Christians. Nobody was maltreated. Cyprian could scarcely have called this exile a persecution. Besides, as Pontius pointed out in his biography of Cyprian, "to the Christian, the whole of this world is one home. Wherefore, though he were banished into a hidden and secret place, yet, associated with the affairs of his God, he cannot regard it as an exile."[4]

But in the summer of 258 Valerian issued his second edict against the Christians, and it was much harsher than the first. Bishops, priests, and deacons who proved recalcitrant were now to be killed. Members of the first two social ranks of the Roman state, the senators and knights, were to lose their possessions to the government if they persisted in being Christian. They were also to be banished and, if they stayed Christian, to be executed. Christian matrons would be exiled, and the government would take over their properties. All people in the direct employ of the emperors, from rich freedmen favored at the court of Valerian on down, were to be sent in chains to work on the imperial estates unless they renounced Christianity.

One of the motives behind the first edict may have been financial. The troops on the ragged frontiers had to be paid, and the church was now prosperous enough to constitute an attractive source of wealth. The confiscation of cemeteries, buildings, and other church properties would help the impecunious government. A financial motive is even easier to see in the second edict, which gave the government the vast estates and fortunes of Christian members of the senatorial aristocracy, matrons, and freedmen at court.

But the second edict must also have been a measure of some desperation. The first one had failed to injure Christianity. By killing churchmen who would not renounce the religion and banishing or executing the most influential Christian laymen, Valerian hoped by the second edict to deprive the sect of all its leaders, both ecclesiastical and secular, so that its heart would die.

What part Gallienus had in either decree was not known; probably he had none. Valerian promulgated both of them from the East while Gallienus was trying to hold the West together. There could have been little communication between father and son, and what there was must have been very slow. Gallienus would naturally have concurred with his father the senior emperor. Although he was not on the most filial terms with Valerian this late in their joint reign, persecution of the Christians was not an issue to split the empire over any more than it was already split. Gallienus was too busy with other matters to push the persecution, but in so far as we know he did nothing to hinder it.

The second stage of the persecution has its quota of questionable stories. Gregory of Tours talks about two missionary bishops in Gaul who, he says, were martyred under Decius but may actually have been killed because of Valerian's edict. One, named Saturninus, was tied behind a bull at the principal temple in Toulouse, which stood on the top of a hill. Then the bull was sent charging down the hill with Saturninus still behind. The other martyr, named Dionysius like the Alexandrian bishop, was dispatched more mercifully by a swordstroke. The French call him Denis. He had come to the town of Paris in the middle of the Seine to preach, and he is now commonly regarded as the patron saint of France. According to the original story his body was thrown into the river but was fished out by other Christians and buried. In the early Middle Ages a legend arose that he was beheaded on Montmartre but that his body, with an angel to lead it, walked two miles to the spot where the abbey of St. Denis was later erected. The body carried its head all that way, while angels sang songs.

Immediately after Pope Stephen's death in 257 a certain Xystus (Sixtus) was elected to succeed him. That testifies to the mildness of Valerian's first edict; during Decius' persecution the Roman church had been too frightened to elect a pope for fifteen months. But Pope Xystus did not last very long after the promulgation of Valerian's second edict. A band of soldiers broke in on him while he was celebrating mass in a catacomb with his congregation and with four of the seven deacons of the Roman church. The story says that he offered his life so that his flock would not be massacred for meeting illicitly. He was beheaded in the catacomb while seated on his episcopal chair. The four deacons were executed too, but the congregation was saved.

Two of his remaining deacons were put to death somewhere else at the same time. That left the Roman church with only one. His name was Lawrence and his days were numbered. But the famous story that Lawrence was fastened to a gridiron and roasted to death over a slow fire is another of the more doubtful tales to come out of this period. All we know is that St. Lawrence died a martyr.

Nearly as famous as the story of St. Lawrence on the gridiron is the one about the so-called **massa candida** or "white mass." It comes down to us in two sermons by St. Augustine and a poem by Prudentius, both of whom lived in the fifth century. At the city of Utica in Africa a massacre of a whole group or mass of Christians must have occurred, probably because they had been meeting illegally. Augustine declares that at least one hundred fifty-three died together. Prudentius makes the whole thing more dramatic. There were three hundred of them, he says, and they were put in front of a deep ditch that glowed and flamed with burning quicklime. The authorities told them that they would either have to drop incense on a pagan altar beside the ditch or be incinerated in the flames. All three hundred jumped into the ditch, and the white glow wrapped the mass of bodies.[5]

Marriage between pagans and Christians who happened to love one another must have been difficult in the best of times, and during a persecution its difficulties intensified. An aristocratic Christian girl named Basilla evidently loved a pagan but declined to marry him because she loved virginity more. After Valerian's second edict her frustrated suitor turned her in. Although the edict stipulated only banishment and confiscation of property for ladies, she was executed.

From Cappadocia in Asia Minor comes a story about a boy named Cyril who was born to heathen parents but turned Christian. His father was a man of substance in Caesarea, capital of Cappadocia. The father and mother, hearing very little out of their rebellious offspring except pious sentiments and the name of Christ, tried to beat paganism back into him. When that did not work they disinherited him and drove him from the house. One of the city magistrates ordered the boy's arrest.

Cyril was found and brought in. The magistrate, wanting to be kind to one so young, promised to return him to his home if he gave up his foolishness. But Cyril responded with more pious sentiments, in the course of which he described himself as a sure candidate for heaven. The magistrate still delayed, but even with a sword hanging over his head Cyril would not recant. All he did was to chastise some of the onlookers for crying. The magistrate condemned him to immediate execution.

Whether or not these tales are accurate, they suggest what must have been going on all over the empire as lovers and families were torn apart by the persecution.

For notorious churchmen the records are fairly full. Dionysius was never made a martyr although he was not treated very kindly. He would live on to guide the Christians of Alexandria for several years after Valerian was dead. But Cyprian, as soon as he reached his place of exile at Curubis, had a vision of approaching martyrdom.

Now Cyprian was able to refute the charges which members of his congregation had made eight years before, in 250, when he fled from Carthage to avoid Decius' persecution. In 258 he certainly wanted to die for the church. He had brought the Christians of Africa through dangerous times, had increased the prestige of the Carthaginian see through the great councils and the force of his own personality, had guarded the morals of his flock and castigated the weak, the slow, and the sin-loving. He had battled for what he considered right in the Christian world—had battled pagans, lay Christians, priests, confessors, sectarians, schismatics, and the pope himself—and he could feel some satisfaction in seeing most of his principles established. Being a soldier of the Lord, as his idol the fierce Tertullian had advocated, had always meant a great deal to Cyprian; and the ultimate victory for a soldier of the Lord was martyrdom with its crown of glory.

In August 258, after he had been in exile at Curubis almost a year, the military came for him. Valerian's second edict had just been published throughout the empire. Cyprian was brought back to Carthage and kept in his own villa, an aristocratic house in the midst of gardens. He had sold this property years before to give the proceeds to the poor, but apparently his rich friends had restored it to him.

Nothing happened. The province had a new governor, Galerius Maximus, and the man was sick with a disease that would kill him very soon. That may have been the reason for the delay of justice. Meanwhile Cyprian seems almost to have held court at his villa, receiving eminent Christians and men of high rank who were not Christians but who admired him as a fighter and a friend. He could tell these people that he looked forward every day to execution, the sweet stroke of the sword. When his friends urged him to hide somewhere before it was too late, and offered their own houses as places of refuge, he could say that he had been summoned to heaven and that he hoped he would be killed while talking about God.[6]

Galerius Maximus finally did send for Cyprian, but the bishop had vanished. He had taken advantage of the offer of one of his friends and gone into hiding for the second time in his life. It looks almost as if the fervor of martyrdom was cooling in his veins at the last minute. But the reason he gave was surely not an excuse. The governor happened to be at Utica, about twenty miles from Carthage. Cyprian did not want to be tried and probably executed in a strange place, where his own people could not gather around. He was bishop of Carthage; he must set an example of Christian courage for his own clergy and congregation. If at the moment of martyrdom he said anything important, anything inspired directly by God, his words should not be wasted on Uticans. When the governor got back to his capital Cyprian would consent to be tried.

Galerius soon moved to a villa just outside Carthage. On September 13th he sent two centurions to Cyprian's residence. Cyprian was there this time, and he went cheerfully along with the officers, riding between them in a chariot.

Again there was a delay. Galerius Maximus, perhaps because he was too sick, postponed the trial until the next day. Cyprian spent the night in the house of one of the officers. It stood in a part of Carthage named after Saturn, ancient Italic god whose festival in December was a sexual explosion. Nearby on one side was a temple to Public Welfare, one of several abstractions worshipped by Romans for the good of the state, and on the other side was the Temple of Venus, goddess of unchaste love.

Cyprian was treated more as a guest than as a prisoner. His deacon Pontius and other Christians were allowed to be with him. Meanwhile a great crowd, hearing where Cyprian had been put, gathered outside. They stayed there all night, waiting. Still very much the Christian administrator, Cyprian issued orders for the safety of the young virgins in this multitude.

By morning the crowd was even greater. Pagans as well as Christians pressed up as close as they could since this bishop was famous with the city's whole population. Some heathens remembered that Cyprian had been active at relieving the sick, regardless of their religion, a few years ago when the plague was at its height in Carthage. Others anticipated a spectacle. Everybody followed when Cyprian was brought out and taken to the governor's court.

His robes were sweaty from the ride under the hot sun. A minor officer in the court—a messenger for the governor—had once been a Christian. Knowing that the relics of martyrs were supposed to have magic powers, he offered to exchange his own clothes for Cyprian's sweaty ones. But the bishop remarked that today's annoyances would probably not be bothersome very long.

The man who would die that day was now judged by the man who had a few more days to live. It was a short trial. Galerius Maximus probably felt too ill to prolong it, and Cyprian's guilt was evident anyway. With Roman formality the governor inquired as to the prisoner's identity and urged him to sacrifice to the gods. Cyprian said he would not consider it. The governor read the sentence; it condemned Cyprian as the leader of an illegal group and as an enemy of the gods, which he certainly was. It said that Cyprian would serve as an example to other malcontents. The laws would be confirmed by his blood. He would die by the sword.

Cyprian thanked God.

The crowd moaned and cried and it looked as if an attempt at rescue might be made. But the guards and officers, who knew what to do at the first sign of trouble, closed in around Cyprian and moved him toward his execution, with the crowd still following. For the Christians of Carthage he was now the great champion, this man whom many had reviled and called a coward eight years before. The hour of his glory had come. He would wear the martyr's crown.

"Now the place itself where he was about to suffer is level," wrote Pontius, "so that it affords a noble spectacle, with its trees thickly planted on all sides. But as, by the extent of the space beyond, the view was not attainable to the confused crowd, persons who favoured him had climbed up into the branches of the trees...."[7] Meanwhile Cyprian, with Pontius and his other disciples close by, took off his cloak, knelt and prayed. Gravely he removed his outer garment and presented it to his deacons. Standing in the middle of his friends and enemies, he issued his last command—that his fellow Christians should give the executioner twenty-five gold coins. They spread linen cloths on the ground in front of him, and he helped a priest and a subdeacon tie a handkerchief over his eyes.

He had certainly done right to avoid being executed at Utica. The governor's sentence had said that Cyprian would serve as an example of how Rome dealt with malcontents. But Cyprian was actually providing an example of Christian courage to the unconverted and of heroism to his clergy and his flock. Only one thing did not happen. He did not utter any divinely inspired words, as he had hoped to do. The priests and deacons around him, the members of his congregation, and even some of the pagans had probably been expecting an ultimate speech from Cyprian, but nothing came.

He merely showed impatience at the executioner's slowness. Evidently this functionary could not bring himself to raise his right arm and swing the blade. His hand faltered and held the sword loosely.

Roman authority felt as impatient as Cyprian. A centurion grabbed the sword and put it to use. Cyprian's head fell away and his body sank to the grass.

The body was placed on exhibition for curious pagans to see. But the Christians came at night by the light of candles and torches, took it to a graveyard, and buried it with prayer.

After everything was over his friend and deacon Pontius, in writing Cyprian's biography, expressed the feelings that many other Christians must have had as they thought back on the martyrdom. Jubilation at Cyprian's glory, a bitter loneliness, and envy, perhaps, that he had achieved what they had not:

> What shall I do now? Between joy at his passion, and grief at still remaining, my mind is divided in different directions, and twofold affections are burdening a heart too limited for them. Shall I grieve that I was not his associate? But yet I must triumph in his victory. Shall I triumph at his victory? Still I grieve that I am not his companion....Much and excessively I exult at his glory; but still more do I grieve that I remained behind.[8]

The persecution intensified at Carthage after Cyprian's execution.

Christians and probably other Carthaginians rioted against the man who took over as acting governor when Galerius Maximus died. Christian clergymen were arrested, and the kindness shown to Cyprian was not shown to them. They were imprisoned, chained, and denied food and drink. They went to death denouncing heathens and heretics or radiating cheer. One young man had a hard time becoming a martyr: since he was neither an aristocrat nor, apparently, a churchman, he did not come under Valerian's edict. He kept claiming to be a deacon, but the crowd, with misdirected pity, shouted that he was a layman and that he should live. After a wait of three days he succeeded in getting executed.

In Numidia the bishops and priests who had been banished under the emperor's first edict were brought back and put to death. New offenders were apprehended. One of them, according to the story, was tortured by being hung up by his thumbs, with weights dangling from his feet to increase the pull. Over North Africa there were many visions; in several of them Cyprian figured. At the Numidian capital the Christians were lined up in neat rows and beheaded in order.

Through the eastern part of the empire the persecution was, in so far as we know, less severe. In Palestine we hear only that three peasants who longed for martyrdom gave themselves up and were fed to the beasts of the arena along with a woman of the Marcionite heresy. Valerian himself was in Syria, but perhaps the Persian war did not leave him or his administrators much leisure for persecuting Christians. Asia Minor, overrun first by Persians, then by Borani and then by Goths, was probably too harassed to do much persecuting.

But at Tarraco (Tarragona), the city on the Spanish Mediterranean coast that would be flattened by the rampaging Franks before the year was out, the bishop and two deacons were tied to stakes in the arena early in 259 and burned. And there is a tradition that Novatian was made a martyr about this time, although it may not be true.

Valerian's persecution extended from 257 to 260, but even after the edict of 258 it was not as violent as Decius'. To be a churchman or a lay Christian of high social position was to live in danger of immediate death, but thousands of ordinary laymen did not need to worry as long as they were not caught at religious assemblies, especially in cemeteries. Like Valerian's other policies, the persecution was not a great success. It did not reunite or even strengthen the state. It did not stamp out Christian meetings or eliminate the clergy. It may have put money into the treasury, but in terms of the enormous expenditures for war and government the financial benefit must have been small. It added to the suffering of a cracked and bleeding empire, and it gave the Christians more martyrs to emulate.

Notes to Chapter 7

1. With regard to the laying on of hands see Duchesne, **Early History of the Christian Church**, p. 306; W. H. C. Frend, **The Early Church** (Philadelphia and New York, 1966), p. 114; and W. H. C. Frend, **Martyrdom and Persecution in the Early Church** (Garden City, New York, 1967), pp. 314-15.

2. Stephen, during this controversy, was the first bishop of Rome to have recourse to the "Thou art Peter" text. See Henry Chadwick, **The Early Church** (Baltimore, 1967), p. 120.

3. Quoted from Dionysius' **On Promises** by Eusebius, **Ecclesiastical History**, with English translation by Kirsopp Lake and J. E. L. Oulton, Loeb Classical Library (London and New York, 1926-32), II, 195.

4. Pontius, **Life and Passion of Cyprian**, in Cyprian, **Writings**, I, xxiii.

5. A rather full treatment of the **massa candida** may be found in the Rev. Patrick J. Healy, **The Valerian Persecution: A Study of the Relations between Church and State in the Third Century A.D.** (Boston, New York, and Cambridge, Massachusetts, 1905), pp. 200-04. Healy dates this holocaust to August 258, whereas Frend dates it to August 259 (**Martyrdom and Persecution**, p. 321).

6. In contrast to Benson (**Cyprian**, pp. 494-95) and Healy (**Valerian Persecution**, pp. 190-91), Joseph H. Fichter attributes these conversations to the end of the Curubis period rather than the return to Carthage; see his **Saint Cecil Cyprian: Early Defender of the Faith** (St. Louis and London, 1942), p. 262. Pontius is unclear.

7. **Life and Passion of Cyprian**, in Cyprian, **Writings**, I, xxx.

8. **Ibid.**, I, xxxi.

8 The Closing Years

One of Gallienus' generals in the Rhineland was a certain Postumus—
"a man of very obscure birth," according to the fourth century historian
Eutropius.[1] On coins he is depicted with a kindly, jovial, almost elf-like
face, a short, tip-tilted nose, a flowing mustache, and a full, curly beard.

His portrait reveals very little about his character. Postumus must have
been an outstanding military commander and politician and a clever opportunist. The opportunity was to make himself emperor. The factors that
created this opportunity were the absence of Gallienus, who had ridden
east toward the Danube with part of the Rhine army to fight barbarian
invaders on that front and perhaps to deal with a usurper named Ingenuus
in Pannonia;[2] Valerian's preoccupation with the Persian war; the disgruntled attitude of some of the soldiers in the Rhineland, who felt that
Valerian and Gallienus should have put more troops on the Rhine to help
them combat the Germans; and very likely the discontent of the civilian
population of that region and Gaul after several years of barbarian depredation.

In 258 or 259, when Gallienus set off for the Danube frontier, Postumus
probably governed Lower Germany. Gallienus left his son, still a boy, as
the imperial representative at Cologne, with a guardian named Silvanus
to watch over him. What apparently happened is that Postumus stopped
a new Frankish raid and, like any general who wanted to be an emperor,
grandly gave the loot to his own soldiers. Silvanus sent him a protest on
behalf of Gallienus and the prince. The soldiers, afraid of being deprived
of their booty, proclaimed Postumus emperor, as he no doubt expected
and perhaps had arranged for them to do. He marched to Cologne and
besieged the city. Cologne surrendered and handed over the young prince
and Silvanus. Postumus had them both killed.

He made Cologne or Trier his capital and ruled unopposed.³ Gallienus was far too busy in the area of the Danube to consider waging war against him immediately. There were now three reigning emperors—Postumus on the Rhine frontier, Gallienus on the Danube frontier, and Valerian on the Persian frontier. Soon after his usurpation Postumus sent Gallienus a message saying that his aim was only to defend Gaul from the barbarians. It seems he also suggested that his rule be combined with Gallienus' but received the rebuff which, quite possibly, he had hoped for. He was now free to set up his own empire, which is sometimes called the Roman Empire of the Gauls. The forces of division were widening the cracks.

Later—some time after Valerian's death—Spain and Britain were to join Postumus' dominions. But even at the beginning of his reign Postumus' power extended far beyond the Rhineland. All of Gaul except the southeastern portion acknowledged him as emperor. Devastated though large parts of it were by this time, Gaul was still, potentially, a very wealthy land. Its many cities, such as Narbonne, Nîmes, Lyons, Autun, and Bordeaux, might not have been as old as the cities of the East and might not have had as many ingenious Greeks living in them, but they had been centers of Roman civilization for a long time and had reached a high degree of sophistication. Their richer citizens held dinner parties in the Roman fashion, with nine diners lying three to a couch and watching jugglers or acrobats while they ate and drank; and on their vast estates they used their Celtic hounds in the aristocratic pastime of the hunt, with deer, bear, wolves and wild boars as game. There were circuses for chariot races, theatres and ampitheatres, and even special cockpit theatres for watching cock fights and bear baiting.

Southern Gaul was rich in figs and olives. In spite of an edict of Domitian restricting viticulture, grapes were grown in Gaul and wines similar to what we call Burgundy and Bordeaux were made. Plentiful flocks of sheep and herds of pigs grazed and foraged in northern Gaul until they became meat for the military. Wheat raised in the fields of Gascony, the Garonne region, and the valley of the Rhone had been exported to Italy for a long time.⁴ Perhaps under Postumus the wheat was not exported any more, and in that case Italy must have suffered. In any event, Postumus had cut away an invaluable piece of the empire.

During the first several years of his reign he must have been gone from his capital for long periods, since his initial problem was to drive out the barbarians or at any rate contain them. There seems to have been a new outburst of barbarian incursions into Gaul about 259. We know as little about Postumus' wars against the Franks and Alemanni as we know about Gallienus' wars against them. But it is evident that Postumus, trained in Gallienus' battles, campaigned with strength and efficiency. After a few years the invasions dwindled off, partly, perhaps, because the Germans felt they had taken all that was worth taking from Gaul, and partly because

Postumus (Gallic Empire, c. 259-268), radiate. Obverse of an antoninianus struck at Lyons or Cologne. 21 mm.

they would rather not cope with Postumus. Bands of Germans, having slipped past Postumus' guard or slaughtered an outpost of soldiers, still roamed the land from time to time wreaking local havoc; but the large scale invasions were over.

On the Danube front Gallienus apparently succeeded in his efforts against the Marcomanni, the Quadi, and the Sarmatians, the tribes that were pushing against the empire in this area. Although we know about his great victory over the Alemannic hordes near Milan in 258, whatever victories he may have achieved in 259 in the remote Danubian borderland are unrecorded. We do know, however, that just as he formed a treaty with some of the Germans along the Rhine several years before, inducing them to help Rome against other Germans, he now entered into a treaty with a Marcomannic king so that this barbarian would help Rome against other barbarians. He had to give the king's tribe a tract of land in Pannonia on the Roman side of the river in return for their military assistance, and he had to seal the bargain by taking the king's daughter, Pipa, as his wife or at any rate his concubine.

Gallienus was already married to a lady named Salonina, mother of the prince whom Postumus ordered to be killed about this time and mother also of an older son who had died several years before. According to all accounts, Gallienus and Salonina loved each other with a strength not very common in fashionable Roman marriages. Perhaps the empress had enough understanding to accept the barbarian girl as a political necessity. In Roman eyes Pipa must have been a concubine rather than a wife. As for the Marcomanni, their distinction between a concubine and a wife may have been cloudy, and if they were satisfied with Pipa's status that was all that mattered.

As a possible precedent for the high place accorded barbarians at court in the Later Roman Empire it would be nice to know something of Pipa's position in the imperial household—the honors given her, the reactions she elicited among Roman senators and their wives, and the extent to which she lived with Gallienus. The only indication comes from Pollio, who presumably wrote Gallienus' biography for the **Augustan History.**[5] Pollio says that because of this princess Gallienus and his associates dyed their hair yellow, apparently so that they would look more like Germans. But Pollio is seldom reliable.

The coins of the emperor Valerian had legends such as "Restorer of the East," "Restorer of the Human Race," "Public Hope," and "Perpetual Security." Aging and harassed, he tried at times to justify these propagandistic mottoes. In 258 or 259 he decided to march from Samosata into Asia Minor and do something about the invading Goths. He headed for the western part of the peninsula but did not get that far. The decision was, like his others, not a happy one. In Cappadocia his army came down with the plague. It was the same plague that had struck Alexandria and Carthage in Gallus' reign and spread over the empire. It was still hitting various parts of the empire; it would withdraw and reappear, taper off and then break out with greater virulence, year after year. With his men sickening and dying around him Valerian had no choice. He turned around and struggled back to Samosata in a painful march.

Safe behind the walls of this city, he probably hoped to rebuild his ruined army or at least to give it rest, but he had to come out and fight the Persians. King Shapur chose this time as the most propitious for another onslaught on the empire. There may have been one battle or there may have been several; again we are in the dark. The only certainty is that as a climax to the Roman fiasco, probably in the summer of 260, the emperor Valerian was captured by the Persians.

He may have been taken in battle or he may have fled to King Shapur on the chance that his enemy would grant him asylum from his own soldiers, tired of this war and mutinous. But the most persistent story is that he was fooled by the Persian king.

The story goes that Valerian decided that it was impossible to hold out against the Persians with his sorry army any longer and that consequently he had better negotiate. He dispatched messengers to the King of Kings with an offer of money if Shapur would call off the war. Shapur sent the messengers back but said that he would discuss the matter if the emperor came in person for a conference. The demand was a proud one and, in Roman terms, insolent. But Valerian, who must have been desperate, complied. With only a small suite to guard him he went to meet Shapur. He and the Persian monarch started to talk about what Valerian hoped would be the treaty. Suddenly the Persians seized the emperor and carried him off. He never was heard from again.

Notes to Chapter 8

1. Eutropius, **Abridgment of Roman History**, in **Justin, Cornelius Nepos; and Eutropius**, translated by John Selby Watson (London, 1890), p. 519.

2. Dates proposed for Ingenuus' revolt range from 258 to 260. See Alföldi in **Cambridge Ancient History**, XII, 184; Homo, "L'Empereur Gallien," pp. 5, 14, 20; David Magie in **The Scriptores Historiae Augustae**, with English translation by David Magie (London and New York, Loeb Classical Library, 1921-32), III, 69, n. 3, and 82, n. 1: and Parker, **History of the Roman World**, pp. 167-68. I have preferred to treat this revolt early in Chap. 9.

3. La Baume (**Colonia Agrippinensis**, pp. 17, 28) says it was Cologne. But Alföldi in **Cambridge Ancient History**, XII, 188, supposes Trier to have been his capital, and Grant (**Climax**, p. 17) follows Alföldi. MacKendrick (**Romans on the Rhine**, p. 215) also names Trier. Edith Mary Wightman

(**Roman Trier and the Treveri**, pp. 53-54) suggests that the Gallic court sometimes resided at Trier, otherwise at Cologne.

4. Excellent accounts of the sociology and economy of Gaul are to be found in Brogan, **Roman Gaul**, especially pp. 59-60, 75-81, 130-36, 156, and Mommsen, **Provinces: European**, pp. 111-14.

5. It is the thesis of Sir Ronald Syme, as of Dessau before him, that the **Augustan History** was written not in the period of Diocletian or Constantine and not by the six men usually credited with its authorship, one of them named Pollio, but by a single author about the year 395. See Syme's **Ammianus and the Historia Augusta** (Oxford, 1968), especially pp. 176-219, and his **Emperors and Biography**, especially pp. v-vi, 1-16, 52-53, 248-62, 281-90. Questions of the authorship, date, method of composition, and possible editorship of the **Augustan History** are among the most complex and tortuous in historical scholarship. For convenience rather than from conviction I will continue to refer to the author of the life of Gallienus as Pollio, the name traditionally assigned him.

Hercules standing with club, lion skin, and bow. Reverse of an antoninianus of Postumus struck at Lyons. 23 mm.

9 Son of the Captive Emperor

As the news of Valerian's capture spread through the empire, so did an overwhelming sense of shame. Never before had a Roman emperor, head and symbol of the state, been carried off by a foreign power. Military reverses, payments to barbarians, and even the loss of land looked minor in comparison with this disgrace, the greatest single indignity that Rome had endured for centuries. All the misfortunes of recent years climaxed in the seizure of Valerian.

Beyond the imperial borders, especially in the East, Roman prestige dropped to a new low. Within the empire people who were not actually disloyal felt defeatist; it did not make much difference what happened now, since the worst had happened already. The view of the Roman world as doddering and decrepit intensified. In allowing himself to get caught Valerian had been a foolish old man, and he represented the empire.

In the depths of the national gloom the Christians felt justified. The divinities who were supposed to safeguard the emperor, the gods of the state whom the pagans kept placating with incense and sacrifice, had been proven powerless. Valerian's capture was a punishment visited on the emperor by God for the persecution of the Christians. Stories circulated about what was happening to Valerian in Persia. People said that he was languishing in prison encumbered with chains—that he had to grovel in the dust before Shapur—that whenever Shapur wanted to get on a horse he stepped on the bent neck of the elderly ex-emperor. No one, of course, knew how Shapur really treated Valerian, and no one knows today. Persian rock carvings showing Valerian on his knees in front of the mounted King of Kings are probably only allegories. But the Christians welcomed the stories.

Gallienus, still on the Danube frontier, must have lamented his father's capture as much as anybody in authority, but he probably did not feel it as a great personal loss. Father and son had been in chronic disagreement too long for that. Gallienus certainly made no attempt to rescue Valerian from the Persians. But this may have been because he knew rescue was impossible. Shapur with his great nobles, his armored knights, and his tens of thousands of peasant soldiers was waging a vicious offensive war that made it hard enough for the battered Roman legions to defend themselves, much less try to save an emperor whose whereabouts were secret. The political situation within the empire, besides, became chaotic with Valerian's capture. As might have been expected, men realized that this time of shock was an excellent time to try usurping the throne.

Probably without having to cope with much resistance, Shapur took Antioch again. Perhaps he was accompanied by the rich former citizen Mariades if, as some ancient historians imply, Mariades betrayed the city to him on this occasion rather than in 256, but more than likely Mariades was already dead.[1] The second taking of the Syrian capital is recorded as confusedly as the first taking.

Ammianus Marcellinus, who lived in Antioch in the fourth century, tells a dramatic story that may have reference to the second capture and may not be true at all. He says that some of the citizens were gathered at the theatre watching a play, as Antiochenes liked to do. Behind them rose Mount Silpius, which overlooked the city. But suddenly one of the actors, happening to glance out past the audience toward the mountain, saw the Persian army assembled on its peak. Abandoning his lines for an ad lib, the actor asked the audience whether he was dreaming or whether the Persians had arrived. The playgoers looked over their shoulders toward the mountaintop, and the Persians answered the actor's question by shooting arrows into the city. That ended the performance. Shapur's army swarmed down the mountain and into Antioch, set fires raging, killed, took prisoners, and looted what they did not burn.

Then Shapur invaded Asia Minor in a campaign of plunder and destruction. His army took towns in the southeastern part of the peninsula, including the splendid merchant city of Tarsus, and marched up through the mountains into Cappadocia. The capital of this province, Caesarea, contained a large population and had been a military center for a long time. Shapur besieged it. A man named Demosthenes was in command of the military units in Caesarea. He was old-fashioned enough to defend the place heroically, but a physician betrayed it. The Persians piled up the dead in the valleys and added to their already enormous loot. They had been scattering off in various directions on this whole Asia Minor expedition, raiding the countryside until it was depleted.

In the **Augustan History** the man calling himself Pollio writes as if thirty people tried to usurp the **imperium** during Gallienus' reign. The number is reminiscent of the "Thirty Tyrants" of ancient Athens, but is not based on fact; many of Pollio's "Thirty Tyrants" were not usurpers at all. But there is no doubt that Valerian's capture provoked a rash of attempted usurpations and that at the beginning of his sole reign Gallienus was in great danger of being overturned.

Some of the revolts are very obscure. The first, that of Ingenuus, may even have occurred before Valerian was captured, although it probably took place shortly after the news of the disaster reached the Danube. As governor in Pannonia, Ingenuus had troops at his command, and they were angry at Gallienus for paying more attention to the Rhine frontier than to the Danube frontier for the past several years. Ingenuus made Sirmium in southern Pannonia his capital. Gallienus, who had previously trusted him in spite of the empress Salonina's suspicions, sent his new mobile cavalry corps against him. The Moorish javelin men distinguished themselves for their deadly accuracy and Ingenuus' reign was over. It cannot have lasted more than a couple of months, if that long. But a military commander named Regalianus took his chance immediately afterwards—in what is now Austria, to judge by coin finds.[2] In a few weeks he was dead, possibly killed by his own troops in fear of Gallienus' vengeance. Disaffection was curbed on the Danube frontier.

In the East Shapur suddenly decided to withdraw. One of the generals in Valerian's army had been a certain Callistus, nicknamed Ballista, which was the term for a Roman military machine that could hurl rocks into enemy towns. Ballista had rallied the Roman soldiers insofar as they could be rallied and handed the Persian forces a series of defeats on the southeast coast of Asia Minor, where various detachments of them were besieging cities or ranging the land for booty. This is apparently one reason Shapur decided to retire. The Persian king also seems to have been as much interested in preserving his heaps of stolen riches as in anything else; and he may have realized that his nobles were anxious to get home with their own share of the spoils. If Shapur had tried to retain the conquered territory he could possibly have added a large part of the Roman East to Persia, which was presumably one of his objects. As it turned out he even had to give up a portion of the loot at Edessa east of the Euphrates before the inhabitants would let his army pass.

An officer named Macrianus had served under Valerian at the imperial headquarters at Samosata. Elderly like Valerian himself and lame besides, he had evidently not done much fighting but had been in charge of troop supplies. After Valerian's capture Macrianus seems to have worked along with Ballista at putting some discipline and spirit back into the Roman army. According to the account given by Pollio, who as usual is open to suspicion, Macrianus and Ballista determined that some new emperor should be chosen. Ballista, not wanting the office, suggested Macrianus himself. But Macrianus protested that he was too old: "'I must bathe too often and eat too carefully, and my very riches have long since kept me away from practicing war. We must seek out some younger man, and not one alone, but two or three of the bravest....' "[3] Since Macrianus had two sons, it was obvious which young men he had in mind. Ballista immediately proposed them but said that Macrianus must act as their advisor if they became emperors since he was a man of much wisdom and experience.

Macrianus agreed and promised a double bonus to the troops out of his own purse. The troops naturally thought the plan an excellent one. The two young men were proclaimed co-emperors and Ballista became their Praetorian Prefect. This was probably in the autumn of 260. Pollio thinks that Macrianus was proclaimed emperor along with his sons, but this is almost certainly wrong. No coins were struck in his name, as they would have been if he shared the **imperium** with his sons. Macrianus seems to have been content to sit back in fatherly pride and offer counsel with fatherly anxiety.

One of the sons was named after his father, the other was called Quietus. Neither seems to have been a man of compelling qualifications, but we know scarcely anything about the personal lives or characters of these adventurers. Pollio says that they were brave but remarks that Macrianus the Younger would never have been made emperor if it had not been for his father. Pollio also mentions—and there is no reason not to believe this—that the whole family of the Macriani traditionally used likenesses of Alexander the Great as magic charms. They wore the portrait of the young Macedonian conqueror in intaglio on their rings. The same portrait decorated their table silver and their wives' gold bracelets and other jewelry. The superstition that the representation of Alexander the Great could be called on for help was evidently not a rare one in an age that cultivated superstitions and looked on Alexander as a god. For a while, it seems to have worked with the Macriani.

Their revolt was, for Gallienus, much more serious than the revolts of Ingenuus and Regalianus in the Balkans and Austria. Gallienus was not in Asia, where he might have been able to stop it at once, but was apparently still in the Danube region. There was, besides, a great deal of sympathy for the Macriani in the Orient. The two young men were recognized as the legitimate rulers not only by the troops but by the populations of Syria, Egypt, and Asia Minor, eager for anybody who might possibly lessen the present distresses and the threat of more war and depredation. At Alexandria, at Antioch, and at cities in Asia Minor coins were struck hailing Macrianus the Younger and Quietus as emperors. Syria was the heart of their empire; cities such as Antioch, Laodicea, and Emesa considered them a most welcome improvement over the ineffectual Valerian and also over Gallienus, too preoccupied in other parts of the world to care for his subjects in the East. If the Persians came again,

Macrianus Junior (260-261), radiate. Obverse of an antoninianus struck at Antioch. 19 x 22 mm.

Macrianus and his sons might know how to defend the people of Syria.

Just as there had been three Roman emperors when Postumus first rebelled against Valerian and Gallienus, there were now three entirely separate Roman Empires: that of Postumus in Gaul and the Rhineland, that of the Macriani in the East, and that of Gallienus. Each claimed to be the true one. Gallienus held Italy, central Europe below Germany, the Balkans, northern Africa except for Egypt, and Spain and Britain if they had not already gone over to Postumus. Harassed as he was by enemies within and beyond his borders, he must expect to cope with Macrianus soon, because Macrianus had decided to invade Europe.

With the Persians now out of Asia Minor, Macrianus could march unopposed through the peninsula toward Europe with his first-born son, his namesake. The younger son, Quietus, stayed in the East to take care of things there. Probably accompanied by much adulation, Macrianus the father and Macrianus the emperor proceeded westward through Asia Minor, requisitioning food, drink, and transport when necessary from land that was already pitifully depleted. When they crossed the water into Europe they could hope to meet and beat Gallienus' legions. Then all Europe except Postumus' empire would lie at the feet of father and sons.

They marched through Thrace without encountering opposition. As in Asia Minor, they must have taken what they needed from the inhabitants. The legions in Pannonia joined them just as those legions had formerly supported Ingenuus and Regalianus. But the emperor sent against the invaders his general Aureolus, the skilled warrior who led the new mobile cavalry corps. Somewhere in the borderland between Thrace and Illyricum there was a battle. The legions from the East, even with the Pannonians to support them—even though they were between 30,000 and 45,000 strong—were no match for the fighting men under Aureolus' command. One of the Eastern standard bearers in the press of battle happened to drop his standard, and the other standard bearers immediately lowered theirs. The war was over.

Father and son did not survive that day. According to the twelfth century historian Zonaras they asked some of their own soldiers, more loyal than the ones who had lowered the standards, to kill them. Gallienus would have killed them otherwise, and it was better not to wait for that.

Meanwhile Gallienus had acquired a friend in the East.

Halfway between the Euphrates River and the city of Damascus, stretched out in the hot desert sands, lay a broad oasis with springs of sulphur water. Here a town called Tadmor sprang up in Old Testament times. It stayed unimportant for a long period, even after Greeks from Seleucid Syria began calling it Palmyra because it was a city of date palms. Caravans would stop there occasionally, and the tribe that held the city would benefit from the caravans. But Palmyra was by no means a great caravan center like Damascus, two hundred miles to the southwest. It did not come into prominence until late in the first century B.C., when much of the trade between Syria and Mesopotamia, which had probably abandoned old routes because of Arab raiders lying in wait along them, passed through the oasis.

About A.D. 17, under the emperor Tiberius, Rome annexed Palmyra. Both Rome and her enemy Parthia, the nation that was later to become Persia, realized that maintaining Palmyra as a trading city was to their economic advantage.[4] Palmyra flourished under their favor. The wealth of Rome was now open to her. Caravans from the Euphrates valley, the Iranian hills, Damascus, Antioch, Sidon, Beirut, or the Persian Gulf stopped here and paid their tariff. The city increased in size as Arab merchants, Syrians, Greeks, and Iranians moved in. Great temples arose, broad streets were laid. The merchants built luxurious dwellings. The emperor Hadrian (117-138) watched over Palmyra's prosperity with special care. A strong Roman garrison occupied the city, largely to protect her commerce, and native Palmyrene archers on horseback or camelback served as auxiliaries with Roman armies. Technically under the government of Rome, Palmyra was ruled largely by her own senate as a republic of merchant chiefs. She sent out her own caravans all over the East. She sent agents to Parthia, Damascus, Rome, even cities in Gaul and Spain as she expanded her commercial empire. Many prominent Palmyrenes were granted Roman citizenship before it became almost universal under Caracalla in 212.

Like other Eastern cities Palmyra suffered from the unsettled conditions of the 240s and 250s, though probably less than most. With Roman legions fighting one another or fighting the Persians there was no one to protect the caravans against the marauding Bedouin, and her trade somewhat declined. But beginning around 260 she was to experience a flaming resurgence, first under a man and then under a woman.

The man was Odenath, member of one of the most distinguished families in the Palmyrene nobility. His grandfather had been honored with Roman citizenship by the emperor Septimius Severus. His father sat in the city's senate and ranked as exarch of the Palmyrenes, a title whose exact meaning is obscure but which in any case implies some leadership in the state. Odenath himself was born to lead. He was alert and physically hard, with the fierce spirit of his desert ancestors scarcely overlaid by the sophistications of his city. From boyhood on "he expended his sweat, as is the duty of a man, in taking lions and panthers and bears and other beasts of the forest, and always lived in the woods and the mountains, enduring heat and rain and all other hardships which pleasures of hunting entail."[5] This would serve him well when he went to war.

First he made war on the Persians. Palmyra was typical of those cities near the empire's eastern border that felt the strong pull of Persia although they were nominally Roman. If Antioch had a considerable body of Persian sympathizers there must have been even more at Palmyra, where the dress, the sculpture, and the local gods were notably Oriental. Especially after Valerian's capture influential Palmyrenes must have thought that Persia might make a better friend than Rome. According to the story told by the sixth century writer Petrus Patricius, Odenath dispatched to King Shapur a procession of camels carrying exquisite presents. These were the embellishments for a letter in which he offered his friendship to Persia. But Shapur asked in scorn who this arrogant Palmyrene was, although he must certainly have known. He may have figured that since Odenath was, after all, a Roman and an enemy, no correspondence between them was possible. Or he may have felt offended that any man, particularly an aristocrat from a city of traders, should presume to offer amity to him, monarch of Persia and King of Kings. Odenath, he said, should fall on his face before the Persian throne, with his hands tied behind his back like a prisoner of war. Otherwise Persia would descend on Palmyra and crush it. As for the gorgeous gifts, they were to be thrown in the Euphrates. But Odenath had as fierce a pride as the Persian did. He dedicated himself to smashing Shapur.

It may have been about this time, perhaps a little later, that he himself took the title King of Kings. For a Roman citizen to hold so exalted and unrepublican a rank was of course unusual, although the rulers of the Bosporus under Rome were called kings and many barbarian chiefs within the empire could claim to be kings too. Whether Gallienus actually gave his permission is not known, but in any case the emperor could hardly object. Since "King of Kings" was a Persian title its appropriation by a Roman citizen was a great insult for Rome's greatest enemy. Odenath had probably meant it that way.

Besides, Gallienus did not want to anger his new and energetic ally by questioning the title. Odenath proved his loyalty by setting out against the Persians.

Shapur, after paying part of his loot to the people of Edessa so that they would allow his troops to pass, had continued on down through Mesopotamia, heading for his capital, Ctesiphon on the Tigris. Odenath cut him off near the Euphrates with an army gathered in eastern Syria and Arabia and containing mounted Palmyrene bowmen as well as knights copied after the Persian cataphracts. He defeated the Persians, chased them all the way down to Ctesiphon and defeated them again, seizing a great deal of their remaining loot. He even captured Shapur's concubines, who had gone along on the expedition against Rome for the regal pleasure. Odenath could now feel that he had paid the proud Persian back.

But revenge had no doubt been only one of Odenath's motives for attacking Shapur. Whether the story of his rebuff by the great king is true in its dramatic details, it suggests that he had been shopping around for an alliance that would do him the most good. When Shapur rejected

Emperor in military dress, right, receiving wreath from Orient or, more likely, Sol. Reverse of an antoninianus of Gallienus struck at an Asiatic mint, perhaps as early as 259. Inscription: ORIENS AVG. 19 mm.

his offer he must have decided that the best hope for his own future lay in Rome. If Rome regained some of her lost power the Palmyrene part of the empire would gain too. A strong Rome, with legions guarding the caravan routes instead of having to fight the Persians, would stabilize the caravan trade and Palmyra would prosper. Therefore Odenath would fight for Rome as hard as he could.

In addition to gathering glory and fame as a warrior he was collecting titles that made him, in Roman terms as well as in Arab terms, the most important man in the eastern part of the empire. Not long after becoming King of Kings of Palmyra, for instance, he became **Dux Romanorum** or "Leader (Duke) of the Romans," a term that indicated his military hegemony. Gallienus, in political gratitude, also allowed him to be called **Imperator.** This, the term from which our word "Emperor" comes although it actually implied "Commander-in-chief," had been borne by generals during republican times and had been one of the imperial titles since Augustus. It permitted Odenath to wear a laurel wreath like the wreath that Gallienus himself wore on gold coins and portrait busts.

Perhaps at about the same time, though we do not know exactly when, Odenath received the title **Corrector totius Orientis,** "Corrector of All the East." Although the denotations of this title are vague, presumably it gave him the responsibility of supervising civil and military affairs throughout the Orient in the emperor's name.[6] Gallienus may have feared that in handing Odenath so much authority he was raising up another potential threat to his own authority. But now was not the time to worry about that. For the moment Odenath was not only useful, he was necessary.

Odenath had taken his wife and young sons along on the campaign against Shapur, arduous as the expedition must have been. His wife was not the kind of woman to be left behind. Her name was Zenobia and she would later challenge the empire. Even now she must have been constantly beside Odenath, inciting his ambition, praising his successes, and, obtrusively or unobtrusively, putting her fine intelligence to work on his problems and plans. Eager for increase of power, she must have thanked the gods of Palmyra that she had such a husband.

From the defeat of Shapur, Odenath whirled around and, under orders dispatched by Gallienus, headed back toward Syria to squash Ballista and the older Macrianus' remaining son, Quietus. He was probably delighted to receive these orders. In effect, they confirmed him in his position as supreme military commander in the East, the man that Rome relied on to crush trouble. The extermination of the Macriani, besides, would make for a stronger Rome, which would protect the caravan routes to Palmyra and make for a stronger Palmyrene state. Odenath may have contemplated betraying Rome eventually and turning his subkingdom into an entirely independent nation. He was as ambitious as his wife, and he had the shrewdness of an Arab trader along with the fierceness of a desert sheik. But for the present it was to his advantage to cultivate Gallienus just as it was to Gallienus' advantage to cultivate him.

Conquering Ballista and young Quietus did not prove difficult for the king of Palmyra. For one thing, once the Syrian cities heard about the deaths of the older and younger Macriani in Europe they quickly lost their faith in the whole rebellion. There was no future in supporting Quietus now that his father and brother were dead, even if the stern Ballista still stood at his side as Praetorian Prefect. So the cities transferred their loyalty to Gallienus. Quietus and Ballista themselves were holed up in Emesa, cult center of the sun god. Odenath proceeded to lay siege to it. The townspeople, whom Ballista seems to have intimidated into staying true to his cause, finally managed to express their own political feelings by killing Quietus and tossing the body over the wall. Odenath had Ballista put out of the way. The greatest rebellion that had threatened Gallienus' sole reign was wiped out in Syria.

But meanwhile there was civil war in Egypt. When one reads the ancient historians on this period one has the impression that the empire, like a masochist, delighted in tormenting itself. The Egyptians had originally sided with the Macriani. When the news of the defeat of the Macriani in Thrace reached Alexandria, the city did not do so simple a thing as resuming loyalty to Gallienus, like the cities of Syria. Some of the inhabitants did want to rejoin Gallienus—probably from fear of his vengeance as much as from affection—but others wanted to support Quietus and Ballista, whom Odenath had not yet besieged.

The two factions fought in the streets, and people who were afraid of being punished by Gallienus were killed defending his cause. The second largest city of the empire, mistress of the Mediterranean, was raked with terror. Quarter blocked quarter. Bishop Dionysius, having returned from exile now that the persecution was over, found it impossible to communicate by letter with Christians in other parts of the city; correspondence between enemy countries would have been easier. A man risked his life if he tried to cross the great main street. Partisans murdered partisans in the alleys. Areas that were usually busy with Alexandria's daily pursuits— the blowing of glass, the making of papyrus, the weaving of linen, the fashioning of jewelry, and the vending of anything to anybody who would buy—grew quiet. People stayed in their homes if they could, listening for sounds of slaughter. The twin harbors, where the great maritime traffic of the empire came and went, were pink with blood.

On top of everything else the plague revisited the city. Perhaps it would not have been so violent if there had not already been so many corpses rotting in the sun. The time was Easter. Dionysius writes that every house had its dead and that wailing sounded through Alexandria. The bishop praises the conduct of the Christians during the whole thing. The pagans, he says, threw the sick into the streets before they were dead to get the contamination out of the houses, and did not dare to bury the corpses but let them putrefy instead. But the Christians in all charity served their sick brothers and sisters and performed the necessary offices for those just dead, "'closing their eyes and shutting their mouths, carrying them on their shoulders and laying them out; they would cling to them, embrace them, bathe and adorn them with their burial clothes, and after a little receive the same services themselves, for those that were left behind were ever following those that went before.'"[7]

The governor of Egypt was still Aemilian, the man who had sent Dionysius into banishment during Valerian's persecution. He did nothing about the plague, but he played an active part in the war of the factions. Apparently he took the side of the Macriani and prevented ships from sailing to Rome with the grain grown along the Nile. Since Egypt and North Africa were Rome's two great sources of cereal, and since without cereal the poor in the capital would collapse with famine or riot against the government through discontent, the revolt of Egypt was one of the most acute problems proliferating for Gallienus.

Pollio tells this story concerning Aemilian: A slave at Alexandria boasted that he owned better sandals than a certain soldier did. The soldier, indignant, killed him. A mob formed, as might have been expected in this excitable city, and it sympathized with the murdered slave. Waving whatever weapons were handy, the outraged people went to Aemilian's house and threw rocks at it.

Because the soldiers in Egypt were under Aemilian's command the street rabble probably held him responsible for the death of the slave. But the whole incident may also have been part of the general strife in Alexandria at the time, and the mob may have consisted of Gallienus' supporters. According to Pollio, Aemilian reasoned that the only hope for himself was to assume the title of emperor. Whether he actually went this far we do not know. He struck no coins in his own name, but the mint may have been in a part of Alexandria held by adherents of Gallienus.

We do know that Gallienus sent a general named Theodotus against him. Aemilian must have gone south from Alexandria to the area around Thebes, partly because some marauding tribes needed to be defeated and partly because many people in this area favored Quietus and Ballista. Gallienus himself, in the Balkans, advanced east as far as Byzantium, where he waited, ready to throw his own forces against Aemilian if this traitor-governor succeeded in defeating the general Theodotus.

But Aemilian lost. He was captured in battle—no one records how or where—and shipped alive to Gallienus. The emperor put him in prison, and there he died by being strangled. The last champion of the Macriani was out of the way. Postumus in Gaul, Odenath in the Orient, and the triumphant Gallienus were the three strongest men in the Roman world.

When life allowed Gallienus a little time off from warfare during the opening year or two of his sole reign he devoted it to counteracting his father's measures. Having disapproved of Valerian's policies while they ruled jointly, he could now reverse them without dividing the empire against itself. The first one he reversed was Valerian's policy toward the Christians.

He issued an edict giving back to the Christians their places of worship and forbidding anyone to disturb these places, and another edict restoring their cemeteries. In other words the church's possession of property was for the first time acknowledged as legal by the government. It was because of these edicts that Bishop Dionysius could return to Alexandria to find the city ruptured by factional war. Other bishops in hiding or banishment also went back to their flocks. The Christians were now relatively secure, although, knowing the whimsicality of emperors, they no doubt continued to feel apprehensive for a while. Their religion was still technically illicit and it was still possible for a man to be executed for refusing pagan sacrifice. But the Christians' freedom to worship as they wished and own what they wished would not be interrupted for at least four decades. After the tribulations inflicted by Decius and Valerian, they would have time to strengthen themselves and consolidate their gains before the worst persecution of all, beginning in 303.

Gallienus had no sympathy for Christianity; he probably disliked it as much as his father had. But he realized that it could not be extinguished by imperial edicts and brute methods. Since the reign of Marcus Aurelius one hundred years before, not many men had worn the Roman purple who by any forcing of the imagination could be called intellectuals. But Gallienus, in the middle of an age of warrior emperors, maintained an interest in literature and philosophy. He was particularly attracted to Greek culture. Perhaps he felt that if Christianity was to be fought successfully it would have to be fought on the subtle level of ideas. Greek thought, in the opinion of most Romans, surely had the strength and truth to overcome Christianity.

In these years of turmoil and agony the Alexandrian philosopher Plotinus, greatest living exponent of Greek philosophy, was interpreting Plato for the modern world in lectures that Rome flocked to hear. Gallienus knew him well and admired his genius. Men such as Plotinus might erase the influence of men such as Origen and Cyprian.

The senate, which had been Valerian's most enthusiastic source of support at the beginning of his reign, had continued to support him even when he no longer seemed to have the qualifications of a great emperor. But the senators looked with some suspicion on Gallienus, and he looked on them with no esteem. About this time the inscription "S C" disappeared from Rome's bronze coins.[8] The letters stood for **Senatus Consulto,** "By Decree of the Senate," as if the senate was responsible for issuing the bronze coinage. Actually the senate had not had much to do with bronze money for more than two centuries. The abandonment of the fiction may simply have been part of the general de-emphasis on bronze coinage under conditions in which the pseudo-silver coins were almost as base as bronze, but it may also have reflected the emperor's low view of a senate so unmanned that its claim to national leadership was a fiction in itself.

Gallienus' principal blow at the senate was to exclude senators from posts of command in the army. Although he belonged to the senatorial class himself, Gallienus recognized that the army was the major force in the empire. The most important men at his mobile court were military men. Courtiers closest to the emperor were already called his **comitatus,** the term we still apply to the military band of eager youths surrounding a German war chief. The functionaries in the spreading imperial bureaucracy belonged to the army. It was an anachronism for senators, a basically unmilitary class, to command the legions. The equestrians—the knights—should issue orders to the soldiers. The emperor Septimius Severus (193-211) had created three new legions at the beginning of his reign and had put knights at their head. Knights could do the best job.

Besides, in an empire as disunified as the Roman Empire now was, the exclusion of senators from offices of high military importance was desirable. Because of their great wealth in an increasingly impoverished state the senators could still exert considerable influence, but much of their influence amounted to interference.

Hostility between emperor and senate was an old tradition. Bred on it, the senators were too often a disruptive element in the nation. They opposed what a given emperor was trying to do; overtly or clandestinely, they tried to subvert him. If senators commanded armies the consequence of their discontent might be revolution and usurpation. That was how Valerian himself had obtained the **imperium.** Philip, it was true, had been a knight, but the danger of usurpation by senators was greater because they were in general more powerfully connected than knights, possessed enormous wealth, and had abundant opportunity for starting trouble. More unity and more coherence within the empire would be possible if the senate's ability to divide the state was kept to a minimum.

Not many aristocratic voices seem to have risen in ire or sadness at Gallienus' policy. If senators complained at all, their outrage is unrecorded. Gallienus certainly made no sudden announcement that senators were not qualified for military commands. The policy only gradually became evident, so that it no doubt took a while for many senators to realize what was happening.

Most senators, besides, would not have wanted to ride at the head of a legion against yelling Germans or armored Persians. They remembered that during the republic and the early empire senators had become heroes by winning battles for Rome, but their memories were only the occasions for bittersweet nostalgia or the swelling of family pride. The sense of dissolution was apparently so overwhelming that one more instance of it did not cause great regret. There may have been resentment that an emperor who came from their own class could treat them in this fashion. But without protesting tyranny—without even whimpering, so far as we know—they gave up one of the most illustrious parts of their heritage. They did not care that much.

Some of the empire's provinces—the so-called senatorial ones—were governed by proconsuls, senators who had already held the consulship and who were not commanders of legions. These provinces were not in great danger of attack from beyond the borders; they did not need legions and their military protection consisted of small units of soldiers at best. They were not much affected by Gallienus' anti-senatorial policy, at least immediately. The provinces where legions were necessary were called imperial provinces and were governed by senators who did command troops. Even here there does not seem to have been much change right away, although eventually—after Gallienus' death—senatorial governors in some of the imperial provinces were replaced by members of the knightly order.

Because of Gallienus' customary severity toward the senate it would be convenient to believe that his object was to deprive senators of their current gubernatorial posts, but this is not borne out by the facts. Occasionally a knight had been temporarily substituted for a senator as governor of some province, senatorial as well as imperial, even before Gallienus' reign. The trend does not seem to have accelerated very much during his years as sole emperor. It increased after his reign, perhaps as a result of his exertions, and possibly Gallienus himself would have encouraged it if he had lived to be an old man. But the climax was not to come until toward the end of the century, when the emperor Diocletian drastically revised the whole provincial administration. What Gallienus perhaps did want to do was to separate the civil from the military power in the provinces by making the knights who now commanded the legions independent of the senators who still functioned as governors. That would deprive the senators of a great deal of political strength.[9]

One thing is clear in any case. Whatever the immediate causes may have been, the senators were relinquishing their administrative functions along with their military functions—more slowly but just as surely. In time they would have little left except their money.

In the Rhineland and throughout Gaul, Postumus continued to be emperor.

After the Germanic invasions of Gaul petered out Postumus seems to have been overcome by grandiose designs, perhaps the hope of some day taking over the whole empire. He either forced or persuaded Spain and

Britain, inhabited mainly by Celts like Gaul itself, to join his domain, so that Gallienus' empire now included nothing west of Italy except the southeastern corner of Gaul, which had never gone over to Postumus. For propaganda, Postumus placed the figure of Hercules on the reverse of many of his coins and tried to associate himself with that god in the minds of his people as the emperor Commodus had done at Rome seventy-five years before.

Postumus was probably of Gallic origin and certainly had the support of the Gallic populace. His Roman Empire of the Gauls looks at first glance like an assertion of Gallic or Celtic nationalism, an attempt at regional independence, an ethnic revolt against the domination of the Roman state. Instead, it **was** the Roman state in Postumus' conception and probably in the opinion of most of his subjects.

When setting it up, Postumus followed the traditional Roman forms exactly. It had a senate and two annually appointed consuls. It had its own Praetorian Guard to defend Postumus, and the office of Praetorian Prefect was one of considerable importance just as it was in the Roman empire of Gallienus. The magistrates who administered the affairs of Postumus' provinces were no different from provincial magistrates in Africa or Syria. The organization of the legions remained the same. The coins were Roman coins—principally brass **sestertii** and the double **denarii** or **antoniniani** that were flooding the rest of the Roman world in all their baseness. Postumus' **antoniniani** may have looked a little better than Gallienus'. At least they had a slightly larger diameter. But they were ragged, cheap, and artistically poor, so that they did not differ very much from those used in Gallienus' provinces. On them Postumus styled himself **Imperator** and **Pius Felix Augustus** in the Roman fashion. To celebrate defeating the barbarians he even termed himself **Restitutor Orbis**, "Restorer of the World," implying that he was the rightful ruler of the whole Roman world rather than merely the holder of power in its western segment.

Some time after the extirpation of the Macriani—probably not until 263—Gallienus with his army invaded the rival Roman empire. His soldiers were probably all from Pannonia and the Balkans, since the Eastern legions could not leave the Persian frontier and the troops of the Rhine frontier and Britain were of course the soldiers of Postumus' realm. It was a sad situation, Gallienus' Roman legions fighting Postumus' Roman legions, which had recently followed Gallienus himself to war against the Germans. If we are to believe Pollio, Postumus had many Celtic and Frankish auxiliaries in his forces. Gallienus had two generals tested and proved in battle. One of them was a hard soldier named Claudius. The other was Aureolus, efficient commander of the mobile cavalry unit, who had already won distinction against Ingenuus and the Macriani in the Balkans.

According to the twelfth century Byzantine chronicler, Zonaras, however, Aureolus did not exert himself as vigorously against Postumus as he could have done, allowing the Gallic emperor to recuperate after defeat when crushing him was feasible. Perhaps Aureolus already contemplated the treachery that he would eventually perpetrate against Gallienus in an attempt to seize the throne for himself, and thought that Postumus might be of help when the time came. At any rate Gallienus' campaign against his rival was inconclusive.

Gallienus is said to have challenged Postumus to single combat at one point during the war so that the lives of many men on both sides would not be needlessly cut off, but Postumus haughtily replied, "I'm no gladiator." The story illustrates the magnanimity that Zonaras, unlike the ancient Latin historians, ascribes to Gallienus, but it sounds too close to romantic idealism. Another story has Gallienus shot by an arrow while besieging a walled city with Postumus inside. The wound was so serious that Gallienus could not continue conducting the siege, and so the war was lost. There may be some truth in this. All we really know is that at the end of the campaign Postumus still ruled in Gaul.

Gallienus returned to Rome. For the moment his wars were over. The first two or three years of his sole reign had not turned out as disastrously as many people expected. They were hectic and frantic years of course, but far from unsuccessful. The Persians had been humiliated, the would-be usurpers had been exterminated; only Postumus remained alive. Barbarians across the Danube frontier stayed relatively quiet for a change, perhaps partly because of Gallienus' "marriage" to the Marcomannic princess. The mobile cavalry corps that he had organized during his joint reign with Valerian had demonstrated its effectiveness. The politically unwise persecution of the Christians was over and, possibly, the divisive influence of the senate was already being checked.

Late nineteenth and twentieth century historians, in their eagerness to rescue Gallienus' reputation from ancient slanders, may sometimes give him a little more credit for all this than he deserves. He certainly had a great deal of help—from Odenath, from Aureolus until the Gallic campaign, and even from his enemies, since Ballista attacked the Persians and Postumus carried on the war against the Germans. But Gallienus had exerted himself strenuously, had made wise decisions unlike his father, and had delegated authority to highly competent men. Most of the credit is rightly his. In his middle forties in 263, he could point proudly to what he had already accomplished and expect to accomplish more. His contemporaries would hardly have admitted an upswing. The times were still too terrible for that, and at any moment a new calamity might fall on the empire. It could be argued, besides, that his triumphs over usurpers were personal ones, bringing more benefit to himself than to the state. But 263 was, in broad terms, a better year than 260. There was some slight reason for hope.

Notes to Chapter 9

1. See Chap. 6, n. 7 and pp. 82-86.
2. See Michael Grant, **Roman History from Coins** (Cambridge University Press, 1968), p. 60.
3. **Scriptores Historiae Augustae**, III, 97. **Tyranni Triginta** XII. 7-8.
4. See M. Rostovtzeff, **Caravan Cities**, translated by D. and T. Talbot Rice (Oxford, 1932), pp. 31-32, 103.
5. Pollio, **Tyranni Triginta** XV. 7, in **Scriptores Historiae Augustae**, III, 107.
6. On Odenath's titles see Alföldi in **Cambridge Ancient History**, XII, 175-76; Charles Simon Clermont-Ganneau, "Odeinat et Vaballat, Rois de Palmyre et leur Titre Romain de Corrector," **Revue Biblique**, XXIX (1920), 382-419; Magie, **Roman Rule in Asia Minor**, I, 709, and II, 1569-70; Parker, **History of the Roman World**, pp. 173-74; and Rostovtzeff, **Caravan Cities**, p. 117.
7. Quoted from Dionysius by Eusebius, **Ecclesiastical History**, Loeb Classical Library, II, 187.
8. See Alföldi in **Cambridge Ancient History**, XII, 183-84.
9. See Ensslin in **Cambridge Ancient History**, XII, 376-77; Magie, **Roman Rule in Asia Minor**, I, 711, and II, 1571; Parker, **History of the Roman World**, pp. 179-80, and Warmington's note, p. 394; and especially Clinton Walker Keyes, **The Rise of the Equites in the Third Century of the Roman Empire** (Princeton, London, and Oxford, 1915), pp. 49-52.

10 Gallienus at Rome

Counting the joint reign with his father, by the autumn of 262 Gallienus had finished his ninth year of rule. The beginning of a tenth year was traditionally an occasion for great celebration at Rome. People renewed their vows for the emperor's safety, prayed to the gods to prosper the empire, and watched processions and games. The emperor himself performed sacrifice at the altars of the national divinities.

There had not been any such celebration for a generation. Since Severus Alexander (222-235), no emperor had stayed alive as long as nine years. Whether Gallienus in the fall of 262 had already completed his campaign against Postumus or still faced that war is not known, but in any case a decennial could not be overlooked and he went to Rome for it.

In spite of his achievements the year was not particularly appropriate for a decennial. The troops at Byzantium revolted earlier in the year and slaughtered the citizens, and Gallienus asserted his authority by having the soldiers executed. The plague apparently struck Rome again in 262, killing several thousand people in the city every day. It may have been in 262 that the Goths streamed into Asia Minor from the Aegean Sea, raiding famous old Ionian cities and wrecking the great temple of Diana of the Ephesians, one of the prides of the East.[1] Earthquakes cracked the streets of Asian and Libyan towns and sucked the houses and screaming people into the ground, and sometimes the sea roared in and flooded what remained. Prayers went up to Jupiter the god of safety.

But even if all these troubles did occur in 262, and we are by no means certain that all of them did, the Roman populace must still have welcomed so important an event as a decennial with some of the old enthusiasm for patriotic holidays. Perhaps the plague had not yet come; Gallienus would not have held the celebration while it was raging. As for the troubles in far-away places such as Asia Minor, they could not have worried the inhabitants of the capital a great deal. Even the privilege of seeing Gallienus was a reason for interest if not for rejoicing. The emperor had been at war so much of the time since 253 that only his shoddy coins reminded the citizens of Rome what he looked like.

Gallienus felt justified in staging a triumphal procession as extravagant as those held during the republic or early empire to celebrate signal military victories. Through streets edged with the thick-packed populace —citizens, slaves, freedmen and women—he proceeded to the Temple of Jupiter on the Capitoline Hill to execute the ritual prescribed by the state religion. The mob ran ahead, waving torches over their heads, honoring this man who was still their emperor after nine years. Two hundred oxen preceded him, with golden cords wound around their horns and magnificent multi-colored cloths of silk draped over their pure white hides. Ten exotic elephants, apparently the only ones in Rome at the time, and two hundred other animals, all in gorgeous trappings, were shown off to the people. So were twelve hundred gladiators, splendidly equipped with the shields, helmets, and weapons of the profession of death. Wagons carried boxers, actors, mimes and buffoons to delight the mob. The buffoons put on performances, probably as pornographic as they were farcical, having to do with the ludicrous figure of the Cyclops, and the crowd loved the whole thing. Gallienus must be a good emperor if he could provide such pleasure for his people.

Grave, playing the role of a victor in battle, he rode in his chariot toward the Capitoline. He wore the vestments of triumph—a purple toga embroidered with gold and, under it, a tunic embroidered with palm leaves. With him, according to custom, went the senators in their white togas with the broad crimson border and the knights in their narrow-bordered togas.

The soldiers all wore white. Five hundred gilded spears and one hundred military banners were carried proudly on each side of Gallienus, plus the flags belonging to units of barbarian auxiliaries, the sacred disc-embellished standards of every legion outside Postumus' empire, and the imperial statues from legionary shrines, where the soldiers practiced the cult of the deified emperors. All of this emphasized the loyalty of the army—an important point. There were also the flags of the city's guilds of tradesmen and artisans, demonstrating the loyalty of the working classes. Throngs of men dressed as Gothic, Sarmatian, Frankish, and Persian prisoners represented nations that presumably cowered before the might of Gallienus.

Jokers in the crowd went up to the pseudo-Persians and started examining them carefully—running from one to another, gazing intently into face after face, shaking their heads and scrutinizing somebody else. People naturally asked what was going on. The comics said that they were looking for the emperor's father. But this was not a planned part of the celebration. When Gallienus heard about it he had the jokers burned alive.

At least, that is the incident as reported by Pollio. Like all Pollio's stories this one is subject to suspicion, but it has the virtue of illustrating the official mood of the decennial.[2] Gallienus resembled many sensible emperors before him in using a state celebration to point up his own excellence as well as to please the people and satisfy the gods. Amusing allusions to the captivity of his father could not be tolerated, especially since Gallienus had made no effort to rescue his father.

For the next few years Gallienus lived mainly at Rome, perhaps some of the time at Milan. He may possibly have been losing a little of his old vigor. Eutropius, writing in the next century, says that even earlier, after the defeat of Ingenuus and Regalianus, he was "for a long time quiet and gentle; afterwards, abandoning himself to all manner of licentiousness, he relaxed the reigns of government with disgraceful inactivity and carelessness." Eutropius like Pollio tries to denigrate Gallienus, but he admits that Gallienus had formerly "performed many gallant acts in Gaul and Illyricum...."[3]

It may be the Roman period that Pollio is talking about when he characterizes Gallienus as irresponsible, affected, frivolous, prodigal, luxurious, and lecherous, a man "who, born for his belly and his pleasures, wasted his days and nights in wine and debauchery...."[4] Instead of wearing a toga at Rome, according to Pollio, this emperor wore a purple cloak fastened with begemmed brooches, a purple-and-gold tunic, a swordbelt encrusted with precious stones, and jeweled laces in his boots, and he powdered his hair with gold dust. In the summer, when Rome is hot and men sweat, he took six or seven baths a day, but he felt that he needed only two or three a day in the winter. Too exalted to touch his lips with glass, he drank his wine from cups of gold and changed the kind of wine after every cup. His concubines lay around in the dining room while he was indulging his appetite, and his favorite actors and buffoons had their own tables close to his. Beautiful girls came in to delight him at his banquets, and scrawny old harridans were sent in for his guests.

Pollio says that Claudius, the general who had helped Gallienus greatly in the campaign against Postumus, felt unhappy at his emperor's dissolute life. In order to regain Claudius' esteem, Gallienus is supposed to have loaded him down with gifts. The letter listing the gifts was probably devised by Pollio himself, but like his examples of Gallienus' self-indulgence, it suggests the luxury that was still possible for the very rich, certainly for the richest man in the empire, even during this age of financial insecurity. Among the presents were embossed silver dishes and silver platters weighing between twenty and thirty pounds each, Persian slippers, Phoenician handkerchiefs, silver pitchers chased with gold, striped tunics from Dalmatia, purple-bordered cloaks, and gold tankards decorated with jewels.

Pollio's picture of Gallienus plays up his vanity as well as his luxury. The emperor apparently ordered a group of statuary, much larger than life, to be erected on the top of the Esquiline Hill. It would consist of a chariot pulled by horses and containing the enormous figure of Gallienus himself as the god of the sun. But this work of art was never finished.

He liked to display what he considered his sharp wit. At the arena one day he watched a man try to kill a bull in the games that simulated actual hunts, but fail again and again. The bull had to be led into the arena ten times, while the spectators no doubt snickered and shouted down comical observations. Gallienus displayed his sharp wit by awarding the embarrassed competitor a wreath of flowers and explaining that to miss a bull ten times was a rare accomplishment.

It is impossible to say whether any of Pollio's portrait of Gallienus is true. The picture contradicts all that we know about the major part of Gallienus' reign. Like the other Latin historians, the less expansive Eutropius and Aurelius Victor, Pollio may have felt resentful toward Gallienus for handling the senate so roughly. If by any chance Gallienus did become a less exemplary ruler after the first few years of his sole reign, however, he would not have been unique in Roman annals.

At least during these years of relative inactivity at Rome he may have relaxed enough to furnish raw material that Pollio and the other Latin historians would later exaggerate, distort, and supplement from their own imaginations.[5] Political and military pressures had eased off that much. In the East he could let Odenath of Palmyra continue to fight the Persians, and Odenath did just that, leading the Eastern legions into Persia as before, winning many victories, and even attacking the capital city, Ctesiphon. Although he did not take Ctesiphon, the Palmyrene ruler provided Gallienus with the right to assume the title **Persicus Maximus** or "Supreme Victor over the Persians," ride in a four-horse chariot in a triumphal procession at Rome, and strike coins commemorating the event about 264.

If Odenath had made a bid for total independence from the empire at this period Gallienus would probably have had to go on the march again, but the king remained loyal. Apparently he still reasoned that the greatest threat to Palmyra's prosperity was Persia, and that he needed Roman troops to keep the Persians on the defensive. He and his wife Zenobia actually controlled Syria by this time anyway, even Antioch, although their control was subtle and the province was of course nominally no part of the Palmyrene kingdom.

It may have been at this period, rather than earlier, that Gallienus concentrated on reducing the influence of the senate. About 265 he fortified Verona with a strong wall in case the barbarians came down that far[6] — an indication that he was not really neglecting his duties as emperor during these years of relative quiet. There were, admittedly, problems that he did not even try to do anything about, but this may have been because he saw that remedies were impossible or too costly to be worthwhile. For instance, there was no use in trying to break Odenath's hold over Syria as long as Odenath was serving Rome valiantly on Persian soil. There was also no use in starting another campaign against Postumus, with insufficient troops to win it.

Inflation and the appearance of the coinage had grown so bad that no way out of the mess could be anticipated. The "silver" **antoniniani** or double **denarii** were by now over 95% copper, and more and more people resorted to barter for ordinary commercial transactions. Cities and even relatively unimportant towns in Asia Minor had customarily struck their own bronze coins, some of them as large as **sestertii,** for local use—token coins with the community's honorific titles, patron gods and goddesses, symbols, temples, and shrines displayed in civic conceit. But these local currencies now dropped off one by one, as they had begun to do even before Valerian and Gallienus came to the purple. Since the **antoninianus,** used all over the empire, had become so base, it was unnecessary and probably unprofitable for the Asiatic cities to issue other base coins containing more metal but officially worth even less. By the end of Gallienus' reign only a very few cities in the East would cling to their own coinages.

For the same reason the imperial denominations in brass and copper, in other words the **sestertius,** the **dupondius,** and the **as,** were less frequently struck—except in the Roman Empire of the Gauls, where Postumus defiantly coined **sestertii** in quantity. A few gold coins or **aurei** still came from Gallienus' mints, and the emperor apparently made some effort to standardize their weight, which had fluctuated wildly during his joint reign with his father. But Gallienus, looking over this disordered monetary scene, may have realized that a long period of peace, uninterrupted trade, and general recuperation would be necessary before the coinage could really be revised; and that tranquil time was still hard to visualize.

Perhaps one reason the Greek historians Zosimus and Zonaras treat Gallienus more kindly that do the Latin historians is his enthusiasm for Greek culture. Now, for the first time since becoming emperor, he had the leisure to indulge his taste for things Greek. In marble portrait busts, reliefs on the sides of sarcophagi, and engravings on gemstones, many artists of the mid-third century were trying, consciously or unconsciously, to recall the philosophic calm, the undisturbed beauty, and the spiritual conviction of classical Greek art. The violence that they eschewed was perhaps the violence of their own age; their art may have been escapist. For that reason, possibly, they did not succeed to the extent that the Greeks had succeeded; even in stone they could not always come close to their sentimental ideal of tranquillity. Some of their contemporaries did not seek the ideal at all, preferring a harsh, almost primitive stylization or the clutter of detail. But for a while the attempted return to the classical

Greek manner—in the sculptures on sarcophagi, for instance, or even some of the coin dies carved at Alexandria—made enough progress to qualify as a minor renaissance.

Gallienus went to Athens at some time during this portion of his reign. In that city, still intellectually active and laden with the greatness of its past, he was elected **archon** or chief magistrate like the philhellenic emperor Hadrian before him. The election must have been a piece of flattery. But the office had existed in the days of Athens' glory, Solon had been an **archon,** and Gallienus probably accepted the title with a real sense of its ancient dignity. Outside Athens, at Eleusis, he was initiated into the cult of Demeter, goddess of ripening fruit and maturing grain, whose daughter Persephone rose each year from the home of the dead to bring in the fertile spring. The cult of Demeter was a mystery religion. We still know very little about it, but we know that it stressed a life after death. In this way it differed from the formal state religion of Rome, the religion of which Gallienus was high priest.

He composed poetry in Greek and Latin. What purports to be part of one of his Latin poems, an **epithalamimum** written for the wedding of a niece and nephew, is cited by Pollio. Gallienus held the hands of the young couple and spoke these suggestive lines:

> Come now, my children, grow heated together in deep-seated passion,
> Never, indeed, may the doves outdo your billings and cooings,
> Never the ivy your arms, or the clinging of sea-shells your kisses.[7]

According to Pollio, many people had written verses for this fashionable wedding but Gallienus' were the best. The emperor apparently enjoyed renown among the poets of the age. That is not saying a great deal, since the age did not excel in poets. Whoever really composed the lines Pollio attributes to Gallienus, they are typical of late classical verse in their sweet effeminacy. But Pollio disapproves of Gallienus' high literary reputation. An emperor who devotes himself conscientiously to affairs of state should not have time for writing verses.

Gallienus also shone as an orator, Pollio says, rivaling the most polished rhetoricians of the period. Pollio is probably not talking about public addresses but about private readings, given to a circle of friends. If these recitals reflected the taste of the age they must have been verbose, profusely decorated with figures of speech and turns of phrase, and very artificial. In Pollio's view the same criticism applies: an emperor should not have time for such literary exercises.

But again, from our limited knowledge Gallienus does not seem to have indulged these interests to the neglect of government. He was certainly no Nero, posturing, proclaiming, and displaying his creative abilities for the edification and wonder of Italy and Greece. He probably deserves some credit, too, for being an individual—an emperor unlike the others, persistently cultivating his intellect in an era of battle.

Notes to Chapter 10

1. See pp. 164-70.
2. Pollio's whole description of the decennial, in fact, is subject to suspicion. Syme suggests that it is a borrowing from and parody on Ammianus' account of Constantius' entry into Rome (**Ammianus and the Historia Augusta**, pp. 40-41). But it is the only description we have.
3. **Abridgment**, p. 519.
4. **Scriptores Historiae Augustae**, III, 51. **Gallieni Duo XVI. 1.**
5. Grant, however, evidently accepts as true the story of the projected statuary group; see his **Climax**, p. 178.
6. See Homo, "L'Empereur Gallien," p. 255; Millar, **Roman Empire and its Neighbours**, p. 129; and Syme, **Emperors and Biography**, p. 244.
7. **Scriptores Historiae Augustae**, III, 41. **Gallieni Duo XI. 8.**

Gallienus as sole emperor (260-268), radiate. Obverse of an antoninianus. 21 mm.

11 The Philosopher

The most convincing indication of Gallienus' cultivation of his mind during these years at Rome is his friendship for and patronage of the philosopher Plotinus. In this man's thought the ancient Greek genius glowed for perhaps the final time, against the troubled, shifting background of his own age.

Plotinus had been born along the Nile somewhere north of Thebes about the year 205. The only detail from his childhood is a singularly uncontemplative one. At the age of eight, according to his student and biographer Porphyry, he had not been weaned. He still liked to uncover his nurse's breast and suck the milk out of it. But he did this so greedily that she raised objections, and the habit stopped.

He was twenty-eight by the time he went to Alexandria to study philosophy. The men at whose feet he sat disappointed him until he discovered Ammonius Saccas, once a porter, possibly a renegade from Christianity, now an expounder of Plato. The young Origen, a generation earlier than Plotinus, had studied under this man. After Origen left Alexandria to carry on the work of the church in Palestine, Ammonius Saccas was probably the greatest teacher in the city. For almost eleven years Plotinus listened to the Alexandrian discuss the Platonic world of ideal forms of which this world of the senses is only a crude suggestion, the demons who are intermediaries between the divine and the human, and the importance of soul over body.

Plotinus must have had the respect of the philosopher's other disciples, though not necessarily for his wisdom. The intense superstitiousness of the age pervaded philosophical circles just as it pervaded the streets and the fields. One of Ammonius Saccas' other followers, jealous of Plotinus, tried to bewitch him. But Plotinus would not be charmed, and the rival, whose name was Olympius, discovered that his magic was ricocheting on himself. For example, "The first time that Olympius attempted to harm him, Plotinus having noticed it, said, 'At this very moment the body of Olympius is undergoing convulsions, and is contracting like a purse.' As Olympius several times felt himself undergoing the very ills he was trying to get Plotinus to undergo, he finally ceased his practices."[1] He also admitted that Plotinus' magic was greater than his own.

When Ammonius Saccas died in 242 or 243 Plotinus, impatient to increase his knowledge, went with the expedition of the boy-emperor Gordian III against the Persians. In Persia he could learn about Zoroastrianism; perhaps he had also heard of the dualism between light and dark that a young man named Mani had just begun to preach there, and was curious concerning it. On the Indian side of the Persian dominions he might even be able to ask questions about Brahminism. But when Gordian was killed by the soldiers and Philip the Arab became emperor and made peace with the Persians, the seeker after Oriental wisdom returned to the Roman world. After a short stay at Antioch he went to Rome, probably in 244, about the time Philip himself arrived there.

Close to forty now, Plotinus opened up his own philosophical school at Rome like Ammonius Saccas' school in Alexandria. When Gallienus and Valerian became emperors in 253 he was already well known as a lecturer. He would stay in or near Rome until he died, becoming famous, arguing patiently with his detractors, inspiring his devoted followers, persuading the curious, and enlightening the sympathetic, such as Gallienus.

The philosophy he taught, which is now called Neoplatonism, revolves around the idea of an Essential Being, an ineffable One, superior to gods, perfect and indescribable. Man cannot conceive of the One, since thought and the objects of thought are limited. The One has always existed and will always exist—beyond time and space, beyond morality and immorality, without properties, qualifications, contradictions, distinctions, or disparities, "neither thing nor quantity nor quality nor intellect nor soul; not in motion, not at rest, not in place, not in time: it is the self-defined, unique in form or, better, formless, existing before Form was, or Movement or Rest. .."[2] Plotinus spoke of it analogically as an inexhaustible pool from which water keeps streaming, an irradiating sun, or the life-giving root of a great tree. These images suggest the creative function of the One. All being proceeds from it in emanations that are continuous. Unlike Judaism or Christianity, Neoplatonism does not regard creation as a single act performed at a specific time. The One is constantly emitting reality.

The emanations exist in several stages, something like concentric rings around a planet, growing less and less perfect as they get farther and farther from the One. The first great stage is **Nous**—Intelligence or Divine Mind, pure and totally lucid, the "source of all knowing."[3] Like the essential being from which it comes it is a oneness, but paradoxically it is also a multiplicity because it enters into every individual human mind, different from every other human mind.

The next stage is **Psyche** or Soul, an intermediary between the Divine Mind and the Physical World, the world of bodies in which man exists. Soul resembles the Divine Mind in being both a unity and a multiplicity. Since it informs and animates the Physical World, which is an area of dazzling diversity, and since it enters into every human soul, which is distinct from every other human soul, it must be a complexity as well as a oneness. Because its immediate progenitor is Divine Mind it partakes of thought, but a somewhat less elevated kind of thought than pure lucidity. Its objects are sensations and ideas, and it walks the labyrinth of reason.

Within an individual man it is the cardinal element. But its housing in the human bodies filling up the Physical World is the Soul's misfortune. That world is the farthest stage of being from the One—the outermost ring. Beyond it lies the stark expanse of uncreation. The lower reaches of the Physical World, although they are not vile, contain a very diluted residue of the perfection which is the One. The soul in man is as superior to the body as the spiritual is to the corporeal in Plato's scheme, but through association with the body it can suffer and be soiled. "What Soul could contain Evil unless by contact with the lower Kind?"[4] Lust, hate, and avarice can stain it. As Plotinus looked around him at the ordinary citizens of Rome—the shopkeepers and smiths and bakers, rowdy at low taverns, raucous at the circus on holidays, and lecherous always—he must have seen little uncontaminated soul.

This whole structure may sound arbitrary, artificial, and far too fanciful to be taken seriously, but there is more to it than hierarchic arrangement. Plotinus' cultivated contemporaries were intrigued by complicated systems (such as the mythological appurtenances of Gnosticism) and would besides have felt pleased to recognize overtones of Plato's world of ideas in the suprahuman scheme, yet even they might have lost interest except for the impulse at the core. Neoplatonism is made beautiful by the same desire that makes Hinduism and Transcendentalism beautiful. The thrust of vitality, Plotinus believed, is not only outwards from the One through the successive rings of reality but also back through them to the One. Man has an urge, an overwhelming ardor, to return to his ultimate source. He feels "that love-passion of vision known to the lover come to rest where he loves."[5]

Plotinus liked to speak of the One as a father. A polluted human soul was a daughter who had fallen off in her affection for him because of the allurements of the world. "But one day coming to hate her shame, she puts away the evil of earth, once more seeks the father, and finds her peace."[6] In reuniting his soul with the central Essential Being a man can achieve not only the peace of the soul but his highest potential. He can fully realize himself by fully losing himself in the One.

This supreme goal can be reached simultaneously at the greatest height to which his soul can climb and in the inmost depths of his own being, because the One pervades everything like the Hindu Brahman or the Emersonian Oversoul. But first a man must scrupulously practice virtue in his relationships with other human beings and then he must lead an ascetic life, a life of simplicity and withdrawal from the coils of the world that drag one down. By virtue and asceticism he can divorce himself from the world's wild passions, temptations, differences, disappointments, commitments and attachments—from the struggles and troubles of the age, the demands of time and space, the self-multiplying swarms of details that distract a man from contemplation. Through thought—through the undivided application of his reason—he can advance toward the area of Divine Mind.

But here the efficacy of reason ends, because "with reasoning we are already in the region of separation and movement"[7] rather than immutability and unity. The rest of the way is by intuition and the end is rapture. Having divested himself of everything of this world—having become void, selfless, unconscious of objects, sounds, emotions, drives, and needs—the man enters a state of vision, an ecstasy. Then he is at his goal. Perfection bursts on him in a luminous blaze and immerses him, so that his soul becomes "that very light, pure, buoyant, unburdened, raised to Godhood or, better, knowing its Godhood, all aflame then...." He is no longer a man but the One itself, the Everything, the Source of his own being, "merged with the Supreme...."[8]

Even for Plotinus this mystic experience was rare. During the five or six years that Porphyry studied under him at Rome, Plotinus achieved it only four times.

In spite of his conception of the physical universe as the lowest grade of creation, he did not, like the Gnostics, consider the world rotten and unrelievedly repellent. He did not long to escape from it because it was a filthy cell. In his system the world has abundant beauty, as it must if it comes, no matter how remotely, from the One. He felt impatient with the Gnostic contention that it was made by a malevolent or bungling god. The world is part of the perfect whole—the outermost part, but still necessary, like a low note in a harmony. Even poisonous reptiles serve a purpose, since without them, as without any other given form of life, the harmony would be incomplete. Evil is pretty much a negative factor, "the required faint image of Being,"[9] the lack of relationship with the One. The Gnostics would have called it very positive.

In addition to conceiving of creation as a constant efflux rather than as something that happened once and for all, Plotinus differed from the Christians in not thinking a Savior necessary. According to his system every man can save himself as long as he has the compulsion and intelligence to unite with the One and the leisure to follow the requisite steps. A Redeemer is a superfluity if not an impediment.

But these differences between Neoplatonism and Christianity did not, as early as Gallienus' reign, make the two creeds confirmed enemies. That would happen later. Soon after Plotinus' death his pupil Porphyry would write a treatise, **Against the Christians**, attacking the Christians for their doctrines of Creation, Doomsday, Incarnation, and Resurrection, and claiming that they had distorted the principles of Jesus, whom Porphyry considered a most admirable but grossly misinterpreted man.

Although Neoplatonism could not embrace Christianity it was elastic enough to accommodate the old gods, the dying patrons of the state and the full-bodied deities from the East. Plotinus did not object to worshipping such figures. They were emanations from the One—mystic revelations that had been sent from the divine as aids to man. Through their worship man could develop a stronger sense of the divine, approach closer to it.

Neoplatonism had considerably less appeal for the masses than Christianity or the cults of Mithra, Isis, and Cybele. It was scarcely a discipline for people with untrained minds or people who had to spend their waking hours at brutal, brutalizing work. Its adherents were, like Christian leaders, usually men of cultivation. But among these literati it soon achieved prominence, partly because it offered a philosophical release from the world's gross preoccupations and frequent horrors. Visitations of pestilence, the savage sack of cities, the news of revolution, the grasping greed, the hunger, and other distractions could be forgotten—in fact had to be forgotten—by the seeker after the One.

Passionate religious feeling, as has been remarked before, was the trend of the age. The Stoicism and Skepticism that had been fashionable in the first and second centuries were, like the ritualistic national religion and in some degree like logical argument, giving way before the sweep of religiosity, best represented in the creeds of the East. Everybody believed in something, if only the magic that Plotinus' rival Olympius believed in, and the favored cults were above all else irrational.

Plotinus could speak of the yearning of the soul for union with the One as a love, a passion. Neoplatonism too, then, had a strongly emotional, ultimately irrational appeal. People welcomed the idea that reason could carry a man only so far on the trip through the rings of reality. They liked to hear Plotinus describe, in so far as it was describable, the ultimate visionary state. What Neoplatonism lacked, however, was the exotic ritual of the Eastern faiths, with their priests, their perfumes, their blood-baths, and their music. This doctrine was, after all, much less a religion than a philosophy. It could not organize.

The physical world—the world of immutable laws and mechanical processes that had fascinated the Ionian Greeks and later the Alexandrians—did not hold tremendous interest for people in the mid-third century. They ploughed, sowed, and ground their grain as their great-great-grandfathers had, and they did not try to improve on nature or manipulate it in new ways. They were not especially curious about their bodies either. Galen, who died early in the century, was the last great ancient physician. What drew these people was their souls, and, as a corollary to that, the life of the soul after death. One of the greatest attractions of the religions from the East, including Christianity of course, was their stress on the soul and their assurance of an immortal life for it. The Neoplatonic journey of the soul to the Absolute One fell in with the age's quest for spiritual satisfaction.

Plotinus' conception of the One also corresponded with an intellectual tendency of the period. Tired and confounded by the rich diversity of classical gods and goddesses, the third century tended to combine them in the process called syncretism. For example, Serapis, the husband of Isis in the late Egyptian pantheon, was also Jupiter in his capacity of supreme god and also Pluto in his capacity as god of the Underworld. On coins struck at Alexandria he was sometimes depicted with the trident of Poseidon and the serpent of Aesculapius, god of health. To push it further, all the deities were particular aspects of an unknowable divine entity. The age leaned toward monotheism. Plotinus' One was an important answer to the search for the Ultimate, that which transcended individual divinities. Everything was synthesized and undifferentiated in the One.

Plotinus, according to Porphyry, neglected to deliver his ideas in finely wrought, formally structured, smooth and exquisite lectures of the kind so admired during the period. In fact his presentation impressed some people as disorganized. He used a seminar system. He would allow his students to interrupt him with questions, and sometimes these questions would, as in modern classrooms, lead to less than relevant discussions. But he answered objections pertinently, and when he really became excited about a point his face seemed almost to shine with intelligence, a light sweat stood on his forehead, and he spoke eloquently.

Only detractors with little soul could criticize his Greek for being ungrammatical. His learning could not be denied. He displayed considerable knowledge of fields such as geometry, optics, and music as well as the various Greek philosophies ancient and recent. He was interested in astronomy—though not from a mathematical viewpoint, Porphyry comments—and it is to his credit that unlike his contemporaries he put no faith in astrology, which he carefully investigated before dismissing it.

Disciples hurried to his lectures after he became famous. But although some of them came from Italy, a significantly large number came from the East—Palestine, Egypt, Syria, and Arabia, the regions where mystic, ecstatic creeds flourished best. Porphyry, for instance, had been born at Tyre in Phoenicia.

Several of the students practised medicine. Other fields of learning represented in this intellectually elite group were poetry, criticism, and rhetoric. One of Plotinus' earliest and most devoted adherents, a man named Amelius, had been a Stoic philosopher before joining the circle, and it is revealing that he abandoned the unflinching rationality of Stoicism for Neoplatonic ecstasy. The circle also included some philosophical women as well as senators.

Plotinus tried to persuade his richest, most avaricious, or busiest disciples to rid themselves of their worldly concerns, the possessions and involvements that stuck to them and kept them back from the One. An Alexandrian rhetorician named Serapion was the most hopeless; his passion for money pulled much harder than his hunger for mystic union. A prosperous doctor with an estate north of Naples evidently found it too hard to relinquish the public affairs in which he was both active and excellent. So did a public figure named Castricius, in spite of his veneration for his teacher. These were men of the surface whom Thoreau might have pitied, and perhaps Plotinius pitied them too.

But Rogatian, a senator, was a much better pupil. Rogatian really opened himself to the One. According to Porphyry, he "abandoned all his possessions, dismissed all his attendants, and renounced all his dignities.... He even failed to dwell in his own house (to avoid needless pomp); he visited his friends, boarding and sleeping there...."[10] Every other day he ate nothing, and as a result he recovered from gout of the hands and feet. He renounced his political career, refusing to make an appearance at his inauguration as a praetor or justice and probably embarrassing high-ranking Roman bureaucracy by his absence. Plotinus pointed him out to others as an example of what a man should be.

The philosopher's quarters were full of the cries of children. Dying parents with plenty of money gave over their sons and daughters to his guardianship and their property to his trusteeship. In spite of his low opinion of the desirability of property for the spiritual man, he conscientiously took care of the estates as well as the children, going over the accounts that the stewards submitted and making sure that nothing was mismanaged or misappropriated.

His own life was one of extreme simplicity. Like the Pythagoreans he practiced vegetarianism, since he believed that human souls which choose the lowest and most lustful aspects of the Physical World transmigrate into animal bodies after death. Sometimes he did not even eat bread. He paid little attention to his body, and when people tried to persuade him to have his portrait painted he would remark platonically that a portrait is nothing but an image of an image. Although he suffered from complaints of the digestive tract (Porphyry is not very specific about them) he did not try to treat them with the medical remedies of the day, and that may have been a good thing.

He never took a bath, although he did care enough for his body to have it massaged from time to time. But when the masseur died of the plague —probably the fearful recurrence of the pestilence at Rome in 262—he did not hire another one. As a consequence, Porphyry thinks, he contracted an inflammation of the throat that hung on for the rest of his life.

He must have been a very gentle and likable person, one of those teachers who inspire devotion by their character as well as their knowledge. Only one of his statements seems really to have perplexed his pupils as the remark of a proud man. When his student Amelius, who scrupulously kept the monthly festival of the New Moon, invited him to participate in that rite, Plotinus said: "'It is the business of those divinities to come and visit me, and not mine to attend on them.' We could not understand why he should make an utterance that revealed so much pride, but we dared not question the matter."[11]

It was through Amelius that Porphyry of Tyre met Plotinus in 263. Amelius had been studying under him for eighteen years by that time. Porphyry, a man of thirty, studied under him for the next five or six. He must have proved a very apt pupil. Plotinus, though not much given to parties, entertained his friends on the birthdays of Socrates and Plato. These birthday celebrations were, it appears, more intellectual than convivial. The guests were supposed to prepare essays ahead of time, and to read them to the group.

At one dinner for Plato's birthday a rhetorician read an essay attempting to prove that to be virtuous a disciple should always be amenable to his teacher's wishes, and that he should stay amenable even if his teacher happened to be in love with him. It was clear that Plotinus did not like the essay. He asked Porphyry to refute it, and Porphyry came up with a paper that he read before the same people. Plotinus considered it brilliant.

Another indication of Porphyry's excellence is that Plotinus chose him to edit his lectures. Many people wanted the lectures preserved as Socrates' discussions had apparently been preserved by Plato. For a number of years Plotinus had been putting down his lecture notes in a disorganized manner, and he circulated these among his friends in twenty-one brief books. Fron 263 to 268, while Porphyry was with him, he wrote twenty-four more books, probably under the impetus of his pupil. Later, after Porphyry had gone to Sicily, Plotinus sent him nine further books.

Porphyry's editorial job was not easy. Plotinus had messy handwriting and was a poor speller and grammarian, and in the rush of thought he did not bother to separate words. He refused to look over what he had written, so that what came to Porphyry was unrevised and even uncorrected. Porphyry tried to make sense out of this material and to arrange it logically according to subject matter.

The result was the **Enneads**, six groups of nine books each, the most important religio-philosophical document to come down to us between

Marcus Aurelius' **Meditations** and Augustine's **City of God.** Partly because of this work, and partly because the doctrines were transmitted orally from teacher to student for generations though inevitably modified in the process, Neoplatonism continued to exist long after Plotinus was dead. It was taught in philosophical schools at the great cities of the East until the fifth century and occupied the attentions of the Platonic Academy at Athens even longer.

Porphyry would have been surprised to find that after the empire became Christian much of Neoplatonism was gradually synthesized into the Christian framework. The denial of a need for a Savior and of a creation in time could not be accepted, of course, but Christian mystics seized on the most important element in Neoplatonism, the mystic union with the divine. The emphasis on the soul, on an ascetic life as a preliminary to union, on the relative unimportance of the things that make men busy, and on the conquest of lust—all of this also appealed to Christians of the late empire and far beyond. Neoplatonism was to flower most luxuriantly in the Renaissance.

Porphyry tells us little about the relationship between Plotinus and Gallienus. The ruler in his palace was surrounded by what Plotinus thought of as distractions—the gold and jewels of imperial luxury, the political and economic problems assailing a man at the vortex of public affairs. It would be interesting to know whether Plotinus pointed out to him that these material possessions and these current concerns held a man fast on the rim of reality, prevented his soul from journeying toward the One. For years, at the Rhine, at the Danube, and in Gaul, Gallienus had been preoccupied with events of the moment, leading the hectic life that the times imposed on him. The idea suggests itself that if he did start paying less attention to the affairs of the empire now, it was partly because of Plotinus' influence. But the likelihood is remote. Attracted though he was toward intellectual pursuits and a life of quiet contemplation, Gallienus had been trained too long in the tradition of immediate intervention and violent exertion. Toward the end of his reign he would give up the relaxation of Rome once more to struggle with events of the moment.

But the relationship between these disparate men must have been close, and the empress Salonina stood by to encourage it. Plotinus felt so confident of their friendship that he asked Gallienus to reconstruct a ghost town in Campania, the warm and pleasant region that includes the Bay of Naples, and to give the town to him and his followers. They would call their community Platonopolis, "City of Plato." Here, removed from the insistent diversions of Rome, they could contemplate in rural peace and advance toward vision.

Platonopolis did not become an actuality any more than the Pantisocracy that Coleridge and Southey dreamed of. A cabal of courtiers, perhaps jealous of Plotinus' influence over the emperor, perhaps afraid of where that influence might lead, kept the project from being carried out. One would like to know more about this intrigue against the philosopher, and one would like to know whether his friendship with the emperor stayed intact after the City of Plato was denied him. The passions of the world had in any case defeated his fond hope.

Notes to Chapter 11

1. Porphyry, **Life of Plotinos**, in Plotinus, **Complete Works**, edited by Kenneth Sylvan Guthrie (London, 1918), I, 17.
2. Plotinus, **The Ethical Treatises**, translated from the Greek by Stephen Mackenna (London, 1917-30), V, 241. Enneads VI.9.3.
3. **Ibid.**, V, 243. **Enneads VI.9.5**.
4. **Ibid.**, I, 108. **Enneads I.8.12**.
5. **Ibid.**, V, 242. **Enneads VI.9.4**.
6. **Ibid.**, V, 250. **Enneads VI.9.9**.
7. **Ibid.**, V, 243. **Enneads VI.9.5**.
8. **Ibid.**, V, 250-51. **Enneads VI.9.9-10**.
9. **Ibid.**, I, 94. **Enneads I.8.3**.
10. Porphyry, **Life of Plotinos**, in Guthrie (ed.), Plotinus, **Complete Works**, I, 14-15.
11. **Ibid.**, I, 18.

Sol standing, radiate, hand raised and holding globe. Reverse of an antoninianus of Gallienus struck at an Eastern mint, c. 267. Inscription: SOLI INVICTO. 21 mm.

12 Chaos Compounded

The last two or three years of the reign of Gallienus rank among the more conjectural years of recorded history. There are very few facts to rely on. The Greek and Latin chronicles make vague and meager reference to this period, the statements of one writer sometimes contradict those of another, what one writer mentions another omits, and nobody pays much attention to time, place, or causal relationship. Modern historians who have tried to untie the tangles have offered various theories all of which are supportable but none of which is provable. Many scholars have reached no firm conclusions as to just what happened or when it happened. This chapter will attempt only to state the alternatives without adding to those already hazarded by authorities on the period. The whole morass of uncertainty reflects the confusion of the empire at the time. Events were building up that would end Gallienus' quiet and then his life.

In 266 or early 267 Odenath of Palmyra was assassinated. His murderer was a relative named Maeonius—his cousin according to Pollio, his nephew according to the twelfth century Greek Zonaras. If we are to believe Dexippus, an Athenian who lived at the time, Odenath was on his way to the city of Heraclea Pontica, on the Black Sea coast in the part of Asia Minor called Bithynia, when he was killed. But the fifth century Zosimus says that he was killed at the Syrian city of Emesa during a banquet celebrating the birthday of a friend.

If the murder did occur at Emesa it was an open and violent affair. Maeonius and several confederates stabbed the Palmyrene king to death in plain sight of the guests at the feast, and at the same time they killed his oldest son, Prince Herodes. From Pollio's characterization the prince does not sound like much of a loss. Unlike his warlike father, "he was the most effeminate of men, wholly oriental and given over to Grecian luxury, for he had embroidered tents and pavilions made out of cloth of gold and everything in the manner of the Persians,"[1] and his indulgent father had given him the jewels and concubines taken from the king of Persia. But Pollio's description may not be reliable. He also affirms that Maeonius set himself up as ruler for a short time after the murder, and that is almost certainly wrong. Maeonius was more likely mobbed at the banquet, as Zonaras says, and died immediately. No inscriptions or other evidence exists to show that he ever reigned.

Zonaras gives the most dramatic motive for the assassination. The king's party had ridden out on a hunt and spotted a lion, and Maeonius threw the first spear. This was a serious breach of etiquette because the right of throwing the first spear belonged to the king. Odenath, proud hunter from boyhood, rebuked him. Maeonius responded by throwing another spear. Furious at such insubordination in a relative, Odenath ordered Maeonius to get off his horse and imprisoned him briefly. To unhorse a nobleman was a bitter insult at the Palmyrene court, which seems to have had an almost Persian regard for riding as a mark of aristocracy. Maeonius, in whom the insult ached and grew, took revenge by killing Odenath the first chance he got.

The story may not be entirely true, but it sounds like a possible culmination to a series of clashes between Maeonius and Odenath, some long-festering family irritation. Perhaps Maeonius felt that the king had passed him over in handing out rewards and offices.

Pollio, however, speaks of a conspiracy between Maeonius and Odenath's wife, the strong-willed Zenobia. According to him, Zenobia resented the partiality that Odenath showed toward his oldest son, the luxurious Herodes, who was not Zenobia's offspring but had been born to some former wife of the king. The passions and maneuverings, jealousies and intrigues of the Palmyrene court are lost to us. It is possible, though, that Zenobia, from hatred of Herodes or for some other reason, contrived to have Maeonius murder her stepson and her husband. A wilful woman with imperial designs, she may even have felt that Odenath with his unswerving loyalty toward Rome was moving too slowly and thwarting her hungry ambition.

But there is still another theory that deserves mention—the supposition that the governor of Roman Arabia, alarmed at the extent of Odenath's power in the East, instigated the murder.[2]

If so, he could not have consulted the imperial government first. In the death of Odenath, Gallienus lost his own greatest source of strength in the Orient, the man who kept beating the Persians on their own ground. Odenath's son Vabalath, who succeeded to the Palmyrene throne, could not be expected to carry on a very vigorous policy against Persia: he was a boy of ten or twelve. The real power lay in the tense grasp of Vaballath's mother, Zenobia, who would rule as regent. Even though she had not yet revealed the length of her ambition, Gallienus knew that she was less friendly than her husband had been. He must have feared that some day, probably quite soon, Rome would have to reckon with her.

His immediate reaction, if we can credit Pollio, was to send an army through Palmyrene territory toward Persia. Ostensibly this was a show of force so that the Persians would not think that Rome was sleeping on its eastern borders now that Odenath was dead. But Zenobia intercepted the Roman army and cut it up.

Since Pollio is the only source for this story its validity is doubtful. Zenobia would probably not have resorted to such an extreme measure so soon, unless she suspected that the announced campaign against Persia was only a disguise and that Gallienus actually intended to reduce Palmyrene control over the East. If he ever did send out such an army, that may very well have been his intention. But it is more likely that Pollio, anxious as always to denigrate Gallienus, made up the whole affair simply to show Gallienus being beaten by a woman.

About the same time that Odenath was killed, the Goths may have attacked Asia Minor and, in the midst of much other damage, demolished the great Temple of Artemis at Ephesus. There are two traditional dates for this Gothic assault, 262-3 and 266-7.[3]

The early date is based mainly on a statement in Pollio which would appear to place the attack in the administration of the two consuls for 262, one of whom was Gallienus himself. If this date is right, the attack occurred partly while the emperor was at Byzantium prior to celebrating his decennial, and the Goths may still have been destroying buildings and people when Gallienus, at Rome, rode to the Temple of Jupiter in his chariot. But there is no reason to hope that Pollio is more trustworthy about relating events to consular dates than about other matters. Depending on him for support is like clinging to a feather.

The later date, 266-7, is based on a statement by the ninth century Greek historian Syncellus that Odenath's death, which we know occurred at that time, prevented him from coming to the rescue of the city called Heraclea Pontica, which the barbarians were assailing. Dexippus, the Athenian who lived during these events, had said that Odenath was marching toward this port in northwestern Asia Minor when the assassination occurred. But even if Dexippus' account was right, the barbarian raid on Heraclea Pontica may not have been connected with the raid on the Temple of Artemis at Ephesus, which is the point around which the obscurity swirls. We do not know how many separate attacks the Goths made at various spots in Asia Minor during the 260s. Odenath may have been trying to stop a later Gothic army than the one that destroyed the Ephesian temple. Or he may not have marched to combat the Goths at all. He may have been killed at

Facing statue of Diana of Ephesus, fillets hanging from her outstretched arms, a deer on each side looking up at her. Reverse of a cistophorus struck at Ephesus under Hadrian (117-138). Inscription: DIANA EPHESIA. 28 mm.

the birthday banquet in Syrian Emesa rather than on a campaign.

At some time during this doubtful period—perhaps as early as 263 or 264, perhaps not until 267—the Goths swooped down on the more central and eastern parts of Asia Minor, devastating northern Galatia and Cappadocia. There were few large cities here; peasants worked the land, herded the sheep, and huddled together in hamlets when people from the outside came to raid. The Goths also invaded areas farther to the west—Lydia and Phrygia, which were studded with cities. And, probably in the same year as the attacks on Ephesus and other places on the Ionian coast of the peninsula, they descended like a plague on the great towns of Bithynia

In other words, at one time or another they overran most of Asia Minor.

If the majority of these incursions took place while Gallienus was living at Rome from 262 to about 266—and it should be stressed that they may not have occurred quite that early—again the charge can be leveled that the emperor was neglecting his empire. He certainly does not appear to have sent much help to the distressed citizens until Odenath presumably marched to the relief of Heraclea Pontica in 266-7 and did not get there. But once more the charge of negligence can be answered more or less satisfactorily. The barbarian raids were probably sporadic and widespread, making it hard for a methodical army to act. Besides, these were the years when Odenath was keeping the Persians occupied in defense of their own home ground, and most of the troops were with him, where they were needed sorely.

Although the countryside of Asia Minor attracted the Goths as a vast storehouse of food that could be had for the taking, the cities offered the greatest temptation. Just as the barbarians who raided Asia Minor in 256-8 seem to have aimed primarily at the cities, so did these Goths of five or ten years later. The western parts of the empire that the Franks and Alemanni attacked could boast important communities too, such as Cologne, Trier, Lyons, and Arles. But it was in the East, much longer civilized and more heavily populated, that cities flourished. Some of them dated back twelve or fifteen centuries, others were the more modern foundations of Hellenistic kings or Roman emperors. Though they were small by today's standards, the ancients thought of cities as the highest expression of society. To the East Germanic tribesmen, these splendid centers of civilization scattered over Asia Minor, crowding its western provinces and fringing its coasts, must have been a fantastic world.

Here stood great things that the Goths could not make—theatres with their marble seats rising in a semicircle, many-columned basilicas where offenders against Roman law were put on trial, and gymnasiums for the cult of the body, with baths and latrines included. Streets and squares were paved with stone and bordered with covered porticoes so that walkers would not be inconvenienced by the hot sun or the rain. Aqueducts poured water into central reservoirs from which it was channeled to various parts of town, and drainage systems washed away the filth. Libraries such as the famous one at Ephesus shelved thousands of manuscript rolls for those who could read. The public baths had rooms for sweating and undressing, for dips into waters of various temperatures, and even for hearing lectures. They also had amazing statuary in bronze and marble—standing deities, recumbent river gods, lion heads with water streaming from their mouths. The homes of the powerful, the cool rooms of marble and mosaic off sunny courtyards, held precious objects to carry away. But most of all there were the temples, altars, shrines and sanctuaries to gods whom the Goths did not honor. Their treasuries were rich with bowls and plates of gold and silver, vessels of ivory, jeweled ornaments, and great cult statues of costly materials.

With no basis for comparison, the Goths could not see that the civilized centers of Asia Minor had attained their apogee a while ago and were now in decline. The glorious buildings were by no means new. At Ephesus, for instance, the gymnasium and the library had been erected in the second century A.D., gifts of prosperous citizens in the age before prosperous citizens tried to avoid generosity toward their towns. The Temple of Serapis, with its eight red-painted monolithic columns across the front, had also risen in the second century, and so had the Temple of Hadrian and the Fountain of Trajan. The marble gate to the market had been set up under Augustus, the huge theatre was already undergoing renovations when St. Paul preached to the Ephesians in the mid-first century A.D., and the Temple of Artemis in its final version had been under construction when Alexander the Great invaded Asia Minor in 334 B.C. Since the maintenance of public buildings was not as scrupulous as it had been in more affluent times, some of these structures must have been showing their age before the Goths came through.

Judged by both Gothic and Roman standards, the cities of Asia Minor were very soft. In the third, second and early first centuries B.C. some of them had become involved in the complicated struggles of the Hellenistic princes, and in the 270s B.C. some had had to withstand the terrible onrush of the Gauls into Asia Minor. But the Roman Peace had endured a long time. The rivalry among the various cities was still fierce, like the rivalry among Greek city states of the archaic and classical periods. But instead of training men for battle the cities strove and jostled for high-sounding titles awarded by the imperial government—"Metropolis," "First in Asia," "Temple Warden of the Augustus for the Second Time." Tarsus and Anazarbus in Cilicia, emulous for empty praise, both called themselves "the First, the Greatest, the Best."[4] The peacock cities of the peninsula repeated their titles in official inscriptions, squeezed them onto their bronze token coins, and coveted the titles of neighboring cities.

They also tried to beat one another at games. For a long time athletic competition, supplemented by competition in music and drama, had been a mania in the cities of the East. Men who would not fight raced or wrestled or played the flute against one another. Almost every self-respecting metropolis in Asia Minor had its games, generally held every fourth year. These were the furthest extension of the games of more ancient times—the Olympics and other religiously oriented contests of the Greeks. The participants were now professionals, traveling from festival to festival and trying to win bags of money.

An athlete who performed extremely well received much honor in his home town and became a hero, but it was the bags of money and the greedy appetite for spectator sports that kept the games going. Cities would sometimes publicize their festivals by showing wreaths of victory or prize urns and vases on their coins, or groups of athletes or even the money bags themselves. All of this can be defended as more civilized than the bloodthirsty enthusiasm for gladiatorial combat in the western provinces. But onlookers at the degenerate athletic spectacles of Asia Minor could hardly be depended on to defeat the Goths, especially without soldiers to help them.

The city of Chalcedon on the Propontis, which the Goths had already looted in their expedition of 257-8, fell to them again, and so did the Bithynian capital of Nicomedia, also for the second time. Having plundered these places, they sailed down through the Hellespont into the Aegean Sea and ravaged the city-laden coast of western Asia Minor. According to the Gothic historian Jordanes, their leaders were Respa, Veduc, and Thuruar—names which, even if not strictly accurate, have a convincingly barbaric ring. They headed for Ephesus, greatest city on the coast. What the Goths did to it we do not know. Because the Roman fleet in the Aegean had lost much of its authority in recent years, pirate raids along the Ionian shores had probably not been infrequent, and Ephesus may therefore have been readier than some of these luxurious cities to defend itself against the Goths. If the barbarians did break into Ephesus bringing terror, the memory of that calamity has been eclipsed by their destruction of the Temple of Artemis, the Diana of the Ephesians.

This renowned building stood outside the city proper. It was not the first temple on the spot to suffer ill luck. The earliest one had been destroyed by barbarian raiders called the Cimmerians in the seventh century B.C. A later temple, which had taken one hundred twenty years to build, was burned down in 356 B.C., supposedly on the day when Alexander the Great was born, by a lunatic who wanted to make his own name famous. (His name, which is less famous than his deed, was Herostratus.)

The edifice that the Goths assailed had been started soon after the burning. Its columns rose more than sixty feet high and people called it one of the Seven Wonders of the World. In the mid-third century A.D. there was probably no more illustrious temple in the Graeco-Roman world except the one to Jupiter on the Capitoline at Rome. The goddess whom it honored, Artemis to the Greeks and Diana to the Romans, was more than the divine virgin of classical legend—the huntress with bow and arrow, protectress of chastity, patroness of wild creatures, lady of the moon.

She had become amalgamated centuries earlier with the Anatolian mother-goddess that the Greeks learned about from the native population when they arrived on those shores about 1000 B.C. Her great cult statue, with the legs seemingly fused together, the arms outstretched, and beasts depicted in the panels on her robe, did not look Greek. From the upper part of her body hung many protrusions representing either breasts or, according to a more recent theory, eggs. Whether she was the Many-Breasted or the Many-Egged, she was an ancient fertility goddess, far different from the fiercely pure Artemis of the Greek mainland. In classical times the Ephesians had symbolized her on their coins as a bee. Her worship included a number of virgins, however, as well as a eunuch from abroad and men who walked on tiptoe.

This was the goddess who figures in the Book of Acts. A smith at Ephesus had been selling little silver replicas of her shrine in the mid-first century A.D. while Paul preached Christianity through the city. Resenting Paul as an enemy to the goddess and to business, the smith initiated a protest. An anti-Christian mob, roused to fanatic indignation by him and his colleagues, gathered in the theatre and yelled "Great is Diana of the Ephesians!" until a city official restored order. But two centuries later Diana of the Ephesians was great no more. The Goths burned her house to the ground for the last time. They also ransacked it and loaded themselves down with her treasures, the pious gifts of governors and princes, senators and kings. Repairs were probably attempted sooner or later but the splendor was gone.[5]

The news that the temple at Ephesus lay in ashes must have fallen on the Mediterranean world as a tremendous blow. Centuries later, chroniclers who skim over these Gothic incursions and omit a great deal are sure to mention the destruction of this building. Christians—and there were many in Ephesus—probably looked with pleasure on the toppled fragments of idolatry, but to others this desecration was so enormous as to be hardly comprehensible. After the earlier temple had been burned by the arsonist at the time of Alexander's birth, people had explained how such a thing could happen. Some said that it signalized an event of terrible importance, the entry of the godlike conqueror into the world. Others said that the goddess would not have allowed her temple to burn if she had known what was going on, but that she was off in Macedonia at the time acting as midwife for Alexander's mother. But the only explanation for the Gothic violation of the sanctuary was strength. The gods of the Goths were stronger than the gods of Rome.

The barbarians went on to attack anciently illustrious Miletus, a short distance to the south. The Milesians even in the third century A.D. had enough spirit to throw together a makeshift wall and beat the barbarians off. Eleven miles south, an easy walk along a road that Trajan had built, stood the vast and mighty Temple of Apollo at Didyma. It had been started by Seleucus, former cavalry commander under Alexander the Great, about 300 B.C., the same time he founded Antioch. In 278 B.C. the wild Gauls who had invaded Asia Minor had cleaned it of almost all its treasures, but since that time it had grown rich and notorious. It flourished especially in the second century A.D. People came here to consult the oracle of Apollo. The Goths came to spoil.

Like the Milesians, the people at Didyma threw up a wall in a hurry, converting Apollo's holy structure into a fort. The Goths gathered in a rapacious, unruly throng outside the double row of massive pillars that surrounded the building. The defenders resisted strongly, but they ran out of water. In their mounting thirst they prayed to the god, and in contrast to his sister at Ephesus he helped. He showed them a spring in the **cella,** a very large chamber eighteen feet lower than the building's preliminary rooms. Too huge to roof, the **cella** was open to the sky but protected by walls over seventy feet high. The prophetess-priestess would dip her feet or the hem of her garment in the spring, or inhale sacred fumes, before uttering the oracle of the god. It seems that prophecy was no longer practiced at Didyma in the mid-third century A.D. and everybody had forgotten about the spring until Apollo pointed it out.[6] With water to drink, and with the god's obvious favor to encourage them, the defenders of the temple carried on their resistance until they drove the barbarians off.

After withdrawing from Didyma the Goths turned north for the trip back home, plundering Ilium near the site of long-dead Troy, crossing the Hellespont and sacking Thrace. Near the Thracian city of Anchialus they stopped to romp and revel in the hot baths. These medicinal waters in which they sported were a different refinement from any they had enjoyed in Asia Minor.

Lured by the comparative ease of conquest and the gleam of gold and gems, the East Germanic peoples soon struck two more blows at the empire. One started about 267 while Gallienus was still reigning, the other started about 269 after he was dead. In the ancient chronicles these two invasions are entangled with one another; perhaps even their contemporaries could not see them as distinct calamities.

We know that one of the invasions was much larger than the other and that in it the Heruls, an East Germanic people who had recently moved down from the north, collaborated with several other East Germanic-Gothic nations. The entire fighting force may possibly have amounted to over 300,000 men and included between 2,000 and 6,000 ships manned by the Heruls, who were practiced sailors. It was the largest barbarian expedition yet to be launched against the Roman world.

Setting out from the Sea of Azov, the barbarians crossed the Black Sea, failed to take the cities of Tomi and Marcianopolis south of the Danube, and captured Chrysopolis and probably Byzantium. In the Propontis the swift current played havoc with the grand array of boats, ramming the vessels into each other so that some of them split and sank with their men or had to float helplessly to shore. But many of the ships survived the current, and the land army that must have been accompanying the fleet was not affected anyway. The barbarians went on to plunder Cyzicus on the Asiatic side, then brought their ships through the Hellespont and like a scourge of insects overran the little Aegean isles of Lemos and Skyros, consuming everything in their path. Others apparently plundered the mainland to the north of the Aegean and besieged the great city of Thessalonica.

It is most or all of these events that some modern authorities place late in Gallienus' reign and others in the reign of his successor.[7] No matter which dating is true—no matter whether this great incursion or a somewhat smaller one came first—there was an expedition of Heruls and other East Germans that swarmed into the Aegean about 267, to Gallienus' alarm. The emperor may not have been able to do much about the recent Gothic assault on Asia Minor, but he could attack ships with ships. Early in the invasion he put an officer named Venerian in charge of a fleet that fought the barbarian navy in the Bosporus, but Venerian was killed in the battle and the Romans lost. The emperor himself prepared to leave Rome for the front. Two Byzantine engineers whom he had appointed as naval commanders worried the boats of the Heruls in the Aegean, doing what harm they could, which was probably considerable. But now the Heruls and their allies attacked Greece; and even more than Asia Minor, this land was incapable of defending itself.

People had been emigrating from Greece since the time of Alexander the Great, when they left their thin-soiled, rock-strewn farms and war-weary cities for the warmth and riches of the Oriental lands Alexander had conquered. Augustus had tried to stem the depopulation by sending Italian colonists to Corinth and Patrae, but although these places had stirred a little, most Greek cities were sleepy and shrunken. Sparta and Thebes were provincial towns. Athens itself, though it remained an intellectual center of great prominence[8] and a museum of art and architecture, was hardly vibrant any more except in terms of philosophy, esthetics, the recital of ancient glory, and the manufacture of clay lamps for oil. The Piraeus, once Athens' busy port, had dwindled into a village. The farmers who stayed in the countryside still raised grapes, olives, grain, and, in Attica, honey bees, but it was not hard to find fields where the weeds had taken over. Roads had been in poor condition for a long time and would not be repaired until the end of the century. Temples decayed and rituals languished for lack of funds.

In the midst of all this decline the Greeks assiduously cultivated the past. They idolized the Spartan heroes of Thermopylae, remembered the brave fighting men at Salamis and Plataea, honored those who fell in the Peloponnesian War. They showed proudly to outsiders the serene statues conceived by nameless craftsmen in bronze and marble, the temples to Olympic gods and goddesses, the venerable cult objects, and the historic spots. They pointed out places touched by legend in the brilliant spring of gods and heroes. The towns retained the priesthoods and magistracies that had existed in pre-Roman times.

This constant rehearsal of the past was partly for the benefit of the tourist trade, which still brought money into Athens and other places full of history and beauty, but it was also sincere. The Greeks knew that even in brash republican days the Romans had felt boyish and inferior before Hellenic culture, and that emperors from Nero to Gallienus had revered it. And even though Hellenic civilization had spread all over the East Mediterranean area, this rocky little land was its home. Nothing could equal what its people had once done.

Athens was of course the center of the cult of the past, with her claims to preeminence in drama, philosophy, oratory, architecture, sculpture, in fact almost everything except the epic. Since classical times Athens had been embellished by her rich citizens, such as Herodes Atticus, and by Greek-lovers from the outside world, such as King Antiochus of Commagene and the Emperor Hadrian. Athenians lived in the midst of art. Aristocratic youths from Rome and the East were sent there for the best possible education. The city had become a symbol of the highest achievements of civilized life, as perhaps she still is. But it was on Athens that the fleet of the Heruls and their Gothic allies bore down.

The barbarians sacked the city. They broke into the homes, hot after loot, and they plundered the wealth of temples. They flattened the buildings of the Agora, the great business plaza north of the Acropolis, burning and stripping its temples and setting aflame the Stoa of Attalus that lined the east side with columns under which buyers strolled and merchants sold their goods. They turned the city's heart into a desert and wiped out a life style that had lasted many centuries.[9] The news that Athens had been ravaged must have shocked the Graeco-Roman world as much as the news that the Temple of Artemis had been burned.

But there was one thing to be proud of. After the sacking the Athenians rallied under a fellow citizen named Dexippus, elderly scion of an aristocratic family, holder of civic and priestly posts, author of historical works on Alexander the Great and Romans from mythical times forward—the man who later recorded these events of his own lifetime in a history of the barbarians from which only a few fragments survive. Under Dexippus, two thousand volunteers, inspired with the remembered valor of their long-dead ancestors, attacked the overconfident barbarians repeatedly from ambush in the woods, guerilla fashion. Helped by the naval commander Cleodamus or Cleodemus (one of the engineers Gallienus had appointed), they defeated the Heruls at the Pireaus and had their moment of glory for future Greeks to treasure.[10]

The barbarian mass, however, was like some monster made of hot jelly. Beat it in one place and it oozed on somewhere else to burn and suffocate. The Heruls and other Goths roved over Greece, spilling into the valleys and occupying the towns. They despoiled Corinth, Argos, and Sparta. It seems that they also overran Olympia, where the games were still held every four years.[11] A wall was built hurriedly around the **Altis,** the sacred grove where statues of Olympic champions and the temples of Zeus and Hera stood. Inside Zeus's temple the gold-and-ivory statue of the god himself, designed by Phidias, sat enthroned in motionless majesty while the barbarians ravaged.

Having sated themselves on civilization, they retired northeastward through Greece. Either at the Nestus River or farther north at Naissus, or possibly at both places, they fought the Romans and lost. The fact that we cannot definitely credit either Gallienus or his successor Claudius with this most important defeat of the Goths in the third century illustrates the chaos of these years. That Gallienus achieved this Roman victory is now perhaps the more widely accepted view.[12]

Pollio in his biography of Gallienus in the **Augustan History** attributes a defeat of the Goths in Illyricum to Gallienus, and Syncellus places the battle at the Nestus River, which runs between Macedonia and Thrace. Zosimus talks about a battle at Naissus in Moesia (now Nish in Yugoslavia) in which 50,000 barbarians were killed, but he says the battle was fought under Gallienus' successor Claudius. The author of the biography in the **Augustan History** also speaks of Claudius as winning a great battle against the Goths. The similarity in names (Nestus/Naissus) suggests that the two battles were actually one. In addition, similar details accompany them—for instance, a preliminary encounter in which 3,000 barbarians were slaughtered by Roman troops (probably Dalmatian horsemen) and, after the great battle, the retreat of the barbarian remnants through the mountains, where they rallied to defend themselves behind a barricade of wagons but were ultimately defeated again by the Romans.

If there was only one great battle rather than two, it is at least likely to have taken place under Gallienus, since he apparently reached the front about this time and since a success is ascribed to him there. The transferral of a great victory from him to his successor would not be very surprising, given the animus of ancient Roman historians against him. Claudius bears the title **Gothicus,** "Conqueror of the Goths," but the title may have been given to him because he was ultimately responsible for driving the Goths out of the empire, not because he won the Battle of Naissus. Gallienus may therefore be one of the few monarchs in history whose greatest single military achievement is obscurely remembered and often credited to another man.

We can tell a little more about his death than about most of his life. Some time after the victory, whatever it was, he had to leave the Gothic front because of the news that his general Aureolus had revolted against him and joined Postumus, who still ruled the Roman Empire of the Gauls.

Aureolus was probably Gallienus' most valuable officer—commander of the mobile cavalry corps ever since its creation about ten years before, victor over men who had tried to usurp the purple in the crisis following Valerian's capture. During Gallienus' war against Postumus he had apparently not pushed the campaign as vigorously as he might have. Several people had suspected him of treachery that early, but Gallienus would not believe him unfaithful.

After Gallienus went to Rome Aureolus evidently continued conspiring with the Roman Emperor of the Gauls, and the period when Gallienus was preoccupied with the Heruls in the Balkans was the best time to make his defection public. Coins were struck in Postumus' name at Milan, headquarters of the mobile cavalry corps. Gallienus, leaving it up to his general Marcian to chase the beaten East Germans out of the empire and harry them on their retreat, hastened toward Italy with whatever troops could be spared.

Aureolus had been at the time in what is today western Austria, ostensibly guarding the empire against incursions from both Postumus' realm and the West Germanic tribes. He now marched toward Milan, where he was probably as highly esteemed as anywhere. Not far from the city Gallienus came up with him and beat him in another of the dark battles of this age, no details surviving. Aureolus retreated within the walls of Milan, and Gallienus settled down to a siege of the city. It was at about this time—the spring or early summer of 268—that Aureolus had himself declared emperor. His soldiers probably realized that there was nothing else to be done. This way they could at least claim to be fighting for the legitimate ruler of the Roman world. Otherwise they were nothing but insurgents.

In Gallienus' own camp outside the walls a conspiracy took shape. His principal officers decided that Gallienus should be murdered. What prompted them—personal ambition, dissatisfaction with his reign, some recent incident that rankled—is not clear. Heraclian or Herculian, his Praetorian Prefect, instigated the conspiracy. It was apparently agreed that if the plot succeeded the next emperor should be Claudius, the officer now second in command to Gallienus himself. Claudius had already demonstrated his military and administrative abilities; he was an excellent choice. Other members of the cabal appear to have been Aurelian, who had been leading the loyal members of the mobile cavalry unit since Aureolus' treason, and a certain Cecropius, who commanded a squadron of Dalmatian horsemen.

While the emperor was at dinner Cecropius came up to him with the false story that a scout had spotted Aureolus approaching with his troops from Milan. The announcement threw the dinner into confusion—real or feigned, depending on whether the listeners were in on the plot. Gallienus jumped up, called for his battle gear, and leaped on his horse. There might still be time to spoil the surprise attack. Ordering his soldiers to arm themselves and follow behind, he rode off to a battle that was not to be. Not even his bodyguard accompanied him.

The assassins were waiting, and they rushed him and killed him. It seems that Cecropius himself ran a spear through his emperor.

He had reigned for fifteen years, from 253 to 268, about half of that time with his father and the other half alone. With the barbarians overwhelming supposedly Roman lands first in the Rhine area and Gaul and then in the East, with Postumus consolidating his own Roman Empire of the Gauls, and with Odenath and Zenobia tightening their hold on Syria, he actually ruled far less than all of the Roman world, and at the end of his reign his empire included less than it had at the beginning. But he had not been a bad emperor; certainly he had worked hard. The nadir of his rule had been the shameful period when his father was captured by the Persians and an assortment of usurpers tried to establish themselves in the purple.

He had surmounted all of that and had even been able to encourage intellectual pursuits in his spare time, and to talk with Plotinus. He had stopped the persecution of the Christians, which was doing the empire no good, and had beaten the Persians by means of Odenath. He had deprived the presumptuous senatorial class of military commands and founded the mobile cavalry corps, to which imperial armies of the future were to look as a model. The final two or three years had been horrible for Asia Minor and the Balkans, but he had left the barbarians in retreat when he went to Milan. Unsolved problems loomed on all sides, but the empire was a little better for his having been its chief.

Notes to Chapter 12

1. **Scriptores Historiae Augustae**, III, 107-09. **Tyranni Triginta** XVI. 1.
2. See Alföldi in **Cambridge Ancient History**, XII, 176.
3. For theories and arguments relative to the chronology, see Alföldi in **Cambridge Ancient History**, XII, 148-49, 721; Bang in **Cambridge Medieval History**, I, 204; George E. Bean, **Aegean Turkey: An Archaeological Guide** (London, 1966), p. 237; Magie, notes to **Scriptores Historiae**

Augustae, III, 26-27 (n. 3), 28 (n. 2), 30 (n. 4), 38 (n. 1), 42 (n. 1); Magie, **Roman Rule in Asia Minor**, I, 706-07, and II, 1567, n. 28; Millar, **Roman Empire and its Neighbours**, p. 217; and Parker, **History of the Roman World**, p. 176 and p. 346, n. 25, with Warmington's note, p. 393.

4. See George Francis Hill, **A Catalogue of the Greek Coins in the British Museum: Lycaonia, Isauria, and Cilicia** (London, 1900), pp. lxxxviii, civ, and D. H. Cox, **A Tarsus Coin Collection in the Adana Museum, Numismatic Notes and Monographs** No. 92 (New York, 1941), pp. 18-19.

5. For the material on Ephesus, though not necessarily the opinions, I am especially indebted to Bean, **Aegean Turkey**, pp. 161-73.

6. The latter is the view of Bean in **Aegean Turkey**, p. 237. For his illuminating discussion of the temple at Didyma see pp. 231-41.

7. For the earlier date see, for example, Alföldi in **Cambridge Ancient History**, XII, 149; for the later date, Bang in **Cambridge Medieval History**, I, 205-06.

8. See Fergus Millar, "P. Herennius Dexippus: The Greek World and the Third-Century Invasions," JRS, LIX (1969), 21.

9. See Homer A. Thompson, "Athenian Twilight: A.D. 267-600," JRS, XLIX (1959), 62-63, 65-66, and on Athens' lamp industry, 70-71.

10. See Millar, "P. Herennius Dexippus," pp. 20-28.

11. See Ludwig Drees, **Olympia: Gods, Artists, and Athletes**, translated by Gerald Onn (New York and Washington, 1968), pp. 156-57, and Thompson, "Athenian Twilight," p. 61, n. 5.

12. See, for example, Alföldi in **Cambridge Ancient History**, XII, 721-23; Grant, **Climax**, p. 33; Magie, **Roman Rule in Asia Minor**, I, 710, and II, 1570-71; Warmington's note in Parker, **History of the Roman World**, p. 393; and Syme, **Emperors and Biography**, p. 205, n. 5.

13 Claudius Gothicus

Before the murder of Gallienus the conspirators had apparently considered two of themselves as possible replacements for him. One, Aurelian, had fought with distinction in many campaigns but was a fierce disciplinarian. The men respected him but they did not love him. Claudius, the officer they chose, also held an illustrious military record but had a milder disposition. Many of the soldiers were outraged by the assassination of their supreme commander; some of them muttered mutiny. The more cynical —and there were plenty of these—realized that a mutiny would afford fine opportunities for looting. To put a military tyrant like Aurelian over such troops might kill their dangerous restlessness, but on the other hand it might provoke a real revolt.

The conspirators immediately promised the soldiers twenty gold coins each to quiet them, and the money was quickly paid. Although the weight of **aurei** was unstable in this unstable period, at least these coins had not been debased like the silver. Emperors on campaign in the mid-third century customarily carried a large supply of gold coins along to pay the troops or, if necessary, buy them. Gallienus' gold bought the army for Claudius. To make the succession surer, the conspirators circulated the story that the expiring Gallienus had said he wanted Claudius to be the next emperor. The troops acclaimed him.

In his middle fifties when he received the highest office in the empire, Claudius had been born into obscurity somewhere in the Balkan provinces, perhaps in what is now Yugoslavia. He was the second of the so-called Illyrian emperors, the aristocratic Decius having been the first. He had worked his way up in the army of the Danube frontier, the tough Illyrian-Pannonian army where old Roman valor now burned. Under Gallienus he had fought against Postumus in Gaul. Such a man, the professional soldier that Gallienus had not been, might do much to rescue the empire.

He even looked the part of the born commander—tall, straight, and muscular, with the popular short, bristly beard. Stories of his great strength passed from soldier to soldier. Men said that with his fist he could knock the teeth out of a horse. During the reign of Decius, according to one story, he wrestled in military games honoring Mars; but his opponent grabbed his testicles, and Claudius in rage hit the man in the mouth and made him toothless with one blow. Decius lauded him for so manfully defending his modesty, gave him arm rings and collars of precious metal awarded as prizes, but ordered him not to participate in any more of the bouts since there was no point in damaging good soldiers.

Claudius' most immediate problem was of course Aureolus, still holed up in Milan. An embassy came from Aureolus to talk about terms of peace, but Claudius responded in the only way he could: he rejected the overtures. Aureolus must have decided that his own cause was hopeless because in a little while he yielded up both himself and Milan, perhaps on condition that he be allowed to live.

The sequel is uncertain, but somehow this rebel was killed. According to Pollio, presumed author of his life for the **Augustan History,** he fell in battle against Claudius; but that is very unlikely since we do not know of such a battle. Perhaps Claudius' soldiers murdered him, with or without the new emperor's approval. Or his own troops may have turned on him and assassinated him to prove their renewed devotion to legally constituted power. Possibly, as the so-called Vopiscus suggests in the biography of Aurelian for the **Augustan History,** Aurelian insisted that the rebel be done away with. No matter where the responsibility lay, it was a good thing that Aureolus was dead. He had performed invaluable services in charge of the new mobile cavalry under Gallienus, but the empire did not need an ex-pretender.

With Aureolus out of the way, Claudius confronted the constant barbarian menace. The Alemanni had to be dealt with at once. They had perhaps been invited into northern Italy by Aureolus to help him against Gallienus. At any rate they were now overrunning the land. Claudius dispatched some cavalry against them, but the cavalry were defeated. Then he himself marched against the Alemanni at the head of his troops. Near Lake Benacus—now the Lago di Garda, west of Verona—the Romans under their new emperor massacred the Germans. Only half the Alemanni left the battlefield to retreat northward into their forested valleys.

Presumably Claudius hurried down to Rome to be acknowledged as emperor by the senate. The senators liked him, no doubt finding him a welcome relief from the dead emperor who had treated them with such indignity. It may have been at this time that the incident related by the Byzantine chronicler Zonaras occurred, if it occurred at all.

Gallienus had sometimes given his officers, to reinforce their loyalty, properties confiscated from subjects who had been implicated in treasonable activities such as rebellions against his rule. There must also have been cases in which the confiscation and redistribution of estates was not entirely excusable. After Claudius was declared emperor an elderly lady came up to him to complain humbly and respectfully about an officer who, under Gallienus, had for no just cause appropriated her patrimony and left her destitute. The rapacious officer had of course been Claudius, no more averse to sudden profit than his fellow commanders. But now that he was an emperor, his innate sense of fairness or an urge to look equitable prevailed. Manifesting embarrassment, he restored the lady's property.

The Alemanni had been cleared out of northern Italy, but many bands of Heruls and other East Germans still sacked the Balkan provinces. It was in the Balkans, the rough land where Claudius had been born and brought up, that he would pass the latter part of his reign, making the country safe again for Romans. He must have marched there directly from Rome. Even if the great invasion of the Balkan provinces occurred under Gallienus rather than Claudius, and even if Gallienus and not Claudius actually won the tremendous victory over the Goths at Naissus in Yugoslavia, the new emperor was urgently needed in this bitter war which Gallienus had had to leave unfinished in order to deal with Aureolus' revolt.[1]

Fresh Gothic hordes may have swept into the Balkans in 268-9 to make Claudius' job harder. Whatever battles he fought in this region, including or excluding Naissus, he accomplished enough to deserve the name **Gothicus,** "Conqueror of the Goths," bestowed on him by the grateful senate. The stern Aurelian, whom he had put in supreme command of the cavalry in place of Aureolus, no doubt served him well, though we have no details.

After their defeat at Naissus many of the Goths took refuge in the Haemus mountains between Moesia and Thrace, and here, either under Gallienus' general Macrian or under Claudius himself, they were surrounded and again chewed up. Their remnants scattered north and east toward the safety of the Danube, with the Romans following them and battering their undisciplined, unorganized bands. Because they had as usual made no long range plans for provisioning their army, the Goths were probably running short on supplies. Many of them had temporarily lost their enthusiasm for war and were only eager to slip away with what they had managed to seize.

The Romans also seized what they could. Pollio remarks that they captured enough barbarian women to give each man two or three. But he tells of one instance in which some of Claudius' victorious soldiers surrendered themselves so thoroughly to the joy of looting that they forgot to stay on guard against the barbarians. A few Goths sneaked back, surprised the legionaries, and slaughtered two thousand.

In general, those Goths who did not turn tail and flee out of the empire were settled peacefully as farmers in Moesia and Thrace. And these provinces themselves, virtually lost to Rome for the past several years, came once again under substantial imperial control. That alone more than justified the title **Gothicus**.

While Claudius was preoccupied in the Balkans, the strong and capable Postumus died in the Roman Empire of the Gauls. He had shaped and hardened that maverick Roman state with its own senate and consuls, its own Praetorian Guard, its own Roman-style coinage in base metal, its beautiful gold coinage, and its capital at Trier or Cologne. He had finished Gallienus' job of driving back the Germans, and as recently as 267 he had apparently fought off Germanic raids by ship along Gaul's northern coast. In 268 or 269 a certain Laelian claimed to be emperor, made Mainz his capital, and issued coins. Postumus defeated him and took Mainz, and Laelian died in the process. But Postumus forbade his own exultant soldiers to pillage and strip the city, which lay at their mercy. Many of these soldiers were certainly men he had led to triumph against Gallienus and against the Germans. They murdered him because he would not let them loot.

Marius, the officer who quickly had himself proclaimed Postumus' successor, was a former smith, a forger of weapons and armor. He had joined the army and climbed to a position of command. If Pollio's inventions contain any residue of fact at all, Marius must have been an officer of extraordinary digital development. He could, according to Pollio, push back onrushing wagons just by sticking out his finger, and a blow with his finger was enough to make a man think he had been hit by a chunk of iron.

Marius did not last long. Pollio credits him with three days as emperor of the Gauls; the historians Aurelius Victor and Eutropius give him two. Actually he must have ruled somewhat longer, since he had time to strike quite a few coins bearing his own name and portrait. He was stabbed to death by a soldier who had once worked in his smithy and was disgruntled at having been brushed off. Pollio, no doubt with a stronger sense of poetic justice than of truth, suggests that Marius himself had forged the sword that ended his life, and that his murderer told him so.

Victorinus, who had been one of Postumus' principal officers, now seized the throne in Gaul and associated his son in his reign. He was prompted by his ambitious mother, Vitruvia or Victoria. But her belief in Victorinus' capacity to be an effective emperor was only a mother's dream. He devoted himself to love and lechery, and his paramours were the wives of the men who served him.

Meanwhile the Roman Empire of the Gauls was cracking. It would not be able to survive the death of Postumus very long unless a man with some of Postumus' ability took control. Spain, which like Britain had joined it under Postumus, defected about this time and returned to the legitimate Roman Empire, as is shown by inscriptions to Claudius found there. The city of Augustodunum or Autun, west of the Rhone and northwest of Lyons, revolted against Victorinus' rule. Autun was a rich commercial center, with a theatre accommodating at least 10,000 people and an already ancient school for educating the young sons of the Romanized Gallic nobility. Victorinus sat down outside this city with an army eager to loot it.

If Claudius had been able to take advantage of the situation he could probably have killed the languishing Roman Empire of the Gauls. But he could not spare the troops and money for a Gallic campaign, much less conduct one himself, until the Balkan crisis was definitely settled. Autun did ask him for help, but all he could do was to send an officer named Placidian with some soldiers from Rome. Since the force was too small to raise the siege, Placidian did not advance as far as Autun but camped at Grenoble in the southeast part of France, which still belonged to Rome. Grenoble was considerably east of the Rhone and a long way from the siege. Situated here, Placidian could perhaps protect southeast Gaul or Italy against an incursion by Victorinus' army, which was unlikely, or guard Claudius' troops if Claudius marched into Gaul soon, which was also unlikely.[2]

The siege of Autun lasted for seven months, and by then Claudius had probably died. The citizens gave up only when Victorinus' men broke their aqueducts, depriving them of water. Exasperated by the long wait and by frustrated greed, Victorinus' army rushed into the town, plundered and destroyed. But Victorinus himself was not to reign much longer. Perhaps he tampered once too often with the wife of an officer. Whatever the reason may have been, a cabal developed against him and he was murdered at Cologne.

While the Roman Empire of the Gauls grew weaker, Palmyra in the East grew stronger. The Palmyrene kingdom was of course still nominally subject to Roman control, but Queen Zenobia chafed under even this light subordination. The death of her gallant husband Odenath had left her enormously rich and powerful — mistress of wide domains, far-flung commerce, and a strong veteran army. If she acted vigorously enough in this period of Rome's feebleness she might make Palmyra an entirely independent state, a Roman Empire of the East, free of all attachments to the sick monster for which her dead husband had fought so loyally. She might also stretch out Palmyra's boundaries. Like the great Cleopatra, to whom she enjoyed comparing herself, she was inordinately acquisitive; and Rome possessed the territory she wanted.

Claudius' involvement with the Goths in the Balkans gave Zenobia the opportunity to start spreading her kingdom. Technically she did not break with Rome at this point. But in the winter of 268-9 she may have sent troops to occupy Antioch, which perhaps had still not entirely recuperated from its occupation by the Persians eight or nine years before. Since coins seem to have been struck for Claudius at Antioch throughout his reign it is likely that Zenobia never actually took over there.[3] But her influence must have been predominant in the great city. She also seems to have sent troops into Cappadocia in eastern Asia Minor, and perhaps even deeper into the peninsula. And it was presumably before the death of Claudius that she invaded Egypt.[4]

She sent into Egypt an army of 70,000 men, according to Zosimus. There were native Palmyrene bowmen and heavy-armed horsemen, half-wild desert fighters, and men from the Syrian cities who would rather serve Zenobia than Rome. At the head of this massive force rode Zabdas, her competent and loyal general. The Roman governor of Egypt was away, challenging seaborne hordes of Goths on the Aegean. Expecting Zenobia's army in Egypt was a certain Timagenes, who had been undermining whatever affection his fellow Egyptians might feel toward Rome, and perhaps even collecting a band of soldiers to join Zabdas.

Timagenes' job of subversion may not have been too difficult. The exotic Palmyrene queen, a second Cleopatra risen in the East, must have had a strong appeal for many Egyptians. Smoldering resentment toward Roman tax gatherers, Roman soldiers, the confiscation of property, and Roman authority in general, plus the chance of pillage that an army life always offered, probably inclined the people of Egypt to hope for a Palmyrene triumph or to fight for one. The historian Zosimus says that the Romans managed to muster 50,000 troops to oppose Zenobia, but under Zabdas her army won a clear victory. Perhaps because Zabdas felt sure of the support of most of the population, or perhaps on orders from Zenobia, he left a garrison of only 5,000 men in Egypt and retired with the rest of his forces.

That was a mistake. Down swept Probus, the Roman governor, who had by this time sunk many Gothic ships in the Aegean and was riding the crest of success. He quickly overthrew the small Palmyrene garrison. The main Palmyrene force turned around to combat this new enemy. Probus gathered an army of Egyptians and Africans, with which he defeated the Palmyrenes. He set off after them to harry their retreat, and seems even to have outmarched them. A short distance south of where Cairo now stands, he encamped on the side of a hill, where his troops could block the Palmyrenes' withdrawal across the desert toward Syria.

But the battle for which he waited never happened. He did not know the land as well as Timagenes did. With 2,000 Palmyrenes, Timagenes silently occupied the top of the hill. The Palmyrenes swarmed down on Probus' camp taking his soldiers by surprise and butchering them. Probus killed himself, either to relieve his sense of shame or to avoid a cruel death dealt out by Timagenes.

Zenobia retained her power in Egypt. It was less than total; in Alexandria at any rate the mint continued to operate for Rome. But her authority in Lower Egypt as a whole was well established. Claudius had stopped the Alemannic depredations in Italy and the Gothic spoliation of the Balkans, but it was the old story: while sores were healed in one part of the ailing old empire they festered and bled in another part.

One of Zenobia's most valuable supporters at Antioch was a Christian called Paul. He had been born at the Graeco-Oriental trading city of Samosata, northeast of Antioch on the Euphrates—the same city in which the satirist Lucian had been born in the preceding century. When Paul of Samosata moved to Antioch he must have been unknown and he probably was poor. But he had energy, ambition, eloquence, intelligence, and apparently charisma. In 260, the depressing year when the emperor Valerian was captured by the Persians, Antioch's Christians elected Paul their bishop. Little is known about his early tenure of the see. It was a time when the Syrian capital was still reeling from the recent Persian raids, when Gallienus was fighting the Macriani and other usurpers for possession of the purple, when Roman prestige in the East had sunk very low, and when Odenath of Palmyra was beating the Persians because Rome could not do it on her own. Paul may already have been looking toward Palmyra as the source of his security.

Although the Persian army had taken many intelligent Christians back to Persia along with Paul's predecessor as bishop, the Christian community at Antioch was still one of the largest and most intellectually active in the empire. Its members held diverse theological views, at times heretical ones. Paul himself thought that Christ had been born essentially human, not divine, and had not descended from heaven to take on the form of man. We know little more than that about his opinions, but he seems to have felt that this human Christ deserved to receive more of the divine spirit than other human beings and did so at his baptism. He may also have believed that after the Resurrection Christ was adopted into full divinity.

No records exist of how Paul's congregation as a whole reacted to his theories, but we know that he had a core of feverishly devoted followers. Orthodox churchmen in the rest of the empire were of course shocked. They called Paul a blasphemer and defiler of Christ. About the year 264 a synod met at Antioch to decide whether he should be condemned and thrown out of his see. Bishops, presbyters, and deacons came from all over the Roman East. The elderly, illustrious Firmilian, bishop at Caesarea in Cappadocia, traveled to Antioch. So did Gregory Thaumaturgus, the enthusiastic convert who ministered in the backwoods of Pontus, and Helenus, bishop of Tarsus, and Hymenaeus, bishop of Jerusalem, and Maximus, who led the flock at Bostra in Arabia. The fine and venerable Dionysius of Alexandria pleaded his age and poor health, but although he could not make the journey to Antioch he sent a letter stating his views on Paul. Dionysius died soon after.

Against the background of the beautiful and hectic Syrian metropolis, old in worldliness, where Persian sympathizers, Roman sympathizers, and friends of Palmyra kept tense watch on public affairs, where Syrians and Arabs and Greeks followed their various gods, the grave synod looked into the bishop's theology. The clergymen tried to expose Paul's heresies in their grotesque nakedness, while Paul's adherents covered up the nakedness and tried to present him as an exemplary Christian.

In an East where faith crowded on faith and a man could sample many creeds, there may have been some Palmyrenes who found Paul's brand of Christianity interesting. King Odenath does not seem to have been fascinated by religion, but Zenobia evidently felt curious about Paul's doctrines. Whether Palmyra exerted an influence on the synod is not known; it may have exerted none. But when the synod broke up it was apparently satisfied as to Paul's orthodoxy, or at least his intention to be orthodox in the future. He continued to hold the see of Antioch.

During the next few years he prospered. He obtained the Roman office of **procurator**, which carried a high salary. Unfortunately for Paul's reputation no documents favorable to him have survived, but like many other officials he seems to have used his post for his own profit. According to a letter that was presumably written by his enemy Malchion and is quoted by the fourth century church historian Eusebius, Paul plundered and blackmailed his fellow Christians. He promised (for a remuneration) to help people who were tangled in lawsuits and easily forgot about them after they had paid him in advance. He strutted around town followed by a bodyguard, says Malchion, and dictated letters as he walked.

Even granting that Malchion exaggerated the situation, there is no doubt that Paul wielded great power at Antioch in these years, the latter part of Gallienus' reign, and that much of Paul's power was secular. He may have remained a sincere clergyman, but the church engrossed only a part of his attention. It was in these years too that he courted Palmyra. Queen Zenobia patronized him. In return for patronage, he must certainly have been required to promote the Palmyrene cause at Antioch. He was a Palmyrene agent there, if nothing more.[5]

But clergymen continued to be bothered by Paul's views and possibly also by his secular activities. At least one more synod, perhaps two, convened at Antioch to probe into these matters. The last one probably met in 268 or 269, during Claudius' reign, although it may not have occurred until after Claudius' death in 270.[6] Perhaps as many as eighty bishops gathered at Antioch. The aged Firmilian of Cappadocian Caesarea did not make it this time. Word came to those already assembled, who were waiting for Firmilian's arrival before starting the meeting, that he had died on the road, at Tarsus.

Malchion, presumed author of the letter against Paul that has already been mentioned, spearheaded the attack. Malchion was a presbyter at Antioch, apparently respected for his piety, but he also conducted a school of rhetoric on the Greek model. He therefore represented the Greek element that was so strong in the city and had the most prestige; the school itself helped to disseminate Hellenic culture in this place that Greeks had founded. Paul, on the other hand, represented the Semitic element, as his attachment to Palmyra suggests. The learned Malchion must have played on this division. He must also have used against Paul the oratorical flourishes, turns, tricks, and postures so prized in the day, and they were effective. He had secretaries take down his debates with Paul so that there would be a record.

Paul's avarice and pride of place were brought before the synod. He overawed the lowly with his elevated throne, accusers said. He had his congregation applaud him, wave handkerchiefs in his honor, and jump up and cheer him; and all this did not befit a Christian flock or its pastor. According to Malchion's letter he prohibited hymns from being sung to Christ, but he had hymns sung to himself. Although he instructed the congregation that Christ had not descended from heaven, some of his ardent adherents believed that Paul himself had come down from there, being actually an angel; and he did not contradict this persuasion. Malchion was not sure that Paul carried on like a lecher with any of his pious sisters in God, but evidently Paul did not bother to keep himself clear of suspicion, as a good bishop should do.

There is no way to tell how much of the attack was true, but Paul's manner of life must in many ways have been flagrant. The synod had heard all it needed to hear. If Zenobia tried to exert her influence in favor of her agent, she failed. Paul was excommunicated. Domnus, son of the bishop who had been dragged away to Persia, was appointed to replace him. The letter presumably by Malchion, describing Paul's heresies and crimes and the synod's decision, went out to the pope and to bishops through the Roman world.

But Paul was not defeated. Excommunicated or not, he still had his congregation, or at least its most loyal center. He refused to give up the ecclesiastical buildings and carried on as usual. In this matter at least, Zenobia with her tremendous strength in Antioch could support him. If Domnus tried to function as bishop somewhere else in Antioch the result must have been chaotic, like the situation at Carthage almost two decades before.

Assuming that the final synod against Paul did take place in Claudius' reign, that emperor probably never heard of it. Squabbles among the Christians were not his problems. He had not quite finished mopping up the Goths to his satisfaction when he received word that the Juthungi, already subsidized by Rome but hungry for new land, were getting ready to invade the province of Raetia, now roughly part of Switzerland and western Austria. In addition, the Vandals were gathering for an inroad into Pannonia, or Hungary. The menace of the Juthungi, he decided, could wait. Deputing Aurelian to take care of whatever warlike Goths were left in the Balkans, Claudius rushed to Sirmium, the great Roman military and administrative center in southeastern Pannonia.

The camp at Sirmium was a grim one. His army had caught a plague from the Goths and the plague had spread among the soldiers. Men died of it at Sirmium as they prepared to fight off the Vandals. In January of the year 270 Claudius died of it too. He had been emperor for about twenty-one months.

When the senators learned of his death they gave him a place among the gods. They had not liked an emperor so much in a long time. They hung a gold shield in the senate house in his memory and set up a gold statue in his honor in the Capitol. They may have been right to venerate him as they did. In his short reign he had, undeniably, left a great deal unaccomplished. The coinage was, if possible, worse than ever, without even a pretense of being silver. The economic situation as a whole had not improved. In the West the Roman Empire of the Gauls hung onto its independence, and in the East Palmyra was beginning to assert hers. Egypt had dropped out of Roman control, and so, perhaps, had Antioch and much of Syria and Asia Minor. But Claudius had beaten the Alemanni and the Goths, had built roads to facilitate his wars, had charmed the senate, and like the great Marcus Aurelius had died in camp defending the imperial frontiers. He had done as much as he could. The golden shield and the golden statue were not mere tokens. Claudius was the first emperor in a long time whom Romans could love, the first one in whom they could really believe. Psychologically his effect had been tremendous. If more men like him held the staff of office, the empire might still be saved.

Notes to Chapter 13

1. It should be remembered that the attribution of the victory at Naissus to Gallienus is by no means certain. Like other historians until recent times, Gibbon unquestioningly gave the victory to Claudius; see **Decline and Fall**, Chap. XI. Theodor Mommsen accepted two Gothic expeditions, one defeated by Gallienus at the Nestus River, the other defeated by Claudius at Naissus; see **Provinces: European**, pp. 259-60. See also Bang in **Cambridge Medieval History**, I, 205; Magie in **Scriptores Historiae Augustae**, III, 162-63, n. 3, expressing a view that Magie modified in **Roman Rule in Asia Minor**, II, 1570-71, n. 34; Millar, **Roman Empire and its Neighbours**, p. 237; and Parker, **History of the Roman World**, pp. 177-78, 188-90.

2. See Parker, **History of the Roman World**, p. 188.
3. See Downey, **History of Antioch**, p. 265, n. 153, and Andreas Alföldi, "Die Römische Münzprägung und die Historischen Ereignisse im Osten zwischen 260 und 270 n. Chr.," **Berytus**, V (1938), p. 56. But see also Parker, **History of the Roman World**, p. 190, and Warmington's note, p. 395.
4. See Magie, **Roman Rule in Asia Minor**, II, 1575, n. 44. But see Alföldi in **Cambridge Ancient History**, XII, 180, for the view that her invasion of Egypt occurred after Claudius' death.
5. For the opinion that Paul actually amounted to Palmyrene viceroy in Antioch, see Downey, **History of Antioch**, p. 264.
6. For the earlier date see F. C. Burkitt in **Cambridge Ancient History**, XII, 491.

Claudius Gothicus (268-270), radiate. Obverse of an antoninianus. 19 mm.

14 The Advent of Aurelian

Claudius had a brother, Quintillus, who commanded troops in northern Italy. Possibly these troops recognized him as emperor on the news of Claudius' death, but it is more likely that the senate recognized him first. Either the senatorial enthusiasm for Claudius extended indiscriminately to his relatives, or the senators thought that they could use Quintillus as their tool. He seems to have been a good, moderate, upright man but not much of a leader.

In the Balkans Aurelian, at the head of the mobile cavalry, quickly completed the Gothic war by rescuing the cities of Nicopolis and Anchialus in Thrace from barbarian siege. Then he marched to Sirmium, where the troops, Claudius' men, thunderously proclaimed him emperor.

If the senate had wanted to demonstrate its independence of the army by selecting Quintillus, it had made a foolish move. The senators may have counted on Claudius' popularity to ensure popularity for his brother. But when the report of Aurelian's accession reached Italy even Quintillus' own soldiers deserted him. A leader might have tried to make a stand; Quintillus did not. In the tradition of noble Romans, he opened his veins.

Pollio, Eutropius, and Zonaras say that Quintillus was emperor for seventeen days. Like Marius in the Roman Empire of the Gauls, however, he had time to strike coins in some quantity—at Rome, at Milan, at Siscia in western Pannonia and Cyzicus on the Asian side of the Propontis. His reign probably lasted for six weeks to three months. Except for issuing coins he does not appear to have done much at all. Meanwhile barbarian bands straggled down through the Tyrol into northern Italy to raid, rape and kill.

Aurelian must have become undisputed emperor sometime in the late winter or very early spring of 270. His stern sense of discipline did not seem to displease the soldiers as much as the conspirators of 268 had feared when, having murdered Gallienus, they passed over Aurelian for Claudius. In 270 at any rate, the troops hailed him with faith and conviction as a worthy successor to Claudius. The next few years were to prove them right.

Probably in his middle fifties, with short, graying hair and beard and alert little eyes, Aurelian may not have been quite as commanding a figure as Claudius but he had the same military gravity and, if we can believe his biographer, a tall and muscular physique to set it off. Like Claudius he was an "Illyrian"—born, perhaps, in Pannonia or modern Hungary, near Sirmium, the same outpost of Roman civilization where the army proclaimed him emperor.[1] Like Claudius also, he was an entirely self-made man. His father worked as a tenant farmer on the lands of an aristocrat.

Vopiscus, who presumably wrote Aurelian's biography for the **Augustan History,** is our principal source for his life. Unfortunately Vopiscus is no more dedicated to truth than Pollio.[2] But the general picture he gives of Aurelian is, in so far as we know, accurate even though some of the details may be embellished or invented.

In the territory of Sirmium the young Aurelian would have seen plenty of soldiers, veterans of the tough, well trained, businesslike Illyrian-Pannonian legions. Inevitably he felt attracted toward a military career. An athletic boy, he practiced hurling the spear and shooting arrows even on festival days, when other people relaxed.

His mother, according to Vopiscus, was a priestess of the Sun in their village. Modern scholars tend to discount this statement. Vopiscus, they say, probably put it into the biography because the Sun later turned out to be Aurelian's principal god. But the statement has a chance of being true even so. For the soldiers in the Danubian provinces the Sun was an extremely important divinity. Some of them worshipped him as Mithra, the heroic champion of goodness imported from Persia, whose mysteries were in most cases forbidden to women. Others worshipped him as Sol the Unconquered, radiant deity with a whip in his hand, borne across the sky in his four-horse chariot. Retired veterans who stayed in the Danubian provinces as farmers must have spread the cult of the Sun, in one form or another, among the civilian population. Aurelian's mother certainly might have been a priestess in some temple to the Sun near Sirmium, just as Aurelian himself might have owed his later veneration of ths Sun to his boyhood environment.[3]

Less credible are the omens of Aurelian's future reign, which Vopiscus surely felt were necessary paraphernalia in the biography of a great emperor. When Aurelian was a baby in swaddling clothes, according to Vopiscus, an eagle—Rome's imperial bird, the symbol that topped the emperor's sceptre—grabbed him out of his cradle and flew with him to an altar where no fire happened to be burning. Also a big white calf with spots of imperial purple was born on his mother's farm. The spots on one flank were arranged to spell out the word **Ave**, or "Hail." The spots on the other flank were arranged like a wreath or corona. Such portents—and Vopiscus included several more—testified to Aurelian's coming splendor.

He joined the army as a common soldier and rose through various commands by means of his love for army life and his bloodthirsty military skill. His exploits are no doubt highly exaggerated by Vopiscus, but they may have been legends among the troops even during his lifetime. In one day, Vopiscus says, he killed forty-eight Slavic barbarians. Over a period of several days he killed 950 men. Boys would compose verses praising him, like the verses celebrating the victories of David, and would dance to them in his honor. As an officer serving in Thrace under Valerian he plundered the Goths, bringing back 1,000 mares, 2,000 cows, 10,000 sheep, 15,000 goats, and 500 Gothic slaves to stock one of Valerian's private estates. During Gallienus' wars against the Franks in the Rhineland he took another 300 slaves, whom he sold for his own profit, and slaughtered 700 Franks. By the latter part of Gallienus' reign he was one of the most illustrious generals in the Roman army. With other high-ranking officers he took part in the plot against Gallienus' life. Under Claudius, as commander-in-chief of the cavalry, he distinguished himself in the final stages of the war against the Goths in his own native Balkans.

Sometime during all this activity he married a lady named Severina. Except for her portrait on coins—a grave small face, the hair swept in plaits over the head and back behind the neck in the fashion of the period—she is unknown. Aurelian the military leader dominates the picture; his wife retires.

Although he sometimes drank too much red wine for his dignity, he must have earned a reputation for personal austerity. He did not believe in doctors; if he felt sick he dieted. Very little amused him. But he did enjoy watching actors perform, and he also enjoyed watching a professional eater who, in one day, swallowed a sheep, a pig, a wild boar, one hundred loaves of bread, and over a cask of wine, which was run into his mouth through a funnel. If this story is true in any degree, it suggests that Aurelian's taste in entertainment was not very sophisticated.

The soldiers nicknamed him "Sword-in-Hand" because he was ready to whip out his sword on any provocation. According to Eutropius he had a flaring temper and a cruel streak. If one of his slaves happened to be put to death for some criminal act, he always wanted to be on hand to watch. His emphasis on discipline made him famous and feared throughout the legions. It came to his attention once that a soldier had violated the wife of a man whose home had been requisitioned as quarters for troops. Some commanders would genially have overlooked this abuse of compulsory hospitality, but Aurelian punished the offender by a device that Alexander the Great had used. He had two supple young trees bent

Aurelian (270-275), laureate. Obverse of a dupondius. 23 mm.

Severina (wife of Aurelian), diademed. Obverse of an antoninianus. 22 mm.

towards each other until one of the man's feet could be tied to each of them. While the man hung there the trees were suddenly released and sprang upright. The man of course was ripped in two.

Vopiscus quotes a letter supposedly written by Aurelian to a subordinate officer. It enjoins the subordinate to enforce discipline rigorously if he wants to be promoted to tribune, or, in fact, if he wants to stay alive. The letter was probably written by Vopiscus himself rather than Aurelian, but it gives a good picture of the areas of army life where severe discipline could be applied. The soldiers should not take for themselves the grapes or firewood of the provincials through whose lands they marched, or thresh the grain, or appropriate the chickens and sheep. They must keep their armor and weapons polished, curry their horses themselves, stay out of taverns, and waste no money on prophets. Any man who started a brawl would have to be whipped.

Not surprisingly, Aurelian's first movements as emperor were military. Rome's abandonment of the Germano-Raetian **limes** or line of fortifications during Valerian's reign, when the Alemanni had swept through toward southern Gaul, had opened the passes out of the Alps to any Germans enterprising enough to attempt them. This meant that Italy lay unguarded against invaders from the north. The West Germanic tribe called the Juthungi, whose homeland was somewhere in northern Bavaria, had by now poured through the Brenner Pass. Claudius had died in the Balkans before even attempting to stop them. They were tasting the spoils of northern Italy, which the Alemanni, their relatives, had stripped two years before.

Aurelian seems to have gone straight from Sirmium to northern Italy to put down the Juthungi, who turned around when they heard of his approach and started retreating north through the Tyrol. The emperor chased them all the way to the Danube, defeating them and making them seek refuge in their own free Germany north of the river. At one point they sent him an embassy to discuss terms of peace. Aurelian said he would see them the next day. The reception he staged was calculated to impress these barbarians with the warlike might of Rome. Dexippus, the Athenian aristocrat who had rallied his fellow citizens to ambush the Heruls during their terrible attack on Athens several years before, has left a description of this audience. It is one of the few intimate pictures of Roman-barbarian relations to remain to us from the third century.

Aurelian, in his cloak of purple, mounted a high platform or tribunal, where he sat in majesty as commander of the Roman world. The great efficient army from the Danube, weapons gleaming and ready, stood rigid in a vast crescent—a silent, superbly drilled, merciless fighting machine. On each side of the tribunal the officers sat their horses. To the rear rose the sacred standards of the military units—gold eagles and images of wild beasts, legionary banners with letters sewn in gold, portraits of past emperors, all affixed to silver-coated spears. Into this military magnificence the ambassadors from the Juthungi were introduced. They fell to the ground. Graciously they were ordered to get up and state their case.

With the help of interpreters they said what they had been told to say, boasting of the battle skill of the Juthungi and asking a sizable subsidy if they were to renew the alliance for which Rome had previously paid them. Aurelian rejected their alliance, refused their demand for subsidy, and promised them war.

When these people had been driven back into Germany Aurelian proceeded south to Rome to be recognized without enthusiasm by the senate, disgruntled over the suicide of its own candidate, Quintillus. He did not spend much time in Rome but marched to Pannonia, his own country. The Vandals were now invading it in force together with a Slavic tribe called the Iazyges, splendid horsemen from central Asia who had already fought Rome several times.

The Vandals and the Iazyges probably broke into Pannonia somewhat north of where the Buda of Budapest now stands — or Aquincum as it was then called, a flourishing Roman administrative, commercial, and military center of perhaps fifty thousand people with a great amphitheatre and a camp nearby.[4] Aurelian sent orders on ahead that the provincials were to bring their grain, cattle, and other food supplies into defensible cities such as Aquincum so that the barbarians would not be able to live off the countryside as they had expected to do. Then Aurelian apparently defeated the Vandals and Iazyges in another battle of which scarcely anything is known. The barbarians sent envoys to talk about peace. According to the settlement the two kings gave their sons over to the care of the Romans as hostages. Two thousand barbarian horsemen were ceded to the Roman army as auxiliaries. The rest of the invaders set out on the peaceful trek back to their own country. A band of five hundred violated the treaty by going off on a private plundering expedition, but Aurelian sent his newly acquired horsemen after them. The five hundred men were destroyed.

It was probably not much later that Aurelian decided to abandon the province of Dacia. This was the vast territory, now roughly Roumania, that lay north of the Danube, across from the two Moesian provinces that stretched along the south side of the river. Dacia had once been the boast of the empire, won for Rome by the deified Trajan over a century and a half ago in a brutal, persistent war against the native king. Soldiers, merchants, and planters had Romanized it in some degree, although the fierce Dacians, people of Thracian blood, proudly maintained their own highly developed culture in the presence of Roman manners and arts. No part of Europe was added to the empire after Dacia. Situated beyond the Pannonian-Moesian frontier, thrusting forth into the barbarian world, Dacia was uncomfortably exposed to raids. In the barbarian wars of the third century she had been tramped over, fought over, ravaged and robbed until many of her towns were ruined and her fields bare. During the past several years the Goths had appropriated more and more of her territory and Roman citizens had been moving out.

Total abandonment of so vulnerable and wasted a country was not an admission of defeat but an act of necessity, a wise move by an intelligent tactician and statesman. There were four legions in Pannonia and four in Moesia as well as the two in Dacia itself. These legions, which would have to rush to Dacia's defense in the crises that chronically disrupted the land, could be used to better effect against Zenobia of Palmyra, who would have to be encountered soon.

Aurelian created a new Dacia south of the Danube in the middle of what had been Moesia, forming it out of parts of Moesia and Thrace. He gave it for a capital the city of Serdica, now Sofia in Bulgaria, where a great imperial mint was soon established. He pulled out of the old Dacia the two legions traditionally stationed there and placed them at Oescus and Ratiaria, posts on the south side of the river in the new province.[5] Along with the legions, most of the Roman civilians remaining in the old Dacia must have crossed the Danube, although a few chose to stay for business reasons or perhaps from sentimental attachment to this endangered area. The region into which they moved had been severely depopulated by the barbarian incursions, so that bringing more Romans into it had a practical advantage.

As in any evacuation, there must have been hardship, sadness, and confusion as the Roman landowners, townspeople, and peasants, their families, household furnishings, sheep and cattle, tools and fineries, were all transported south of the river. But in so far as we can tell the whole process of withdrawal was effected with as little fuss as possible. And in spite of the inconvenience and worry, many of the evacuees must have felt glad to be going to an area where life would perhaps be a little less chaotic. Coins with the legend **Dacia Felix,** "Dacia the Fortunate," may have been struck at this time with reference to the newly fashioned province.

With as many troops as he could spare from the Danube, including the two thousand barbarian horsemen, Aurelian had to hurry back to northern Italy late in 270 because the Juthungi were again looting lustily. They had evidently not been scared enough by Aurelian's earlier victory over them or his reception of their envoys.[6] Joined by the Marcomanni and the Alemanni, the Juthungi had swarmed back into Italy through the Brenner Pass and were spoiling the fields around Milan. When Aurelian reached northern Italy he must have gained a sufficient advantage over them, psychological or military, to suggest that they surrender. The details are obscure, but it is clear enough that for once he had miscalculated. Near the city of Placentia, as night was coming on, the barbarians jumped out of the thick forests at his unsuspecting soldiers. Aurelian was badly defeated.

There was now nothing to prevent the Germanic hordes from sweeping down to Rome herself and sacking her. They were already advancing south along the Aemilian Way. The panic that had gripped the Roman citizens under Valerian twelve years before, when the Alemanni threatened to attack Rome, returned intensified. The invaders who threatened this time were apparently a much larger mass, and Rome was as defenseless as she had been then, without natural barriers to protect her, without a military force or adequate walls. The terrorized people roamed the streets in mobs on the point of riot, and Aurelian's reputation was low.

During the emergency under Valerian the senate had rallied an army of citizen volunteers. This time it decreed that the Sibylline books must be consulted. In these sacred volumes were recorded the ecstatic utterances of the Cumaean prophetess from the deep past, rhapsodic pronouncements to be relied on when the state was in peril.

Purified, sanctified, and veiled in white, the priests entered the high temple. Boys whose parents were both living, and who therefore qualified to assist, sang the prescribed songs. With veils over their hands the priests unwound the ancient scrolls. They read the divine words and interpreted for the people.

The Sibyl enjoined rituals that involved the chanting of hymns, the leading of animals in solemn procession around the edges of the city to cleanse it, and the sacrifice of the animals. It was thought that enemies would not be able to cross the places made pure by these ceremonies. The rituals were gravely performed, but in a city where belief in the efficacy of the traditional rites was fading, there must have been many whose panic was not allayed.

As it turned out, the ceremonies were not needed. The Germans did not get near enough to Rome to try to cross the purified borders of the city. Aurelian quickly rectified his mistake. He defeated the barbarians at Fanum Fortunae (Temple of Fortune) on the Adriatic at the mouth of the Metaurus River; he chased them as they retreated and beat them again at Ticinum, modern Pavia. Those not captured turned their backs on the allurements of Italy and limped home to the northern woods.

Aurelian went on to Rome. Most of the senators now felt obliged to admit that he was an adequate emperor, although many of them still did not like him very much. A few had even been plotting against him. With swift army-type justice he saw to it that the traitors were executed and their property confiscated.

This sojourn in Rome was probably the period when the mystifying rebellion of the mint workers occurred. According to the ancient historians the mint workers were adulterating the coins, already hopelessly adulterated of course. They seem to have been keeping for themselves some of the minimal amount of silver that went into the base money. Aurelian apparently shut down the Roman mint for the time being, perhaps to look into the situation or to prevent more underhandedness, and his interference with the mint workers' activities sparked their revolt. But there may have been other causes, such as wretched working conditions, the sorry economic state in general, or clandestine encouragement by senators opposed to Aurelian. At the head of the insurrection was a high mint official named Felicissimus, who may have organized the whole thing in self-defense, to keep from being punished for fraudulent practices of his own. It is not often, even in the chaotic third century, that one finds a group of people rising in revolt for a reason neither political nor military. But the issues of this revolt, if there were any aside from tampering with the currency, have been lost.

The Roman mint must have employed a large body of workers to make the great masses of coins that it, like other imperial mints, had to turn out in these inflationary times. The rebellion was therefore not a mere uprising, even if other people opposed to the government did not join it, as they quite possibly did. The insurgents seem to have collected on the Caelian Hill, not far from the mint itself. Aurelian wasted no time in repressing them, but according to Vopiscus they killed 7,000 of his soldiers before he stopped the rebellion.

Rome was still quivering from the recent threat of sack by the Juthungi. To prevent more seizures of panic in the empire's capital, and to prevent it from actually being entered by barbarian hordes during the reign of some emperor less watchful or warlike than himself, Aurelian started to build a wall around the fourteen districts of the city. He consulted the senate about its construction, perhaps in the hope of improving his relationship with the senators by asking for their advice in the great design.

The wall, which was not finished until after his death, extended for twelve miles and was at least twenty feet high and twelve feet thick. Along its length stood eighteen gateways and bastions for heavy artillery. The gates had semicircular crenellated towers and single or double arches. In spite of these rather impressive figures, however, the barricade was not intended to withstand a sustained siege by forces equipped with sophisticated siege engines. The artillery could not be lowered at a sufficiently sharp angle to hit men crowding close underneath. Defenders were not even expected to line up on top of the ramparts and fight off an enemy trying to scale them. The wall would serve its purpose if it discouraged barbarian tribesmen from making an attack or from prolonging a siege they had already begun. That would be enough to keep the city safe.

Parts of it stand today as testimony to the tenseness of those years. Unpretentious, stark, with no fancy variations or elaborate details, it was meant to perform a function, to fill a desperate need. Those who worked on it were not soldiers but members of the builders' guilds and slaves; the soldiers could not be spared. But although it was a civilian undertaking it had somewhat the same effect as the walls of camps and military posts. It turned Rome, like many smaller cities throughout the empire at this period, into a military fortification, shrinking from onslaught behind a modern barrier.[7]

Notes to Chapter 14

1. Syme, following Eutropius, prefers Dacia Ripensis. See **Emperors and Biography**, pp. 209-10.

2. For Syme's extremely plausible thesis that the **Augustan History** was actually written by one man under six pseudonyms, see above, Chap. 8, n. 5. Although for the sake of convenience I will call Aurelian's biographer by the traditional name Vopiscus, it should be remembered that he and Pollio may be two masks for the same author.

3. On this supposition see Léon Homo, **Essai sur le Règne de l'Empereur Aurélien (270-275)** (Paris, 1904), p. 28.

4. See Ramsay MacMullen, **Soldier and Civilian in the Later Roman Empire** (Cambridge, Massachusetts, 1963), pp. 99, 102-03, and Millar, **Roman Empire and its Neighbours**, pp. 231-32.

5. For the view that the new Dacia almost at once became the two provinces of Dacia Ripensis and Dacia Mediterranea, or perhaps was two provinces to begin with, see Syme, **Emperors and Biography**, p. 223.

6. For the possibility that there was only one Juthungi war in 270, occurring after the defeat of the Vandals and Iazyges, see Alföldi in **Cambridge Ancient History**, XII, 152. But for the more widely held view that Aurelian fought the Juthungi twice in 270 see Harold Mattingly in **Cambridge Ancient History**, XII, 298-99.

7. On the wall see especially Ian A. Richmond, **The City Wall of Imperial Rome: An Account of its Architectural Development from Aurelian to Narses** (Oxford, 1930), pp. 56-67, 241-50.

15 The Overthrow of Zenobia

The other item that occupied Aurelian's attention during his visit to Rome was his projected war against Palmyra. Queen Zenobia had rendered this war unavoidable. Pleased by his troubles with barbarians, she had decided to make the final, long-planned break with Rome. It was time to turn her territory—northern Arabia, most of Egypt, Mesopotamia, Syria including Antioch, Asia Minor as far west as Ancyra or modern Ankara, and the heartland of Palmyra itself—into a totally independent nation, a Roman Empire of the Orient like the Roman Empire of the Gauls.

She had already been striking coins at Antioch and Alexandria with Aurelian's portrait on what may have been considered the reverse and her son Vabalath's boyish portrait on the obverse. Vabalath's bust was surrounded by the titles that Gallienus had granted to his father Odenath and that Claudius has refused to renew for Vabalath:[1] **Vir Clarissimus, Rex, Imperator, Dux Romanorum,** or "Man of Most Illustrious Rank, King, General, Duke of the Romans." Either Aurelian endorsed this grandiloquent coinage as signifying accord between his empire and the subsidiary kingdom of Palmyra, or else he realized that he could do nothing about it for the time being and so did not object.

But now, in the spring or summer of 271, Zenobia dropped Aurelian's portrait from coins minted at Antioch and Alexandria. Copper **antoniniani** from the Antioch mint, for example, substituted the figure of Victory for Aurelian's bust. Even more flagrant, the inscription around the head of Vabalath on the obverse gave him Aurelian's own imperial title, **Augustus.** Base tetradrachms appeared at Alexandria with Zenobia's portrait in a tiara on the obverse and the bust of Selene, goddess of the moon, on the reverse. Zenobia's coins called her **Augusta** since she was the mother of **Augustus.** By means of these coins the new Roman Empire of the Orient

Vabalath, king of Palmyra, laureate. Inscription: VABALATHVS V(ir) C(larissimus) R(ex) IM(perator) D(ux) R(omanorum). 21 x 19 mm.

Aurelian (270-275), radiate. Reverse (?) of an antoninianus struck at Antioch with Vabalath's portrait on other side. 21 x 19 mm.

was announced to the world. Zenobia's son, not Aurelian, ruled as Roman emperor in the East. She could expect Aurelian to respond.

When his military preparations at Rome were completed, probably in the late summer or early fall of 271, he set out for this war that would make him or break him—Illyrian against Arab, emperor against queen, man against woman. If he felt any gallantry toward his opponent he did not show it: she must be shattered. The major part of his army, which probably joined him at the Danube, came from the Celtic legions guarding the Alpine provinces of Raetia and Noricum and from the Pannonian and Moesian legions with which he had spent so much of his life. He could trust these men to follow his orders and to die for him. There were also the horsemen from Dalmatia and North Africa, the splendid mobile cavalry that he had commanded under Claudius. These men too had faith in his leadership and could be relied on.

It was in fact a changed army that backed Aurelian, an army that had lost interest in setting up new emperors. Soldiers were coming to realize that rapid changes of regime—political confusion and internal war—did not serve their own interests best. The feeling was growing that if an emperor was a fine military leader he should not be cut off in the midst of his reign. Such a man could do more for the soldiers than a usurper supported by part of the army. The shift in attitude had probably started under Gallienus, whose assassination by his officers had evidently not had the approval of his troops. Gallienus' successor Claudius was a general whom the legionaries could admire. So was Aurelian, old Sword-in-Hand. Besides, his campaign against Palmyra promised the looting of opulent Eastern cities.

Marching through the Balkans, this army took time off from its main objective to defeat a Gothic king called Cannabaudes. He had been raiding on the south side of the Danube in Moesia. Aurelian's troops chased him across the river and killed him there along with 5,000 of his warriors. Then they continued on toward Byzantium and Asia Minor.

The population of Zenobia's realm may not have looked forward with patriotic pleasure to the war with Rome. The battles waged by Odenath against the Persians had been another matter; Odenath had taken the war into Persia itself and had fought like a lion, gathering glory for the Palmyrene name under Roman auspices. But now the Roman army under a great soldier threatened to invade the Palmyrenes' own territory, and that meant robbery and ruin; and Odenath was represented only by his young son and his widow.

Besides, many of Zenobia's newly acquired subjects—Syrians, Cappadocians, even some Egyptians—had no great love for the Palmyrene state and valued their Roman citizenship too highly to endorse the split from Rome. That was one reason the queen used Roman terms such as **Augustus** and **Augusta** on her coins: these subjects must be made to feel that in spite of the split they were still under Roman rule. But many of them saw clearly that Zenobia's overreaching ambition alone had brought about this war with the true Roman Empire. Others no doubt were indifferent: one master was as good or as bad as another. In the city of Palmyra itself, especially among the courtiers and the military, there must have been a core of nationalism that welcomed the war, and among the tribes of the desert the anti-Roman sentiment was strong. But Zenobia's kingdom as a whole could not have been enthusiastically behind her.

If we can believe the fifth century historian Zosimus, by far the best chronicler of these events, the omens did not encourage the Palmyrenes. At Aphaca in Syria, between Beirut and the sun-worshipping city of Heliopolis or Baalbek, stood a shrine to an Oriental equivalent of the goddess Aphrodite. There was a pool in its grounds. People would come every year at festival time and drop gifts into the pool—cloths of fine linen and precious stuffs, offerings of silver and gold. If the goddess liked these gifts they sank to the bottom. But if she rejected them they floated—even, says Zosimus, the objects of silver and gold. Presumably she accepted the presents most of the time. But in the year when the war with Rome began she rejected them all.

At the city of Seleucia in Cilicia, one of the territories in eastern Asia Minor recently taken over by Zenobia, stood a temple to the local version of Apollo. The Palmyrenes went to the oracle in this temple and inquired whether they would rule the East, but the reaction was even more disturbing than Aphrodite's refusal of the gifts in the pool. The oracle said that the Palmyrenes pained the gods, and he ordered them off his property. It almost sounds as if the priests at this temple were opposed to Zenobia's policies. "And when certain men made inquiry concerning Aurelian's campaign against the Palmyrenes," Zosimus tells us, "the god gave this answer:

> 'A single hawk is the precursor of chill woe
> For many doves; they shiver at this murderer.'"[2]

Crossing over the Bosporus from Thrace into Asia Minor, the hawk proceeded through Bithynia in the northwestern part of the peninsula and down through Galatia, where the city of Ancyra renounced its allegiance to Zenobia and returned to Rome. He marched southeast through Cappadocia to Tyana, a metropolis in territory still loyal to Zenobia. Tyana had to be taken, partly because it lay on the road through the Cilician Gates, the northern entrance to the pass through the Taurus Mountains. His army would have to file through this pass, then through the Syrian Gates on the southern side of the Taurus, before it could spread out on the Syrian plain, take Antioch, and if necessary march on Palmyra itself.

But Tyana shut the Roman emperor out. In one of his rages Aurelian exclaimed that by the time he finished with it not even a dog would be alive there.

He immediately laid siege. Tyana might have put up a stiff resistance and seriously checked his progress southeastward if one of its citizens, named Heraclammon, had not betrayed it. Heraclammon probably figured that the eventual conquest of Tyana was inevitable. If the city fired Aurelian's anger by a stubborn resistance, when the Romans finally did break in there would be mass murder. To betray the city was a way for Heraclammon to ensure the lives of his fellow citizens as well as his own, and maybe also gain a reward from a grateful emperor.

So he showed Aurelian a point where the ground rose gradually up toward the top of the wall. Aurelian mounted this slope in his armor and stood at the top, holding up his purple imperial cloak. It was a dramatic gesture, like the reception of the ambassadors from the Juthungi the previous year. The townspeople inside and the soldiers outside looked up at their invincible emperor, and the city yielded with no more trouble.

Aurelian immediately ordered the death of Heraclammon. If the traitor had known the emperor better, he might have expected this.

Tyana was a rich and populous place. The troops naturally were itching to loot it, to burn it, to kill its inhabitants, to perform the proper offices of war. But Aurelian refused permission. They respectfully reminded him that he had said not even a dog would be left alive in the city. He told them to go ahead and kill the dogs.

There had been born at Tyana in the first century A.D. a sage named Apollonius, for whom the city was famous. Apollonius had walked over the East preaching love, simplicity, and the transmigration of souls. He had lived on vegetables and worn shoes of bark, had exorcised many demons, read the future, raised the dead, and talked back to the emperor Domitian. Early in the third century a rhetorician named Philostratus had written his biography, which increased his reputation. Apollonius had by this time become a god; there were temples to his worship. The emperor Severus Alexander (222-235) may even have put his image in a private shrine to virtue, along with images of Alexander the Great, Abraham, Orpheus, and Jesus Christ. According to Vopiscus, the ghost of Apollonius came to Aurelian as the emperor was going to his tent. Realizing that Aurelian was not good at Greek, the apparition addressed him in Latin. It told Aurelian plainly to spare Tyana. That was why the emperor refused to let his soldiers pillage and destroy.

This story may have been invented by Vopiscus, or it may have been invented by Aurelian. If Aurelian made it up, his purpose was probably to give the army a supernatural, unanswerable reason for his order of clemency. But the real explanation of his mercy toward Tyana is that he wanted to appear in the role of savior, not of conqueror. He was not supposed to be wreaking his terrible revenge on a criminal city — he was delivering the city from Palmyrene oppression and restoring it to the Roman family. If his soldiers did not quite understand all this, at least they obeyed him.

With Tyana secured, Aurelian proceeded south through the Taurus Mountains and out via the Syrian Gates onto coastal Asia Minor. Antioch in northern Syria was only a short distance away. Zenobia waited for him there.

Although she had not seriously defended Asia Minor against him, and although certain oracles may have condemned her war, she was not an unworthy opponent for a general like Aurelian. Pollio in the **Augustan History** talks about her Arab beauty—her swarthy complexion, arresting black eyes, and perfect white teeth—but in some ways she resembled a man. Her voice was one of clear command. Early in life she had inured herself to hardship. She preferred riding her own horse to being conveyed in a carriage, and sometimes, according to Pollio, she tramped several miles with her infantry. For public appearances she wore a helmet and did not always bother to cover her arms. Like her virile husband Odenath she loved to hunt. When it suited her dignity she drank with her generals, and she outdrank Persians and Armenians to prove that she could do it. But Pollio may be fabricating when he says that she would deny her body to Odenath except when she had just menstruated and knew she was not pregnant.

A hunger for incalculable wealth and vast dominion was not the only respect in which she resembled her favorite historical figure, the great Egyptian queen. As Cleopatra had been a female intellectual, so was Zenobia. Aramaic was her native language—her own people called her Bat Zabbai—but she spoke Egyptian fluently and, like other upper class Asiatics, was proficient in Greek. Although she never entirely mastered Latin she used it anyway, and had her sons talk in Latin until their Greek suffered. Pollio mentions that she wrote an epitome of Oriental history, and even though the work has not survived there is no real necessity to discount his statement.

But she seems to have operated more as a patroness of learning than as a learned lady. Her favor toward Paul of Samosata had an intellectual side as well as a political side; she was countenancing a man with interesting religious concepts. In the years after Odenath's death she made Palmyra a center for late Greek culture. About 268 she attracted to her court the famous Longinus, a Syrian who had been teaching at the Platonic Academy at Athens for the past several years. The critical treatise **On the Sublime** used to be attributed to him. Although he did not write this work he was one of the most erudite men of the age. Rich and widely traveled, he had known Ammonius Saccas, teacher of Origen and Plotinus, and at Athens he knew and admired the ardent intellectual Porphyry, who would go on to Rome and become Plotinus' pupil and biographer. Students from all over came to Longinus at Athens to hear him discourse on Plato. But when the Goths swarmed into Athens toward the end of Gallienus' reign he decided to take advantage of Zenobia's invitation and expound Greek philosophy in an Oriental setting. Turning from wisdom to politics, he soon became one of her principal counselors. He may have advised her to start the war on Rome, although she probably would have undertaken this struggle even if he had discouraged it.

She had Zabdas to command her army as during the Egyptian campaign. It was a seasoned fighting force, one which she could depend on as Aurelian could depend on his. Former Roman foot soldiers stationed in the area belonged to it. So did Palmyrene archers mounted on horses and camels, auxiliaries from Armenia and from the Saracen tribes, and the cataphracts on whom the Palmyrenes like the Persians placed such reliance—the armored men on their great armored horses.[3]

Antioch, where the army was quartered, was no more friendly toward Zenobia than most of her other recent acquisitions. There was still of course a pro-Palmyrene party in the city. Paul had no doubt encouraged it while he was legitimate Bishop of Antioch. Now that he refused to give up the episcopal office and exercised it illegitimately, he probably continued to encourage the party. Zenobia attracted not only Paul's avid adherents, but other Antiochenes who were disenchanted with Roman rule, some of them perhaps the same ones who had favored Persia under Valerian. But Christians who listened to the legitimate Bishop Domnus would have been opposed to Zenobia, and so would those elements in the city's population that retained some loyal feelings toward Rome—the Graeco-Roman upper class, perhaps. So would the many who feared Aurelian's army or had heard of his clemency toward Tyana. Aurelian's psychology was working as he had planned: he was undermining the people's resistance with mercy. They hoped that if Antioch admitted the Roman emperor it would be treated as generously as Tyana. If the gates stayed closed, when he finally did force his way in he would undoubtedly plunder and kill.

Antioch lay mainly on the east side of the Orontes River. Aurelian evidently approached the city from the east along the road leading to Berea. Somewhere on this road, probably near the town of Immae where Roman legions had won the empire for the boy Elagabalus fifty-eight years before, he encountered the Palmyrenes.[4] Zenobia's general Zabdas, on hearing that the Romans were coming toward the city, had dispatched against them the pride of the Palmyrene forces, the cataphracts. Aurelian, afraid that his foot soldiers would fall before this metal-plated machine, sent them across the Orontes River out of the way of the cataphracts, where they could perhaps intercept more of Zenobia's troops coming from Antioch. That left his own numerically inferior cavalry on the east side to deal with the Palmyrene knights, surging forward on their war horses.

When the mailed Palmyrenes struck, Aurelian's cavalry pretended to retreat toward Immae, according to instructions. The cataphracts thundered after them. The strong Syrian sun beat down on the knights' conical helmets, their glittering bronze or iron plates, and the armor of their mounts. As the metal got hotter and heavier, men and horses sweated inside it and tired fast. When Aurelian felt sure that they were exhausted he had his own cavalry wheel around and charge. The Palmyrenes broke, fell from their horses, let themselves be trampled by the horses of the enemy, let themselves be struck by Roman swords. Their hot mail burdened them, clung to them, hampered their movements. They could not remount by themselves.

It was a total rout. Aurelian had not yet won the war, but he had gained an important victory. He did not enter Antioch right away, however. In fact Zabdas went back to Antioch. Knowing that the city had not yet learned how the battle had turned out, and wanting to delay the news of his own defeat until he could remove all his troops from this largely inimical, potentially dangerous metropolis, Zabdas devised a ruse. He found a middle-aged man who vaguely resembled Aurelian in appearance, dressed him up as the emperor, and paraded him through the city as a captive. Temporarily, the Antiochenes accepted the idea that Palmyra had triumphed over the Romans. That night Zabdas clandestinely led his army out of the city. Zenobia of course stole out of Antioch with the rest.

The Palmyrenes headed south, through the flowered suburb of Daphne toward Apamea and eventually toward Emesa. They did not hurry. That was because Aurelian would presumably be preoccupied in Antioch for the next several days and because Zenobia had asked Persia, the enemy over whom her husband had so valorously triumphed, to help her against Rome. She and Zabdas expected to be joined by Persian contingents if they lingered on the way.

When Aurelian entered Antioch the citizens greeted him rhapsodically. Here was the man who had restored their city to her place in the empire. Zenobia's most ardent supporters had fled in fear of the imperial wrath, so that the remaining population was mainly a loyalist one; and those who were not especially loyal kept their mouths shut or shouted for Aurelian like the others.

The emperor extended his mercy over Antioch. Like Tyana, the city was spared all spoliation. His soldiers were not to touch anything. He even proclaimed a general amnesty, inviting back Zenobia's supporters who had fled. Again he preferred to play the part of deliverer. It is proof of his power over the army that his men did not grumble at his decision even though from their point of view he was making the war uninteresting.

The Christians in Antioch who did not side with Paul permitted themselves to hope. They asked Aurelian to arbitrate on the matter of Paul versus Domnus. These Christians probably expected that since Paul was a creature of the Palmyrenes, Aurelian would not decide in his favor. They were right, but Aurelian justified his ruling on very defensible grounds. He said that the episcopal house belonged to the man whom the bishops in Italy, including the pope, recognized as bishop of Antioch—and that man was unquestionably Domnus. Paul was finally and irrevocably driven from his see.

This was the first time that Christians anywhere in Roman lands had asked an emperor to intervene in a question concerning the church. Whether or not Aurelian realized the implications of his ruling, he was advancing the authority of the Western bishops. It had been the Eastern bishops assembled at Antioch who had condemned Paul and tried to deprive him of his office; but what mattered to Aurelian was how the Western prelates felt about Paul. In particular, the emperor was augmenting the prestige of the Roman see.

After putting Antioch in order Aurelian proceeded south through Syria in pursuit of Zabdas and Zenobia. Zabdas had left a detachment of Palmyrenes four or five miles south of Antioch at Daphne, the city's notorious suburb, dedicated to Apollo and pleasure—a spacious area of gardens, temples, groves and cool waters, where people came to worship the god and have sex with the prostitute population.

Zabdas had posted his Palmyrenes on a rocky height above Daphne to incommode the Romans whenever they should decide to march. Aurelian had his legionaries hold their shields above their heads, locked together like the plates of a turtle shell in the **testudo** formation traditional since the army of republican times. Under this shell the soldiers climbed the hill, and the stones and missiles sent down by the Palmyrenes bounced off. When the Romans got to the top they dislodged the Palmyrenes, stabbed them to death or threw them down the sides of the hill to be bruised, ripped, and broken by the rocks.

South along the Orontes through the cities of Apamea, Larissa, and Arethusa. These cities rushed to come back into the empire and hailed Aurelian as their savior, just as he had intended. On south toward Emesa (modern Homs), where Zabdas and Zenobia were encamped, more than a hundred miles from Antioch and close to the western edge of the desert. Emesa was famous for the glass perfume bottles, oil containers, and drinking vessels that it exported to far parts of the empire, and for the worship of the Sun, known there as Elagabal. For centuries, even under Roman control, Emesa had been ruled by priest-kings dedicated to the Sun. In the late second century a female descendant of these priest-kings had introduced their blood into the imperial family as wife of the emperor Septimius Severus, and the house of Severus that continued to rule the empire until

A.D. 235 retained its blood ties with Emesa. In 272 this city with its imperial Roman connections was perhaps even less sympathetic toward Zenobia than the other cities through which Aurelian had passed. Aurelian's image was very popular there. The Emesans must have known about his own strong faith in the Sun, so fervently worshipped by the Pannonian-Moesian legions in which he had been bred. They begrudged their city to the queen from the desert.

The army with which Aurelian had entered Asia Minor had by this time been swelled by troops from Tyana, Mesopotamia, Syria, Phoenicia, and Palestine. But it was not nearly as large an army as Zenobia's, which, according to Zosimus, had 70,000 men. This probably did not yet include the contingents from Persia that Zenobia had been expecting. When Aurelian approached, her great force was drawn up under Zabdas on the plain outside Emesa. While the townspeople waited behind their walls for an imperial victory, the Romans and the Palmyrenes fought.

Aurelian's cavalry fell back under the threat of Zenobia's cataphracts. This was somewhat the same tactic that Aurelian had used in the battle outside Antioch near Immae. It seemed necessary now because the Palmyrene horsemen, seriously outnumbering the Roman cavalry, could have surrounded them otherwise and, riding around and around them, gradually pulled the circle tighter until the Romans were a tangled, hysterical mass in the center. As he did outside Antioch, then, Aurelian was trying to cope with a larger force in the best way he knew. But the tactic did not work as well as at Immae. The cataphracts soon caught up with Aurelian's horsemen and, invincible in their heavy mail, slashed at them and cut them down. In the swirling dust the Romans died of their wounds or were trampled to death by the armored horses.

But now the infantry, the great body of the Roman army, attacked the Palmyrenes and their allies. The line of Zenobia's army had broken up when the cataphracts spurred off in pursuit of the Roman cavalry; it was simple for the legionaries and the auxiliaries to penetrate and to swarm all over their enemies. The most spectacular auxiliaries were the men from Palestine who had recently joined Aurelian's forces. They fought with clubs, smashing the Palmyrenes on the head and the chest, crumpling iron and bronze that swords did not pierce. The Palmyrenes were terrified of the clubs. They had lost the battle. Their foot soldiers and even their cavalry panicked. They fled across the plain, the cataphracts riding their war stallions over their own fallen comrades, the foot soldiers climbing over their friends. Some of the Palmyrenes got into Emesa and hid out there. Dead horses and dead men littered the plain.

What was left of Zenobia's army turned east toward the city of Palmyra, the last refuge, where they would at least be among friends. Aurelian entered a wildly enthusiastic Emesa.

According to Vopiscus in the **Augustan History**, the turning point in the battle had come when a godlike form appeared to the Roman foot soldiers and horsemen, rallying them and inspiring them to win. Vopiscus says that when Aurelian visited the temple of Elagabal, the Emesan god of the Sun, he recognized the form that had appeared to his men as the Sun himself. Apart from the matter of the epiphany, the story may have some fact behind it. For one reason or another Aurelian may actually have credited the Sun, his own patron deity, with this great victory. Coins of Aurelian often show the Sun, radiate and with cloak flying behind, setting his foot on an enemy of Rome. He had stamped on the Palmyrene at Emesa.

Zenobia's desert capital lay about eighty miles to the east. It may have taken Aurelian's army as long as a week to cross the sands. About this time Aurelian may have been joined by reinforcements from Egypt. At the beginning of his campaign against Zenobia he had dispatched one of his most competent generals, a certain Probus, to reconquer Egypt from the Palmyrenes. This man fared better than the former Probus, who under the emperor Claudius had been tricked into defeat by Zabdas. In fact the assignment was easy, since Zabdas had left only a small body of troops in Egypt. With the province again under Roman control, Probus probably sent part of his army into Syria to help his emperor. At the same time the Persian troops that Zenobia had been waiting for may have succeeded in getting through to her.

As they trudged over the sands toward Palmyra, Aurelian's men were harassed by Arab raiders. For these nomads, if not for the inhabitants of the Syrian cities, Zenobia was ruler and Rome the enemy. Besides, the Romans' baggage train appealed irresistibly to their greed. They kept nipping at the Roman line of march, stealing what they could, killing here and there, fading into the desert, and coming again. They were not a serious menace, but they embarrassed the emperor since they did not stay in one place long enough for him to beat them.

What probably worried Aurelian more than the Arab harassment was the fact that every mile he advanced toward Palmyra put him that much farther from his nearest supply base—Emesa. At Palmyra he would be totally in enemy territory and surrounded by the enemy's desert.

Not that Palmyra faced immediately upon the desert as her honey-colored ruins do today. There were gardens around the city then, and farming villages, and vineyards and fields of vegetables irrigated through the generosity of the merchant aristocracy.

The city had probably never been more splendid than during the reign of Zenobia. Enriched by Odenath's conquests and then by those of his widow, and profiting fully once more from the caravan trade that the uncertainties of Valerian's reign had crippled, Palmyra was affluent and beautiful. She was also one of the busiest marts of the Orient. Her situation at the half-way point between the cities of the Persian Gulf and those of the Mediterranean littoral meant that caravans from both shores came to her.

Some of the caravans, after paying for the rest and refreshment that she offered and the water from her fountains, continued on the long journey from shore to shore. Others used Palmyra as their point of exchange. Merchants from the Gulf would trade their goods—silk stuffs from China, perfumes from Arabia, spices and ivories from the Far East, tigers and slaves, jewels and pearls—to merchants from the Mediterranean, who would turn their caravans around and take their purchases back to Antioch, Caesarea in Palestine, or Beirut. But before they left Palmyra these merchants would unload the salable commodities of the Roman provinces—grain, wine, pickled fish, hides, woolens dyed with Tyrian purple—onto caravans that would carry them to the Gulf ports.[5] Since Palmyra taxed the merchandise that passed through her gates, she flourished exceedingly.

The Palmyrene aristocracy—people of pure Arab descent, a few Iranians and Syrians, and a few transplanted Greeks—had developed a civilization of high sophistication. Many had traveled in the Orient or even in the Roman West. Their culture was a fusion. They lived in houses reminiscent of Babylon with mosaics and thick Asiatic carpets on the floor, worshipped at temples with Corinthian columns, read Greek poetry and philosophy, and spoke Aramaic. The men usually wore embroidered robes and loose Persian trousers, occasionally the Greek tunic and himation. Their wives decorated their persons with massive Oriental earrings, necklaces, rings and bracelets. The most prominent men debated civic affairs in the local senate or council, as in cities throughout the Graeco-Roman world.

Sometimes they went to family tombs to feast with their relatives and the spirits of their dead ancestors, as people did also at Rome. When they died they joined their ancestors in one of the tombs. In the first and early second centuries their bodies probably entered a sandstone tower, rising several stories high, with space for mummified dead in recesses on the upper floors. But the **hypogeum** or underground tomb had come into popularity in the second century and was the kind of burial place in which an aristocrat of Zenobia's time could expect his body to rest.[6] T-shaped or cross-shaped in plan, a **hypogeum** could shelve several hundred corpses in the walls of its galleries. There were frescoes on the principal walls, perhaps showing the dead at banquets. There were diademed busts of the dead in hard limestone—funerary portraits as in Roman tombs but executed in the rigid, impersonal manner of the East—and there were limestone reliefs of the dead lying in rich clothing on their couches and drinking as they had done in life. They could hope for their descendants to come and drink with them in their tombs as long as the city endured.

Palmyrenes crossed their city on one of the most stately avenues to be found anywhere in the Roman world, rivaling the grand boulevard at

Antioch — two-thirds of a mile long, bordered on each side with close to four hundred great soaring columns from which consoles jutted out to support the bronze statues of eminent citizens that looked down on the crowds beneath. This avenue led to Palmyra's main temple, that of the god Bel, set in a broad courtyard lined with double rows of Corinthian columns. As with the street, parts of the temple still stand in ruined magnificence.

The Palmyrenes' religion was typical of their culture in general: a fusion, a mingling of the local and the foreign. In a niche inside the temple were statues of the divine triad — Bel himself, Yaribol, and Aglibol. The Greeks identified Bel, who was often shown armed for battle, with their own Zeus, king of the gods; the Romans likened him to Jupiter; and no doubt there were Palmyrenes who reasoned that Zeus and Jupiter were manifestations of Bel. He seems to have been imported from Babylonia, perhaps by way of the Parthians.[7] Yaribol was the sun god, like Elagabal at Emesa or Helius among the Greeks; and the third member of the triad, Aglibol, was god of the moon. Both of them may have been indigenous, worshipped by the desert tribes and the men on caravan. Definitely local was Arsu, the young caravan god, who rode a camel and sometimes appeared in sculpture as a camel himself. He and the other young caravan god, Azizu, were the Morning Star and the Evening Star, invaluable to men crossing the unmarked sands.

But there were many importations aside from Bel in the conglomerate Palmyrene pantheon. Baal-Shamin, Lord of the Skies — god of lightning, of rainstorms, and of fertile fields — had probably come from Syria. Atargatis, the female reproductive principle, had originated in Asia Minor like her husband Hadad, whom she overshadowed. She related ultimately to the Great Mother venerated by matriarchal Mediterranean peoples before there was a Greece, and as Cybele she had gone to Rome. The great fertility goddess whom the Babylonians knew as Ishtar and the Phoenicians as Astarte also had her Palmyrene devotees.[8]

This diversity of deities — and there were many more — received the prayers of the people as Aurelian drew near with his legions.

The city was well prepared for a siege. Great quantities of arrows, spears, and stones had been stored there. Machines for projecting these missiles, even engines for hurling fire down on the Romans, stood on the walls. Enough water was available to satisfy the needs of citizens and soldiers. In a measure that only the emergency could justify, Zenobia seems to have reinforced the walls with stones from some of the tombs in the necropolises outside the city and from the porticoed building where the senate held its debates. She also seems to have incorporated old mansion-like tombs in new walls hurriedly thrown up.[9]

Psychologically too, in so far as we can tell, the Palmyrenes were ready

Sol, radiate, holding laurel branch and bow and stamping on an Eastern (Palmyrene) enemy with arm upraised. Reverse of an antoninianus of Aurelian. Inscription: ORIENS AVG. In the exergue: XXI (mark of value) R (mint of Rome). 22 mm.

for a siege. They knew how the Romans fought, since Roman soldiers had been stationed at Palmyra for so long and since many Palmyrenes had served in the Roman army. Aurelian could hold no great surprises for them. His men, besides, may have been growing tired of this war without booty or rape. The desert heat was not in his favor either; his Celtic and Pannonian legionaries found it hard to take. The Arabs who wandered the desert between Palmyra and Emesa were loyal to the queen; they could cut off precious supplies dispatched to Aurelian from Emesa. All in all, the situation did not look bad from the Palmyrene point of view.

Aurelian dealt with the desert tribes in the only way possible: he bribed them into shifting their loyalty to himself. Some of the Arabs even began bringing provisions into his camp. Having encircled Palmyra with his army, he set about the siege in earnest. He may have moved siege towers and battering rams against the city, but the historians do not say so.

The Palmyrenes mocked the Romans from the top of the wall, shouting that their city was unconquerable. One Palmyrene, according to Zosimus, yelled out obscenities about Aurelian. A Persian archer who was serving with the Roman army promised to make this insolent Palmyrene a corpse if Aurelian gave the order. Aurelian had no objection. The Palmyrene kept screaming filthy comments, evidently having a good time. The Persian screened himself behind some soldiers, fitted an arrow to his bowstring, and let go. Just as the Palmyrene looked out from behind a parapet the arrow struck. He tumbled down dead to the Romans.

Vopiscus tells us that Aurelian, debilitated by the long hot siege, wrote a letter to Zenobia proposing terms of surrender for herself: she and her allies would not be killed, she would be sent with her children to live in a place selected by Aurelian, and her silks, jewels, gold, camels, and horses would be confiscated. Vopiscus pretends to quote Zenobia's reply, in which she proudly observes that Cleopatra preferred death as queen to capitulation.

But within the city more and more people wanted the war to be over. A peace party developed in opposition to the war party that had been dominant until then. Food was running low. The jeering from the walls lost spirit in the face of Roman stubbornness. Aurelian may have intercepted reinforcements from Persia and in one way or another he made the queen's Armenian and Saracen allies his own allies instead.

Zenobia's advisors must have felt that Persia was the only hope left. Somehow the Persians must be persuaded to send help again. The queen herself was to do the negotiating. Mounted on a camel, she slipped out of Palmyra, crossed the Roman siege line in some fashion, and set off across the desert, eastward toward the Euphrates. We do not know who attended her—slaves, soldiers, or counselors. Zosimus says she rode a she-dromedary because the females are faster than the males, faster even than horses. Presumably she headed for Dura sixty miles away, until recently a Roman frontier post on the Euphrates, once manned by Palmyrenes serving as auxiliaries in the Roman forces, now probably eager to support Zenobia. Across the river she could talk with the Persians. She would not have to sneak back into Palmyra as she had sneaked out; the Persians would be with her and she could fight her way in.

Although Zosimus does not say so, there was probably a second reason for her flight. If things went badly at Palmyra in the meantime, she would be safe on Persian ground. Aurelian might take the city but he would not take the queen.

But her daring accomplished nothing. Aurelian must have learned about the flight fairly soon. He sent horsemen after her, and they chased her for the sixty miles. According to Zosimus, when they caught up with her she was already on the boat to cross the Euphrates. But the boat had not set sail, and the Romans went on board and took her off.

They rode back to the Roman camp, where Aurelian greeted the captive queen. As soon as he got over his elation at seeing his enemy in his power, Zosimus says, a reaction set in. Enemy or not, she was only a woman. How much credit would future generations give him for having defeated a woman? Like other Romans, Aurelian looked on lasting renown as a kind of a life after death. He was winning shabby glory if posterity would know him as the man who had beaten a widow from the East.

Without the queen, the city yielded. The party for peace had been justified. People held olive branches over the wall to show that they were no longer at war. They streamed out of Palmyra loaded down with presents for the emperor and leading animals for sacrifice. Aurelian now entered on the role of magnanimous conqueror at which he was so good. He performed sacrifice and accepted the presents—the heaps of gold, the gems and silks and weapons. He told the people not to be afraid, and sent them back into the city unharmed. Like Tyana and Antioch, Palmyra was a Roman city. The war had been a civil war, not one between two different nations. Aurelian would be gracious to Palmyra now that he had restored it to the empire. No soldiers from his army pillaged its homes or temples.

Since he did not entirely trust its devotion, however, he stationed six hundred archers there under a certain Sandarion. In supreme command was an officer named Marcellinus, with the titles Prefect of Mesopotamia and Governor of All the East. It looked as if the Palmyrenes, under these light reins, could resume their lucrative lives among the splendors of their capital.

Aurelian marched back across the desert to Emesa. What happened to Zenobia's son Vabalath, boy king of Palmyra, is not known, but Zosimus mentions a son of Zenobia as still alive when Aurelian proceeded toward Europe. As for the queen herself, she was brought to Emesa, along with her principal advisors, to stand trial before the emperor. We know next to nothing about the trial; we do not even know the specific charges, except that they were related to rebellion against the Roman state.

Somehow Zenobia kept her life. Vopiscus says that the Roman soldiers clamored for her punishment; perhaps they were entirely disillusioned by this time with a war that was from their standpoint unrewarding, and their frustration fell on the queen. But Aurelian, according to Vopiscus, considered it ungallant to execute a woman. The doubtful glory of having defeated her was apparently all that he could cope with. Or else he realized that if he sentenced this woman to death he would be criticized and shamed. Zosimus implies, besides, that Zenobia was clever and unprincipled enough to throw the blame for the revolt on her counselors. In the terror of the trial she lost her sense of regal responsibility and denounced her advisors for inveigling her into revolt. Several were executed summarily. One of these was the philosopher Longinus.

Although he had lived for many years at Athens, Longinus came originally from Syria, perhaps from Emesa itself, which had been his mother's home town. The Emesans decried the sentence, weeping bitterly. In this instance, they thought, Aurelian had been unjust. But Longinus, admirer of Plato and friend of Porphyry, calmed their lamentations. Then he went quietly to his end.

Though Zenobia's life was spared she did not go free. Aurelian reserved her for the triumph that he planned to hold eventually at Rome. Meanwhile he started on the march back through Syria and Asia Minor to Europe. Eastern potentates brought the great man gifts—jeweled clothing, for example, and the dragon-standards that the Iranians as well as the Scythian and Sarmatian barbarians used, bright-colored strips of cloth cut in the shape of serpents, sewn lightly together and attached to poles. In the wind the fantastic shapes puffed out and twisted like angry monsters.

The sixth century chronicler John Malalas, an Antiochene, says that Aurelian in his progress showed off Zenobia to the populace. At Antioch, for instance, he exhibited her on camelback in the hippodrome, probably during games celebrating his victory, and he put her in a cage for crowds in the streets to jeer at. Living several centuries after the Palmyrene war, John Malalas may have been mistaken, but there is at least a possibility that he was telling the truth. To humiliate the queen in the area that she had tried to entice from Rome would not have been a bad political move.

Many Palmyrene captives accompanied Aurelian through the length of Asia Minor toward Europe. In crossing the Propontis they were, according to Zosimus, drowned. Zosimus suggests that Zenobia died too on the way back to Europe, perhaps by refusing to eat. But in this he is wrong: Aurelian managed to save her for his triumph.

The emperor probably reached the Balkan provinces in the early autumn of 272. He threw his army immediately into another war, this time against the Carpi, barbarians of Dacian stock who were restless as they had been under Decius, Gallus, and Valerian. He conquered them along the Danube, added **Carpicus Maximus** to his other titles, and settled large numbers of them in the provinces of Lower Moesia and Thrace to farm regions that the barbarian incursions of recent years had left desolate. Then the news came from Palmyra. The city was in revolt.

The Palmyrene war party, or party of nationalists, had regained control. A man named Apsaeus headed the faction. He had been an enthusiast for war under Zenobia but had for some reason not been executed at Emesa along with Longinus and other leaders of the rebellion. First he went to Marcellinus, the officer whom Aurelian had left in charge as Prefect of Mesopotamia and Governor of All the East, and proposed that Marcellinus declare himself emperor and lead a revolt. It appeared to be the old pattern of usurpation once more. But either Marcellinus was very loyal to his emperor or he was sensible enough to realize that rebellion against a man like Aurelian would never work. He put Apsaeus off, saying that he could not quite make up his mind. Apsaeus kept coming back but getting noncommittal answers, so he turned elsewhere. He set up as puppet king of Palmyra a certain Antiochus, who claimed to be a relative of Zenobia. The war party massacred the six hundred archers whom Aurelian had stationed in Palmyra, together with their commanding officer, Sandarion. But meanwhile Marcellinus contrived to send the news to Aurelian.

The legions marched rapidly back toward Palmyra, driven on by an emperor who would not rest. They arrived at Antioch while the citizens were enjoying horse races in the hippodrome and marched immediately to Palmyra. The revolt was probably not a major affair. Many Palmyrenes no doubt cringed at the thought of another war with Rome and offered no help to the patriots. There had not been time to repair the fortifications damaged during the siege, or, probably, to gather in a sufficient food supply. Aurelian took the city without any trouble.

This time his soldiers could plunder to their hearts' content. Anything or anybody they could lay their hands on was theirs. Aurelian had evidently determined to make Palmyra a lesson to the Roman world. According to Zosimus he spared the life of "King" Antiochus, considering him too insignificant to bother killing. But Vopiscus says that he slaughtered men, women, children, and peasants—probably farmers from the surrounding fields who had fled into Palmyra for safety when the Romans came near. No doubt he also took many captives.

As for the gorgeous city itself, parts of it must have been destroyed. The proudest buildings stood, but Palmyra never recovered from the ferocity of Aurelian. It sank into a quiet unimportance. Later the emperor Diocletian (284-305) would revive it in some degree by erecting military buildings, baths, and an imperial palace there. But Palmyra's busy, productive life as an Oriental capital and a center for the caravan trade could not be restored. Zenobia had blighted her city.

Not long after the punishment of Palmyra Aurelian created two new legions and stationed one in Phoenicia and the other in Arabia, doubling the number of legions in each of these regions. He apparently wanted to make sure that future rebellions in the Orient would be quashed at once. Instead of raising the legions locally he formed them of Illyrians—Balkan peoples whom he could trust to keep the Easterners in order.

Meanwhile he marched from Palmyra to Egypt. A revolt had broken out in Alexandria. It had started about the same time that Apsaeus began his machinations in Palmyra. Its leader, a merchant named Firmus according to the **Augustan History**, had not proclaimed himself emperor. Most likely, he knew what was going on in Palmyra and was waiting to see whether Marcellinus' would let himself be made emperor. When Marcellinus proved unwilling, Firmus probably decided to support the puppet King Antiochus. His precise motives are not known, but it sounds reasonable that he had been one of those Egyptians who helped Zenobia take over Egypt several years before. Perhaps he felt that his own commercial interests, and those of Alexandria as well, fared better under Palmyrene rule than under Roman rule; and perhaps he was right.

Firmus was immensely rich—so rich that he owned a great private library and the windows of his house had panes of glass. He traded widely —with the Saracens and with the Blemmyes, desert tribes who lived in the Sudan and along the Red Sea. He traded all the way to India, as far fewer Romans were doing in the later third century than in the second, and according to Vopiscus he had two exceptional elephant tusks, each about ten feet long. Vopiscus portrays Firmus as a man who stood out among men. Huge and hairy, with bulging eyes in a swarthy face, he was nicknamed the Cyclops. Although he did not usually drink a lot of wine he had a remarkable capacity for it, and when another man challenged him to a drinking bout he swigged two buckets of wine without noticeably modifying his sobriety. But he preferred eating to drinking; one day he ate a whole ostrich.

Iron-muscled, he liked to perform feats of strength, such as bridging his body while men put an anvil on his chest and started pounding on it. He also rode ostriches and swam among crocodiles, having smeared crocodile fat over his body first so that the reptiles would think he was their relative. Even if Vopiscus' picture of Firmus is fanciful, as it surely is, the general impression of a powerful, successful, aggressive, highly competitive business man sounds genuine.[10]

He occupied Alexandria and prepared for Aurelian's coming. If we are to believe Vopiscus, he stopped the precious shipments of grain to Rome, the shipments that the Roman populace in large degree depended on. But possibly even his charisma could not counter the news that Palmyra had fallen. Many of his potential followers perhaps decided to wait a little while before declaring themselves. When Aurelian arrived at Alexandria he found his histrionic enemy, with an army of adherents that probably was not large, confined to the Bruchium, the central part of the city, with the great harbor to the north and walls on the other three sides.

Aurelian's campaign did not last long. Firmus, realizing that winning out against this emperor was impossible, killed himself. The conqueror appointed his general Probus, the man who had liberated Egypt from Palmyrene control a few months before, as prefect of Egypt.

His wars in his Eastern dominions were now complete. Once again the empire stretched unbroken from the Strait of Gibraltar to the Euphrates. After a job well done, he could turn back to Europe and finish the job there.

Notes to Chapter 15

1. See Downey, **History of Antioch**, p. 265.

2. Zosimus, **Historia Nova**, translated by James J. Buchanan and Harold T. Davis (San Antonio, Texas, 1967), p. 35.

3. For the makeup of Zenobia's army see Harold Mattingly in **Cambridge Ancient History**, XII, 303, and Grace Harriet Macurdy, **Vassal-Queens and Some Contemporary Women in the Roman Empire** (Baltimore, 1937), pp. 119-20.

4. I have followed the interpretation of the ancient historians given by Downey in his **History of Antioch**, pp. 266-67, and in "Aurelian's Victory over Zenobia at Immae, A.D. 272," **TAPA**, LXXXI (1950), 57-68.

5. For a view of Palmyra as a center for this kind of exchange see Kazimierz Michalowski and Andrzej Dziewanowski, **Palmyra** (New York, 1970), pp. 6-7.

6. See **ibid.**, pp. 11, 14-15.

7. See Rostovtzeff, **Caravan Cities**, pp. 140-41.

8. On Palmyrene religion see, in addition to Rostovtzeff, Jean Starcky, **Palmyre** (Paris, 1952), pp. 85-106. For an earlier treatment, see James Germain Février, **La Religion des Palmyréniens** (Paris, 1931). Among the most remarkable photographs of the temples and other antiquities of this often-photographed site are those in Albert Champdor, **Les Ruines de Palmyre**, 3rd edition (Paris, 1953).

9. See Michalowski and Dziewanowski, **Palmyra**, pp. 7-8, 20, 22.

10. Syme, however, doubts the whole portrait. See **Ammianus and the Augustan History**, pp. 29-30, 55, 83, 189, and **Emperors and Biography**, pp. 268-69. Syme points out that the **Augustan History** is the only document naming Firmus in connection with the troubles in Egypt.

16 The Hermit

About the time Aurelian became emperor, a young Egyptian named Antony retired from the life of the world. The emperor no doubt never heard of him, and if Antony heard anything about the emperor he probably dismissed it as Thoreau would later dismiss the kind of information headlined in newspapers. Aurelian's problems—war, money, foreign policy, domestic policy—were the problems of the physical environment, the toils of material involvement. Antony wanted to untie himself from these distractions, and in doing this he unintentionally made himself famous. There are people who have never heard of Aurelian but have heard of St. Antony.

Born about 251, the son of Christian parents, he passed his childhood and early adolescence during the reigns of Valerian and Gallienus. His village on the Middle Nile was perhaps sixty miles south of modern Cairo. Whichever town it was—and we are not sure—it lay among palms and fertile fields irrigated by canals from the Nile; and beyond the line of green stretched the stark, buff, sunbeaten desert. During Antony's boyhood the village must have felt the taxation in coin and kind, the starving poverty, and the blank despair that filled provincial Egypt.

Antony's parents, who owned over two hundred acres of the fertile fields, probably ranked among the most prosperous villagers, whatever that was worth. But they did not send their son to school, apparently because he felt shy about mixing with the other children. As a result he learned no Greek, which was of course the language of the educated in Egypt. He knew only his own native Egyptian or Coptic, and to all appearances he could not read or write at all. Even the inscriptions on the coins struck for Egyptian use would have meant nothing to him.

The village had a Christian community and a church of sorts—most likely a room in somebody's home where members of the suspect faith gathered once a week for prayer, perhaps the Eucharist, and readings from the Bible. They may have suffered under Valerian's persecution in the late 250s, but if so their sufferings were too obscure to be recorded. In Gallienus' sole reign, during much of Antony's boyhood and adolescence, they could practice their religion without fear. The Bible readings were probably done by a priest since Egyptian towns in the third century, unlike towns in Syria and Asia Minor, usually did not have bishops of their own.[1] Antony listened attentively to the readings and did what literate people sometimes lose the ability to do through disuse: he memorized. His Biblical knowledge was therefore considerable, although he probably never encountered a paragraph of theological disputation.

When he was between eighteen and twenty his parents died, leaving him a younger sister and the family property to take care of. This was about the time, late in the reign of Claudius or early in that of Aurelian, when Zenobia's general Zabdas took over in lower Egypt. But political changes may have had little effect on humble country folk and they could not have interested Antony. He had other things to think about. Walking to church one day about six months after his parents' death, he thought about the prosperous people in the fourth chapter of Acts who sold their houses and lands so that the Apostles could distribute the money among the poor. This is what St. Athanasius, who knew Antony later on, says in the biography that is our principal source for Antony's life. And when the young man got to church, according to Athanasius, a verse was read quoting Christ's injunction to an earnest young man: "Jesus said unto him, If thou wilt be perfect, go and sell that thou hast, and give to the poor, and thou shalt have treasure in heaven: and come and follow me" (Matthew 19:21).

Antony sold his acres and his other material possessions and gave most of the proceeds to the poor. The little that he retained was for the maintenance of his sister.

But that was not all. In church again, he listened to another verse with particular relevance to himself: "Take therefore no thought for the morrow: for the morrow shall take thought for the things of itself. Sufficient unto the day is the evil thereof" (Matthew 6:34). He gave away what he had saved for his sister and put her in a house for virgins.

Now there was nothing between Antony and the life of a hermit. Retirement into solitude was already being practiced by Egyptian Christians. He knew an old man in a neighboring village who had been a hermit since youth, and he followed this man's example. It was about the year 270 — perhaps a little later, when Aurelian, having conquered the German barbarians, was fighting Zenobia and struggling to make the Roman world a better place than he found it.

Asceticism—the Greek **askesis**—implied training or discipline. Antony had gone into training for as perfect a life as possible. In this premonastic age of Christianity, ascetics simply lived apart in some bare place, voluntarily divorced from whatever comforts, pleasures, social obligations, business affairs, loves and hatreds their own local world might set in front of them to blot out the spiritual. Antony took up residence near his village, not among men and women but not quite out in the howling desert. He performed manual labor, bought bread with part of his earnings and gave the rest of the money to those who needed it. Other hermits were scattered over the area, and sometimes this young neophyte visited them to learn how they excelled him, how he could be better. Some perhaps were kinder than he, or endured more discomfort, or prayed more steadily, or loved Christ more fervently.

Most of the time he was by himself, reciting the Biblical verses he had memorized, thinking about holiness, praying, devoting his mind passionately to his Savior. People called him the Friend of God. He did not cater to his body. Bread was all he ate, and all he drank was water. He wore the skin of an animal, with the hair on the inside. Like another Egyptian, Plotinus, he never bathed. To wash the body was to coddle it, to commit oneself to the discriminations of the world—and to suggest the foulness of the public baths, where lustful pagans went to play.

Doctrinal points—the arguments and principles that meant so much to Cyprian and other earnest ecclesiastics—did not command his attention. These learned aspects of Christianity were not essential to salvation. The Scriptures—the verses that Antony had memorized—were all that a man had to have. Antony's Christianity was non-intellectual, the faith of the folk. Much later in his life, when some Greek philosophers twitted him for his illiteracy, he asked them which came first, mind or learning; and when they said mind, he replied that therefore a man with a good mind did not need learning. He approached religion intensely, supra-rationally, perhaps even mystically. This approach was just as characteristic of his own time as the highly educated attitude of a Cyprian or a Novatian. In an age that was abandoning the reasonable classical religions for the mystery cults of the East, an age when people sought solace in the ecstatic and when even intellectuals such as Plotinus left reason behind, Antony represents a very significant kind of Christian.

Alone with his prayers and his visions, he was far from lonely. He rarely had a human visitor, but according to Athanasius, the devil paid him a great deal of attention. Satan came in person, offering various specious arguments for abandoning asceticism, the same sort of distractions that Plotinus counseled his disciples to avoid. Athanasius says that Satan mentioned Antony's "property, the care of his sister, the attachments of kindred, the love of money, the love of fame, the myriad pleasures of eating, and all the other amenities of life. Finally he represented to him the austerity and all the toil that go with virtue, suggesting that the body is weak and time is long."[2]

When that did not work, the devil fired Antony's mind with obscene thoughts and lascivious pictures. The man was no more than twenty and, in spite of his piety, not entirely cold to desire. Satan, like inferior devils, could assume various forms. He "even dared to masquerade as a woman by night...." Antony, in response, "filled his thoughts with Christ and reflected upon the nobility of the soul that comes from Him, and its spirituality, and thus quenched the glowing coal of temptation."[3]

After the hermit had done that, the devil resorted to other visions. He came to Antony in his own identity as the Black One and talked conversationally about fornication, calling himself a lover of it. This served no purpose. Antony only burrowed more deeply into his asceticism. He drank water and ate his bread and salt once a day if that—after sunset. Sometimes he ate once every two days, sometimes he went three or four days without eating. The world changed outside—Egypt returned to Roman control and Aurelian conquered Zenobia—but Antony, unconcerned, kept on battling the devil.

For ordinary people in this age, religious notions were often a blend of blind credulity and dark superstition. In Egypt especially, magic permeated men's lives.[4] There were formulas to compel demons to perform certain acts, amulets to ward off sickness from oneself or bring it on an enemy, love potions for the unrequited, and curse tablets with inscriptions to a wide variety of spirits willing to work ill. Charlatans made money practicing magic in the streets, and boys worked as mediums. With the decline in rationalism in the third century throughout the Roman world, belief in demons intensified. Even in earlier centuries people had held that each individual has his own guardian spirit, his personal demon, not evil but protective. Now the demons multiplied beyond all bounds, until the world was thick with them. Some were beneficent, but malign ones lurked everywhere—behind rocks, in the marketplace, above one's bed. An Egyptian boy learned something about demonology if he learned no other science.

Christians were as impressed by demon lore as anybody else. Many Christians conceived of every human being as attended by both a good spirit and a bad one. They said that demons infested the air and swarmed over the earth. Some of the evil spirits played the parts of pagan gods; some hid under the statues in temples, entered the minds of seers, determined the utterances of oracles, or governed the flights of birds by which augurs interpreted the future.[5] Christ had come to earth to fight these servants of Satan: "He preached in their synagogues throughout all Galilee, and cast out the devils" (Mark 1:39).

Sometimes a malignant spirit would utterly possess a Christian, inhabiting his body and controlling his soul. The spirit would make him sick—give him aches, cripple him, convulse him—or pollute his soul, rendering him wretched, willful, lecherous, and hateful if not crazy, so that he screamed and tore his hair and scratched his friends. Then an exorcist would have to be called on to drive the demon out. He might be an unprincipled practitioner of magic greedy for money but aware of the common Christian remedies for devils, such as making the sign of the cross or invoking the name of Christ. He might be a functionary attached to some large church for the express purpose of dealing with demons.[6] Cyprian, who never doubted the prevalence of demons, described their exit from their hosts when exorcised in a Christian manner:

> You may see them at our voice, and by the operation of the hidden majesty, smitten with stripes, burnt with fire, stretched out with the increase of a growing punishment, howling, groaning, entreating, confessing whence they came and when they depart, even in the hearing of those very persons who worship them, and either springing forth at once or vanishing gradually, even as the faith of the sufferer comes in aid, or the grace of the healer effects.[7]

In his retirement the devil's demons, like the devil, did not leave Antony alone. Much later, when he was already famous among Christians, he gave a talk to his followers in his native Coptic. The address, quoted lengthily by Athanasius, told among other things about his experiences with demons. These trials apparently lasted over many years if not throughout his life. He must have fought demons from the early years of his asceticism on. They came, he said, as beasts, as soldiers, as reptiles, as women, as pious men. They whipped him as he lay on the ground; they burst through the walls of his bare room and attacked him in the shapes of leopards, bulls, and scorpions.

About the year 285 he moved to an empty tomb in a desolate region and lived for a time in the darkness behind its locked door; the demons beleaguered him there. He moved to an abandoned Roman fort on a mountain in the desert. They clustered around him, talking, laughing, hissing, chanting psalms, quoting Scripture, capering, rattling, hammering, grimacing, pretending to prophesy, and wailing when he paid no attention. He resisted them by reciting the Psalms. He got rid of one tall demon by blowing at him while calling on Christ's name. He got rid of another by rising to pray, and the devil took the form of smoke as it vanished through the door.

There is of course no way to tell how much of this picture is Antony and how much is his biographer Athanasius. Even supposing that Athanasius added occasional details, however, the hermit's struggles with demons are the most vivid aspect of his long life of solitude. But these demons were, at any rate, external. Although they might maul him unmercifully, they shrank away when he used Christianity against them. They did not get inside him and possess him, as they did with the sufferers from sickness and the mad people who had to rely on exorcists. He triumphed every time.

Long after Aurelian's reign Antony would develop his hermeticism into a way of life for others. About the year 305 he came down from his fort on the mountain, where a man had brought him bread twice a year for the past twenty years and where his unflinching asceticism had made him notorious. Devout visitors had picked their way to the fort from time to time to talk with so admirable a man, and he had shut them out. But now, in the hills in the part of Egypt called the Fayoum, he established a cluster of cells for men who wished to live as he did. Later he established a second cluster of cells not far from the Nile. He is therefore credited with having founded monasticism. Occasionally he looked in on his anchorites to advise them and help them spiritually, but most of the time he still kept alone, leaving the monks to take care of themselves.

Although Antony may have originated monasticism as an institution, he did not originate monasteries. The monks lived as hermits, their cells being widely apart. They prayed and recited psalms in private, and they did not follow a strict set of rules for communal life. Antony was less their supervisor than their inspiration, the model after whom they hoped to form themselves. His intense presence lay behind the monastic movement. That presence would continue into the Middle Ages as a vital symbol of self-abnegation, oneness of purpose, and unadulterated devotion.

For greater solitude he moved farther south to an even less accessible mountain in broad desert country about twenty miles west of the Red Sea. But people found him anyway—his monks, other pious persons, the sick, and the demon-ridden—so that he did receive visitors at intervals. He made two brief returns to the world of affairs, both for religious reasons. In 311, during the fiercest of all persecutions of the Christians, he traveled to Alexandria to tend those in prison, encourage them at their trials, and watch them become martyrs. And at some unknown date, perhaps in the middle or later 330s, he journeyed to Alexandria again to talk against the Arian heresy that was troubling Christianity then—the only time he ever engaged in religious controversy.

When he grew very old he had two monks living with him on the mountain. He kept his eyesight and all his teeth to the end of his long life. In so far as he could, he maintained the old ascetic regime. He still ate scarcely anything and did not bathe. When he knew that he was going to die he instructed his two attendants to bury his body in some secret place. Egyptian Christians liked to preserve the bodies of their eminent dead by mummifying them, but Antony disapproved of the practice, perhaps because it overemphasized the physical. He was afraid that unless his burial place was secret, someone would dig him up and keep him above the ground to be venerated.

He also disposed of his material possessions. One sheepskin and the cloak that he spread on the ground at night went to Athanasius. His other sheepskin went to a Bishop Serapion of whom he thought highly. His two attendants could have his hair shirt.

Early in 357 he died quietly at the approximate age of one hundred and five.

Notes to Chapter 16

1. See Adolf von Harnack, **The Mission and Expansion of Christianity in the First Three Centuries**, translated and edited by James Moffatt, 2nd ed. (London, 1908), II, 474.

2. St. Athanasius, **The Life of Saint Antony**, translated and annotated by Robert T. Meyer (Westminster, Maryland, 1950), p. 22.

3. **Ibid.**, p. 23.

4. See MacMullen, **Enemies of the Roman Order**, p. 103, and Grant, **Climax**, p. 191.

5. See Cyprian, Treatise VI, **On the Vanity of Idols**, in **Writings**, I, 447.

6. See von Harnack, **Mission and Expansion**, I, 132.

7. **Writings**, I, 447-48. From Treatise VI.

Valerian (253-260), laureate. Obverse of a sestertius. 29 mm.

17 Aurelian Triumphant

After the recovery of Egypt and the defeat of Palmyra, only one area remained to be reunited with the empire. This was of course the declining Roman Empire of the Gauls. Since it was becoming consistently weaker, Aurelian could afford to let it wait.

In 270 the control of Gaul, which had been shifting dizzily from one would-be emperor to another since the death of Postumus a year or two before, was seized by a man called Tetricus. His immediate predecessors, a father and son both named Victorinus, had evidently been murdered by soldiers at Cologne.[1] According to Pollio the elder Victorinus' mother, Victoria, persuaded Tetricus to make himself Gallic emperor just as she had been instrumental in elevating her son and grandson before him. Almost nothing is known about this emperor-making woman except that she had taken the title Mother of the Camp, often assumed by legitimate empresses at Rome. She did not live to see the end of Tetricus' reign.

He was of senatorial rank and already knew something about ruling, having governed the province of Aquitania. But although his reign lasted for several years it was not a successful one. The Germanic tribes were making expeditions into Gaul again for plunder, some along the eastern borders and others via sea raids along the coasts. The population had little respect for an emperor who could not protect them against the barbarians. The army, demoralized by the flickering loyalties of recent years, was inclined to mutiny, and for a while part of it apparently was seduced into insurrection by the governor of one of the provinces. No doubt people contrasted Aurelian's victories with their own emperor's placid inactivity. The feeling was growing that it might be a good idea for Gaul to rejoin the rest of the Roman Empire. Tetricus knew that his dominion was slipping away from him.

Victorinus (Gallic Empire, 268-270), radiate. Obverse of an antoninianus struck in Gaul. 16 mm.

Tetricus (Gallic Empire, 270-273), radiate. Obverse of an antoninianus struck in Gaul. 17 mm.

Aurelian's activities after the sacking of Palmyra are not clear, but he does not seem to have set out for Gaul as soon as he got back to Europe. Perhaps he was waiting to see how the Gallic situation developed on its own. According to a story handed down by the early fifth century churchman Orosius, Tetricus wrote secretly to Aurelian, asking to be delivered from his difficulties and even quoting a line from Book VI of the **Aeneid:** "Invincible one, snatch me out of these evils." Aurelian marched to Gaul, probably early in 274.[2]

Tetricus drew up his legions against him near Châlons. But when his men and Aurelian's men had started to slaughter each other he abandoned his troops and gave himself up to Aurelian. His soldiers fought on until they were cut down. The Roman Empire of the Gauls was finished.

In return for his treachery Tetricus received his life. Not only that; he also gained the patronage of Aurelian, who later appointed him the **corrector** or governor of Lucania in southern Italy, as Vopiscus says in his biography of Aurelian for the **Augustan History**, or possibly **corrector** of all Italy, as Pollio says in his biography of Tetricus for the **Augustan History**.

The Roman Empire, which had been dismembered by Postumus' rebellion under Valerian about 258, was now whole again. Aurelian had achieved something that had seemed impossible only a few years before, and he could march back to Rome in glory. The senate awarded him the title "Restorer of the World," which appeared on his money. His coins also called him "Restorer of the Age," "Restorer of Mankind," "Peacemaker of the World," and with reference solely to his Palmyrene victory, "Restorer of the East" and "Peacemaker of the East." The magniloquence that had sounded pitiful when applied to less successful emperors was only his due. Within the memory of living Romans, no man had accomplished so much.

When Aurelian arrived at Rome in the role of the hero come back to his capital, he staged a triumph suited to the occasion, the greatest show that the city had seen in many years. It lasted several days and included chariot races in the Circus Maximus, theatrical productions, and a variety of games to please the populace, such as gladiatorial combats, the pursuit and killing of wild beasts by professional huntsmen in a forest improvised on the arena, and even a battle between warships in the flooded Colosseum. But the first day of the triumph consisted of a long, elaborate procession that all of Rome turned out to watch. The Secular Games of Philip the Arab in 248 had been highly publicized but, in view of the sorry state of the empire, hardly convincing. Aurelian's triumph in 274 was a very real thing, an event to believe in and be proud of.

The crowds saw four splendid chariots, three of which were symbols of the majesty of empire. One was a gift to Aurelian from the Persian King of Kings. Traditionally a triumphal procession displayed the spoils of conquest before the populace: two of the other chariots came from

Palmyra. One, of gold and silver glittering with precious stones, had belonged to Odenath. The other, ornate and expensive, had belonged to Zenobia herself. According to Vopiscus she had ordered it made so that she could visit Rome in it some day.

The emperor did not ride in any of these gorgeous constructions. His own chariot had belonged to the Gothic king whom he defeated three years before in the Danube region on the march to Palmyra. Instead of the usual four horses, four stags pulled this barbaric war carriage. In it Aurelian rode past the excited throngs and up to the temple of Jupiter the Best and Greatest, center of the state religion, at the summit of the Capitoline Hill.

Behind him came the long procession—tigers, elephants, elks, giraffes, animals from Libya and Palestine, all with their keepers, and sixteen hundred gladiators in pairs, who would soon be trying to kill each other in the games. Also, the representatives of strange nations from beyond the borders, here to acknowledge the glory of Rome, dressed according to their own tastes, and carrying gifts for the emperor—Arabs from the southwest corner of Arabia where the power of Palmyra had never stretched, Blemmyes from Nubia, Axumites from Ethiopia, Hiberians from south of the Caucasus, Saracens and Bactrians, Persians and Indians. A placard was carried in front of each nation explaining who these fabulous peoples were.

There followed captive Germans and Asiatic barbarians wrapped in the furs of their homelands, with their hands tied behind their backs. Again, placards identified them for the crowd—Goths, Franks, Vandals, the Sarmatians and Roxolani and Alans whose home had been the Russian steppes, the Juthungi and Alemanni whom Aurelian had beaten when they broke into northern Italy and threatened Rome. With these warriors in skins marched Egyptians, since Egypt had rebelled against the empire, and eminent men from Palmyra whom Aurelian had taken prisoner in the sacking of the city. There were also ten women advertised as Amazons. They had been captured with the Gothic prisoners and probably were Gothic wives who had been fighting along with their men.

Tetricus had to walk in the procession too, as well as the son whom he had made his associate in his moribund empire. Tetricus wore a red cloak over a yellow tunic and the tight trousers, gathered in at the ankles, that were favored by the Gauls and not unpopular at Rome. It was scarcely a dignified situation for a man who had recently been an emperor, but it was better than death. Some of the senators felt sorry and outraged. Tetricus was a Roman of senatorial rank; making him shuffle along with the other captives like some brutish barbarian was, according to these aristocrats, an insult to the senatorial class. The upstart who had succeeded in the imperial office, they said, was trying to humble the leaders of the state through Tetricus.

This may or may not have been Aurelian's wish; it was probably not. Tetricus was a defeated enemy and must march in the triumph. Aurelian's subsequent appointment of Tetricus to the office of **corrector** may have been an attempt to heal the wounded sensibilities of the senators.

The focal point of the whole procession, the person whom the Romans had come particularly to look at, was of course Zenobia. Whatever humiliations she had undergone in the past year or so fell away before the supreme humiliation of walking, chained, in Aurelian's triumph, with the curious Roman crowds gawking and jeering in vulgar delight. Those responsible for the procession had made sure that the mob would not be disappointed by this part of the display. The chains on her hands and feet were gold, and the gold chain around her neck was so heavy that a Persian fool had to follow along behind carrying it. The cumbrous jewels of Palmyra had been loaded on her until she could hardly stand. Pollio, expanding on Vopiscus' picture of her in the procession, says that "she was adorned with gems so huge that she laboured under the weight of her ornaments; for it is said that this woman, courageous though she was, halted very frequently, saying that she could not endure the load of her gems."[3]

Shortly after the triumph, Aurelian dedicated the Temple of the Sun God, the most magnificent structure to be built at Rome since the completion of the so-called Baths of Caracalla in the Reign of Severus Alexander (222-235). Aurelian must have ordered the erection of this temple earlier in his reign. Now gold and jewels from Palmyra could be lavished on its decoration. Statues of the Sun as both the Roman god Sol and the Eastern god Belus (Baal) stood inside. Aurelian established the celebration of the Sun's birthday on December 25th, close to the winter solstice, when daylight begins lengthening again and the earth looks toward its flowering time. He also created a new priestly college, whose members came from the senatorial class, to perform the functions sacred to the Sun. It was to rank with the ancient priestly colleges dedicated to carrying on the rituals of the state religion. By means of it, the Sun cult became an official part of the national religion of Rome.

Aurelian had no notion of supplanting the gods of the state with his own patron deity. His intention, it would seem, was to supplement and revitalize the state religion by means of the cult of the Sun, victor over darkness and evil, restorer of life through light and warmth. The deterioration of the official Roman religion, even of emperor worship, was obvious. So was the dismembering effect of the multiplicity of deities inside the empire, with Jupiter, Isis, Cybele, the Christian God, and many others pulling in different directions. The Sun, whether as Roman Sol, Greek Helios, Mithra of the soldiers, or some Eastern Baal, was as universally adored a divinity as any; even at Palmyra he had his temple, as at Emesa and Baalbek (Heliopolis). The Sun might serve to bring the empire together through a common devotion just as Aurelian had reunited it politically through war.

Elagabalus, boy-emperor from Syria between 218 and 222, had tried to introduce the Emesan version of the Sun as the prime deity at Rome, but the attempt was childishly executed and extremely undiplomatic. Aurelian's establishment of the Sun as a national god was the act of an astute statesman; it gave the Sun a place. Sol would continue to receive official worship throughout the empire from then until Christianity became dominant. Even late in the reign of the Christian Constantine (307-337) bronze coins bore the image of the Unconquerable Sun, radiate, with cloak and globe.

A tendency to associate emperors with the Sun is noticeable in the radiate imperial portraits on **dupondii** in the late first and second centuries and on **antoniniani** in the third century, also in the inscription "**Oriens Augusti**," "the Rising of the Augustus," often placed on third century coins relating to victories in the East. The historian Petrus Patricius, who lived in the sixth century, says that Aurelian once informed some insurgent soldiers that his imperial office did not come from the army, it came from the god. The story is very suspect, however, and even if by chance it is true, it does not necessarily imply that Aurelian thought of himself as sharing in divinity. There is no real indication that he encouraged this idea in his empire except the inscription "Born Lord and God" on coins minted at Serdica, modern Sofia, and one inscription out of the various legends on the coins of his reign is weak evidence. So it is very improbable that in building the temple to the Sun, Aurelian was making an effort to identify himself with his god. The boy Elagabalus, apparently, had tried to do this earlier in the century and had failed. Aurelian had too much sense to repeat the attempt.

Alongside the conception of the emperor as a god, however, there grew up during the third century the notion that he was not yet a god himself but the delegate of the gods, their viceroy over affairs on earth, below divinity though above ordinary humanity. Aurelian's presumable statement to his soldiers may have meant just that. Many of his **antoniniani** showed him receiving the orb of worldly dominion from **Jupiter**. Reverses of his brass coins depicted him and his wife Severina standing with the radiate head of Sol between them, as if the Sun was blessing the vicegeral pair. With his strong sense of duty Aurelian may easily have believed himself to be the deputy of the gods and particularly of the Sun, chosen to execute the divine wishes for the empire. His temple to his patron, through whom he had won at Emesa and even at Palmyra, and the introduction of his patron into the official circle of Roman gods, may have been an expression of this belief.

Aurelian (left) receiving globe from Jupiter; each holds a sceptre. Reverse of an antoninianus. It is noteworthy that the emperor is about as tall as the god. 23 x 20 mm.

In the late second century the mad Commodus sometimes tried to identify himself with Hercules but sometimes claimed to be only the companion or comrade of Hercules. Like the idea that an emperor had been delegated by divinity to administer the affairs of the world, the conception of the emperor as the comrade of a specific god spread in the third century. It is possible that Aurelian, in his attention to the Sun, wanted to suggest such a relationship. Many of his subjects would certainly have been willing to believe that Aurelian was the elected comrade of the Sun. His friendship with his patron, they would have said, had made Aurelian the champion of good and right. It had allowed him to triumph over his enemies.

Notes to Chapter 17

1. See La Baume, **Colonia Agrippinensis**, p. 17.
2. For the date, see Mattingly in **Cambridge Ancient History**, XII, 306.
3. **Scriptores Historiae Augustae**, III, 141. **Tyranni Triginta** XXX. 24-25.

Severina (left) and Aurelian clasping hands; radiate head of Sol between. Reverse of a dupondius. 23 mm.

18 Reform, Benevolence and Death

The time was coming when the city of Rome would be little more than a provincial capital. The eastern half of the empire would be ruled from Constantinople, the western half from Milan or Ravenna. But even in the fifth century, when barbarians ransacked her, Rome could still dominate the minds of men by her former greatness and the physical splendor that remained to her. Here it had all begun. She was a symbol of glory long after she had outlived her political authority. And if she was still so compelling in the fifth century, she was demanding in the late third. The fact that Aurelian had spent little time in his capital is significant of the decline in the city's actual power. But after his wars were over and he took up temporary residence in Rome, Aurelian turned his attention to benefiting these favored citizens, the crowds of the capital.

Over 100,000 of these citizens[1] held **tesserae** or base metal tickets entitling them to free distribution of valued commodities such as grain. Aurelian seems to have changed the grain dole, which occurred once a month and had been going on since 58 B.C., into a daily distribution of two pounds of bread per citizen. Except for these free loaves, the price of bread at Rome was controlled by the state. By leveling a special tax in kind on Egyptian grain Aurelian added an ounce, at no extra cost to the purchaser, to every loaf sold in the city.[2] He also provided free distributions of pork, oil, and salt, and according to Vopiscus he reserved for Rome the tax in kind on Egyptian hemp, paper, linen, and glass.

Vopiscus mentions three distributions of coins during his reign and the gift of long-sleeved white tunics for the citizens, as well as handkerchiefs to wave in approval. These instances of the emperor's generosity toward his capital are somewhat doubtful, except that he must have made at least one distribution of coins. He also apparently dredged the Tiber to expedite navigation, rebuilt its banks, and laid plans for erecting a bath on the western side.

Vopiscus claims that he contemplated doling out free wine. This is very questionable, but Vopiscus may be right in saying that he intended to buy up lands that had gone out of cultivation in the part of Italy north of Rome —in Etruria or Tuscany—and settle on them the families of war captives. These involuntary settlers were to plant grape vines on the Tuscan hills, so that gradually the region would be wine-producing as in the past.

In spite of the monumental implications of Aurelian's triumph, the amount that would have to be done before the empire had really recuperated was gigantic. Aurelian's military victories had shown that recovery was possible, but the emperor must have seen as vividly as anyone that in other fields this recovery would have to be slower and much less dramatic.

Economic recuperation was still a crying need. It is not at all certain how much good soil throughout the empire had lapsed into weedy desolation like the vinelands of Tuscany, but agriculture in some areas must have declined considerably.[3] Trade had to be stimulated, especially between parts of the empire where revolts or barbarian inroads had broken off the normal processes of moneymaking. In many parts of the Roman world the great estates were retreating within themselves, becoming self-sufficient, raising their own foodstuffs, making their own bricks and tools and clothes, keeping their own standing army of peasants that could be armed in a moment against barbarians or other invaders. In these areas the broad and lively trade of the first and second centuries was being succeeded by a closed house economy that anticipated the manorialism of the Middle Ages.

The financial burdens on the decurions or members of the councils in the provincial cities had grown no lighter; liturgies still squeezed these men to desperation. The armies of Zenobia, marching through Syria and Asia Minor, had added to the general havoc in the East; and Aurelian's own troops, quartered on the populace and confiscating what they needed, had increased the poverty of their fellow citizens. (Another great privilege of the city of Rome was that large armies were not imposed on her.) Meanwhile inflation swept on unchecked. The coinage was as poor as before; the crude copper **antoniniani** that had been struck by Tetricus in the last days of the Roman Empire of the Gauls were matched by miserable money from Aurelian's own mints.

As, perhaps, an initial step in remedying the economic situation, Aurelian tried to do something about the coinage. The new **antoniniani** or whatever they were called that started appearing in 274 looked better than the old ones. They were broader and weighed a little more, their designs tended to be more carefully executed, and the silver wash that covered them was apparently applied in an improved manner so that it did not wear away as soon. But the coins were still basically copper, only 4 or 5 percent silver.[4] Aurelian called in the old **antoniniani** but perhaps at an unfavorable rate in relation to the new ones; many people seem to have buried these old coins rather than turning them in to the government, and large hoards of them are still being unearthed.[5]

There is no certainty among scholars as to the value that Aurelian attached to his new pieces. He put on some of them "XXI" or "XX.I" as a sign of value — on those struck for a Greek-speaking population, "KA." He also minted some smaller coins that bore the legend "VSV." The inscriptions on the larger coins have been taken to mean "Twenty to one," but twenty of what to one of what remains a matter for conjecture. "VSV" is sometimes interpreted as an abbreviation for "VSVALIS" (**usualis** or usual") — in other words the "usual" unit of value.[6]

Since we do not know what Aurelian's new coins were worth we cannot very well estimate how successful his monetary reform was. Presumably the improved appearance of the new pieces gave people a little more confidence in Roman money and in the government behind it. But if citizens sometimes stashed away hoards of their old **antoniniani** rather than turning them in for new, they must have thought the new coins were overvalued by the government. Real confidence could not be restored until coins of real silver and gold were once more in general circulation. Aurelian's reform may even have worsened the inflation.[7] But at least it did give the empire a currency with a fixed standard of value, whatever that standard may have been, in place of the fluctuating values that had contributed to the confusion of the last few years. And it helped prepare for the more drastic monetary reforms that would occur under Diocletian (284-305) and Constantine (307-337). The tendency was toward amelioration even if the immediate results were far from spectacular.

We know very little about Aurelian's other policies. Vopiscus says that he was particularly severe on informers, dishonest provincial officials, and those who brought false charges, but Vopiscus, as usual, does not inspire confidence. Certainly the military agents throughout the empire, the dreaded secret police, were as ruthless in his reign as in previous reigns toward people who neglected to pay their taxes, avoided making compulsory contributions of food, or tried to escape compulsory labor. A time had not yet come when officialdom could pretend to leniency or understanding.

But Aurelian at least performed some grand gestures of benevolence. He forgave those who had committed crimes against the state and he canceled some debts owed to the state by burning the records in the Forum, as the emperor Hadrian had done before him. It was possibly because of the surrender of Tetricus but more probably because of the Palmyrene war that Aurelian could convert into smoke the records of financial obligations to the government. This was the first profitable war that Rome had fought in a long time. The wealth of Palmyra helped to replenish the national coffers.

Aurelian's measures regarding clothes may be the fabrications of Vopiscus although at least some of them ring true to his character. Vopiscus says, for example, that he forbade men to wear purple boots, ivy colored boots, or even boots of white or wax color. He permitted these delicate fashions for women, however, and also let matrons wear purple clothes. As for his personal preferences, he disliked residing in his palace at Rome but enjoyed the villas and extensive gardens on the bank of the Tiber, near where Hadrian's tomb was built, and on the north side of the Quirinal Hill. He added a portico 1,000 feet long to the buildings on the Quirinal and used to ride his horse there every day.

According to Vopiscus he planned to reinstitute the Senate of Matrons, a group of noble ladies that had existed in republican times to legislate on matters of importance to women. The boy emperor Elagabalus seems to have revived it briefly during his reign (218-222). Whether Aurelian actually envisioned a ladies' senate is highly questionable. Almost as doubtful is the claim of the ecclesiastical historian Eusebius that the emperor contemplated a new persecution of the Christians. But it is not impossible that he did. Attaching so much importance to the reunification of the empire, first by war and then by worship of the Sun, he may have felt that the time had come to make the Christians conform.

Meanwhile his wars were not over. Before the end of 274 or early in 275 he had to return to Gaul and attend to more troubles from barbarians. Very little is known about this campaign, if it amounted to one. But he had greater military designs on hand. He had decided to make war on the Persians.

Shapur, the king of kings who had bothered the Roman Empire so long and so seriously, was dead. The son to whom he had left the throne was also dead, and another son reigned. There was bound to be some internal confusion in Persia as a result of these shifts in kingship, and the time looked propitious for a campaign there. A really successful war against Persia would add much glory to Aurelian's glorious name and much more gold to his chests. He assembled his army—not of great size, Vopiscus says—and set off in the summer of 275. He planned to march through Thrace, then eastward through Asia Minor as on the campaign against Zenobia, and down into Persia itself. But he did not even get all the way through Thrace. At the town of Caenophrurium, about fifty miles west of Byzantium, he was murdered.

The man responsible was called Mnestheus according to Vopiscus, but according to Zosimus and Zonaras his name was Eros, or Love. He was the emperor's private secretary or one of the officials of the court. He had been remiss at his duties, whatever they were. Probably he indulged in the peculation that Aurelian punished so severely in his staff. Aurelian had found him out and threatened him. To save himself he devised a plot based on his ability to counterfeit the emperor's handwriting.

Vopiscus says that he forged a list of names of men slated for death by Aurelian, including his own name among them for the sake of credibility. Zosimus' version is that he forged letters from Aurelian that would lead to the execution of some men who were guilty of offenses against the emperor and some who were not. The result was of course a cabal of desperate officials afraid of death. According to Zosimus, "Having watched the Emperor leave the city without enough of a bodyguard, they all charged him with swords unsheathed and killed him. Then he was buried on the very spot by his army, in magnificent style on account of the works and the dangers he had undergone in behalf of the commonwealth."[8] So much for the Restorer of the World. With no preamble, the empire was informed that the great Aurelian was dead. Here, it seemed, was an end of conquest. The glory was over.

Notes to Chapter 18

1. See Grant, **Climax**, p. 52.

2. See Parker, **History of the Roman World**, pp. 206-07. But Mattingly in **Cambridge Ancient History**, XII, 307-08, relates this extra ounce only to the free bread, which is an entirely possible interpretation of Vopiscus' unclear account.

3. The extent to which land went out of cultivation has perhaps been exaggerated. See, for example, Oertel's discussion of the matter in **Cambridge Ancient History**, XII, 260, 278.

4. The usual explanation for the small amount of silver in coins of the mid-third century is that the mines had been exhausted. But Rostovtzeff's view—that in this age of disruption the empire lacked not silver but workers to mine it—should be mentioned (**Social and Economic History**, I, 343).

5. See Harold Mattingly, **Roman Coins From the Earliest Times to the Fall of the Western Empire** (London, 1928), p. 192, and Grant, **Climax**, p. 47. But it should not be forgotten that the large finds still coming to light also result from (1) the hiding of silver because of barbarian invasions and (2) the enormous amount of coinage struck during this inflationary period. Aurelian's rate of exchange is, after all, unknown.

6. See Jones, **Later Roman Empire**, I, 26, suggesting that the larger new coin equaled 20 **sestertii** or 5 **denarii** and the smaller coin 2 **denarii**; Grant, **Climax**, p. 47, tentatively accepting that view; Parker, **History of the Roman World**, p. 206, suggesting that the larger coin equaled 20 **libellae** or 2 **sestertii** and the smaller 1 **sestertius**; Mattingly in **Cambridge**

Ancient History, XII, 307, tentatively agreeing with Parker, and his **Roman Coins**, pp. 129-30, expanding on that view; Percy H. Webb, **The Roman Imperial Coinage**, edited by Harold Mattingly and Edward A. Sydenham, V, Part I (London, 1927, reprinted 1972), pp. 8-14, maintaining that 20 of the larger coins equaled 1 **aureus**; David Sear, **Roman Coins and Their Values**, revised ed. (London, 1970), p. 270, mentioning that theory without endorsement; and Magie in **Scriptores Historiae Augustae**, III, 263, n. 2, mentioning without endorsement a 20-to-1 relationship between the larger new coin and the **aureus** or the silver **denarius** or the debased **denarius**.

7. Jones, **Later Roman Empire**, I, 27, says that it did. But see also Grant, **Climax**, p. 47.

8. Zosimus, **Historia Nova**, p. 38.

Tacitus (275-276), laureate. Obverse of a potin tetradrachm struck at Alexandria. 22 x 18 mm.

19 The Next Hero

Aurelian's murder did not result from either the disloyalty of the army or the discontent of the ruled. It was simply a personal matter, not indicative of national trends or feelings, not important for an assessment of Aurelian except that it might never have happened if he had been less severe toward subordinates. The army, devoted to a general who won battles, was appalled and hastened to disclaim any part in the assassination. The civilian population, accustomed to seeing emperors come and go rather quickly, probably felt little astonishment, but it genuinely lamented the passing of this illustrious prince as it had lamented the passing of few in recent times. The senate perhaps experienced relief and a sense of freedom but could show only sorrow.

The Illyrian soldiers, the ones surrounding Aurelian when he was murdered and buried, apparently declined to suggest a successor. Soldiers in the rest of the empire seem to have made no suggestions either, although those in the East could logically have put forth Aurelian's best general, Probus, who was in Egypt. Nobody knew better than the troops that in the present age the legions, rather than the senate, made emperors. But the army evidently asked the senate to name a new emperor anyway.

If this was actually the situation, it was one without precedent in the memory of living Romans. An army too shocked, almost too embarrassed, to choose a leader on its own. But the senate did not want to commit itself to designating Aurelian's successor either. It would be willing to approve someone hailed by the army, but it shrank from taking the first step. The shadow of the great Aurelian fell over his empire, freezing men in their tracks. An interregnum was proclaimed while senate and army negotiated. Each tried to foist off on the other the privilege of selecting a ruler for the Roman world. The negotiations probably lasted through September of 275.¹ Finally, reluctantly, the senators appear to have resumed their ancient initiative in the state. They named one of their own number, a certain Tacitus, as emperor.

It looked almost as if the senate had achieved some independence, and the selection of a non-military emperor might suggest an intentional cut at the army or at least at the memory of Aurelian. But as a senatorial champion Tacitus had little to recommend him. His time of vigor was already over; according to Zonaras, he was seventy-five. He lived so mildly, Vopiscus says, "that in a whole day he never drank a pint of wine, and frequently less than a half-pint. Even at a banquet there would be served a single cock, with the addition of a pig's jowl and some eggs." But he did have one enthusiasm: "In preference to all other greens he would indulge himself without stint in lettuce ...."²

He had no desire to be emperor, and when rumors circulated that he would be nominated he retired to his villa at Baiae on the Bay of Naples. But they came for him there and brought him back to Rome. The senate overwhelmed him with acclamations and there was nothing he could do. According to Vopiscus he protested that he was old and feeble, extremely unlike Aurelian, and sure to displease the army. Whether he actually made such a speech, the contrast to Aurelian was plain enough.

The army, however, did not object.³ Tacitus attempted to bring Aurelian's murderers to justice, which meant death, and although he did not succeed in catching all of them, his effort no doubt pleased the soldiers. In other ways too, once he was elected, he tried sincerely to rule as an emperor should. Like Aurelian, he carried out measures for the public welfare. If we can believe Vopiscus he transferred 280,000 **sestertii** from his private fortune to the nation, contributed from his cash on hand to the soldiers' pay, ordered his house to be torn down and a public bath to be put up in place of it, gave the city of Ostia one hundred columns of Numidian marble, donated his table silver for use in banquets at the temples, devoted the income from his Mauretanian estates to the maintenance of the Capitoline Hill where the Temple of Jupiter stood, and freed some of his slaves.

Tacitus even went to war against the barbarians, apparently Goths. When Aurelian was planning the Persian campaign he negotiated with Gothic tribes to help him. His death meant that they were left waiting, unoccupied and unrewarded, in southern Russia. Their idleness soon turned into another raid on Asia Minor. They assailed the eastern part of the peninsula from Pontus on south to Cilicia. Tacitus girded on his armor and marched forth like a younger man to protect the empire. So did his brother or half-brother Florian, whom he had appointed Praetorian Prefect. Somehow—we know no details—they were victorious, probably by the late spring of 276. But the old man who tried his best did not live to return to Rome.

Either he died of natural causes aggravated by exhaustion, or like Aurelian he was murdered.[4] He had appointed a relative named Maximin as governor of Syria. The man was flagrantly oppressive, and some of his soldiers formed a conspiracy and killed him. Then, according to the story, they killed Tacitus to prevent their own execution. There is no way of determining whether this story is essentially true or whether Tacitus succumbed to a fever. We are not even certain where he died, but it was most likely at Tyana. That was the city which Aurelian had besieged on the way to Antioch, telling his soldiers to kill all the dogs.

He had been a good emperor during his half-year of office—had tried honestly and earnestly to carry on in the monumental post suddenly thrust on him by the senate. But his reign had only delayed the uncertainty caused by Aurelian's death.

Tacitus' brother or half-brother Florian, Praetorian Prefect, did not share Tacitus' disinclination to rule. He had been engaging some barbarians in western Asia Minor at the Bosporus at the time of the emperor's death. Now he announced that he was emperor. That he sent to the senate ahead of time for its approval is doubtful. The senate at any rate gave its approval sooner or later, reduced to endorsing **faits accomplis** as usual rather than acting in free concert with the army. Florian's troops, near the end of a victorious campaign, must have been behind him, and he was accepted as emperor through the European provinces, in Asia Minor, and in North Africa west of Egypt.

But Egypt itself, Syria, Palestine, and Phoenicia held out for another man. The troops of the East had proclaimed Probus emperor—Aurelian's loyal officer, general of great capacity. At the head of his men Probus marched toward Asia Minor to encounter Florian. The empire was split in two once more.

Florian had encircled the barbarians at the Bosporus, but now he forgot about them and turned east to meet Probus. The Goths, many of whom would have been killed or enslaved otherwise, sailed unmolested back to the Crimea. Florian and his army progressed toward Tarsus. On the southeastern coast, close to where Asia Minor joins Syria, Tarsus was almost at the border of Florian's dominions. His army was larger than Probus', and its seasoned Illyrian-Pannonian soldiers were still, by and large, the best fighting men in the empire. But Probus had a reputation as an exceptional military leader, brave, stern, and intelligent. He was the man whom Aurelian had esteemed above all others, and Florian's troops must have felt this as keenly as Probus' own legions. Again the shade of the dead emperor fell across the living.

At Tarsus an intense heat wave added to the unhappiness of Florian's army. These man from the cool valleys, plains, and forests of the Balkans, working away at the strenuous duties of Roman military life, could hardly tolerate the fierce Cilician summer. If the heat had bothered them even under the redoubtable Aurelian in the Palmyrene war, it bothered them more under the uninspiring Florian. Some of them sickened. But Probus' men, being Easterners, were used to hot weather.

Probus laid siege to Tarsus and there were occasional minor engagements, but not a great deal was done. He preferred to wait a while and see how the matter developed. The development was the murder of Florian, apparently by men under his own command. Probus may have had a guiding hand in this, but his contribution is vague at best.[5] The empire was again united, and Probus ruled it all.

Notes to Chapter 19

1. The interregnum is sometimes assumed to have contained about six months. Coins were struck announcing it. But Syme plausibly maintains that it was of very short duration and did not involve much shuttling back and forth between senate and army. See **Emperors and Biography**, pp. 237-38, 241. Parker calculates that it lasted approximately a month; see **History of the Roman World**, pp. 212, 352-53, n. 2.

2. **Scriptores Historiae Augustae**, III, 315. Tacitus XI. 1-2.

3. Syme, following Zonaras, stresses that Tacitus was actually the army's choice more than the senate's. He even speculates that Tacitus had a military career behind him and belonged to the Danubian soldiery. See **Emperors and Biography**, pp. 237, 242-45, 247. Syme also (pp. 239-40) dismisses as fiction the personal details about Tacitus set forth in the **Augustan History** and (pp. 276-77) the statements about his domestic policy.

4. Mattingly prefers the story that he died from disease (**Cambridge Ancient History**, XII, 312), whereas the theory that he died from assassination is preferred by Magie (**Scriptores Historiae Augustae**, III, 319, notes 6 and 7), by Parker (**History of the Roman World**, p. 214), and by J.H.E. Crees, **The Reign of the Emperor Probus** (London, 1911), pp. 86-87.

5. The account in Zosimus, **Historia Nova** I.64 (Buchanan and Davis translation, p. 39) that some men serving under Probus deposed Florian and kept him under guard, that they later let him resume the purple, but that when Probus' intentions were made clear Florian was killed by his own followers, makes little sense.

20 Probus

Like his mentor Aurelian, Probus came from Sirmium, the great military and administrative center in Pannonia close to the Danube. Like his mentor too, he was of peasant stock, the sturdy native stock from which so many legionaries came. At the time he took the throne he must have been in his early forties. "He was," says the fourth century chronicler Eutropius, "a man of spirit, activity, and justice, equalling Aurelian in military glory, and surpassing him in affability of manners."[1] His affability did not mean that he had none of Aurelian's army severity, but he apparently lightened his strictness with a little graciousness and tact.

He entered the army young and must have risen in it fast, although the honors and exploits assigned to him by Vopiscus in the **Augustan History** are all suspect since Vopiscus' life of Probus is little but a long laudation. He became a tribune before he had a beard, according to this account, and was put by Valerian in command of the Legion Three Felix, which in fact never existed. "It would be a lengthy task," Vopiscus remarks, "were I to enumerate all the exploits of so great a man, which he performed as a commoner under Valerian, under Gallienus, under Aurelian, and under Claudius, how many times he scaled a wall, tore down a rampart, slew the enemy in a hand-to-hand fight, won the gifts of emperors, and by his valour restored the commonwealth to its ancient condition."[2]

Under Valerian, according to Vopiscus, he rescued a noble youth from captivity among the Quadi, a Germanic tribe. In Africa he defeated a man in single combat and, because the man had been brave, buried him magnificently. Whatever his actual achievements may have been on the battlefields of the empire in the mid-third century, Vopiscus' stories suggest that he had attained an almost legendary renown. His career parallels Aurelian's in being one of swift, uninterrupted rise in rank and honor through the military. At the time of Tacitus' death he had apparently been promised the consulship for the coming year.

Just as the capture of Valerian by the Persians in 260 had been the low point in Roman fortunes, the great defeat of the Heruls at Naissus in 268, whether it was one of the last efforts of Gallienus or should be credited to Claudius, marks the upswing in Roman fortunes that Gallienus had been working toward since he became emperor. In the short reign of Claudius (268-270) Rome had continued to revive, and in the five and a half years under Aurelian she had regained much of her self-confidence and even considerable glory in spite of the heavy problems still unsolved. The confusion after Aurelian's assassination had done little harm if any. Tacitus had managed a very creditable reign, and the break in the empire at his death was short and easily mended. Probus, so much like Aurelian in so many respects except savage austerity, resolved to carry on Aurelian's work. The empire needed more military victories, for example, and Probus felt that he could supply these.

In some ways he could improve on Aurelian. He was, for instance, careful to obtain the approval of the senate for his elevation to emperor, and when he reached Rome he treated the senate deferentially, with the tact that Aurelian usually lacked. He may even have tried to include the senate, which had lost so many of its rights and privileges over the years, as an active participant in civil government. Vopiscus says that he made the senate a court of appeal for provincial governors, gave it certain powers of appointment, and let it count his laws as its own enactments. Although these particulars may not be correct, they probably reflect some attempt on Probus' part to increase the senate's role in government. Perhaps he realized the importance of maintaining at least an appearance of continuity between the Roman constitution of the past and that of the present, and certainly he saw how desirable it was for the head of the state to show respect for the most reverend body in the state, ancient symbol of the greatness of Rome.

Shortly before or after his visit to the capital Probus committed an act that would gain him public esteem: he brought down retribution on those murderers of Aurelian whom Tacitus had not been able to execute as well as on the murderers of Tacitus. According to Zosimus he invited these men to a banquet and had them slaughtered there, a tactic which, if true, says little for his conception of Roman justice. He did not stay long at Rome; like Aurelian and other emperors of this period, he was to rule mainly from the provinces. He seems to have been at his home town of Sirmium in May of 277,[3] probably to attend to the affairs of the Danube frontier, and then he marched to Gaul.

The Germans were swarming into Gaul again, roving through this land that had recently come back into the empire and wreaking their usual havoc. There probably had been intermittent raids ever since the death

Probus (276-282), radiate, wearing imperial mantle and holding sceptre surmounted by eagle. Obverse of an antoninianus. 20 mm.

of Postumus, increasing during the weak reign of Tetricus and intensifying now. Paris shrank into the Ile de la Cité and other towns relied on their fortifications—to no purpose, if there is any truth behind Vopiscus' allegation that Probus had to retake sixty communes from the barbarians. The emperor chased the Alemanni east of the Upper Rhine to the Neckar while, farther north, his generals dealt with the Franks. Zosimus tells a marvelous tale in which Probus' army, during a famine, is relieved by a tremendous tempest that rained grain as well as water. The soldiers were afraid to touch the food at first, but later their hunger overcame their superstition. They baked the bread, satisfied their appetites, and won battles.

The **limes,** the fortified wall marking the edge of civilization, had been abandoned by the time Probus gained the purple. He did not attempt to rebuild this old line of no trespass, but possibly he established camps in German territory on the east side of the Rhine to discourage future inroads.[4] He apparently defeated some people called the Longiones, who may have been an Alemannic tribe or may just be a name invented by Zosimus, and captured their chief and his son. He defeated the Burgundians and Vandals, who had evidently gone to the aid of the Franks.

According to Vopiscus, bounty hunters came to him every day carrying barbarian heads, and the bounty was one **aureus** or gold coin per head. The terms of peace, Vopiscus says, included hostages, grain, sheep, and cattle, and Probus took many recruits to distribute as auxiliaries among his frontier forces. The Germans on the east side of the Rhine outnumbered the Roman soldiers on the west side, Zosimus affirms, but the Romans kept challenging them until some of the barbarians came over. Without their friends to help them, they were either captured or slaughtered. As the price of peace, the Germans promised to give back the Roman soldiers and possessions that they had seized. But they withheld a percentage of both. Probus attacked them again, killed more of them, captured one of their chiefs, captured many of their men, and sent the prisoners to Britain.

The accounts by Zosimus and Vopiscus have very little in common, and the accounts by other historians, such as Eutropius and Zonaras, add no details if they mention the Gallic campaign at all. It is clear, however, that Probus had rescued the Rhineland and Gaul from barbarian invasions.

The chronology of Probus' reign is almost as dubious as that of Gallienus' reign. One reason is that several things were going on at about the same time in different parts of the empire. But that does not explain the uncertainty surrounding the revolt of a man named Saturninus, which Zosimus places toward the beginning of Probus' reign—before the Gallic campaign, in fact—whereas Vopiscus puts it several years later. Since there are no other events to relate this rebellion to, it could conceivably have occurred at any time during the reign.[5]

Saturninus was a Moor according to Zosimus and Zonaras, a Gaul according to the less credible Vopiscus. Apparently he governed Syria. He seems to have decided that usurpation was possible, got recognized as emperor by the troops in Syria, but was murdered by them fairly soon because they had lost faith in his leadership and wanted to please Probus. That is Zosimus' version. Vopiscus tells an improbable story: that Aurelian had warned Saturninus not to visit Egypt because Egyptians are excitable and so was he; that he went to Alexandria during Probus' reign anyway and was hailed as emperor there by the excited Egyptians; that when he arrived back in Palestine he seized a purple robe from a statue of Venus and, wrapping it around himself, had his soldiers hail him; that Probus kept sending him kind letters offering forgiveness but his soldiers, distrusting Probus' sincerity, would not let him resign the office; and that Probus finally sent soldiers who stabbed him to death although the emperor had not expected them to go that far. Zosimus' account is certainly to be preferred.[6] In any case it sounds as if the rebellion was never a serious threat to Probus. Even if the Syrian legions were briefly in revolt, their disaffection did not spread. Probus did not have to go to Syria to stop it.

When affairs in Gaul were settled he marched eastwards, pausing in Raetia to deal with barbarians there either diplomatically or belligerently.[7] This was probably in 278. Farther east, in Illyricum and Thrace, perhaps in 279, he somehow made sure that the Sarmatians and the Goths would be peaceful for at least a while. These Goths may have come into Thrace from the Dacia that Aurelian had relinquished to barbarians.

In all these exploits Probus, like Aurelian, associated himself with the Sun. He carried on the religious policy of his predecessor as well as his militarism. The Sun frequently appeared on Probus' coinage, placing his foot on a conquered barbarian or even riding above the clouds in a four-horse chariot.

There were still unquiet cities and frontiers. At Athens the citizens were at work on an inner defense wall enclosing the Acropolis and a small area north of it. They built it of stones from the temples and other structures on the Agora that the Heruls had ruined in the catastrophic invasions of 267, and they could retreat behind it if barbarians swept into Athens again.[8] A body of adventurous Franks, anticipating the Northmen of a later age in their far-ranging exploits, sailed to Greece, to Syracuse in Sicily, and to North Africa, raiding all the way. The southern border of the empire in North Africa was perennially crossed by Moorish peoples who had to be fought off or conciliated. Probus did what he could. In Egypt, land was falling out of cultivation because poor management and the cupidity of the bureaucracy kept the irrigation system in disrepair. Probus had the soldiers drain swamps and clear the clogged mouths of rivers. Bearing down on Egyptian landowners with the oppressive power of the imperial government, he forced them to contribute workmen to rebuild the fallen dykes and clean the canals.[9]

The southern part of Asia Minor also needed Probus' help. In the

Taurus mountains lived some of the most successful of the robbers that infested the empire. The caves in the hills furnished hideouts to which the packs of thieves could return after raids. To many of these bandits, half-wild tribesmen of the highlands and the desert places, depredation was an ancient and even respectable mode of life, though obviously the government disapproved. Others had been forced into raiding their neighbors by the unsettled conditions of the past quarter-century or so. There was no suggestion of romance about these men; they were hard professionals earning a living. Probus, like former emperors, ignored through necessity the brigandage in most parts of the empire. But he either proceeded to southern Asia Minor to do something for the harried population there, or he directed some of his military commanders to march against the marauders.

Vopiscus mentions a bandit chief named Palfuerius, and Zosimus talks about one named Lydius. Although these were possibly the same man, more probably they were the two most troublesome robber barons in the region.[10] If we are to believe Vopiscus, the emperor went after Palfuerius' men in the Isaurian hills in an arduous campaign, rooting them out of their strongholds and killing Palfuerius himself.

Lydius, the other chief, was a leader of exceptional ability and boldness. On the approach of the Roman army he took over the old walled city of Cremna in the hills of Pisidia. The Roman soldiers laid siege. Lydius, evidently forcing the inhabitants to work along with his thieves, tore down buildings in Cremna and planted grain where they had stood, so that his own men and incidentally the citizens would not starve if the siege went on a long time. But meanwhile food was not plentiful, and he drove out the men and women who were too old to work. The Romans, realizing why Lydius had expelled these senior citizens, drove them back into Cremna. This time Lydius got rid of them by throwing them down the precipices.

As the siege continued, Lydius set his men and no doubt the able-bodied inhabitants to work on a tunnel. It extended under the wall of the town and under the Roman camp, emerging in the countryside. Here his men stole cattle, which they brought back through the tunnel to increase the food supply. But a woman informed the Roman soldiers about the tunnel and that source of food was suddenly cut off. Conditions were now desperate in the city, but the ruthless and resourceful Lydius knew how to cope with the situation:

> ... he little by little curtailed his associates' wine and measured out less than the customary ration of grain. Still ... the food was failing, and he was reduced to the necessity of destroying everyone in the town save for a few men who were both his intimate friends and seemed to suffice for keeping watch. He retained also some women,

Sol, carrying whip and globe, in four-horse chariot. Reverse of an antoninianus of Probus struck at Rome. 20 mm.

whom he bade to be shared by all for the necessary function of nature.[11]

But the strain was telling on everybody that still lived. One of Lydius' most valued men, an engineer who could put war machines together and was an almost infallible marksman with them, missed a Roman soldier whom Lydius had ordered him to hit. Lydius, in a rage, had the man stripped and severely whipped, and threatened to have him killed. This was unnecessarily harsh treatment unless, as Zosimus suggests, the marksman had missed on purpose. In any case Lydius had made a mistake by being so severe. The marksman escaped from the city and located some Roman soldiers. He told them about a small aperture in the wall through which Lydius habitually looked to see what the Romans were doing, and he claimed that he could nail his chief with an arrow when Lydius had his head at this hole. The Roman officer encouraged him to try. The marksman set up a siege engine that shot arrows and aimed it at the hole. When Lydius' head appeared he fired. This time he did not miss.

The remnant of Lydius' band, at a loss without their leader, gave up, and banditry languished in Pisidia.

The Blemmyes, wild tribesmen from Nubia who sacrificed human beings to their divinities, periodically swarmed over the southern frontier of Egypt to raid the upper part of the province. About this time they fell on the Egyptian city of Coptos. But Probus' generals defeated them, apparently without the emperor's having to go to Egypt at all. According to Vopiscus, captives were taken for display before the citizens of Rome.

About this time also, Probus received ambassadors from the current Persian king, Vahram II. Probus had evidently intended to march to Persia for another war, perhaps even to retake Mesopotamia from the Persians and in any event to humiliate the rival empire and strengthen Rome's eastern borders. But Vahram, not yet secure on the throne, did not want to risk a war with the reinvigorated Roman Empire just yet. Probus himself may have decided to delay a war, since troubles had sprung up within the empire and they would have to be dealt with first. He and Vahram arrived at some sort of a truce.

After the defeat of Lydius he seems to have settled veterans as farmers in southern Asia Minor, probably as a stabilizing influence against the return of banditry on a large scale. He also settled a great many barbarians in Thrace—100,000 is Vopiscus' figure. Called the Bastarnae, they had gotten into trouble with the Goths and had been forced to leave their Scythian homeland.[12] In search of fresh territory, they had drifted into the empire. By offering them a new home in Thrace Probus precluded their ravaging the land, replenished a depopulated area, and provided the empire with a stock of barbarians to use against future barbarian invaders. He could not see that he was contributing to the transformation of the Roman army and in a lesser degree Roman life itself. Many factors would promote the cultural interchange between Rome and the barbarian world—the process, sometimes called barbarization, that accelerated in the fourth and fifth centuries. Settling the Bastarnae within the empire brought the alien cultures a little closer, eased the infiltration.

In various parts of the empire—Gaul, the Danubian provinces, perhaps even Spain and Britain—Probus promoted the growing of the grape. Late in the first century A.D. the emperor Domitian had issued an edict restricting viticulture in the provinces for the benefit of vine growers in Italy. Domitian's edict does not seem to have been very conscientiously observed, but Probus put an end to whatever was left of it. This was a necessary move in an impoverished empire. Vopiscus says that the emperor used the army to dig up the ground for grape vines on the slopes northeast of Sirmium along the Danube. He probably felt that to keep the forces busy when there were no barbarian wars to fight was to forestall the smoldering of unrest. In any case the cultivation of the vine was obviously one of his favorite measures for the economic recovery of the empire.

The unstable conditions of Gaul and the Rhineland in recent years— the Germanic depredations under Valerian, the establishment of a separate empire, the disintegration of that empire after Postumus' death, the reconquest by Aurelian, the renewal of Germanic depredations under Probus himself, economic uncertainty, sporadic raids by bandit gangs—had ripened the area for insurrection. A double revolt occurred here, adding to the problems that had to be solved before Probus could go to war against the Persians.

Vopiscus in the **Augustan History** gives a romantic picture of Proculus, one of the leaders. The man's homeland was in the Maritime Alps southwest of Genoa, but he liked to say he had Frankish blood. Rich and aristocratic, he derived his wealth from bandit ancestors who had excelled in cattle raids. He himself sometimes lived as a bandit, though he had also served as a tribune in the legions. Far from faithful to his wife, he took his sexual pleasure freely and in heroic proportions. Vopiscus purports to quote from one of Proculus' letters: "'I have taken one hundred maidens from Sarmatia. Of these I have mated with ten in a single night; all of them, however, I made into women, as far as was in my power, in the space of fifteen days.'"[13] Vopiscus depicts Proculus' wife as a lady of masculine force and drive. Named Vituriga, she came to be called Samso. It was she that pushed him in his fight for imperial power.[14]

The other rebel leader, Bonosus, had been born in Spain according to Vopiscus, but his mother was a Gaul. Bonosus' father, less dashing than Proculus' robber-ancestors, had taught rhetoric perhaps, or else he had been an ordinary schoolmaster. He had died during Bonosus' childhood, and the Gallic mother had not given the boy much of an education. He worked his way up in the army until, at the time of his revolt, he occupied a position of command along the Germanic frontier. Aurelian, who respected his military ability, had provided him with a wife — a regal Gothic girl named Hunila.[15] Aurelian gave him this wife so that Bonosus could draw from her various secrets of Gothic strategy. But Bonosus had another way of discovering barbarian secrets. His alcoholic capacity was phenomenal. He could drink savage envoys under the table. Nothing that he himself swallowed stayed in him for long, so his stomach and his kidneys were not incommoded. When the barbarian guests were drunk and drivel-tongued he was still cool and rational, and he could easily pump them for information.[16]

The year of the Gallo-Rhenish disturbances must have been about 280, but there is no certainty as to whether Proculus and Bonosus revolted separately or more or less in conjunction. Vopiscus says that although Bonosus rebelled at Cologne, Proculus rebelled at Lyons.[17] At a banquet in Lyons Proculus won the game of Thieves ten times — a game remotely like chess, in which some pieces were moved straight ahead and others slantwise on a checkered board. The winner was called "Emperor." On Proculus' tenth win somebody shouted "Hail, Augustus" as a joke. The joke caught on and a piece of purple cloth was brought and draped around Proculus' shoulders as an imperial mantle. Suddenly the banqueters grew serious.

Proculus enrolled 2,000 of his own slaves in his insurrectionary army — some of them may have served under him on bandit raids in the past — and tried to make the jest come real. His ambitious wife spurred him on. Presumably the city of Lyons supported him. Vopiscus implies that Lyons was in political disfavor. Aurelian had punished her for some reason, and she feared that Probus would punish her too if he stayed in power. Proculus also sought the help of Frankish tribesmen, and thought for a while that he had secured it. But the Franks betrayed him — Vopiscus does not say how. Probus conquered him — Vopiscus does not say where — and killed him.

Bonosus had been negligent in his post as Roman commander along the Rhine frontier. He had let barbarians burn part of the Rhine fleet that patrolled the river to keep the Germans from coming over. Deciding that it would be better to rebel than to wait for the imperial government to punish him, he established himself at Cologne. Coins were struck in his name as emperor. He apparently held out for some time, fighting more battles against Probus that we know nothing of, but in the end he grew desperate. His final recourse, according to Vopiscus, was to hang himself.[18]

That was the end of the Gallo-Rhenish troubles for Probus. They may have been in part a reminiscence of the Roman Empire of the Gauls, a sentimental reversion to the time, fifteen or twenty years before, when the area had flourished independently under the successful Postumus. There was also a rebellion in Britain at this period, led by its governor, but Probus' consul Victorinus put a stop to it.[19]

For the second time in less than a decade—probably the year 281 or early in 282—the population of Rome could enjoy an imperial triumph. The one that Probus staged was perhaps not quite so magnificent as Aurelian's in 274, but it still set off Probus' victories as the glory of the world. Barbaric nations filed past, each represented by a contingent of up to fifty men. The Blemmyes from Nubia were among them, and so were various Germanic tribes, and even confederations of brigands from Asia Minor.

A forest was planted on a vast platform in the Circus Maximus. A thousand stags, a thousand ostriches, a thousand wild boars, plus wild sheep, ibexes, and other herbivorous creatures were let loose in it, and then the populace was let loose to down these helpless animals among the trees and drag them out, to the extreme delight of the mob in the stands. For another part of the entertainment one hundred Syrian leopards, one hundred Libyan leopards, and one hundred lionesses were freed in the arena to be killed, according to Vopiscus. One hundred lions came out of their dens—but not all of them came out with a rush and a roar, says Vopiscus, as beasts do if they are freed from cages on the floor of the arena itself. They simply emerged into the arena and were drilled with arrows. The gladiators—three hundred pairs—probably afforded better spectacle.

It may have been in connection with the triumph, it may have been earlier, that a minor revolt of the gladiators occurred. About eighty of these death-dedicated wretches killed their overseers and set out on a brief career of independence. Robbery was the only profession open to them; they plundered and other plunderers joined them. But they never seriously threatened the imperial establishment. Probus' soldiers ended their bid for freedom.

After the triumph Probus reversed his recent Persian policy. He marched east from Rome to make war on the empire's primary rival.

He had not been entirely wise toward the army. According to Vopiscus, one of his mistakes had been a speech in which he looked forward to a period when an army was no longer necessary. It would be a new golden age, this time when barbarians would not menace, when agriculture and commerce could be carried on in security, and when soldiers would not have to be fed and paid. If Probus did give such a speech it must not have set well with men who had risked their lives under him.

He had also alienated his soldiers by working them too hard. He made them drain swamps, clear land for crops, enlarge harbors, construct canals. This useful kind of work was of course expected of the Roman military man when he was not fighting. But Probus perhaps overemphasized it in an era when military men had not forgotten that soldiers made emperors. Probus' principles—that a man must earn his rations and that idleness bred discontent in the army—could not be disputed. But unremitting menial labor also bred discontent.

Probus paused in the Danube region, perhaps to gather troops for the descent on Persia. Near Sirmium, his home town, he had his soldiers drain marshes, according to Vopiscus. This was part of a project to construct a canal to the river Save. It was probably late summer of 282, and probably hot. The troops rebelled. Probus had to retreat to an iron-sheathed tower that had been set up for overlooking the drainage work. The troops rushed in after him. As Gibbon envisioned it, "a thousand swords were plunged at once into the bosom of the unfortunate Probus."[20]

Carus, one of his officers, succeeded him. Although Vopiscus says that Carus was not at all involved in his emperor's death, his non-involvement is not that clear. According to Zonaras and John of Antioch, the soldiers under his command were in revolt. Probus had sent some troops toward Austria to stop this rebellion as the other attempts to end his reign had been stopped. But Carus' soldiers hailed Carus as emperor. Either they forced the imperial office on him because they were disenchanted with Probus, or else, scenting profit for themselves, they willingly supported him in his own ambition for power. The troops whom Probus had dispatched put their officers in chains and joined Carus' men instead of fighting them. Again, dissatisfaction with Probus' regime seems evident. It may have been when the news of Carus' success reached Sirmium, and the fever of revolt spread in the camp there, that Probus was killed—either in the iron tower as Vopiscus says, or by his guards as Zonaras says.

Whatever the circumstances of his murder may have been, it was a backward step. Like Claudius and Aurelian before him, Probus left the empire better than he found it. His assassination in camp brought back the precariousness of imperial rule and the whimsical tyranny of the army. He had been a fine general and had probably shown statesmanship in his truce with Persia. He had been able to please the senate. He had understood how to delegate authority, if we can judge from what little we know of the defeats of the Blemmyes in Egypt and of the brigands in Asia Minor. He had crushed several revolts and made strenuous efforts to improve the economy through the encouragement of agriculture. Now he was going to hurl the might of Rome against Persia. But the army was not happy. Therefore Carus reigned instead.

Notes to Chapter 20

1. **Abridgment**, p. 522.
2. **Scriptores Historiae Augustae**, III, 347. Probus VI. 1.
3. See Crees, **Reign of Probus**, pp. 19 and 100, n. 1.
4. See, however, MacMullen, **Soldier and Civilian**, p. 13, n. 35.
5. Crees is inclined to believe Zosimus (**Reign of Probus**, pp. 157-58).

Most authorities seem even less willing than he to commit themselves.

6. See the discussions by Syme in **Ammianus and the Historia Augusta**, pp. 55, 64, 78-79, and **Emperors and Biography**, pp. 18, 269.

7. According to Crees he did not employ force (**Reign of Probus**, p. 104), but see George Kossack in **Roman Empire and its Neighbours** (ed. Millar), p. 318.

8. See Thompson, "Athenian Twilight," pp. 63-65.

9. See Rostovtzeff, **Social and Economic History**, I, 481-82.

10. See Magie, **Roman Rule in Asia Minor**, II, 1577, n. 50. MacMullen (**Enemies of the Roman Order**, Appendix B, pp. 262-63) assumes that they were two individuals. Syme questions the existence of Palfuerius and the presence of Probus in Isauria in an anti-brigand campaign, accepting only Zosimus' account of a campaign against Lydius under an unnamed commander. See **Annianus and the Historia Augusta**, pp. 48-51, and **Emperors and Biography**, p. 277.

11. Zosimus, **Historia Nova**, p. 42. I.69.

12. See Parker, **History of the Roman World**, p. 217. But see also Bang in **Cambridge Medieval History**, I, 206.

13. **Scriptores Historiae Augustae**, III, 407. **Quadr. tyr.** XII. 7.

14. See the discussions of the **Augustan History**'s account in Syme, **Ammianus and the Historia Augusta**, pp. 56-58, 70-71, 76, 174-75, 188, 218, and **Emperors and Biography**, pp. 26, 269. Syme points to Ammianus as a source for much of the material about Proculus and suggests, perhaps not convincingly, that the name Samso is borrowed from that of the Jewish hero Samson.

15. But "Hunila," though Gothic, was apparently a masculine name. See Crees, **Reign of Probus**, p. 120, and Syme, **Ammianus and the Historia Augusta**, pp. 37-38, 174, and **Emperors and Biography**, p. 26.

16. For Syme's skeptical comments on Bonosus' drinking ability and other aspects of his portrait in the **Augustan History**, see **Ammianus and the Historia Augusta**, pp. 58, 67-68, 70-71, 77, 186.

17. Other sources, such as Eutropius and Victor, mention only Cologne. Vopiscus besides is not consistent; compare **Quadr. tyr.** XIII. 1 with **Vita Probi** XVIII. 5. Crees tends toward two separate revolts (**Reign of Probus**, pp. 116-17), Mattingly favors independent revolts (**Cambridge Ancient History**, XII, 316), and Parker treats the revolts as separate (**History of the Roman World**, pp. 217-18). Syme, on the other hand, argues for a single revolt or at least for revolts with a common center at Cologne (**Ammianus and the Historia Augusta**, pp. 55-56, 76-77; **Emperors and Biography**, p. 269). But see Magie (ed.), **Scriptores Historiae Augustae**, III, 406, n. 1.

18. Syme (**Ammianus and the Historia Augusta**, p. 77) gives arguments for considering this suicide a fiction.

19. See Crees, **Reign of Probus**, pp. 121-22, 157; Mattingly in **Cambridge Ancient History**, XII, 316-17; and Parker, **History of the Roman World**,

pp. 218, 354, n. 33. The British revolt may possibly have occurred as early as 277.
20. **Decline and Fall**, Chap. XII.

Probus (276-282), radiate and helmeted, with shield and spear. Obverse of an antoninianus. 21 mm.

21 Carus and His Dynasty

The new emperor may have been born at the city of Narbona in Illyricum, in which case he qualifies along with Decius, Claudius, Aurelian, and Probus as one of the so-called "Illyrian" emperors. Or he may have been born at Narbo (Narbonne) on the south coast of Gaul.[1] In any case his pre-imperial career, like those of the "Illyrians," seems to have been largely a military one. According to Vopiscus, Probus had made him a Praetorian Prefect.

His treatment of the senate was in the tradition of Aurelian and Gallienus. The senate would not take an active part in the choice of an emperor again. Carus sent the ancient body an announcement that the army had elected him emperor in succession to Probus. He apparently did not even request the senators to confirm the election. He was emperor in fact, no matter what the senate did or thought.

He had two grown sons, Carinus and Numerian. Both were raised to the rank of Caesar in the expectation of some day following their father in the supreme command of the empire. Coins issued in their names referred to them as "Most Noble Caesar" and "Prince of Youth." Other coins struck for them celebrated the "Happiness of the Age" and the "Clemency of the Times." Carus clearly saw himself as the founder of an imperial dynasty.

If Vopiscus is right in saying that Probus had made him a Praetorian Prefect, Carus may have possessed a considerable amount of legal knowledge in addition to military experience. From the early third century on, Praetorian Prefects had often been men prominent at law; the great legalists Paulus and Ulpian, under Septimius Severus (193-211) and Severus Alexander (222-235), are the prime examples. Although a prefect's responsibilities were in part financial, including such matters as army rations and allowances and the construction of roads and bridges, they were also in part legal. Prefects judged criminal cases that were appealed to them, and as members of the imperial council they gave the emperor advice on legal questions.

As emperor, Carus brought about quite a bit of legislation beneficial to the provinces, where Roman justice often rode on slow and wobbly wheels. For instance, he ruled that no governor could impose a larger fine than the legal one, and that if a governor designated a man to hear a case the man should hear it without the unconscionable delay that sometimes ensued. With regard to the onerous civic duties required of eminent townsmen, neither abundance of children nor abundance of years constituted a fair cause for exemption from them.[2]

But Carus' most important immediate project was the Persian war to which Probus had already committed the empire. Unless he achieved a victory over Persia he was an unworthy replacement for Probus. First, according to Vopiscus, he handed a severe defeat to the Sarmatians, Slavic barbarians who had been threatening to invade Thrace and Illyricum. Vopiscus says that he took 20,000 Sarmatian men and women captive and left 16,000 warriors dead. He may have defeated the Germanic Quadi at the same time.[3] Then, early in 283, without going to Rome at all, he set his face toward Persia in command of the great army that Probus had mobilized. He brought with him his younger son, Numerian. The other son, Carinus, was supposed to go to Gaul to govern this part of the empire in his father's name. One through war, the other through administration, Carus' sons were being trained for the full imperial duties that they would have to handle some day.

The evidence is scanty, but in so far as we can tell neither of these youngish men had much to offer in the way of imperial material. Carinus, charged with the governance of Gaul, was rabidly dissolute. Numerian was a gentler type. Even on his coins he has a sensitive, almost fastidious, not at all aggressive face. He apparently excelled at the rhetorical flourishes of the day, the figures and other ornaments that made declamation a fascinating thing to hear. He was also, according to Vopiscus, something of a poet. It was not an age when poets shone. The brightest was Nemesian of Carthage, who composed a well known piece on fishing, another on hunting, and another on sailing. When Vopiscus suggests that Numerian was as good as Nemesian, he is not praising the prince in an absolute sense.

Carus' Persian expedition is largely a blank. We do not know how the literary Numerian responded to the rigors of a military life. But there is reason for thinking that he did not acquire the hardness of a Roman officer.

With or without Numerian's help, Carus penetrated deep into Persia. The King of Kings was still Vahram II, who had gained the throne about the same time Probus became emperor. Much of the recent vigor of the

Carus (282-283), radiate. Obverse of an antoninianus. 22 mm.

Carinus (283-285), radiate, as Caesar (282-283). Obverse of an antoninianus. 19 mm.

Persian monarchy was wasted in dynastic struggles between Vahram and his brother. The glow and thrill of refashioning a great nation out of the ruins of the Parthian empire had worn away. Persia would regain her strength, but for the moment she could do little against the Romans.

Carus took back Mesopotamia and advanced down the west side of the Tigris. He captured the city once called Seleucia, on the west bank. The Hellenistic Greeks had founded it and Ardashir I, father of the revived Persian state, had refounded it and named it Ardashir Is Good. Its sister city Ctesiphon, spread out on the east bank of the Tigris, fell next to Carus. This sumptuous metropolis was the capital of the Persian monarchs as of their predecessors the Parthians. Long a center for the trade of the East, it had become even more important commercially since the collapse of Palmyra a decade before. Here caravaneers from Syria and Arabia could exchange goods with caravaneers from India and even China.

With Mesopotamia in Roman hands and the pride of Persia humbled, Carus pushed on farther into Persian territory. According to Vopiscus he was worried by reports that came to him about his older son. He contemplated putting someone else in Carinus' administrative position or even having Carinus killed, says Vopiscus. Most probably his thoughts did not go that far, but he must have been disappointed in this representative of his dynasty.

Carinus at that time shared the title **Augustus** with his father and apparently had charge not only of Gaul but of Spain, Britain, Africa, Illyricum, Italy itself, in fact the whole western half of the empire, much as Gallienus had ruled the western half during Valerian's reign. In Rome now rather than in Gaul, Carinus was not leading a very worthwhile life. Vopiscus' version of that life may be much exaggerated, but since all the sources agree that Carinus was something of a monster, it is probably true in essence if not in particulars.

It sounds as if the transition from private station to immeasurable authority was too sudden for Carinus. Certainly he abused his authority. Toward the senate, if Vopiscus can be believed, he was more arrogant than his father. He told the senators that he was thinking of donating their property to the populace. He employed a man to forge his signature to documents, being too lazy to sign for himself. He selected his officials on the basis of crass favoritism: a doorkeeper became Prefect of Rome, and an old pimp, the servant of his lusts, became Praetorian Prefect.[4] In a short period he got married nine times, divorcing some of his wives while they were carrying his children (but the only wife officially known is a certain Magnia Urbica who appears on some of his coins). For the fullness of life, apparently, he lay with males as well as females.

Like the execrable Elagabalus in the early part of the century, he sported jeweled shoes. Whores, actors, and singers lent color to the doings at his palace. His prodigality took familiar forms: at his banquets he would serve up one hundred pounds of birds or one thousand pounds of meat, and the guests reclined among Milanese roses. When he swam, apples and melons bobbed in the water.

The fourth century historian Eutropius adds to these interesting details. Carinus, he says, carried on with the wives of Roman aristocrats (evidently supplementary to his own wife or wives and his boys). He had men killed for no defensible reason at all. Among his victims were former classmates. Perhaps, as Gibbon suggests, he did away with them because during schooldays they "had not sufficiently respected the latent majesty of the emperor."[5]

Some of these enormities were committed while he was co-Augustus with his father and others later on. But in his exuberant despotism he did not forget to please the Roman populace by holding games. Vopiscus singles out for mention one hundred trumpeters who blew in unison, one thousand practitioners of pantomime and gymnastic exercises, trained bears that put on a farce, a tightrope walker in heavy boots, and a man who climbed up a wall with a bear chasing him. Unpremeditated spectacle was provided by a scaffold designed to open up and reveal performers inside. It burned up instead, and caught the stage on fire. There must have been gladiatorial fights too, possibly with Sarmatian prisoners as gladiators.[6] An eclogue attributed to the poet Nemesian talks about a hunt in the arena for animals such as boar, elk, bison, white hares, Syrian bulls, and the hippopotamus.

Meanwhile Carus died mysteriously somewhere beyond Ctesiphon. A terrific storm arose, and the thunderbolts shot and cracked in the black sky. Carus lay sick in his tent while heaven broke over the camp. A cry went up: the emperor was dead. His tent blazed with sudden fire. Vopiscus thinks that Carus' illness had killed him but that his attendants in their hysterical grief had set the tent on fire. Other sources credit the rumor that circulated through the army that Carus had been struck by lightning. Modern historians attribute his death to assassination, covered up by the story of the lightning.[7] The prime suspect is Aper, his Praetorian Prefect, father-in-law to the poetic Numerian.

Carus had reigned not much more than ten months. Some people believed that Roman emperors were fated not to go past Ctesiphon. He had brought on his death, they said, by defying fate.

The victorious Roman army began a withdrawal toward Europe. The war was no longer approved by the gods, and Numerian had no heart to continue it. If the twelfth century historian Zonaras is right, he may even have suffered a defeat. Numerian apparently became Augustus at this time, the autumn of 283.[8] The Roman world was in the hands of brother emperors, himself and Carinus. Their father's dynastic hopes had been realized, more quickly than Carus would have wished.

Carinus, who may have performed well as a soldier in spite of his many indulgences, carried on campaigns against the Germans and in Britain, evidently with success. They may have occurred at this time or, having completed them earlier, he may already have been back at Rome. Numerian meanwhile was trying to get from Persia to Europe with the army. It was probably Numerian's father-in-law, the Praetorian Prefect Aper, who conducted the march back through Mesopotamia and Asia Minor. The route was slow and tedious, full of hardship for a sensitive and poetic young emperor. Numerian suffered an inflammation of the eyeballs and took to a closed litter.

During the fall of 284 the army drew up to the Bosporus and prepared to cross to Europe. Numerian still rode in the closed litter. But the soldiers noticed a smell that grew more and more nauseous. The emperor had not been seen in several days; Aper, when questioned, explained that sunlight and wind were bad for his eyes. Now the soldiers pulled open the curtains of the litter. Numerian lay inside, dead and stinking.

Aper, evidently, had contrived his murder with the intention of becoming emperor himself. This, at any rate, was what the officers suspected. According to Vopiscus, he was brought before the standards, sacred emblems of the legions, to be judged by a military tribunal. The ad hoc court also chose a man to take Numerian's place as co-emperor with Carinus.

There was among the officers a certain Diocles or Diocletian from Dalmatia. According to Eutropius he was of very low birth. Perhaps his father had been a clerk, perhaps a freed slave.[9] Diocletian, however, had risen to the command of Numerian's household troops, being extraordinarily competent as well as ambitious. The angry officers named this man their next emperor.

Handsome and forceful looking, with square jaw and arresting eyes, Diocletian ascended the tribunal. He swore by the Unconquerable Sun that he himself had had nothing to do with Numerian's death. (Apparently he felt that since his duties had brought him into close contact with Numerian, his own innocence needed to be established beyond doubt.) Then he accused Aper, who stood in chains. This must have been a popular gesture in front of a court that had prejudged the man. He did not give Aper a chance to protest or prevaricate. Instead, he shoved his sword through the murderer in front of all the officers.[10]

Perhaps immediately after the news of Numerian's death reached Europe, an official named Julian revolted against Carinus and had himself declared emperor. He was probably taking advantage of the sudden confusion. At the Pannonian city of Siscia he struck coins advertising the "Victory of the Augustus" (meaning himself), the "Happiness of the Age," and "Public Liberty." Carinus marched against him. Meanwhile Diocletian marched against Carinus.

Numerian (283-284), radiate, as Caesar (282-283). Obverse of an antoninianus. 20 mm.

Diocletian (284-305), radiate. Obverse of an antoninianus. 22 mm.

The last representative of the dynasty of Carus came to an obscure end. He defeated Julian near Verona easily enough, but he did not last very long after that. Quite probably, as Vopiscus says, he fell in battle against Diocletian close to where the north-running river Margus joins the Danube, southeast of Sirmium. Eutropius says that his army betrayed him, and this also sounds likely. But there is a characteristic story that he was killed by an officer whose wife he had slept with.

It was early in 285, and Diocletian was master of the Roman world.

Notes to Chapter 21

1. For comment see Magie (ed.), Scriptores Historiae Augustae, III, 422, n. 3; Mattingly in Cambridge Ancient History, XII, 321; and Syme, Ammianus and the Historia Augusta, p. 275, and Emperors and Biography, p. 247.

2. See Magie, Roman Rule in Asia Minor, I, 722.

3. See Magie (ed.), Scriptores Historiae Augustae, III, 426-27, n. 4, and Mattingly in Cambridge Ancient History, XII, 321. Syme (Ammianus and the Historia Augusta, p. 48, n. 6) considers the Sarmatian war a fiction.

4. But see Syme's conjecture that the late fourth century author of the Augustan History derived the name of this old pimp from that of a man who governed Isauria in 382 (Ammianus and the Historia Augusta, pp. 159-60).

5. Decline and Fall, Chap. XII.

6. See, however, Syme's sceptical comments, Ammianus and the Historia Augusta, pp. 195-96.

7. For example, see Grant, Climax, p. 26; Mattingly in Cambridge Ancient History, XII, 322; and Parker, History of the Roman World, p. 219.

8. Magie (ed.), Scriptores Historiae Augustae, III, 432, n. 2. But see also Parker, History of the Roman World, pp. 219-20, who believes that Numerian became Augustus before Carus' death.

9. On Diocletian's name and origin see Syme, Emperors and Biography, p. 233.

10. Mattingly (Cambridge Ancient History, XII, 323) credits Vopiscus' story of a druidess' prophecy that Diocletian would become emperor when he had killed a boar. (Aper meant "boar.") The story, however, deserves distrust. Vopiscus says that he heard it from his grandfather.

22 Prospect

Carinus had belonged to a tradition already out of date by the late third century and never prevalent, that of the irresponsible ruler, like Elagabalus early in the century or Gallus in the fifties. But Diocletian would be as dead-serious about imperial responsibilities and ideals as most of his recent predecessors, from Philip on through Gallienus, Claudius, Aurelian, and Probus. Like them, he had been made emperor by the army. Like several of them, he came from the "Illyrian" regions and from humble origins. But as a result of their tough and persistent efforts he had a stronger empire to work with than theirs had been.

At the beginning of his reign, the Roman Empire was intact from Britain east into Mesopotamia and south to the Sahara. It had defeated Goths and West Germans, Palmyrenes and Persians, and had recently celebrated two spectacular triumphs. Economically it was far from recovery, but the coinage had slightly improved. Religiously it was more or less at peace. The Christians had now been let alone for some time. Resentment against them stayed within bounds rather than breaking out into government-sponsored terrorism.

Unlike his predecessors, Diocletian would not fall to an enemy army, assassins, or plague. Having been elected emperor late in 284, he would reign until 305 and then, in a move unprecedented in imperial annals, would step from his office into tranquil retirement. Meanwhile he would have been able to build on his predecessors' accomplishments and to change Roman life.

With him the era of the military emperors—emperors created by the soldiery to wage essential war and distribute emoluments to the troops—was over. On the whole, war perhaps lost some importance during Diocletian's reign. The emperor himself was primarily an administrator, only secondarily a soldier. There were, it is true, civil conflicts. Britain and part of Gaul separated from the empire for a number of years under the leadership of Carausius, an officer-turned-pirate; and a usurper took over briefly in Alexandria. But Carausius' revolt was the only one of real significance. Unquiet Franks, Saxons, Alemanni, Burgundians, Heruls, Sarmatians, Saracens, Moors, and other peoples had to be dealt with, but the barbarian inroads could not compare with the horrible ones of the mid-third century.

Imaginative as few men since Augustus, Diocletian drastically revised the army and the provincial administration, starting off from Gallienus' revisions. He altered the empire's economic structure, its social organization, and the imperial office itself. He made that office a post that implied first of all not the supreme military command but supremacy in an Oriental, almost superhuman sense—sacrosanctity, jeweled aloofness from rough soldiery and raucous citizenry. In large measure he froze society, rendering it very difficult for a man to change occupations or climb to a higher social level. His reform of the coinage, much more far-reaching than Aurelian's, increased the weight of goldpieces, introduced a new silver denomination (the **argenteus**, real silver rather than base pretense), and also introduced a new, essentially bronze coin (the **follis**, heavy enough to be impressive). In 301 he put a ceiling on prices, and although it may not have worked extremely well, it was at any rate a bold attempt to combat inflation.

He affiliated with himself a co-Augustus and two Caesars. The plan was that the Caesars would rule under the two emperors and in time would peacefully take their places as the supreme authorities in the state, each with his own special provinces to administer. This arrangement, he hoped, would do away with the chaotic succession problems that still loomed as ghosts from the past to be laid, and would ensure able government of an empire too widespread for one man to rule alone. For the promotion of religious solidarity he identified himself with Jupiter and the co-Augustus identified himself with Hercules. With the two gods working through the two emperors, Rome was bound to prosper.

In many ways, then, Diocletian labored for the durability of the empire. Only toward the end of his reign he became convinced that a renewal of persecution would be a good thing, and at the time of his retirement in 305 the empire was being torn by the fiercest anti-Christian program in her history, and the last. Politically too the empire would be torn in the years after his retirement as the two-Augustus, two-Caesar system fell apart. But throughout these new disorders the essence of his accomplishments would be preserved, and out of the disorders would emerge Constantine. This man would rule until 337 over an empire that Philip and the other soldier emperors could hardly have recognized.

Different though the Roman world was, it had in some form been saved. Partly through change and partly through relentless effort, its leaders had fended off the forces of disintegration. If determined men such as Gallienus, Claudius, Aurelian, and Probus had not come before Diocletian and prepared the way for him and Constantine, the story might have been one of continued rot and repeated surrender. The forces of disintegration would renew themselves and increase. But in the West the empire would live until 476 if not beyond, and in the East, where its capital was the city of Constantine, it would undergo a further transformation, find new enemies, and become the Byzantine Empire. In that shape it would last until 1453, preserving the heritage of Rome and Greece through the tumult of the Middle Ages.

Victory striding left with wreath and palm branch. Reverse of a sestertius of Decius. 28 mm.

Bibliography

1. Ancient Sources

Amminanus Marcellinus. [Res Gestae.] With English Translation by John C. Rolfe. (Loeb Classical Library.) 3 vols. Cambridge, Massachusetts, and London, 1935-39.

Athanasius, St. **The Life of St. Antony.** Newly Translated and Annotated by Robert T. Meyer. (Ancient Christian Writers, edited by Johannes Quasten and Joseph C. Plumpe, No. 10.) Westminster, Maryland, 1950.

Clement of Alexandria. **Writings.** Translated by the Rev. William Wilson. (Ante-Nicene Christian Library, Vols. IV and II, in that order.) Edinburgh, 1867-69.

Cyprian, St. **Select Epistles of St. Cyprian Treating of the Episcopate.** After the Translation of Nathaniel Marshall. Edited with Introduction & Notes by T. A. Lacey. London and New York, n. d.

— — —. **The Writings of Cyprian, Bishop of Carthage.** Translated by the Rev. Robert Ernest Wallis. (Ante-Nicene Christian Library, Vols. XIII and VIII, in that order.) 2 vols. Edinburgh, 1880-82. Includes **Life** by Pontius.

Dexippus, Publius Herennius. **Fragmenta.** In **Fragmenta Historicorum Graecorum,** edited by Karl and Theodore Müller. 4 vols. Paris, 1841-51.

Eusebius. **Ecclesiastical History.** Translated by Roy J. Deferrari. (The Fathers of the Church, edited by Roy J. Deferrari, Vols. 19 and 29.) New York, 1953-55.

— — —. **The Ecclesiastical History.** With English Translation by Kirsopp Lake and J. D. L. Oulton. (Loeb Classical Library.) 2 vols. London and New York, 1926-32.

— — —. **The History of the Church from Christ to Constantine.** Translated with an Introduction by G. A. Williamson. Baltimore, 1965.

Eutropius. **Abridgment of Roman History.** In **Justin, Cornelius Nepos; and Eutropius,** translated by the Rev. John Selby Watson. London, 1890.

Gregorius Thaumaturgus, St. **Address to Origen.** Translated by W. Metcalfe. London and New York, 1920.

— — —. **The Works of Gregory Thaumaturgus, Dionysius of Alexandria, and Archelaus.** Translated by Rev. S. D. F. Salmond. (Ante-Nicene Christian Library, Vol. XX.) Edinburgh, 1871.

Gregory of Tours. **Histoire des Francs.** Texte des Manuscrits de Corbie et de Bruxelles. Publié par Henri Omont et Gaston Collon. Paris, 1913.

Heliodorus. **An Ethiopian Romance.** Translated with an Introduction by Moses Hadas. Ann Arbor, 1957.

Jordanes. **The Gothic History.** In English Version with an Introduction and Commentary by Charles Christopher Mierow. Cambridge and New York, 1960. Photographically Reprinted from Second Edition, Princeton, 1915.

Nemesianus. **The Eclogues of Calpurnius Siculus and M. Aurelius Olympius Nemesianus.** With Introduction, Commentary, & Appendix by Charles Haines Keene. London and Cambridge. 1887.

Orosius, Paulus. **Seven Books of History Against the Pagans.** Translated with Introduction and Notes by Irving Woodworth Raymond. New York, 1936.

Petrus Patricius. **Fragmenta.** In **Fragmenta Historicorum Graecorum,** edited by Karl and Theodore Müller. 4 vols. Paris, 1841-51.

Plotinus. **Complete Works.** Edited by Kenneth Sylvan Guthrie. 4 vols. London, 1918.

–––. **The Ethical Treatises.** Translated from the Greek by Stephen Mackenna. 5 vols. London, 1917-30.

Pontius the Deacon. **The Life and Passion of Cyprian, Bishop and Martyr.** In Cyprian, **Writings,** Vol I, xiii-xxxi.

Porphyry. **Life of Plotinos And Order of His Writings.** In Plotinus, **Complete Works,** edited by K. S. Guthrie, Vol. I, 5-38.

Scriptores Historiae Augustae. With English Translation by David Magie. (Loeb Classical Library.) 3 vols. London and New York. 1921-32.

Tertullianus, Quintus Septimus Florens. **The Five Books of Quintus Sept. Flor. Tertullianus Against Marcion.** Translated by Peter Holmes. (Ante-Nicene Christian Library, Vol. VII.) Edinburgh, 1868.

–––. **Writings.** Translated by the Rev. S. Thelwall and Rev. Dr. Peter Holmes. (Ante-Nicene Christian Library, Vols. XI, XV, and XVIII.) Edinburgh, 1869-70.

Victor, Sextus Aurelius. **Liber de Caesaribus . . . Subsequitur Epitome de Caesaribus.** Edited by Fr. Pichlmayr. Leipzig, 1966.

Zonaras, Johannes. **Epitome Historiarum, cum C. Ducangii suisque annotationibus edidit L. Dindorfius,** 6 vols. Leipzig, 1868-76.

Zosimus. **Historia Nova.** Translated by James Buchanan and Harold T. Davis. San Antonio, Texas, 1967.

2. Modern Works

Adcock, F. E. **The Greek and Macedonian Art of War.** Berkeley and Los Angeles, 1967.

Alföldi, Andreas. "Die Hauptereignisse der Jahre 253-61 n. Chr. im Orient im Spiegel der Münzprägung," **Berytus,** IV (1937), 41-67.

–––. "Die Römische Münzprägung und die Historischen Ereignisse im Osten zwischen 260 und 270 n. Chr.," **Berytus,** V (1938), 47-91.

Atlas of Ancient and Classical Geography. (Everyman's Library, edited by Ernest Rhys, No. 451.) London and New York, 1942.

Baynes, Norman H. **Byzantine Studies and Other Essays.** London, 1955.
Bean, George E. **Aegean Turkey: An Archaeological Guide.** London, 1966.
Benson, Edward White. **Cyprian: His Life, His Times, His Work.** London and New York, 1897.
Bourguet, Pierre du, S. J. **Early Christian Painting.** Translated by Simon Watson Taylor. New York, 1965.
Brogan, Olwen. **Roman Gaul.** Cambridge, Massachusetts, 1953.
Burkitt, F. C. "Petra and Palmyra," in **Palestine in General History** by Theodore H. Robinson, J. W. Hunkin, and F. C. Burkitt. London, 1929. Pp. 85-106.
Bury, J. B. **The Invasion of Europe by the Barbarians.** New York, 1967.
Butler, Alban. **Lives of the Saints.** Complete Edition. Edited, revised, and supplemented by Herbert Thurston, S. J. and Donald Attwater. 4 vols. New York, 1956.
The Cambridge Ancient History. Vol. XII: **The Imperial Crisis and Recovery, A.D. 193-324.** Edited by S. A. Cook, F. E. Adcock, M. P. Charlesworth, and N. H. Baynes. Cambridge University Press, 1956. The following chapters:
Alföldi, A. "The Invasions of Peoples from the Rhine to the Black Sea," pp. 138-64.
— — —. "The Crisis of the Empire (A.D. 249-270)," pp. 165-231.
Baynes, N. H. "The Great Persecution," pp. 646-77.
Bidez, J. "Literature and Philosophy in the Eastern Half of the Empire," pp. 611-45.
Burkitt, F. C. "The Christian Church in the East," pp. 476-514.
— — —. "Pagan Philosophy and the Christian Church," pp. 450-75.
Christensen, Arthur. "Sassanid Persia," pp. 109-37.
Collingwood, R. G. "Britain," pp. 282-96.
Ensslin, W. "The Senate and the Army," pp. 57-95.
— — —. "The End of the Principate," pp. 352-82.
Leitzmann, Hans. "The Christian Church in the West," pp. 515-43.
Mattingly, H. "The Imperial Recovery," pp. 297-351.
Nock, A. D. "The Development of Paganism in the Roman Empire," pp. 409-49.
Oertel, F. "The Economic Life of the Empire," pp. 232-81.
Rand, E. K. "The Latin Literature of the West from the Antonines to Constantine," pp. 571-610.
Rodenwaldt, G. "The Transition to Late-Classical Art," pp. 544-70.
The Cambridge Medieval History. Vol. I. Planned by J. B. Bury, edited by H. M. Gwatkin and J. P. Whitney. Cambridge University Press, 1964. The following chapters:
Bang, Martin. "Expansion of the Teutons," pp. 183-217.
Lindsay, the Rev. T. M. "The Triumph of Christianity," pp. 87-117.
Chadwick, Henry. **The Early Church.** Baltimore, 1967.

Champdor, Albert. **Palmyre.** Préface de M. G. Peytavi de Faugères. Paris, Neuchâtel, 1934.
— — —. **Les Ruines de Palmyre.** 3rd edition. Paris, 1953.
Charlesworth, M. P. **Trade-Routes and Commerce of the Roman Empire.** 2nd edition, revised. Cambridge University Press, 1926.
Clermont-Ganneau, Charles Simon. "Odeinat et Vaballat, Rois de Palmyre et leur Titre Romain de Corrector," **Revue Biblique,** XXIX (1920), 382-419.
Cox, D. H. **A Tarsus Coin Collection in the Adana Museum.** (Numismatic Notes and Monographs No. 92.) New York, 1941.
Crees, J. H. E. **The Reign of the Emperor Probus.** London, 1911.
Donaldson, T. L. **Architectura Numismatica: Ancient Architecture on Greek and Roman Coins and Medals.** Chicago, 1966.
Doppelfeld, Otto. **The Dionysian - Mosaic at Cologne Cathedral.** Translated by Barry Jones. Chicago, 1969.
Downey, Glanville. "Aurelian's Victory over Zenobia at Immae, A.D. 272," **TAPA,** LXXXI (1950), 57-68.
— — —. **A History of Antioch in Syria from Seleucus to the Arab Conquest.** Princeton, 1961.
Drees, Ludwig. **Olympia: Gods, Artists, and Athletes.** Translated by Gerald Onn. New York and Washington, 1968.
Duchesne, Monsignor Louis. **Early History of the Christian Church from Its Foundation to the End of the Third Century.** Rendered into English from the Fourth Edition. New York and London, 1909.
Dussaud, R., P. Deschamps, and H. Seyrig. **La Syrie Antique et Médiévale Illustrée.** Paris, 1931.
Encyclopaedia of Religion and Ethics. Edited by James Hastings. With the Assistance of John A. Selbie . . . and Other Scholars. 13 vols. Edinburgh and New York, 1908-27.
Février, James Germain. **Essai sur l'Histoire Politique et Économique de Palmyre.** Paris, 1931.
— — —. **La Religion des Palmyréniens.** Paris, 1931.
Fichter, Joseph H., S. J. **Saint Cyprian: Early Defender of the Faith.** St. Louis and London, 1942.
Frend, W. H. C. **The Early Church.** Philadelphia and New York, 1966.
— — —. **Martyrdom and Persecution in the Early Church: A Study of a Conflict from the Maccabees to Donatus.** Garden City, 1967.
Frye, Richard N. **The Heritage of Persia.** London, 1962.
Gibbon, Edward. **The History of the Decline and Fall of the Roman Empire.** Edited by J. B. Bury. 7 vols. London and New York, 1897-1902.
Grant, Michael. **The Climax of Rome: The Final Achievement of the Ancient World A.D. 161-337.** Boston and Toronto, 1968.
— — —. **Roman History from Coins: Some uses of the Imperial Coinage to the Historian.** Cambridge University Press, 1968.

Harnack, Adolf von. **The Constitution & Law of the Church in the First Two Centuries.** Translated by F. L. Pogson. Edited by H. D. A. Major. New York and London, 1910.

―――. **The Mission and Expansion of Christianity in the First Three Centuries.** Translated and edited by James Moffatt. 2nd, enlarged and revised edition. 2 vols. London and New York, 1908.

―――. **Outlines of the History of Dogma.** Translated by Edwin Knox Mitchell. New York, London and Toronto, 1893.

Hayes, Carlton Huntley. **An Introduction to the Sources Relating to the Germanic Invasions.** (Columbia University Studies in History, Economics and Public Law, Vol. XXXIII, No. 3.) New York, 1909.

Healy, the Rev. Patrick J. **The Valerian Persecution: A Study of the Relations between Church and State in the Third Century A.D.** Boston, New York, and Cambridge, Massachusetts, 1905.

Hill, George Francis. **A Catalogue of the Greek Coins in the British Museum: Lycaonia, Isauria, and Cilicia.** London, 1900.

Homo, Léon. "L'Empereur Gallien et la Crise de l'Empire Romain au IIIe Siècle," Revue Historique, CXIII (May-August 1913), 1-22, 225-67.

―――. **Essai sur le Règne de L'Empereur Aurélien (270-275).** Thèse pour le Doctorat. Paris, 1904.

Jones, A. H. M. **The Cities of the Eastern Roman Provinces.** 2nd edition. Oxford, 1971.

―――. **The Later Roman Empire 284-602: A Social Economic and Administrative Survey.** 2 vols. Norman, Oklahoma, 1964.

Keyes, Clinton Walker. **The Rise of the Equites in the Third Century of the Roman Empire.** A Dissertation Presented to the Faculty of Princeton University in Candidacy for the Degree of Doctor of Philosophy. Princeton, London, and Oxford, 1915.

La Baume, Peter. **Colonia Agrippinensis: A Brief Survey of Cologne in Roman Times.** Translated by Barry Jones. Chicago, 1969.

―――. **The Romans on the Rhine.** Chicago, 1969.

Latourette, Kenneth Scott. **A History of the Expansion of Christianity.** 7 vols. New York and London, 1937-45. Vol. I, 1937: **The First Five Centuries.**

L'Orange, H. P. **Art Forms and Civic Life in the Later Roman Empire.** Princeton, 1965.

MacKendrick, Paul. **Romans on the Rhine: Archaeology in Germany.** New York, 1970.

MacMullen, Ramsay. **Enemies of the Roman Order: Treason, Unrest, and Alienation in the Empire.** Cambridge, Massachusetts, 1966.

―――. **Soldier and Civilian in the Later Roman Empire.** Cambridge, Massachusetts, 1963.

Macurdy, Grace Harriet. **Vassal-Queens and Some Contemporary Women in the Roman Empire.** (The Johns Hopkins University Studies in Archaeology, No. 22.) Baltimore, 1937.

Magie, David. **Roman Rule in Asia Minor to the End of the Third Century after Christ.** 2 vols. Princeton, 1950.

Mattingly, Harold. "Palmyrene Princes and the Mints of Antioch and Alexandria," **Num. Chron.**, Fifth Ser., Vol. XVI (1936), 89-114.

— — —. **Roman Coins From the Earliest Times to the Fall of the Western Empire.** London, 1928.

Michalowski, Kasimierz, and Andrzej Dziewanowski. **Palmyra.** New York, Washington, and London, 1970.

Millar, Fergus. "P. Herennius Dexippus: The Greek World and the Third Century Invasions," JRS, LIX (1969), 12-29.

— — —. **The Roman Empire and its Neighbours.** New York, 1968.

Mommsen, Theodor. **The Provinces of the Roman Empire from Caesar to Diocletian.** Translated by William P. Dickson. 2 vols. New York, 1887.

— — —. **The Provinces of the Roman Empire: The European Provinces.** Edited and with an Introduction by T. Robert S. Broughton. Chicago and London, 1968.

Muir's Atlas of Ancient & Classical History. Edited by George Goodall and R. F. Treharne. New York, 1961.

New Catholic Encyclopedia. 15 vols. New York, 1967.

The New Century Classical Handbook. Edited by Catherine B. Avery. Editorial consultant, Jotham Johnson. New York, 1962.

The Oxford Classical Dictionary. Edited by M. Cary, J. D. Denniston, J. Wright Duff, A. D. Nock, W. D. Ross, and H. H. Sculland. With the assistance of H. J. Rose, H. P. Harvey, and A. Souter. Oxford, 1949.

Parker, H. M. D. **A History of the Roman World from A.D. 138 to 337.** Revised with additional Notes by B. H. Warmington. London, 1958.

Perowne, Stewart. **The End of the Roman World.** New York, 1967.

Queffélec, Henri. **Saint Anthony of the Desert.** Translated from the French by James Whitall. New York, 1954.

Ramsay, Sir William Mitchell. **The Cities and Bishoprics of Phrygia, Being an Essay of the Local History of Phrygia from the Earliest Times to the Turkish Conquest.** 2 vols. Oxford, 1895-97.

— — — (ed.). **Studies in the History and Art of the Eastern Provinces of the Roman Empire.** Aberdeen, 1906.

Réville, Albert. "Le Christianisme Unitaire au Troisième Siècle: Paul de Samosate et Zénobie," **Revue des Deux Mondes,** LXXV (May-June 1868), 73-106.

Richmond, I. A. **The City-Wall of Imperial Rome, An Account of Its Architectural Development from Aurelian to Narses.** Oxford, 1930.

Rohde, Theodor. **Die Münzen des Kaisers Aurelianus, seiner Frau Severina und der Fürsten von Palmyra.** Miskoloz, 1881.

Rostovtzeff, M. **Caravan Cities.** Translated by D. and T. Talbot Rice. Oxford, 1932.

———. **The Social and Economic History of the Roman Empire.** 2nd Edition. Revised by P. M. Fraser. 2 vols. Oxford, 1957.

Seaby, H. A. **Roman Silver Coins, IV: Gordian III to Postumus.** London, 1971.

Sear, David R. **Roman Coins and Their Values.** Revised Edition. London, 1970.

Seyrig, Henri. **Antiquités Syriennes.** Paris, 1934-38.

Sprengling, Martin. **Third Century Iran: Sapor and Kartir.** Prepared and distributed at the Oriental Institute, University of Chicago, 1953.

Starcky, Jean. **Palmyre.** Paris, 1952.

———. **Palmyre: Guide Archéologique, Mélanges de l'Université Saint Joseph** (Beyrouth), XXIV (1941).

Stark, Freya. **Rome on the Euphrates: The Story of a Frontier.** New York, 1967.

Swete, H. B., D. D. (ed.). **Essays on the Early History of the Church and the Ministry.** By Various Writers. London, 1921.

Syme, Sir Ronald. **Ammianus and the Historia Augusta.** Oxford, 1968.

———. **Emperors and Biography: Studies in the Historia Augusta.** Oxford, 1971.

Thompson, Homer A. "Athenian Twilight: A.D. 267-600," **JRS**, XLIX (1959), 61-72.

Turner, Cuthbert Hamilton. **Studies in Early Church History.** Oxford, 1912.

Vogt, Joseph. **The Decline of Rome.** Translated from the German by Janet Sondheimer. New York, 1967.

Webb, Percy H. **The Roman Imperial Coinage** (ed. Harold Mattingly and Edward A. Sydenham), V, Part I. London, 1972.

Wightman, Edith Mary. **Roman Trier and the Treveri.** New York and Washington, 1971.

Syncretistic head of Zeus Ammon wearing horn of Ammon, rays of Sol, and hemhem crown; to left, trident of Poseidon entwined with serpent of Aesculapius; to right, cornucopiae. Reverse of a potin tetradrachm of Philip the Arab struck at Alexandria. 22 mm.

INDEX

Abrittus, 56-57
Abraham, 14, 202
Aemilian (emperor), 66-67, 69, 75
Aemilian (governor of Egypt), 112-13, 138
Aeneid, 39, 227
Aesculapius, 106, 157
Africa, 20, 40, 47, 63, 64, 94, 97-98, 112, 115-19, 132, 138, 142, 200, 241, 243, 247, 260
Agape, 26-27
Against the Christians, 156
Aglibol, 210
Agri Decumates, 79, 80
Ahura-Mazda, 80
Alamanni, see Alemanni
Alans, 228
Alemanni, 75, 78-80, 87, 92-94, 122, 124, 166, 178-79, 186, 192, 194, 228, 246, 266
Alexander the Great, 14, 53, 80, 130, 167-72, 190, 202
Alexander Severus, see Severus Alexander
Alexandria, 7, 24, 28-35, 38, 40, 42, 46, 49, 61, 70, 90, 98, 99, 100, 102, 111, 112, 125, 130, 137-38, 139, 150, 152-53, 156-57, 183-84, 198, 216-17, 223, 247, 266
Amelius, 158, 159
Ammianus Marcellinus, 128
Ammonius Saccas, 152-53
Anazarbus, 167
Anchialus, 91, 170
Ancyra (Ankara), 198, 201
Andernach (Antumnacum), 77
Antioch, 7, 8, 14, 20, 24, 27-28, 40, 49, 81, 82-87, 89, 90, 94, 102, 128, 130, 133, 153, 170, 181-82, 183-85, 186, 198, 201, 204-7, 209-10, 213-15, 241
Antiochus (king of Commagene), 172
Antiochus ("king" of Palmyra), 215, 216

Antoninianus, 10-11, 54-56, 69, 142, 149, 198-200, 230, 234-35
Antony, St., 2; childhood and youth, 218-19; retirement near village, 219; temptation, 220-21; and demons, 221-23; retirement to tomb and fort, 222; and monasticism, 223; retirement west of Red Sea, 223; death, 223-24
Apamea (Phrygia), 92
Apamea (Syria), 205, 206
Apelles, 106
Aper, 261, 262
Aphaca, 201
Aphrodite, 201
Apollo, 4, 170, 201, 206
Apollonius of Tyana, 202
Apostolic romances, 102
Apsaeus, 215, 216
Aquincum, 193
Aquitania, 225
Arabia/Arabs, 4, 11, 28, 83, 94, 133, 203, 208, 209, 212, 216, 228, 260
Ardashir, 80, 260
Arethusa, 206
Argaith, 14
Argenteus, 266
Argos, 173
Arianism, 223
Arles, 80, 97, 166
Armenia, 11, 64, 81, 89, 204, 212
Army: under Philip, 6, 12; in Pannonia, 19; and Christianity, 26, 35-36; in Rhineland, 75-76; Persian, 81-82; in East, 82-83; at Trebizond, 89-90; under Valerian and Gallienus, 94-95; exclusion of senators from posts of command, 139-41, 175; revolt at Byzantium, 145; in Gallienus' triumph, 146; Palmyrene, 182, 204, 207; and Sun, 189; under Aurelian, 192, 200, 207; in Gaul, 225; and Aurelian's successor, 239-40;

under Probus, 253-54; **see also** individual emperors.
Arsinoë, 100
Arsu, 210
Art, 1, 27, 149-50
Artemis, and Temple at Ephesus, 89, 164, 167-69, 172
As, 149
Asceticism, 102-3, 155, 160, 219-20, 221, 223
Asia Minor, 16, 20, 24, 27-28, 49, 51, 64, 80, 82, 87-92, 94, 98, 99, 100, 102, 104, 106, 108, 110, 115, 119, 124-25, 128, 129, 130, 132, 145, 146, 149, 162, 164-71, 182, 186, 198, 200, 201, 203, 210, 214, 219, 234, 236, 240, 241, 247-50, 253, 254
Astarte, 210
Atargatis, 210
Athanasius, St., 219, 220, 222, 223
Athens, 27, 70, 87, 112, 129, 150, 160, 171, 172-73, 203-4, 214, 247
Augustan History, 78, 124, 128-29, 132, 173-74, 178, 189, 203, 216, 227, 243, 251; **see also** Pollio, Vopiscus
Augustine, St., 115, 160
Augustus, 13, 22, 54-56, 57, 91, 167, 171, 266
Aurelian, 2, 218, 244, 254, 265, 266; and death of Gallienus, 174-75, 177, 190; and death of Aureolus, 178; and East Germans, 179, 186, 188, 200, 228, 240; becomes emperor, 188-89; and senate, 193, 195, 227, 228-29, 239-40, 257; background, 189-92, 243-44, 257; character, 174-75, 190-92, 243; and Juthungi, 192-93, 194-95; Pannonian campaign, 193, 228; abandonment of Dacia, 193-94, 247; and Zenobia, 194, 214, 228-29; campaign in Asia Minor, 201-3, 234, 241; campaign in Syria, 204-8, 242; capture of Palmyra, 210-13, 230; capture of Zenobia, 213-14; revolt and punishment of Palmyra, 215-16, 227; finances, 235-36; revolt of mint workers, 195-96; coinage under, 195-96, 208, 227, 230, 234-35, 266; wall of Rome, 196-97; and Christians, 205-6, 229, 236; and Carpi, 214-15; and revolt of Firmus, 216-17; and St. Antony, 219, 221; and Roman Empire of the Gauls, 225-27, 251; triumph at Rome, 227-29; and Persia, 227, 236; dedicates Temple of the Sun, 229-32; benefits Rome, 233-34; and Probus, 208, 217, 239, 243; and Saturninus, 247; and Bonosus, 252; death 236-37, 241, 244
Aurelius, Marcus, 11, 20, 24, 28, 54-56, 139, 160, 186
Aurelius Victor, 17, 148, 180
Aureolus, 132, 142-43, 174-75, 178, 179
Aureus, 149, 177, 180, 246, 266
Austria, 79, 92, 94, 129, 130, 174, 186, 254
Autun, 122, 181
Azizu, 210

Baal-Shamin, 210
Babylas, 28
Babylon, 209
Ballista, 129-32, 136-37, 143
Barbarians, 1, 6, 51, 69, 111, 124, 134, 146, 175, 233, 253; **see also** under names of particular tribes and groups
Basilla, 115
Bastarnae, 250-51
Beirut (Berytus), 27, 81, 90, 133, 209
Bel, 210, 229
Benacus, Lake, 178
Berea (Macedonia), 11
Berea (Syria), 204
Berea (Thrace), 54

Bible, 30-31, 38, 39, 100, 101, 104-10, 132, 219-20, 222
Bithynia, 162, 166, 168, 201
Black Sea, 51-52, 56, 58, 69, 87-92, 94, 162, 171
Blemmyes, 216, 228, 250, 253, 254
Bonn, 76
Bonosus, 251-52
Borani, 87-91, 104, 119
Bordeaux, 122
Bosporus (kingdom), 87-89, 134
Bostra, 183
Brahminism, 153, 154, 155
Britain, 1, 122, 132, 141-42, 180-81, 246, 251, 252-53, 260, 262, 265, 266
Bruchium, 217
Budalia, 19
Burgundians, 66, 246, 266
Burgundy, 122
Byzacium, 47
Byzantine Empire, 64, 111, 267
Byzantium, 91, 138, 145, 164, 171, 200, 236

Cabira, 90
Caenophrurium, 236
Caesar, Julius, 13
Caesarea (Cappadocia), 98, 115, 128, 183, 184
Caesarea (Palestine), 29-30, 209
Callistus, see Ballista
Campania, 160
Cannabaudes, 200
Canonical Epistle, 90-91
Cappadocia, 16, 82, 98, 115, 124-25, 128, 166, 182, 183, 200
Caracalla, 4, 10, 68, 75, 83, 133, 229
Carausius, 266
Carinus, 257-62, 265
Carpi, 12-13, 52, 54, 66, 214-15
Carthage, 28, 38-47, 49-50, 60-63, 70, 97-99, 110, 112, 113, 116-19, 125, 185, 258
Carus: becomes emperor, 254; and senate, 257; coinage under, 257; background, 257-58; legislation, 258; and Persia, 258-60; death, 261
Castricius, 158
Cataphracts, 81-82, 134, 204-5, 207
Catechetical School at Alexandria, 30
Caucasus, 88, 89, 228
Cecropius, 174-75
Celts, 27, 71, 74-76, 142, 212
Cephro, 112-13
Chalcedon, 91-92, 168
Châlons, 227
Christ, 14, 25, 27, 31, 41, 45, 63, 99, 101-10, 156, 183, 185, 202, 219-22
Christianity, 1, 152; and Philip, 13-14; and state religion, 22-23, 25-26, 28-29, 112-13, 117, 128; promise of immortality, 24-25; pagan attacks on, 26-27; expansion of, 27-28; persecution under Decius, 28-36, 56, 90, 106, 111, 112, 114, 119; at Carthage during persecution under Decius, 38-45, 116; problem of the lapsed, 42-47, 50, 62-64; election of Cornelius, 47-50; and Gallus, 60; and plague, 61-62, 137-38; and Novatianism, 64, 97-99; and barbarians, 90-91; and rebaptism of heretics, 97-99, 111; and the Roman see, 99; heresies, 99-111; persecution under Valerian, 111-19; reaction to capture of Valerian, 128; Gallienus ends persecution, 139; and Neoplatonism, 153, 155-56, 160; and Paul of Samosata, 183-85, 204, 205-6; and St. Antony, 218-24; and demonology, 221-23; persecution under Maximinus, 223; and Aurelian, 205-6, 229, 236; and Diocetian, 266
Chrocus, 79-80
Chrysopolis, 171
Chrysostom, 28

Cilicia, 83, 167, 201, 240, 242
Cimmerians, 168
Citizenship, Roman, 4
City of God, 160
Cius, 92
Claudius: commander under Gallienus, 142; supposed gifts from Gallienus, 147; and battle of Naissus, 173-74; and death of Gallienus, 174-75; becomes emperor, 177, 178; background, 177-78, 257; and Alemanni, 178-9; and senate, 178, 186, 188; and Gothic/Herul raids of 268/9, 179-80, 185, 244; and Roman Empire of the Gauls, 180-81; death, 181, 186, 192; and Palmyra, 181-85, 198; coinage under, 182, 183; assessment of reign, 186, 244, 254, 265, 266; and Aurelian, 190, 200; and St. Antony, 219; and Probus, 243
Clement of Alexandria, 30
Cleodamus, 173
Cleopatra VII, 181, 182, 203, 212
Clermont, 80
Clibanarii, **see** Cataphracts
Coinage: under Philip, 3, 10-11, 13; under Decius, 54-56; under Valerian, 69, 70, 86, 124; Persian, 84; Bosporan, 87-88; of the Macriani, 130; under Gallienus, 139-40, 149; under Postumus, 142, 149, 180; Alexandrian, 150, 157, 198-200; under Claudius, 182, 183; under Aurelian, 195-96, 208, 227, 230, 234-35; of Zenobia, 198-201; and the Sun, 230, 247; under Probus, 247; under Carus, 257; of Carinus, 257, 260; of Julian, 262; under Diocletian and Constantine, 235, 260, 266
Colchis, 88, 89
Cologne, 74, 76-79, 121, 122, 166, 180-81, 225, 252
Comitatus, 72-73, 140

Commagene, 87, 172
Commodus, 20, 142, 232
Confessors, 43-45, 47
Constantine, 2, 64, 230, 235, 266-67
Constantinople, 111, 233, 267
Contra Celsum, 31
Coptos, 250
Corinth, 27, 171, 173, 209, 210
Cornelius, Pope, 47-50, 60, 62-64
Cremna, 248-50
Crete, 27
Crimea, 87, 241
Ctesiphon, 134, 148, 260, 261
Curubis, 113, 115-16
Cybele, 108, 109, 156, 210, 229
Cyprian, 139; becomes Christian and bishop, 38-39, 102; on Carthaginian Christians, 39-40, 110; resentment of him, 40-42; and persecution of Decius, 41-45, 116; and the lapsed, 42-48, 62-64; and election of Cornelius, 50; and plague, 61-62; on world's senescence, 70; and Pope Stephen, 97-99, 112; and rebaptism of heretics, 97-99; and pre-eminence of Roman see, 99; exile to Curubis, 113, 115-16; trial and martyrdom, 116-18; and St. Antony, 220; and demonology, 222
Cyrenaica, 40, 101-2
Cyril, 115
Cyzicus, 7, 171, 188

Dacia, 19-20, 51-52, 66, 69-70, 193-94, 214, 247
Dalmatia, 173, 175, 200, 262
Damascus, 7, 81, 132-33
Danube, 12, 14, 16, 20, 51-53, 56, 69-70, 79, 92, 121, 122, 124, 129, 130, 160, 171, 177, 179, 189, 192, 193-94, 200, 243, 244, 251, 254, 264
Daphne, 7, 205, 206
Decius, Trajan: and Philip, 16,

31, 60; background, 19, 68, 177, 257; the name Trajan, 19-20; attitude toward Christians, 23; persecution of Christians, 28-36, 56, 90, 106, 111, 112, 114, 119; persecution at Carthage, 40-45, 62, 116; results of persecution, 45-46; Gothic war, 51-57, 58, 214-15; coinage under, 54-56; death, 56-58; and Claudius, 178
Decurions, 7-9, 83, 234
Demeter, cult of, 50.
Demetrianus, Bishop, 86
Demiurge, 103
Demons, 42, 220-22
Demosthenes, 128
Denarius, 10, 22, 142
Denis, St., 114
Dexippus, 53, 162, 164, 172-73, 192-93
Diana, 4, 145, 164, 167-69
Didyma, 170
Diocletian, 2, 141, 215; background, 262; becomes emperor, 262-64; and Carinus, 262-64; coinage under, 235, 265, 266; policies, 265-67
Dionysius, Bishop of Alexanddria, 31-35, 41, 44, 49-50, 98-99, 100-102, 111, 112-13, 115, 137-38, 139, 183-84
Dionysius (martyr), 114
Dionysus, 53, 74
Distributions (largesses), 12, 20, 67, 233
Docetism, 105
Domitian, 122, 202, 251
Domnus, Bishop of Antioch, 185, 204, 205-6
Double **denarius, see Antoninianus**
Dupondius, 149, 230
Dura, 82, 212-13

East Germans, 51-52, 71, 170, 174, 179-80; **see also** Goths, Heruls, etc.

Economic conditions: under Philip, 5-12; under Decius, 54-56; under Valerian, 69-71, 113; trade with Germans, 73, 74; Palmyra, 132-33, 208-9; under Gallienus, 149; under Aurelian, 234-35; under Probus, 251; under Diocletian, 265, 266
Edessa, 87, 129, 134
Egypt, 7, 22, 25, 35-36, 40, 60, 83, 100-1, 103, 110, 112-13, 130, 132, 137-38, 152-53, 157, 182, 186, 198, 200, 208, 216-17, 218-24, 225, 228, 233, 241, 247, 250, 254
Elagabalus, 5, 68, 204, 230, 236, 265
Eleusis, 150
Emesa, 81, 82, 130, 137, 162-63, 166, 205-8, 210, 212, 213-14, 229-30
Emperor, cult of, 22-23
Encratites, 102-3, 104
Enneads, 159-60
Ephesus, 8, 20, 27, 29, 40, 145, 164, 167-69
Epiphanius, 30
Equestrians, 113, 140-41
Etruscus, Herennius, 52, 56-57
Eucharist, 25-27, 49, 112, 219
Euphrates River, 28, 82, 129, 132, 133, 134, 183, 212-13, 217
Eusebius, 13-14, 32-33, 184, 236
Eutropius, 121, 147, 148, 180, 188, 190, 243, 246, 261, 262, 264

Fabian, Pope, 28, 46
Fallen, The, **see** Lapsed
Fanum Fortunae, 195
Faraxen, 94
Fate, 4, 24-25
Fayoum, 100, 223
Felicissimus (of Carthage), 42-44, 46, 63-64
Felicissimus (of Roman mint), 196
Firmilian, Bishop, 98, 183, 184
Flavians, 68

Florian, 240-42
Follis, 266
Fortunatus, 63
Forum Terebronii, 56-57
Franks, 75, 77-79, 87, 121, 122, 142, 146, 166, 190, 228, 246, 247, 251-52, 266

Galatia, 166, 201
Galen, 157
Galerius Maximus, 116-18
Gallic Roman Empire, see Gauls, Roman Empire of the
Gallienus: made co-emperor, 68, 69, 153; campaigns against West Germans, 2, 77-80, 82, 86, 122, 160; character, 78, 143-44, 147-51; division of empire with Valerian, 86, 260; defeats Alemanni near Milan, 94; creates mobile cavalry corps, 94-95, 175; and persecution under Valerian, 114; on Danube front, 121-22, 129, 130, 160; and Postumus, 122, 132, 138, 141-43, 145, 174; and capture of Valerian, 128, 146-47; and Persians, 128-29, 133-36, 148-49, 163-64, 175; and revolts of Ingenuus and Regalianus, 129, 132; and revolt of the Macriani, 129-32, 136-38, 183; coinage under, 139-40, 149; and Palmyra, 132-37, 148-49, 163-64, 198; and Aemilian, 138; ends Valerian's persecution, 139, 175; and senate, 139-41, 148, 175, 257; decennial celebration, 145-47, 164; enthusiasm for Greek culture, 149-50, 172; as poet and orator, 150; and Plotinus, 153, 160-61, 175; and Gothic raids on Asia Minor, 145, 146, 164-70; and Gothic/Herul raids of 267/9, l70-74, 179, 204, 244; death, 174-75, 190; assessment of reign, 175, 244, 265, 266; and Paul of Samosata, 184; and St. Antony, 218, 219; and Probus, 243

Gallus, Trebonianus: and Kniva, 53; and death of Decius, 56-58; and peace with Goths and confirmation as emperor, 58; and wife, 60; policies, 60, 265; and plague, 60-61; and Goths, 64-66; and Aemilian, 66-67, 69; and Persia, 81; and Carpi, 214-15
Gaul, 1, 22, 24, 27, 64, 78-80, 94, 97, 114, 121-24, 132, 133, 141-43, 147, 160, 175, 177, 180-81, 192, 225-27, 236, 244-47, 251, 257, 258, 260, 266
Gauls, Roman Empire of the, 1, 121-24, 132, 138, 141-43, 149, 174-75, l80-81, 186, 188, 198, 225-27, 234, 251, 252
Gaza, 7
Gepids, 69-70
Germans, **see** East Germans, West Germans, and names of particular tribes or groups
Germany, 71-80, 94, 121-24, 132, 141-43, 160, 175, 190, 192, 193, 246, 251
Gibbon, Edward, 61, 78, 254, 261
Gnosticism, 103-4, 109, 154, 155
Gordian III, 4, 5, 6, 10, 11, 14, 52, 80, 153
Goths, 1, 71-72, 265; raid Danube region under Philip, 14, 16; raid Balkans under Decius, 51-58, 64-66, and under Valerian and Gallienus, 69-70; raid Asia Minor under Valerian and Gallienus, 91-92, 119, 124; raid Asia Minor under Gallienus **solus,** 145, 146, 164-70; raids of 267/9, 170-74, 179-80, 186, 194; and Aurelian, 190, 200, 228, 240; and Tacitus, 240; and Florian, 241; and Probus, 247, 250; and Bonosus, 252
Great Mother, 25, 27, 108, 109,

169, 210
Greece, 27, 70, 171-73, 247
Gregory of Tours, 79-80, 114
Gregory Thaumaturgus, Bishop, 28, 90-91, 183
Grenoble, 181
Guntheric, 14

Hadad, 210
Hadrian, 89, 133, 150, 167, 172, 235
Haemus Mountains, 52-54, 179
Helenus, Bishop, 183
Heliopolis (Baalbek), 210, 230
Helius, 210, 229
Hera, 173
Heraclammon, 202
Heraclea Pontica, 162, 164, 166
Heraclian (Herculian), 174-75
Hercules, 142, 232, 266
Herennius Etruscus, 52, 56-57
Heresies: proliferation in East, 99-100, 111; of Nepos, 100; Monarchians, 100-2, 103, 109; Encratites, 102-3; Gnostics, 103-4, 109; Marcionites, 104-6, 110, 119; Ophites, 106-8; Montanists, 108-11; Paul of Samosata. 183-85, 203, 204, 205-6; Arianism, 223
Heretics, rebaptism of, 97-99
Herod the Great, 30
Herodes, Prince, 162-63
Herodes Atticus, 172
Herostratus, 168
Heruls, 170-74, 179, 244, 247, 266
Hexapla, 31
Hiberians, 228
Hormizd, Prince, 82, 83
Hostilian, 52, 58-60, 61
Hunila, 252
Hymenaeus, Bishop, 183
Hypogeum, 209

Iazyges, 193
Iliad, 39
Ilithyia, 4, 6
Ilium, 170

Illyricum/Illyrians, 20, 66, 94, 132, 147, 173, 177, 216, 239, 241, 247, 257, 258, 260, 265
Immae, 204-5, 207
India, 69, 80, 216, 228, 260
Ingenuus, 121, 129, 130, 132, 142, 147
Interamna, 66-67
Isauria, 248
Ishtar, 210
Isis, 22, 25, 27-28, 31, 156, 157, 229
Istrus, 52, 91
Italy, 12, 52, 66, 76, 78, 92-94, 122, 132, 142, 181, 192, 194-95, 206, 227, 228, 234, 251, 260

Jerusalem, 27-28, 183
Jews, 31-32, 48, 83, 104-5
John of Antioch, 254
John, St., 108
Jordanes, 14, 16, 53, 56, 168
Jotapian, 16
Judaism, 23, 100, 103-5, 109, 153
Judas, 99, 106
Julian (martyr), 35
Julian (usurper), 262-64
Juno, 4, 20
Jupiter, 1, 4, 20, 39, 74, 145-46, 157, 164, 168, 210, 228, 229, 240, 266
Justinian, 111
Juthungi, 185-86, 192-93, 196, 202, 228

Knights (Equestrian Order), 113, 140-41
Kniva, 52-54, 56, 66
Kyriades, **see** Mariades

Laelian, 180
Laodicea, 130
Lapsed, The, 42-47, 50, 62-64
Larissa, 206
Lawrence, St., 114-15
Lemnos, 171
Leo III, 111
Libya, 33, 35, 46, 101, 112-13,

145, 227, 253
Limes, 78-79, 92, 192, 246
Liturgies, 8-10, 11, 83
Logos, 101
London, 70
Longinus, 203-4, 214, 215
Longiones, 246
Lucania, 227
Lucian (confessor), 44
Lucian (satirist), 87, 183
Lucius, Pope, 60
Luke, St., 105
Lydia, 166
Lydius, 248-50
Lyons, 122, 166, 181, 252

Macedonia, 11-12, 173
Macrianus the Elder, 129-32, 142, 183
Marcrianus the Younger, 130-32, 142, 183
Macrianus (minister of Valerian), 111
Maeonius, 162-63
Magnia Urbica, 260
Mainz (Mogontiacum), 76, 79, 180
Malalas, John, 214
Malchion, 184-85
Mani, 153
Marcellinus (Prefect of Mesopotamia), 213, 215, 216
Marcellinus, Ammianus, 128
Marcian, 174, 179
Marciana, 14
Marcianopolis, 14, 52, 171
Marcion/Marcionites, 29, 104-6, 110, 119
Marcomanni, 124, 143, 194
Mariades, 83-86, 128
Marius, 180, 188
Mars, 1, 20, 39, 178
Massa candida, 115
Mauretania, 47, 78, 95, 240, 247
Maximilla, 109-10
Maximin (emperor), 5, 24, 39, 68, 69
Maximin (relative of Tacitus), 241

Maximinus Daia, 223
Maximus, Bishop of Bostra, 183
Maximus, Novatianist Bishop of Carthage, 63
Maximus, Galerius, 116-18
Meditations, 160
Megaris, 91
Mesopotamia, 11, 80, 81, 82, 103, 133, 134, 198, 207, 213, 250, 260, 265
Metras, 32
Metrodorus, 106
Milan, 94, 95, 124, 147, 174-75, 178, 188, 194, 233, 261
Miletus, 169-70
Minerva, 1, 20
Mithra, 25, 156, 189, 229
Mnestheus, 236-37
Moesia, 12-14, 16, 20, 51-53, 56, 58, 66, 70, 91, 173, 179-80, 193-94, 200, 207, 215
Monarchianism, 100-2, 103, 109
Monophysitism, 102
Monotheism, 157
Montanus/Montanism, 108-11
Moors, 13, 94-95, 129

Naissus, battle at, 173-74, 179, 244
Naples, 158, 160, 240
Narbona, 257
Narbonne, 122, 257
Nemesian, 258, 261
Neocaesarea, 90
Neoplatonism, 153-60
Nepos, Bishop, 100
Neptune, 20
Nero, 23, 78, 150, 172
Nestus River, battle at, 173-74
Neuss (Novaesium), 77
Nicaea, 27, 92
Nicomedia, 27, 92, 168
Nicopolis, 53-54
Nîmes (Nemausus), 122
Nisibis, 82
Noricum, 94, 200
Novae, 53
Novatian/Novatianism, 42, 47-

50, 62-64, 97, 111, 119, 220
Novatus, 46-48
Nubia, 228, 250
Numerian, 257-58, 261-62
Numidia, 47, 112, 119, 240

Odenath, 132-37, 138, 143, 148, 162-64, 166, 175, 181, 183, 184, 200, 203, 228
Oedipus, 39
Oescus, 194
Olbia, 52
Olympia, 173
Olympius, 152-53, 156
On Jewish Meals, 48
On Promises, 100
On the Sublime, 203
On the Trinity, 48
Ophites, 106-8
Origen, 14, 29-31, 90, 102, 139, 152, 203
Orosius, 227
Osiris, 25
Osrhoëne, 28
Ostia, 240
Otacilia Severa, 3, 13
Ovid, 91

Pacatian, 16
Paganism, **see** Religion (Germanic, Oriental, State)
Palestine, 27, 29-30, 119, 152, 157, 207, 209, 227, 241, 247
Palfuerius, 248
Palmyra, 1, 7, 83, 225, 228, 229, 265; growth, 132-33; and Gallienus, 132-37, 148-49, 163-64; murder of Odenath, 162-64; and Claudius, 181-82, 184, 186; and Paul of Samosata, 183-85; the city under Zenobia, 208-10; coinage under Zenobia, 198-200; attitude toward war with Rome, 200-1, 211-12; Aurelian's campaign in Asia Minor, 201-3; Aurelian's campaign in Syria, 204-8, 242; involvement with Persia, 205, 207; capture of capital by Aurelian, 210-13, 230; trial of offenders, 213-14, 215; revolt and punishment, 215-16, 227, 260; and Aurelian's triumph at Rome, 229; and Roman finances, 235-36
Pannonia, 16, 19-20, 94, 121, 124, 129, 132, 142, 177, 186, 188, 189, 193, 194, 200, 207, 212, 241, 243, 262
Paris, 78, 114, 246
Parthia, 6, 80-83, 133, 210, 260
Paternus, 113
Patrae, 171
Patricius, Petrus, 134, 230
Patripassians, 101
Paul of Samosata, 183-85, 203, 204, 205-6
Paul, St., 23, 27, 39, 99, 104-6, 167, 169
Paulus, 257
Pavia, 195
Pepuza, 108-11
Persecution: under Decius, 28-36, 38-45, 90, 106, 111, 112, 114, 116, 119; under Valerian, 111-19, 138; ended by Gallienus, 139; under Maximinus Daia, 223; under Diocletian, 266
Persephone, 150
Persia, 1, 70, 89, 103, 133, 153, 163, 189; and Philip, 4, 6, 11; and Gallus, 64; and Valerian, 69, 80-87, 119, 122, 125, 127-28, 244; and Gallienus, 128-29, 132, 146-47; and Palmyra, 133-36, 148-49, 163-64, 166, 183, 200, 205, 207, 209, 212, 265; and Aurelian's triumph at Rome, 227-29; and Aurelian, 227, 236; and Probus, 250, 251, 253-54, 258; and Carus, 258-61; and Numerian, 258, 262
Peter, St. 23, 99, 102
Petrus Patricius, 134
Phidias, 173
Philip, 68, 140, 153, 265; and Secular Games, 3-4, 20, 227,

266; becomes emperor, 4; and economics, 5-12; and army, 6, 12; policies, 11-12, 60, 80; and Christianity, 13-14; and barbarians, 12-16, 52; and revolt, 14-17, 52
Philip Junior, 13, 17
Philip II of Macedon, 53
Philippopolis (Arabia), 11-12
Philippopolis (Thrace), 53-54, 58, 66
Philostratus, 202
Phoenicia, 27, 157, 207, 216, 241
Phrygia, 64, 108-10, 166
Pionius, 29
Pipa, 124
Piraeus, 173
Pisidia, 248-50
Pityus, 88-89
Placentia, 195
Placidian, 181
Plague, 60-62, 64, 66, 69, 111, 124-25, 137-38, 145, 159, 186
Plataea, 172
Plato/Platonism, 30-31, 101, 152, 154, 158, 159, 160-61, 203-4, 214
Platonopolis, 160-61
Pliny the Younger, 23
Plotinus, 2, 139, 220; education, 152-53, 203; philosophical school, 153; and Neoplatonism, 153-57; as teacher, 157-60; **Enneads,** 159-60; and Gallienus, 153, 160-61, 175
Pluto, 157
Pollio, 78, 124, 128-29, 132, 138, 142, 147-48, 150, 162-64, 173, 178, 179, 180, 188, 189, 203, 225, 229
Polycarp, Bishop, 104
Pontius, 38, 41, 61, 113, 117-18
Pontus, 90, 104, 183, 240
Porphyry, 152, 156-60, 203-4, 214
Poseidon, 157
Postumus: is proclaimed emperor, 121; reign, 121-24, 132, 142, 149, 180; and Gallienus, 122, 132, 138, 141-43, 145, 174,

175, 227, 252; and Aureolus, 174; and Claudius, 177; death, 180, 225, 244-46, 251
Praetorian Guard, 4, 17, 89, 92, 94, 142, 180
Priscilla, 109-10
Priscus (brother of Philip), 16
Priscus (governor of Thrace), 53-54
Probus (emperor): in Egypt under Aurelian, 208, 217, 239; becomes emperor, 241-42, 258; and death of Florian, 242; background, 243-44, 257; character, 244; and senate, 244, 254; and West Germans, 244-46, 251; and Sun, 247; coinage under, 247; and Egypt, 247, 250; and bandits of Asia Minor, 247-50; and Persia, 250, 251, 253-54, 258; and Bastarnae, 250-51; encourages viticulture, 251, 254; and Proculus and Bonosus, 251-52; triumph at Rome, 253; and revolt of gladiators, 253; and army, 253-54; death, 254; assessment of reign, 254, 265, 266
Probus (governor of Egypt), 182, 208
Proculus, 251-52
Prudentius, 115
Prusa, 92
Pythagoreanism, 158

Quadi, 12-13, 124, 243, 258
Quietus, 130-32, 136-37
Quinta, 32
Quintillus, 188, 193

Raetia, 79, 92, 94, 186, 192, 200, 247
Ratiaria, 194
Ravenna, 12, 92-94, 233
Regalianus, 129, 130, 132, 147
Religion (Germanic), 72
Religion (Oriental), 22, 25, 27-28, 156, 157, 210, 220; **see also** Isis,

Sun, etc.
Religion (State): decline, 20-23; cult of emperor, 22-23; and Christianity, 22-23, 25-26, 28-29, 112-13, 117, 128; and Gallienus, 146-47, 150; and Neoplatonism, 156; and Aurelian, 229-32; and Diocletian, 266
Respa, 168
Rhaetia, see Raetia
Rheinzabern, 79
Rhine River/Rhineland, 66, 74-80, 86, 94, 121, 122, 124, 129, 132, 142, 160, 175, 190, 251-52
Rogatian, 158
Rome (city), 3-4, 7, 11, 12, 19, 23, 28, 40-42, 46-50, 52, 58, 60, 61, 64, 68, 70, 92, 99, 102, 104, 110, 111-12, 114-15, 133, 138, 143, 145-48, 153, 154, 164, 166, 178, 188, 193, 195-97, 214, 227-30, 233-34, 236, 244, 250, 260
Roxolani, 228

Sabellius, 101
Saccas, Ammonius, 152-53, 203
Salamis, 172
Salonina, 124, 129, 160
Samosata, 87, 124-25, 129, 183
Sandarion, 213, 215
Sarmatians, 53, 124, 146, 214, 228, 247, 251, 258, 261, 266
Saturn, 117
Saturninus (martyr), 114
Saturninus (rebel), 246-47
Scythians, 52, 80, 214
Secular Games, 3-4, 13, 14, 20, 58
Seleucia (Cilicia), 201
Seleucia (Mesopotamia), 260
Seleucids, 83, 132, 170
Senate: and Philip, 11, 14-15; and Decius, 19; and Gallus, 58; and Valerian, 68; and Maximin, 68-69; and Alemannic invasion, 92; and persecution under Valerian, 113; and Gallienus, 139-41, 148, 175; and Claudius, 178, 186, 188; and Quintillus, 188, 193; and Aurelian, 193, 195, 227, 228-29, 239; of Matrons, 236; and Tacitus, 239-40; and Florian, 241; and Probus, 244, 254; and Carus, 257; and Carinus, 260
Septimius Severus, 6, 24, 30, 39, 68, 133, 140, 206-7, 257
Septuagint, 31
Serapion (Alexandrian Christian), 32
Serapion, Bishop, 224
Serapion (student of Plotinus), 158
Serapis, 31-32, 157, 167
Serdica, 194, 230
Sestertius, 10-11, 56, 142, 149, 240
Severina, 190, 230
Severus Alexander, 5, 14, 68, 145, 202, 229, 257
Shapur, 64, 80-86, 125, 127-29, 134-36, 236
Sibylline Books, 4, 195
Sicily, 247
Sidon, 7, 133
Silvanus, 121
Sirmium, 129, 186, 189, 192, 243, 244, 251, 254, 264
Siscia, 188, 262
Skepticism, 156
Skyros, 171
Slavs, 190, 193, 258
Smyrna, 27, 29, 104, 106
Socrates, 159
Sodomites, 106
Sol, see Sun god
Spain, 1, 27, 64, 78, 119, 122, 132, 133, 141-42, 180-81, 251, 252-53, 260
Sparta, 27, 171, 172, 173
Stephen, Pope, 97-99, 111, 112, 114
Stoicism, 156, 157
Successianus, 88-89
Sulla, 70
Sun god, 22, 148, 189, 206-7, 210, 229-32, 236, 247
Switzerland, 78, 92, 94, 186

Syncellus, 164, 173
Syncretism, 157
Syracuse, 247
Syria, 16, 22, 27, 49, 64, 80, 81, 82-87, 90, 94, 99, 103, 130-37, 142, 157, 175, 183-85, 186, 198, 200-1, 204-10, 213-14, 219, 230, 234, 241, 246-47, 253, 260, 261

Tacitus (emperor), 239-41, 244
Tacitus (historian), 75
Taposiris, 34-35, 44
Tarraco (Tarragona), 78, 119
Tarsus, 7, 128, 167, 183, 184, 241 242
Taurus Mountains, 82, 201, 203, 247-48
Tertullian, 38, 40, 110, 116
Tetricus, 225-27, 228-29, 234, 246
Thebes (Egypt), 138, 152
Thebes (Greece), 171
Theodotus, 138
Thermopylae, 70, 172
Thessalonica, 171
Thor, 72-74
Thrace, 14, 51-54, 56, 58, 66, 70, 91, 109, 132, 170, 173, 179-80, 190, 194, 201, 215, 236, 247, 250-51, 258
Thuruar, 168
Tiberius, 105, 133
Ticinum, 195
Timagenes, 182
Timothy, 33
Tingitana, 47
Tomi, 91, 171
Toulouse, 114
Trajan, 12, 14, 19-20, 23-24, 32, 53, 54-56, 69, 167, 170, 193
Trajan Decius, see Decius, Trajan
Transcendentalism, 154, 155, 158, 218
Trebizond, 89-92
Trebonianus Gallus, see Gallus, Trebonianus
Trier, 74, 76-79, 122, 166, 180
Trinity, 99, 101, 103, 109-10

Triumphs at Rome: of Gallienus, 146-47, 148; of Aurelian, 227-29, 253; of Probus, 253
Tyana, 82, 201-3, 204, 205, 207, 213, 241
Tyras, 52
Tyre, 27, 157, 159, 209

Ulpian, 257
Umbria, 12
Uranius, 16, 82, 86
Urbica, Magnia, 260
Utica, 115, 116, 118

Vabalath, 163, 198-200, 213
Vahram II, 250, 258-60
Valens, 54
Valerian, 111, 121, 122, 251; in command on Rhine, 66-67; becomes emperor, 68, 75, 140, 153; background, 68-69; coinage under, 69, 70, 86, 124; sends Gallienus against West Germans, 77, 86; and war with Persia, 80-87, 89, 119, 204; divides empire with Gallienus, 86, 260; Borani raids, 87-91; Gothic raids, 91-92, 214-15; Alemannic descent into Italy, 92-94, 192, 195; and persecution of Christians, 111-19; expedition into Asia Minor, 124-25; capture by Persians, 125, 127-28, 129, 134, 146-47, 174, 175, 183, 244; and Aurelian, 190; and St. Antony, 218, 219; and Probus, 243
Vandals, 186, 193, 228, 246
Vasso Galatae, Temple of, 80
Veduc, 168
Venerian, 171
Venus, 20, 39, 117, 247
Verona, 17, 19, 148, 178, 264
Vesta, 20
Victorinus (consul), 252-53
Victorinus (emperor in Gaul), 180-81, 225

Vitellius, 78
Vitruvia (Victoria), 180, 225
Vituriga, 251-52
Volusian, 60, 66-67
Vopiscus, 178, 189-92, 202, 208, 212, 214, 215, 216, 227-29, 233, 234, 235, 236-37, 240, 244, 246-48, 250, 251-52, 253, 254, 257-62

West Germans, 1, 51, 71-75, 174, 192, 225, 246, 262, 265, 266; **see also** names of particular tribes and groups

Xenophon, 89
Xystus (Sixtus), Pope, 114

Yaribol, 210

Zabdas, 182, 204-8, 219
Zenobia: as wife of Odenath, 136, 148, 175, 203; and Odenath's murder, 163-64; and Claudius, 181-82; and Paul of Samosata, 184-85; and Aurelian, 194, 214, 219; coinage of, 198-200, 200-201; character, 203-4; and Aurelian's campaign in Asia Minor, 201-3, 234; and Aurelian's campaign in Syria, 204-8; involvement with Persia, 205, 207, 212-13; capture of Palmyra by Aurelian, 210-13; her own capture and trial, 212-14, 215, 221; and Aurelian's triumph at Rome, 228-29
Zeus, 173, 210
Zonaras, 17, 94, 132, 142, 149, 162-63, 178, 188, 236, 246, 254, 261
Zoroastrianism, 80, 153
Zosimus, 17, 56, 58, 60, 88, 89, 90, 92, 149, 162, 173, 182, 200, 212-15, 236-37, 244, 246-50